걸프 사태

유엔안전보장이사회 동향 8

걸프 사태

유엔안전보장이사회
동향 8

한국외교협회

| 머리말

　걸프 전쟁은 미국의 주도하에 34개국 연합군 병력이 수행한 전쟁으로, 1990년 8월 이라크의 쿠웨이트 침공 및 합병에 반대하며 발발했다. 미국은 초기부터 파병 외교에 나섰고, 1990년 9월 서울 등에 고위 관리를 파견하며 한국의 동참을 요청했다. 88올림픽 이후 동구권 국교 수립과 유엔 가입 추진 등 적극적인 외교 활동을 펼치는 당시 한국에 있어 이는 미국과 국제사회의 지지를 얻기 위해서라도 피할 수 없는 일이었다. 결국 정부는 91년 1월부터 약 3개월에 걸쳐 국군의료지원단과 공군수송단을 사우디아라비아 및 아랍 에미리트 연합 등에 파병하였고, 군 · 민간 의료 활동, 병력 수송 임무를 수행했다. 동시에 당시 걸프 지역 8개국에 살던 5천여 명의 교민에게 방독면 등 물자를 제공하고, 특별기 파견 등으로 비상시 대피할 수 있도록 지원했다. 비록 전쟁 부담금과 유가 상승 등 어려움도 있었지만, 걸프전 파병과 군사 외교를 통해 한국은 유엔 가입에 박차를 가할 수 있었고 미국 등 선진 우방국, 아랍권 국가 등과 밀접한 외교 관계를 유지하며 여러 국익을 창출할 수 있었다.

　본 총서는 외교부에서 작성하여 30여 년간 유지한 걸프 사태 관련 자료를 담고 있다. 미국을 비롯한 여러 국가와의 군사 외교 과정, 일일 보고 자료와 기타 정부의 대응 및 조치, 재외동포 철수와 보호, 의료지원단과 수송단 파견 및 지원 과정, 유엔을 포함해 세계 각국에서 수집한 관련 동향 자료, 주변국 지원과 전후복구사업 참여 등 총 48권으로 구성되었다. 전체 분량은 약 2만 4천여 쪽에 이른다.

2024년 3월

한국학술정보(주)

| 일러두기

· 본 총서에 실린 자료는 2022년 4월과 2023년 4월에 각각 공개한 외교문서 4,827권, 76만 여 쪽 가운데 일부를 발췌한 것이다.

· 각 권의 제목과 순서는 공개된 원본을 최대한 반영하였으나, 주제에 따라 일부는 적절히 변경하였다.

· 원본 자료는 A4 판형에 맞게 축소하거나 원본 비율을 유지한 채 A4 페이지 안에 삽입 하였다. 또한 현재 시점에선 공개되지 않아 '공란'이란 표기만 있는 페이지 역시 그대로 실었다.

· 외교부가 공개한 문서 각 권의 첫 페이지에는 '정리 보존 문서 목록'이란 이름으로 기록물 종류, 일자, 명칭, 간단한 내용 등의 정보가 수록되어 있으며, 이를 기준으로 0001번부터 번호가 매겨져 있다. 이는 삭제하지 않고 총서에 그대로 수록하였다.

· 보고서 내용에 관한 더 자세한 정보가 필요하다면, 외교부가 온라인상에 제공하는 『대한 민국 외교사료요약집』 1991년과 1992년 자료를 참조할 수 있다.

| 차례

기록물종류	일반공문서철		등록번호	2020110025	등록일자	2020-11-09
분류번호	731.33		국가코드	IQ	보존기간	30년
명 칭	유엔이라크대량살상무기폐기특별위원회(UNSCOM)의 화학무기폐기작업단 참여 요청, 1992. 전2권					
생 산 과	국제연합1과		생산년도	1992~1992	담당그룹	
권 차 명	V.2 6.10-12월					
내용목차	* 국방부 요원 2명 파견(기간 : 8.24-12.4) * 이라크 지하시설물 건조, 지상건물 신축 등의 공사실적 정보 제공 요청 포함					

0001

관리 번호	92 -669

	분류번호	보존기간

발 신 전 보

번 호 : WUN-1411   920610 1758 FQ   종별 : _____

수 신 : 주   유엔   대사. ♣♣♣♣♣

발 신 : 장 관   (연일)

제 목 : 이라크무기 폐기

대 : UNW-1649

　　　대호 UNSCOM 위원장의 협조요청 서한에 대하여 UNSCOM측으로
부터의 공식적인 독촉이 없는한 회신하지 않는 방향으로 본부입장
검토하고 있는바, 6.10.회신~~요망~~ 기한이 ~~지났예~~으나 UNSCOM측 문의가
있을경우 정부 관련부처에서 검토~~ㅇ략~~하고 있다는 선에서 적의 대응
바람. 끝.

(국제기구국장   김재섭)

예고 : 92.12.31. 일반.

검 토 필 (1992. 6 .30.)

	보 안 통 제	김

앙 고 재	92 년 6 월 10 일	기안자 성명		과 장	심의관	국 장	차 관	장 관		외신과통제
		황로	과		김재섭					

0002

원 본

외 무 부

종   별 :

번   호 : UNW-1662

일   시 : 92 0610 1830

수   신 : 장 관(연일)

발   신 : 주 유엔 대사

제   목 : 이락무기 폐기작업단

연:UNW-1377

이락무기 폐기작업단 참여와 관련, EKEUS UNSCOM 위원장은 본직앞 서한으로 현지 작업단 요원들의 여가시 사용할 하기물품을 제공하여 줄것을 요청하여 왔는바 검토후 회시바람

   -단파라디오 4 대

   -TV 수상기 4 대

   -비데오 레코더 4 대

 ✓ -책 12 권

 ✓ -CD 또는 테이프 12 개

 ✓ -녹화비데오 테이프 12 개

   (대사 유종하-국장)

예고:92.12.31 일반 고문에
의거 일반문서로 재분류됨

첨부:UNW(F)-0534

검토필 (1992. 6. 30)

국기국

REFERENCE

4 June 1992

Excellency,

I have recently written to you on the subject of providing personnel for the overseeing of the destruction of Iraq's chemical warfare capability. I also indicated at the time that I would be writing to you about the provision of equipment.

My experts have now identified the three categories of equipment the Chemical Destruction Group will require to achieve their objective. These are firstly, equipment which will enable them to carry out the business of supervision, observation, monitoring and verification. Secondly, equipment such as detection and protection equipment, which will enable them to work safely in an inherently dangerous environment. Regarding these first two categories, in order to enable the implementation of standard operating procedures and for reasons of safety, maintenance and accountability, I intend standardising equipment wherever possible. The third category is what I have called morale and welfare equipment, items which will allow the Group members to relax and keep fit.

Where possible, I will ask the Government of Iraq to provide equipment. However, in the majority of cases, Iraq will be unable to meet UNSCOM's requirements. I am therefore once again dependent on the generosity of UNSCOM supporters and would request that the Government of the Republic of Korea provide the equipment on the enclosed list. The equipment, whether loaned or donated, will be required for the duration of the destruction programme.

His Excellency
Mr. Chong-Ha YOO
Ambassador Extraordinary and Plenipotentiary
Permanent Representative of the Republic of Korea
to the United Nations
New York, N.Y.

/...

534-3-1

0004

If your Government is also able to undertake to get the equipment to Bahrain or to Germany, at no cost to UNSCOM, for onward transport on UNSCOM scheduled flights, it would be of considerable assistance.

I should be grateful if you could inform us as soon as possible whether your Government will be able to respond positively to this request.

Accept, Excellency, the assurances of my highest consideration.

Rolf Ekéus
Executive Chairman
Office of the Special Commission

Enc.

CHEMICAL DESTRUCTION GROUP
EQUIPMENT REQUEST

1. ### Monitoring and Verification Support Equipment

   Nil.

2. ### Safety Equipment

   Nil.

3. ### Welfare Equipment

a.	Radios, short wave	x	4.
b.	TV monitors	x	4.
c.	Video recorders	x	4.
d.	Books (novels, autobiographies etc)	x	12.
e.	Music cassettes/CDs	x	12.
c.	Video cassettes, pre-recorded	x	12.

534-3-3

0006

주 국 련 대 표 부

주국련 2031- **653**   1992. 6. 11.

수신 : 장관

참조 : 국제기구국장

제목 : 이락무기 폐기 작업단

　　연 : UNW-1642

　　연호 아국 장교 2인의 이락무기 폐기 작업단 참여와 관련, UNSCOM이 제공한
안내서를 별첨 송부합니다.

　　첨부 : 안내서 **2**부.　끝.

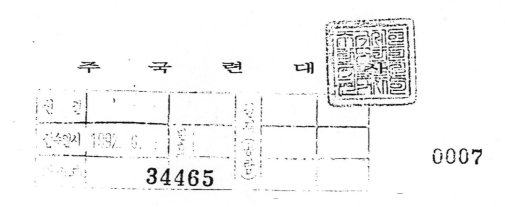

34465

0007

Chemical Destruction
Group Information

Office of the
Special Commission

0008

9 June 1992

CHEMICAL DESTRUCTION GROUP INFORMATION

1.   The enclosed information has been prepared to assist
nominated personnel in their preparations for deployment as
members of UNSCOM's Chemical Destruction Group.

2.   Although some information may have been repeated elsewhere,
it is included for completeness.

Garth Whitty
Chief Inspector
UNSCOM 38/CDG

0009

OFFICE OF THE SPECIAL COMMISSION

7 JUNE 1992

CHEMICAL DESTRUCTION GROUP INFORMATION

0010

INDEX

0011

0013

. . . . .

0014

<u>GENERAL</u>

1.   This background information is provided for the use of
nominated personnel in their preparation for deployment as
members of UNSCOM's Chemical Destruction Group (CDG). Please
treat the information as confidential to CDG personnel and not
for public release.

2.   A recent review of UNSCOM procedures has identified the
requirement for a more detailed medical return and the signing of
an "undertaking", in common with other UN agencies. These are
attachments 1 and 4 to Annex A.

3.   CDG personnel should meet in the lobby of the Holiday Inn at
0915 hrs (9.15 am) on the morning after the nominated Bahrain
arrival date.

4.   The introductory brief will be in the Holiday Inn as
follows:-

        a.   0930 -   Introduction.
        b.   1000 -   Administration brief.
        c.   1030 -   Payment of cash advance.
        d.   1100 -   Break.
        e.   1130 -   Medical brief.
        f.   1230 -   Lunch.
        g.   1400 -   UNSCOM.
        h.   1430 -   Security brief.
        i.   1445 -   Health and Safety brief.
        j.   1500 -   CDG brief and discussion.
        k.   1700 -   Next day's programme advised.
        l.   1930 -   CDG Dinner.

<u>ACCIDENTS</u>

5.   All accidents will be the subject of an inquiry and a
written report.

<u>ACCLIMATIZATION</u>

6.   UNSCOM's medical team will closely monitor the
acclimatization of newly arrived personnel. Beware of overuse of
air-conditioning.

0015

ACCOMMODATION

7.   UNSCOM will book hotel accommodation for personnel in Bahrain and Baghdad.

8.   The hotel currently used by UNSCOM in Baghdad is the Ishtar Sheraton which is situated within 200 metres of the Tigris River and is within walking distance of a number of restaurants.

9.   The UNSCOM compound at Al Muthanna includes office, storage and personnel accommodation.

AIRCRAFT

10. Flights between Bahrain and Habbiniyah Airforce Base in Iraq are by UNSCOM C160 aircraft which are provided by the Government of Germany.

11. The flight time between Bahrain and Habbiniyah is approximately two hours. No refreshments are served during this flight.

ALCOHOL

2.   Alcoholic drinks are available in both Bahrain and Iraq lthough restrictions are imposed during the Muslim observance of madan.

     Alcohol will not be permitted at Al Muthanna or on any other k sites. All personnel will be expected to be sober when they ort for work.

   YSIS

   The CDG will have its own chemical analyst and a limited :al analytical capability.

0016

ARABIC

15. A list of useful arabic phrases will be issued in Iraq.

ARRIVAL

16. UNSCOM personnel will usually be met on arrival in Bahrain. If you are not met, you should take a taxi or courtesy bus to the Holiday Inn unless advised otherwise.

ATTITUDE

17. The Iraqi people are generally tolerant of the presence of UNSCOM personnel in Iraq.

BAGGAGE ALLOWANCE

18. Approval for excess baggage must be sought prior to embarkation.

BARBERS

19. Barbers (hairdressers) are available at reasonable cost in both Bahrain and Baghdad.

BLOOD SAMPLES

20. Blood samples will be taken from CDG personnel at regular intervals to determine cholinesterase, a chemical agent exposure indicator level.

CALL FORWARD

21. Three nominated personnel will be required in Bahrain on 16 June, and half the main group will be required in Bahrain on 29 June 1992. However, because factors outside the control of UNSCOM will dictate the date, the remainder of the CDG will be required, they will be placed on seven days notice to move (NTM) with effect 4 July 1992, ie. from 4 July 1992, personnel will be

0017

given seven days notice of the requirement to arrive in Bahrain on a nominated date.

CASUALTY NOTIFICATION

22. CDG casualties will be notified to individual governments through missions or embassies.

CHEMICAL DESTRUCTION

23. The majority of nerve and mustard agent has been concentrated at Al Muthanna for destruction by caustic hydrolysis and incineration respectively. Alternative means of destruction may have to be employed for munitions too unstable for either road movement or drainage.

24. Chemical agent precursors and ballistic missile related chemicals are also stored at Al Muthanna.

CHEMICAL WARFARE AGENTS

25. Chemical warfare agents located at MSE sites include Sarin (GB, GF or a combination), tabun (GA), mustard (H, HD) and VX. Note: A standardised CW agent prophylactic and treatment regime has been implemented.

26. Precursors include methylphosphoryl dichloride (DF), phosphorous oxychloride ($POCL_3$), phosphorous trichloride, thiodiglycol and thioryl chloride (TC).

CW AGENT DELIVERY SYSTEMS

27. CW agent delivery systems include:

    a.   82 mm mortars.
    b.   122 mm artillery rockets.
    c.   155 mm artillery shells.
    d.   250 kg bombs.
    e.   500 kg bombs.
    f.   Cluster bombs.

0018

CLAIM FORMS

28. Legitimate expenses incurred during official UNSCOM activities are recovered by submission of a form F10.

CLOTHING

29. Information regarding clothing is given at paragraphs 32, 33 and 34 of Annex A. Many personnel find cotton coveralls a useful form of work dress. Also see Annex D.

COMMUNICATIONS

30. UNSCOM has its own communications network which includes hand held and vehicle mounted radios, satellite telephone links and mobile telephones.

COMPASSIONATE PROCEDURE

31. In the event of a serious illness, accident or death in the family of a member of the CDG, this information should be passed via one of the points of contact shown at paragraph 41 of Annex A. Additional telephone numbers will be advised later.

32. Personnel who are required to return to their home country for compassionate reasons will be evacuated from Iraq as quickly as possible.

DECONTAMINATION

33. UNSCOM standardised chemical decontamination procedures utilising standardised equipment will be employed. All UNSCOM personnel will be trained in decontamination procedures.

DEMOLITION

34. Direction of Iraqi demolitions will only be carried out by appropriately qualified personnel on the authority of the Chief Inspector.

0019

DETECTION

35. Chemical detection will be carried out using standardised equipment and operating procedures. All UNSCOM personnel will be trained in the use of the equipment.

36. An array of remote detectors/monitors will be deployed to protect the UNSCOM compound.

DENTAL

37. Personnel should have dental checks before deployment. Dental care is available in Bahrain at individual's expense.

DURATION OF TOUR

38. The duration of tour with the CDG is six months. However, to ensure a 3-month overlap for successive 6-month tours, some nominated personnel from the first tour will serve for three months.

DUTY OFFICER

39. A duty officer roster will be maintained throughout CDG operations. The main function of the duty officer will be as the after duty hours point of contact.

ENVIRONMENTAL CONSIDERATIONS

40. The environmental impact of chemical destruction activities is high on the list of factors considered during planning.

41. The work of the CDG will reduce the environmental threat posed by the presence of CW agents and their precursors.

EQUIPMENT

42. A number of governments have been approached to provide equipment for the CDG. Equipment falls into one of the following three categories:

0020

a.   Role equipment which will enable the CDG to carry out
     the business of direction, observation , monitoring and
     verification.

b.   Safety equipment such as detection, protection and
     decontamination equipment which will enable CDG
     personnel to work safely in an inherently dangerous
     environment.

c.   Welfare equipment for fitness and relaxation and
     consequently assisting in the maintenance of high
     morale.

EVACUATION

43.   Personnel evacuation plans are held.

EXPLOSIVE ORDNANCE

44.   Explosive ordnance falls into one of the following three
categories:

a.   The explosive element of chemical munitions.
b.   Conventional Iraqi munitions.
c.   Unexploded coalition munitions.

45.   Areas where the CDG will work have either been or will be
cleared of scattered explosive ordnance.

46.   Only appropriately qualified EOD personnel, on the authority
of the Chief Inspector, will be involved in the supervision of
EOD operations.

FAUNA

47.   There is a variety of wildlife at Al Muthanna. Birds of
prey including eagles and falcons are regularly seen as are bee-
eaters. Feral dogs, snakes and scorpions are also present.

0021

FAX

48. Authority for the use of fax machines for other than UNSCOM business must be sought from the Chief Inspector.

FLORA

49. In spring, much of Al Muthanna is covered with a large variety of flora including grasses and wild flowers. As summer approaches, the vegetation dies off.

FOOD

50. In Baghdad, food may be purchased in shops and markets although the choice is limited.

51. Bahrain has a wide variety of western type food available although prices tend to be higher than for equivalent products in North America or Europe.

52. There is a modern staff restaurant at Al Muthanna, where CDG personnel will be able to purchase meals.

53. When working at sites which lack alternative facilities, MREs (meals ready to eat) are available.

GOVERNMENT REPORTS

54. CDG personnel work for the UN and should not therefore make reports to their governments. Participating governments will be given regular updates of CDG activities through UNSCOM New York.

HEALTH AND SAFETY

55. All personnel will be required to read and observe the "UNSCOM Policy Memorandum Covering Health and Safety During Operations in Iraq". This document will be made available in Baghdad.

0022

HELICOPTERS

56. The German Government provides CH53 helicopters and crew to UNSCOM for internal Iraq flights. Iraqi escort helicopters accompany flights but leave UNSCOM helicopters flying north of the 36th parallel, which is "Op Safe Haven" airspace.

57. Ear protection is advised during helicopter flights.

HIERARCHY

58. The CDG hierarchy is based on the appointment held within the CDG.

INNOCULATIONS

59. Innoculation requirements are regularly reviewed. Current UN recommendations are given in paragraph 30 of Annex A.

IPE

60. CDG personnel should arrive with their own respirator, canisters and protective suit. Standardised replacement IPE will be held by the CDG.

JOB DESCRIPTIONS

61. Outline job descriptions are as follows:

   a. **Analyst/Safety Officer**
      The Analyst/Safety Officer will be responsible for the implementation of an analytical quality control regime and ensuring the observation of the UNSCOM "Health and Safety Policy Statement".

   b. **Shift Leader**
      In addition to being a member of a Destruction Monitoring Team (DMT), the Shift Leader will be responsible for the day-to-day activities of the shift.

0023

c. <u>Deputy Shift Leader</u>
In addition to being a member of a DMT, the Deputy Shift Leader will assist the Shift Leader and perform the function of Shift Security Officer.

d. <u>Shift Administration Officer</u>
In addition to being a member of a DMT, the Shift Administration Officer will be responsible for shift administration.

e. <u>Technical Storeman</u>
Each shift will have a technical storeman who in addition to being a member of a DMT, will be responsible to the Shift Leader for the control and, where appropriate, maintenance of CDG equipment.

f. <u>Clerks</u>
In addition to usual clerical activities, clerks will maintain the destruction database and have the opportunity of participating in DMT activities.

g. <u>DMT Members</u>
DMT members will be responsible for the directing, monitoring and recording of chemical destruction activities.

<u>LANGUAGE</u>

62. The working language of the CDG is English.

<u>MEDEVAC</u>

63. Medical evacuation plans are regularly updated and tested.

<u>MODUS OPERANDI</u>

64. The CDG will comprise predominantly multi-national, multi-function teams working to UNSCOM standard operating procedures (SOPs) with standardised equipment. UNSCOM SOPs will cover detection, decontamination, demolition, rescue, verification, health and safety and such other activities as is deemed necessary.

0024

65. The basic team will comprise four personnel. However, teams will be combined when specific activities require additional staff.

MUTHANNA STATE ESTABLISHMENT (MSE)

66. The Muthanna State Establishment is the organization which ran Iraq's CW programme. Its principal sites are at:

    a.   Al Muthanna (Samara), 73 km NW of Baghdad.
    b.   Falliyah, 80 km NW of Baghdad.
    c.   Muhammidiyat, 215 km W of Baghdad.

0025

ORGANIZATION

67. <u>HQ CDG</u>

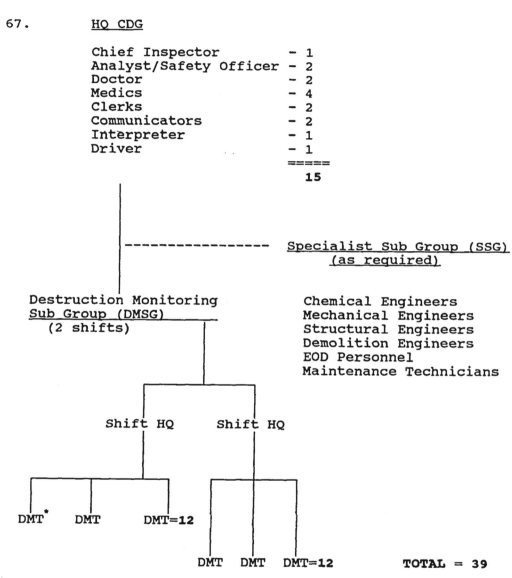

```
        Chief Inspector        - 1
        Analyst/Safety Officer - 2
        Doctor                 - 2
        Medics                 - 4
        Clerks                 - 2
        Communicators          - 2
        Interpreter            - 1
        Driver                 - 1
                               =====
                                15
```

Specialist Sub Group (SSG)
(as required)

Destruction Monitoring
Sub Group (DMSG)
(2 shifts)

Chemical Engineers
Mechanical Engineers
Structural Engineers
Demolition Engineers
EOD Personnel
Maintenance Technicians

Shift HQ   Shift HQ

DMT*   DMT   DMT=12

DMT   DMT   DMT=12   TOTAL = 39

* Destruction Monitoring Team

NB: With the exception of the Chief Inspector, the interpreter and the driver, HQ CDG personnel are split between two shifts.

0026

PASSPORT PHOTOGRAPHS

68.   Personnel should have 10 spare passport photographs with them.

PERSONAL QUALITIES

69.   Personnel nominated for missions should have the following personal qualities:

      a.   Good health.
      b.   Fitness.
      c.   Tolerance.
      d.   Resilience.
      e.   Stability - no personal problems which will affect
           performance.
      f.   A high standard of spoken English and written English
           in appropriate appointments.
      g.   Adaptability to new methods.

POINTS OF CONTACT

70.   The UNSCOM New York CDG Desk Officer is:

      Ms. Agnes Marcaillou
      + 1-212-963-9030

71.   The UNSCOM New York Administrative Officer is:

      Ms. Alice Hecht
      + 1-212-963-5545

PROCEDURES

72.   Standard operating procedures (SOPs) for all appropriate functions are being developed to ensure that the CDG discharges its responsibilities in a safe and effective manner.

0027

PROFESSIONAL QUALITIES

73. Personnel nominated for the CDG should have the following professional qualities in addition to any specialised knowledge or expertise:

   a.   Sound general NBC or equivalent knowledge.
   b.   Confidence when wearing protective NBC equipment.
   c.   Adaptability to new methods and equipment.
   d.   An international driving licence is desirable.

PROTECTION

74. In addition to IPE, impermeable suits and compressed air breathing apparatus *will be available, if required.*

REPATRIATION

75. Repatriation of CDG personnel, before completion of their tour, may occur under any of the following circumstances:

   a.   Accident.
   b.   Chemical exposure limit reached.
   c.   Unsuitability.
   d.   Compassionate.

RESCUE

76. The CDG will have an integral rescue capability.

SECURITY

77. CDG personnel should not be in possession of any documents which are either classified or of a sensitive nature.

78. The likelihood of conversations being overheard should always be considered.

0028

79. The use of a money belt or pouch is recommended.

80. Safe deposit boxes are available in both the Holiday Inn, Bahrain, and the Ishtar Sheraton, Baghdad.

81. Security concerns should be raised with the Deputy Shift Leader.

SHOPPING

82. The markets (souks) in both Bahrain and Baghdad provide a wide range of products including oriental carpets, gold jewellery and copper work.

SOUVENIRS

83. Souvenirs are not to be collected from sites.

SPECIAL COMMISSION

84. On 3 April 1991, the Security Council adopted resolution 687 (1991) setting specific terms for a formal ceasefire between Iraq and Kuwait and the Member States cooperating with Kuwait. In Section C, paragraph 9 (b) (i), of that resolution the Council decided that the Secretary-General should submit to it for approval a plan calling, _inter alia_ for the forming of a Special Commission to carry out the following tasks:

    a.   Carry out immediate on-site inspection of Iraq's biological, chemical and missile capabilities, based on Iraq's declarations and the designation of any additional locations by the Special Commission itself;

    b.   Take possession for destruction, removal or rendering harmless of all chemical and biological weapons and all stocks of agents and all related subsystems and components and all research, development, support and manufacturing facilities items;

    c.   Supervise the destruction by Iraq of all its ballistic missiles with a range greater than 150 km and related major parts, and repair and production facilities;

0029

d.   Assist the Secretary-General in developing a plan for the future ongoing monitoring and verification of Iraq's compliance with its undertaking not to use, develop, construct or acquire any of the items specified above;

e.   Assist the Director-General of the International Atomic Energy Agency (IAEA) in the following:

(1)   Carrying out immediate on-site inspection of Iraq's nuclear capabilities based on Iraq's declarations and the designation of any additional locations by the Special Commission itself;

(2)   Developing a plan for submission to the Security Council calling for the destruction, removal, or rendering harmless as appropriate of all nuclear weapons or nuclear-weapons-usable material or any subsystems or components or any related research, development, support or manufacturing facilities; and carrying out that plan following approval by the Security Council;

(3)   Developing a plan for the future ongoing monitoring and verification of Iraq's compliance with its undertaking not to acquire or develop nuclear weapons or nuclear-weapons-usable material or any subsystems or components or any research, development, support or manufacturing facilities related to the above.

85.   On 18 April 1991, the Secretary-General submitted to the Council his report regarding the establishment of the Special Commission.   In the report, he proposed that the Commission should have an Executive Chairman with a Deputy Executive Chairman to assist the Chairman in carrying out his functions.

86.   Planning and operational direction of the functions of the Commission are carried out by five groups, each under a head of group with appropriate executive experience in the assigned field and each consisting of a small number of experts.   The major areas of responsibility would be: biological and chemical weapons; ballistic missiles; nuclear-weapons capabilities; future compliance and operations support.

0030

STAFFING

87. It is hoped contributing states will continue to support the CDG by providing replacement personnel for the duration of the CDG programme.

STAMPS

88. Individuals are advised to purchase postage stamps in Bahrain.

START DATE

89. CD activity will begin on 8 July 1992.

TELEPHONES

90. Personal use of Inmarsat (International Maritime Satellite) communications is permitted, at designated times, on an immediate repayment basis of US$10 per minute.

91. International telephone calls may be booked through the operator at the Ishtar Sheraton but are usually terminated after five minutes. The cost is usually cheaper than Inmarsat.

92. There is an effective international direct dialling system in Bahrain. Prices are listed in telephone directories.

TRAINING

93. A training programme will be carried out in Iraq to ensure all CDG personnel are competent and confident in the use of CDG equipment and the implementation of SOPs.

TRANSPORT

94. In-country transport will be provided by a combination of:

0031

a.   Helicopters.
b.   Coaches.
c.   Self-drive 4 x 4 vehicles.

UN AGENCIES

95. In addition to UNSCOM, the following UN Agencies are based in Baghdad:

a.   UNDP - UN Development Programme.
b.   UNGCI - UN Guard Contingent Iraq.
c.   UNIKOM - UN Iraq Kuwait Observer Mission.
d.   UNROP - UN Return of Property.
e.   IOM - International Organization for Migration.
f.   IRCU - Inter-agency Release Co-ordination Unit.
g.   WHO - World Health Organization.
h.   WFP - World Food Programme.

96. A number of UN agencies have their Headquarters at the Canal Hotel and accommodation at the Palastine Hotel which is directly opposite the Ishtar Sheraton.

UN MEDAL

97. The UN does not award a medal for UNSCOM service.

UNSCOM BAHRAIN

98. UNSCOM Bahrain (Bahrain Field Office) supports all missions during their time in Bahrain with a full range of administrative and liaison support including the arrangement of all onward flights.

UNSCOM BAGHDAD

99. UNSCOM Baghdad provides administrative, liaison, medical, communication, interpreter and photographic support to all missions.

0032

VERIFICATION

100. The fundamental role of the CDG is the verification of the destruction, removal or rendering harmless of Iraq's CW capability.

WATER

101. When on work sites in Iraq, bottled water is provided. When off duty (off-site), provision of bottled water is the responsibility of the individual.

102. Bottled water should also be used when brushing teeth.

WORK REGIME

103. With the exception of some members of the HQ and assigned specialists, personnel will work a 4-day shift as follows:

   a.   4 days (96 hours) based at Al Muthanna.
   b.   4 days (96 hours) working on chemical tasks at other sites but based in Baghdad.
   c.   4 days off, in Baghdad, every 4 weeks.
   d.   4 days off, out of country (Bahrain or Cyprus), every 8 weeks.

Note: This regime may be modified in the interest of CDG personnel if conditions of climate, work, chemical exposure or general well-being dictate such modifications are necessary.

. . . . .

0033

OFFICE OF THE SPECIAL COMMISSION

JUNE 1992

INFORMATION FOR UNSCOM INSPECTORS

UNITED NATIONS STATUS

1.   While on duty with the United Nations Special Commission
(UNSCOM), personnel will enjoy the privileges and immunities
accorded to experts performing missions for the United Nations
under article VI of the Convention on the Privileges and
Immunities of the United Nations of 13 February 1946.   To be
covered under this Convention, personnel will be requested to
sign a group Special Service Agreement, a type of UN contract,
which identifies them as experts on mission as well as making
them eligible for cover under UN provided special insurances.
Further special arrangements regarding facilities, privileges and
immunities for UNSCOM operations have been negotiated with
Bahrain and with Iraq.   The Chief Inspector will be furnished
with copies of the arrangements.

CONDUCT AND PERFORMANCE

2.   UNSCOM personnel shall, during the term of their
appointment, discharge their functions and regulate their conduct
with the interests of the United Nations only in view and shall
not seek or accept instructions in respect of the performance of
their duties from their own government or from any other
authority external to the United Nations.

3.   UNSCOM personnel must always be completely impartial and
objective, and should avoid any action that might give rise to
doubts about their ability to remain so.

4.   UNSCOM personnel are to exercise the utmost discretion in
respect of all matters of official business.   They must not
communicate to any person any information known to them by reason
of their official position which has not been made public, except
in the course of their duties or with the authorization of the

0034

Chief Inspector. In addition, they must not use such information to private advantage. On taking up their assignment, UNSCOM personnel are required to sign an undertaking, the text of which is attached. These obligations shall not cease after the term of their appointment with UNSCOM.

PRIVILEGES AND IMMUNITIES

5.   The privileges and immunities of UNSCOM personnel are defined under article VI, "Experts on missions for the United Nations", of the Convention on the Privileges and Immunities of the United Nations, which have been acceded to by Bahrain and Iraq.

6.   These privileges and immunities are granted in the interests of the United Nations and not for the personal benefit of individuals. The United Nations or a national authority may take whatever legal or disciplinary action may be warranted against UNSCOM personnel, in accordance with his country's laws and regulations.

FINANCIAL LIABILITIES

7.   UNSCOM personnel may be required to reimburse the United Nations either partially or in full for any financial loss suffered by the United Nations as a result of their negligence or of their having violated any regulation, rule or administrative instruction. This may be done by withholding the mission subsistence allowance.

TRAINING

8.   Members of inspection teams will receive mission training in Bahrain and in Iraq, as required.

BRIEFING

9.   In addition to information provided to nominated individuals, personnel will receive detailed briefings on all aspects of their employment in Bahrain and Baghdad.

0035

TRAVEL

10. a. <u>Bahrain</u>. The United Nations, in accordance with existing United Nations rules and regulations, will provide round-trip transportation on a recognised public carrier, at the most economical rate, via the shortest, most direct route from country of residence to Bahrain. For flights under nine hours duration, travel accommodation will be in economy class; when the duration of a flight exceeds nine hours, accommodation will be in business class. UNSCOM's NY Administrative Office will contact personnel, normally by fax, with information on where to pick up the prepaid ticket, which must be used. Standard time in Bahrain is GMT + 3. Travel to Bahrain, will require, at this time, a national passport and an entry visa for nationals of all countries other than countries which are members of the Gulf Cooperation Council (Saudi Arabia, Kuwait, Oman, Qatar and the United Arab Emirates) and British nationals. Personnel will be met at the airport by an UNSCOM representative and the entry visa will be issued upon arrival in Bahrain. Should you be unable to locate the UNSCOM representative, please telephone as follows:

> UNSCOM Office - 33-6898
> Chief Field Operations - 45-9273
> Movement Control Assistant; - 45-9656.

NOTE: Personnel will be denied entry into Bahrain if their national passport contains an entry/exit stamp from Israel. If this is the case, personnel should obtain a new passport before leaving for Bahrain.

b. <u>Iraq</u>. Standard time in Iraq is GMT + 3. Personnel will fly on a UN aircraft from Bahrain to Iraq and back. Normally, members of inspection teams will enter Iraq on the UN Certificate, a form of "passport" identifying them as a UN expert on mission. These certificates will be given to each inspector in Bahrain. Upon completion of the mission, the certificate will be collected and maintained in Bahrain and be available for any subsequent deployment. UN certificates which have expired will be extended in Bahrain. Thus, if personnel already have a certificate, it should be taken to Bahrain even if expired.

11. In order to obtain this essential travel document for the first time, it is imperative that personnel fill out <u>all</u>

0036

information required on the UN Certificate application form (a
blue original card or a facsimile thereof, as attached), sign the
card or the facsimile, attach 8 passport-size photos and return
immediately by the most expeditious way (DHL or other express
mail if necessary) to:

Ms. Alice Hecht
United Nations Special Commission
Room S-3120D
United Nations
New York, N.Y. 10017
U.S.A.

Telephone: (international access code + 1-212-963-5545)

12. **NO NEW CERTIFICATES WILL BE ISSUED IN BAHRAIN.** New
certificates are issued only at UN Headquarters in New York.

13. **IF THE INFORMATION IS NOT RECEIVED AT LEAST 7 DAYS PRIOR TO
THE TEAM'S ASSEMBLY DATE IN BAHRAIN, IT MAY NOT BE POSSIBLE
TO OBTAIN THE UN CERTIFICATE IN TIME.**

ACCOMMODATION

14. UNSCOM will book hotel accommodation for personnel in
Bahrain and Baghdad.

ALLOWANCES

15. In addition to roundtrip transportation to and from Baghdad,
the United Nations will provide personnel with a per diem
allowance for their stay in Bahrain and in Baghdad. At this
time, the allowance, which is subject to change, for Bahrain is
US$154.00, and for long-term Iraq-based personnel (over 30 days)
it is US$250.00. Personnel selected for a short-duration
mission, less than 30 days, will be entitled to a per diem of
US$335.00. Personnel will receive a cash advance on arrival in
Bahrain. UNSCOM personnel are fully responsible for expenses,
including paying hotel bills before check out, meals, telephone
calls, etc.

16. The exchange rate is very unfavourable making simple
amenities expensive.

17. Final settlement of all entitlements and claims will take
place before departure from Bahrain for the return trip home.

0037

INSURANCE

18.   Personnel are fully responsible for arranging, at their own expense, such ordinary life, health and other forms of insurance cover for the period of their service for the United Nations as they consider appropriate. The responsibility of the United Nations is limited solely to the payment of compensation, if appropriate, under the following 2 schemes:

(1)   Compensation coverage in the event of death, injury or illness attributable to the performance of official duties on behalf of the United Nations.

The death, injury or illness of personnel is deemed to be attributable to the performance of official duties on behalf of the United Nations in the absence of any wilful misconduct or wilful intent when:

a.   the death, injury or illness was the result of a natural incident when performing official duties in the course of a United Nations assignment;

b.   the death, injury or illness was a direct result of the presence of personnel in accordance with a United Nations assignment in an area involving special hazards to the staff member's health or security, and occurred as a result of such hazards; or

c.   the death, injury or illness occurred as a direct result of travelling by means of transportation furnished by, or at the expense of, the United Nations in connection with the performance of official duties only. This provision shall not extend to motor-vehicle transportation provided by the staff member or sanctioned or authorized by the United Nations solely at the request of and for the convenience of personnel.

The compensation payable under the United Nations rules governing entitlement will be the sole compensation payable by the United Nations in respect of death, injury or illness which is not covered by the hazardous duty and malicious acts insurance.

(2)   A hazardous duty and malicious acts personal accident insurance coverage for civilian personnel exclusively is related only to malicious acts, i.e. for death or disability caused directly or indirectly by war, invasion, acts of foreign enemies, hostilities, civil war, revolution, rebellion, military or usurped power, explosion of war weapons, terrorist activities, etc.

0038

Coverage begins when the staff member boards the aircraft for the last leg of the flight to the designated duty station, in this case Iraq, and ceases when the staff member deplanes from a flight departing from the designated duty station.

COMPENSATION

19. **Compensation Claims.** A claim for compensation by or on behalf of UNSCOM personnel should be submitted through the Executive Office of UNSCOM within four months of death, injury or onset of illness. In exceptional circumstances, the Secretary-General may accept for consideration a claim made at a later date. The determination of the injury or illness and the type and degree of incapacity and of the relevant award will be decided on the basis of the documentary evidence and in accordance with the provisions established by the Secretary-General.

20. Except for payment of reasonable medical and hospital expenses, and in case of death, payment of transportation or reasonable burial expenses of the remains, the United Nations will not be responsible and will not pay compensation for death, injury or illness not attributable to the performance of official duties.

21. **Disability Payments.** In the event of disability deemed by the Secretary-General to be attributable to United Nations service, the total compensation awarded by the United Nations will be payable to UNSCOM Personnel under the rules governing entitlement.

22. **Beneficiary.** UNSCOM personnel should provide the name of their beneficiary. For this purpose, personnel are required to complete, in triplicate, a designation of beneficiary form upon arrival in Bahrain.

23. **Death.** In the event of death in the service of the United Nations, the award of compensation will follow a similar procedure, but the payment will be made to the duly designated beneficiary, subject to the requirements of the laws of the individual's own country. If no beneficiary has been named, the payment will be made to the deceased's estate. In either case, payment will be made by the United Nations through the individual Governments.

0039

Compensation for Loss of Personal Effects

24. **Entitlement.** Administrative instruction ST/AI/149/Rev.3 sets out the provisions concerning compensation for loss or theft of personal effects incurred in the course of duty in the mission area. This instruction will be available at UNSCOM Headquarters.

25. **Limitations.** UNSCOM personnel are advised not only to take all possible precautions against loss or theft of their personal property, but to avoid having with them expensive cameras, watches, radios or similar items, or large amounts of cash or traveller's cheques. In cases of loss or theft which qualify for compensation under the terms of ST/AI/149/Rev.3, the maximum payment will not exceed the amount indicated for each of the following items:

		$US
(a)	Camera (still or movie and accessories)	350
(b)	Radio, record player, tape recorder or watch	350
(c)	Binoculars or typewriter	175
(d)	Video camera	600
(e)	Electronic typewriter	300
(f)	Personal computer	1000
(g)	Cash	400

26. These figures are revised periodically in the light of prevailing circumstances. No compensation will be paid for loss of or damage to more than one of each of the articles mentioned.

27. UNSCOM personnel should not encumber themselves with personal household effects, especially in view of the need for mobility in the execution of duties. Moreover, UNSCOM personnel are compensated by receiving a mission subsistence allowance during their entire tour of duty which should be sufficient to cover the cost of accommodation from which personnel can move at short notice. However, long-term personnel (6 months) may be entitled to a baggage allowance of up to 100 kgs., provided prior authorization is obtained from the UNSCOM Administrative Office.

HEALTH/MEDICAL

28. Healthy personnel are essential to the success of the inspection process. Inspection activities will take their toll on everyone, more so in hot weather and on individuals who are not fit. For Bahrain and Iraq, the United Nations recommends immunizations for typhoid, tetanus, and also recommends gamma

0040

globulin. Although there have been cases of cholera reported, it does not appear to be a significant danger in the areas to which UNSCOM personnel will travel.

29. **Initial Medical Examination Before Departure**. UNSCOM Personnel should ensure that, prior to their departure for the mission area, the appropriate authorities of their country forward the appropriate medical form to the Chief Administrative Officer, UNSCOM, at the address listed on page 11, either by DHL or fax, depending upon time constraints. These will be used by the Medical Director of the United Nations for verification of physical fitness and as a record of physical condition upon assignment:

(a) **For missions less than 3 months** - a Health Certificate signed by a physician that the expert is in good health and fit to travel, copy attached.

(b) **For missions over 3 months** - their medical history and the result of their latest medical examination along with the interpretation of the chest X-rays (do not send original X-rays) using United Nations form MS.2, copy attached.

30. Medical, hospital and dental facilities in Iraq are inadequate by UN standards. Emergency medical services will be provided to UNSCOM personnel by a medical support team, which will be provided at United Nations expense. An UNSCOM doctor or medical assistant will accompany each team. Should an individual require hospitalisation outside Iraq, he will normally be evacuated from Iraq into the country appropriate to his condition and the Medical Support Plan.

31. Personnel should bring with them an adequate supply of all personal medications, as re-filling prescriptions may not be possible. They should also bring spare spectacles, as well as sunglasses which are at least 80% UV, A&B protection, with lenses preferrably very dark green or grey. Sunblock (at least #15 waterproof to be reapplied every 2 hours), chapstick, and salves for rashes are advised. Rashes, stomach aches, and diarrhoea are likely ailments. Personnel will be given a complete medical briefing while in Bahrain.

CLOTHING

32. Personnel are responsible for their own personal clothing. Prudent selection of clothing will contribute significantly to comfortable working conditions and should be adapted to the weather. Temperatures in summer are up to 54 degrees Celsius, in

0041

winter, temperatures will drop to zero. In January/March, light-weight daytime clothing with warm sweaters or jackets for the evening will be required. Outerwear providing warmth and rain protection is strongly recommended. It is also recommended that personnel who will be engaged in official meetings with Iraqis bring suitable attire.

33. Natural fibre materials such as cotton are cooler and easier to launder; long-sleeve shirts will afford protection against sunburn and flying insects. A laundry service is available in the hotel in Baghdad. Shoes are a most critical item of clothing. Lightweight, over-the-ankle shoes/boots are advised. Shoes or boots with steel in the sole or toe conduct extremes of cold and heat and can become very uncomfortable. New footwear should be broken in prior to arriving in Bahrain.

34. Personnel may wear/use military items such as boots and canteens, but should not wear military uniforms or insignia. The UN will provide identifying floppy-brimmed hats and armbands.

INDIVIDUAL PROTECTION EQUIPMENT

35. Chemical inspectors only must bring their own individual protection equipment. They must also bring a respirator with two spare canisters/sets of filters and optical inserts if required.

MEDIA

36. Media interest in the activities of the Special Commission continues to be high. The authorised spokesman for the team is the Chief Inspector. Operations will be considered confidential until authorised for release by the Special Commission.

GOVERNMENT REPORTS

37. Team members should not make personal reports to their government prior to the completion of the official mission.

0042

PHOTOGRAPHS

38. The use of personal cameras in Iraq is normally permitted
during leisure activities in civilian areas. However, on the
inspection site itself, or going to and from the inspection site,
photographs will be taken only by the official team photographers
or by individuals specifically designated by the Chief Inspector.
These official photographs will be released only with the
specific authority of the Special Commission. Further details on
the rules relating to the taking of photographs will be provided
during the initial briefing in Bahrain.

MAIL TO UNSCOM PERSONNEL

39. Mail to UNSCOM personnel in Iraq should be addressed as
follows:

> Ms./Mr. _____
> UNSCOM #_____
> United Nations Special Commission
> c/o UNDP Bahrain
> P.O. Box 26814
> Manama, Bahrain

40. Mail from UNSCOM personnel out of Iraq will be collected at
the Baghdad office and will be periodically flown out of Iraq to
the Bahrain office, where it will be dispatched. Appropriate
stamps will be made available.

EMERGENCY NOTIFICATION

41. UNSCOM must have on record an individual or institution,
personal designate as an emergency point of contact. Please
ensure the information provided on the attached Inspector Data
Sheet is accurate. Family members or designated points of
contact may pass urgent messages to personnel through UNSCOM
Headquarters New York (international access code + 1-212-963-
9044/9041) or Field Office Bahrain (international access code +
973-320-936).

0043

POINT OF CONTACT

42. Queries relating to administrative matters should be
directed to:

> Ms. Alice Hecht
> Chief Administrative Officer
> United Nations Special Commission
> United Nations Secretariat, Room 3120D
> New York, New York
>
> Telephone - + 1-212-963-5545
> Fax - + 1-212-963-3922

Attachments:

1.   UNSCOM Undertaking
2.   Inspector Data Sheet
3.   UN Certificate
4.   UN Medical Form (MS.2)
5.   UN Health Certificate

0044

TEXT OF THE UNDERTAKING TO BE SIGNED BY
UNITED NATIONS SPECIAL COMMISSION (UNSCOM) PERSONNEL

I, the undersigned, undertake to avoid any action which may adversely reflect on my status as UNSCOM Personnel assigned to the United Nations Special Commission in Iraq or on the integrity, independence and impartiality which are required by that status.

I undertake to observe the following rules:

(a) Publication of any material or information, whether or not protected by copyright, is forbidden during an UNSCOM assignment, except by the express authorization of the UNSCOM Chief Inspector;

(b) Unless specifically authorised by the UNSCOM Chief Inspector, I shall not accept speaking engagements or make statements to, or grant interviews with the press, radio, television or other agencies of public information during my assignment with UNSCOM;

(c) I shall exercise the utmost discretion in regard to the handling of documents, cables, maps or other UNSCOM papers, and shall follow detailed instructions issued by UNSCOM concerning such documentation. In particular, documents, cables, maps or other papers, copies thereof or notes on their contents will not be taken away from the mission, published or otherwise handled or communicated to others, except with the prior approval of the UNSCOM Chief Inspector in each case;

(d) Without the prior approval of the UNSCOM Chief Inspector in each case, I shall not accept any invitation to visit military or industrial installations or to participate in or be present at official ceremonies sponsored by Iraq;

(e) I shall follow specific regulations issued by UNSCOM regarding the taking of private photographs and the carrying of private photographic equipment. In particular, I shall not photograph restricted subjects;

(f) I shall follow specific regulations issued by UNSCOM regarding the purchase, import and disposal of duty-free merchandise and shall co-operate with measures taken by UNSCOM to prevent the occurrence of any abuse of privileges or facilities accorded to UNSCOM Personnel.

0045

I understand that non-compliance on my part with any of the above rules during my UNSCOM assignment may result in my immediate repatriation.

I further recognise that the following rules may apply after completion of assignment to UNSCOM and undertake to observe them:

(a) Publication of any material or information whether or not protected by copyright, is forbidden after completion of the Iraq assignment, except with the prior approval of the Executive Chairman of UNSCOM in each case;

(b) I, after my UNSCOM assignment, shall not divulge the contents of documents, cables, maps or other papers of UNSCOM except with the prior approval of the Executive Chairman of UNSCOM in each case.

Signature: _____

Name printed in block letters: _____

Date: _____

0046

INSPECTOR DATA SHEET

NAME: _____

ADDRESS: _____

_____

_____

TELEPHONE NUMBERS: OFFICE: _____

FAX: _____ HOME: _____

NATIONALITY: _____ DATE OF BIRTH: _____

PLACE OF BIRTH: _____ SEX: _____ BLOOD TYPE: _____

EMERGENCY NOTIFICATION: NAME: _____

ADDRESS: _____

_____

TELEPHONE NO.: _____

LANGUAGES: _____

PASSPORT: TYPE: _____ NUMBER: _____

DATE OF ISSUE: _____ DATE OF EXPIRATION _____

PLACE OF ISSUE: _____ CURRENT VISAS: _____

PRIMARY AREA OF EXPERTISE: CW, BW, NUCLEAR, BALLISTIC MISSILE

SPECIALITY: _____

PREVIOUS INSPECTION EXPERIENCE: _____

DATES OF AVAILABILITY: _____

UN CERTIFICATE NUMBER (When available): _____

PLEASE FORWARD BY MOST EXPEDITIOUS MEANS THIS DATA SHEET AND EIGHT PASSPORT SIZE PHOTOS FOR UN CERTIFICATE:

Ms. Alice Hecht
United Nations Special Commission
Room 3120-D
United Nations
New York, New York   10017
(212) 963-5545

0047

APPLICATION FOR UNITED NATIONS CERTIFICATE

NAME: _____
       Last   First   Middle

ADDRESS: _____
(Local)
     _____

          Tel. No. _____

DURATION of CONTRACT: _____

PURPOSE of TRAVEL:

Activities pursuant to SCR 687 (1991) UNSCOM.

TITLE: _Adviser to Special Commissio_

NATIONALITY: _____

PASSPORT No.: _____

ISSUED BY (Country): _____

DATE of EXPIRY: _____

TRAVELLING on BEHALF of:
    United Nations
      (Name of Organization)
    UNSCOM
      (Division or Section)

I certify that the above statements are true to the best of my knowledge.

_____   _____
   Date   Signature of Applicant

Certified that the applicant is entitled to a United Nations Certificate. Please issue valid until

_____
(Not exceeding one year)

Date: _____ Certifying Officer: _____

Name: __Alice Hecht__ Office: __UNSCOM__

Do not write below this line

DATE of ISSUE: _____   EXPIRES on: _____   CERT. No.: _____

REVALIDATED: _____   EXPIRES on: _____

0048

FAO	GATT	IAEA	ILO	ITC	ITU	UN	UNDP	UNEP	UNESCO	UNICEF	UNIDO	WHO	WIPO	WMO

CONFIDENTIAL	PERIODIC MEDICAL EXAMINATION	🌐	UNITED NATIONS AND SPECIALIZED AGENCIES

For recruitment do not use this form.	Periodic Examination ☐	Extension ☐	Reassignment ☐	End of Service ☐

Pages 1 and 2 to be completed by the staff member

FAMILY NAME (IN BLOCK CAPITALS)	GIVEN NAMES	MAIDEN NAME (FOR WOMEN ONLY)	SEX ☐ M ☐ F

ADDRESS (STREET, TOWN, DISTRICT OR PROVINCE, COUNTRY) AND TELEPHONE	DATE OF BIRTH
. . . .	
. . . .	NATIONALITY

EMPLOYMENT HELD	SINCE	FAMILY CHANGES SINCE THE LAST EXAMINATION: (MARRIAGE, BIRTHS, DEATHS, DIVORCE; GIVE THE DATES)
YEARS OF SERVICE		. . . .
DEPARTMENT OR UNIT		. . . .
OFFICE OR DIVISION/SECTION		

LAST COMPLETE MEDICAL EXAMINATION

Date: . . . .   Place: . . . .

A. INTERIM HISTORY — Since your last examination:

1. Indicate the illnesses or accidents which you have had, stating their length. Give the place of hospitalization if applicable.

_____

_____

2. Do you consider that your health is altogether satisfactory? _____ If not, for what reason? _____

3. Have you been examined by: Your own doctor? ☐ Yes ☐ No   A specialist? ☐ Yes ☐ No
   If so, when and for what reason? _____

4. Have you consulted: A neurologist? ☐ Yes ☐ No   A psychiatrist? ☐ Yes ☐ No   A psychoanalyst? ☐ Yes ☐ No
   If so, when and for what reason? _____

5. Are you under medical treatment at present? _____
   If so, state treatment followed: _____

6. Have members of your family had any serious health problems? ☐ Yes ☐ No
   If yes, give details: _____

7. Please give any additional information that might help the examining doctor: _____

8. Name and address of your own doctor: _____

TO BE COMPLETED BY STAFF MEMBER	TO BE COMPLETED BY THE DIRECTOR OF THE MEDICAL SERVICE
Place:	Medical Classification: ☐ 1a ☐ 1b ☐ 2a ☐ 2b
Date:	Comments: . . . .
Signature:	. . . .
	Date: . . . . Signature: . . . .

VERY IMPORTANT: Please indicate the Agency or Organization concerned: _____

0049

MS.6 (9-85) - E.

B. PRESENT HEALTH — *Each question requires a specific answer (yes, no, date, etc.); to leave a blank or draw a line is not sufficient. If the questionnaire is not fully completed and enquiries are therefore needed, time may be lost.*

1. Have you suffered from any of the following diseases or disorders? Check yes or no. If yes, state the year.

	YES Date	NO		YES Date	NO		YES Date	NO		YES Date	NO
Frequent sore throats			Heart and blood vessel disease			Urinary disorder			Fainting spells		
Hay fever			Pains in the heart region			Kidney trouble			Epilepsy		
Asthma			Varicose veins			Kidney stones			Diabetes		
Tuberculosis			Frequent indigestion			Back pain			Gonorrhoea		
Pneumonia			Ulcer of stomach or duodenum			Joint problems			Any other sexually transmitted disease		
Pleurisy			Jaundice			Skin disease			Tropical diseases		
Repeated bronchitis			Gall stones			Sleeplessness			Amoebic dysentery		
Rheumatic fever			Hernia			Any nervous or mental disorder			Malaria		
High blood pressure			Haemorrhoids			Frequent headaches					

C. DAILY HABITS

1. Do you smoke regularly?   ☐ Yes   ☐ No

   If so, what do you smoke?   ☐ Cigarettes   ☐ Pipe   ☐ Cigars

   For how many years have you smoked? _____

   How much per day? _____

2. Daily consumption of alcoholic beverages: _____

3. Recreation:

   What kind now? _____
   _____

   How often? _____
   _____
   _____
   _____
   _____

D. FOR WOMEN STAFF ONLY

1. Do you take contraceptive pills?   ☐ Yes   ☐ No

2. When did you last visit a gynaecologist? _____

   For what reason? _____
   _____
   _____
   _____

3. Any pregnancies since last examination? _____

4. Date of menopause (if applicable): _____

0050

- 3 -

TO BE COMPLETED BY THE EXAMINING PHYSICIAN

GENERAL APPEARANCE   Height: cm. _____   Weight: kg. _____

Skin: _____   Scalp : _____

SIGHT, MEASURED VISUAL ACUITY

Gross vision   : Right _____ Left _____   Pupils: Equal? _____ Regular? _____

Vision with spectacles   : Right _____ Left _____   Fundi (if necessary): _____

Near vision   : Right _____ Left _____   Colour vision: _____

With correction   : Right _____ Left _____

HEARING (test by whispering)	Right : Normal: _____ Sufficient: _____ Insufficient: _____
	Left : Normal: _____ Sufficient: _____ Insufficient: _____
	Ear drum : Right: _____ Left: _____

NOSE-MOUTH-NECK   Nose : _____ Pharynx: _____ Teeth : _____

Tongue: _____ Tonsils: _____ Thyroid: _____

CARDIOVASCULAR SYSTEM

                                     Peripheral arteries

Pulse rate   : _____   Auscultation   : _____   –carotid   : _____

Rhythm   : _____   Blood pressure   : _____   –posterior tibial: _____

Apex beat   : _____   Varicose veins   : _____   –dorsalis pedis : _____

Electrocardiogram (if indicated or after age of 45) – Please attach tracing

RESPIRATORY SYSTEM

Thorax: Breasts   RIGHT ⊕   LEFT ⊕

DIGESTIVE SYSTEM

Abdomen: _____   Spleen: _____

Liver : _____   Hernia: _____

               Rectal examination: _____

NERVOUS SYSTEM

                                    Plantar reflexes : _____

Pupillary reflexes: – To light: _____   Motor functions : _____

              – On accommodation: _____   Sensory functions : _____

Patellar reflexes : _____   Muscular tonus : _____

Achilles reflexes : _____   Romberg's sign : _____

MENTAL STATE

Appearance: _____   Behaviour: _____

GENITO–URINARY SYSTEM

Kidneys: _____   Genitals: _____

SKELETAL SYSTEM

Skull : _____   Upper extremities : _____

Spine: _____   Lower extremities: _____

LYMPHATIC SYSTEM

CHEST X-RAY (Full size film – Please send film itself, the radiologist's report is not sufficient. Lateral film not necessary unless indicated medically.)

0051

LABORATORY

cept by prior agreement, only the investigations mentioned are done at the Organization's expense.

'tine :   Albumin _____   Sugar _____   Microscopic _____

.ood :   Haemoglobin : _____ % _____ grams/1   Leucocytes: _____

   Haematocrit : _____ % _____   Differential count (if indicated) : _____

   Erythrocytes : _____   Blood sedimentation rate : _____

.lood chemistry (if these tests can be carried out on the spot):

   Sugar   : _____   Urea or creatinine : _____

   Cholesterol : _____   Uric acid   : _____

Serological test for syphilis (if indicated):

ool examination (if indicated):

COMMENTS (Please comment on all the positive answers given by the staff member and summarize the abnormal findings):

ONCLUSIONS (Please state your opinion on the physical and mental health of the staff member):

The examining doctor is requested before sending this report to verify that the questionnaire, page 1 and 2 of this form, has been fully completed by the staff member and that all the results of the investigations required are given on the report.

tame of the examining physician (in block capitals) :

_____

Address: _____

_____

Signature: _____

Date: _____

0052

HEALTH CERTIFICATE

_____ is in good health and is
physically fit to travel to Bahrain and Iraq to carry
out inspection activities as required by the United
Nations. All required inoculations for the travel area
have been administered.

_____
Physician

_____
Date

0053

BAHRAIN

GEOGRAPHY

1.   Bahrain consists of an archipelago of thirty-three islands, having a total area of 691.2 square kilometres, situated halfway down the Arabian Gulf, 28 km from the western coast of Qatar and linked by a 25 km causeway from the eastern coast of Saudi Arabia.

2.   There are six main islands in Bahrain; the largest is Bahrain, the principal island is about (578 sq km) 50 km long and 13 to 25 km wide, from which the state derived its name. It is linked by a 3 km causeway to connect Manama the capital on the northern tip, with the neighbouring town and second largest island, Muharraq. Halfway down the east coast of Bahrain Island, a bridge joins it to Sitra Island. Other islands of significant size include AL-Nabeeh Saleh to the east, and Jiddah, Umm El-Nassan and Umm El-Subban to the west coast, and Hawar Islands to the south-east of Bahrain.

3.   There are numerous other tiny islands in the archipelago but they are uninhabited, and are best known for the rich variety of migrating birds which live there for part of the year.

4.   Most of Bahrain is low-lying and its surface is limestone rock, covered by varying densities of saline sand which will support only the hardiest desert vegetation. Along the northern coast is a 5 km wide fertile strip.

5.   From the shore line the topography gradually rises towards the centre where it again drops off into a basin surrounded by steep cliffs. Towards the centre of the basin, there is the highest point in the island (122.4 m) known as Jabal Al-Dukhan, the Mountain of Smoke, because of its vague and hazy appearance, especially during the hot summer months. The majority of Bahrain's oil wells are situated around this area.

6.   Dates, loaz (Indian almond), pomegranate, banana, fig trees and a variety of vegetables are grown on the fertile strip to the north, and are irrigated from natural springs and artisan wells. The remainder of the state is covered in varying degrees by low-lying desert shrub and ground plants which thrive in the south.

0054

7.   There are no rivers in Bahrain and the country depends solely on ground water.

MAIN CITIES

8.   Manama (the capital city), Muharraq, East and West Rifa'a, Jid Hafs, Isa Town, Hamad Town, Hidd and Awali.

CLIMATE

9.   Bahrain's climate is pleasant except during summer months (June, July, August and September) when it becomes hot with high humidity. Most rainfall occurs during the cold season (December, January, February and March), usually in the form of a number of heavy storms, often accompanied by a strong wind from the north-west, known as the Shamaal, or the south-east, known as the Kaws. It is often cold enough, during cold season, for electric heaters, warm clothes and the use of blankets.

   Monthly average temperatures in Manama are as follows:

	Jan	Feb	Mar	Apr	May	Jun	Jul	Aug	Sep	Oct	Nov	Dec
Day	20	21	24	28	33	35	37	38	36	32	27	22
Night	14	15	17	21	26	28	29	30	27	24	21	16

POPULATION

10.   According to the latest census of the Central Statistics Organization in 1986, the population of Bahrain was about 420,000 of which 70% were Bahrainis and 30% expatriates.

11.   About 32% of the total population lives in the capital city Manama, on the north-eastern tip of Bahrain.

LANGUAGE

12.   Arabic is the official and mother tongue language in Bahrain. However English is the second spoken language and widely used in work and commercial areas. Other spoken languages in the society are French, Persian, Urdu and Hindi.

0055

RELIGION

13. The national religion of the country is Islam. However, as Bahrain is known for its tolerance, other religious communities living on the island also enjoy freedom to practice their religious faiths. In addition to mosques, there are Christian churches (St. Christopher's church [Anglican], Sacred Heart church [Roman Catholic], National Evangelical church and Syrian Orthodox church), as well as a Hindu Temple.

HISTORY

14. The thousands of flints that lie scattered on the desert flats bear witness to the existence, some thirty to forty thousand years ago, of Palaeolithic and Mesolithic hunters. With the rise of rich city states in Mesopotamia and the Indus Valley and the growing market in Mesopotamia for the copper of Oman, the fishermen and pearl divers of Bahrain began to engage in maritime trade and with the wealth that it brought the land, they built the first unfortified city at Qalat Al-Bahrain, where there were continuous city settlements from the beginning of the third millennium B.C. down to Neo-Babylonian times (circa 650 B.C.).

15. Babylonian and Sumerian records frequently mentioned a place called Dilmun, known as the "land of immortality", an ideal land, the terrestrial paradise, and archaeological finds support the identification of Bahrain as ancient Dilmun.

16. The first historical reference appeared at the time of Sargeon of Akkad's conquest of the island and its neighbouring lands. Under the successive suzerainty of the Sumerians, Semitic Babylonians, Amorites from the Syrian deserts and the Kassites, a partly Indo-European people from the Iranian highlands, Bahrain continued its prosperous mercantile activities uninterrupted until the invasion by the Aryans of the Indus Valley civilizations. Prosperity returned to the island once more with the rise of the Assyrian Empire in Mesopotamia and continued under Babylonian rule; it is not known whether Bahrain formed part of the Persian Empire following the conquest of Babylonia by the Persians.

17. Alexander the Great sent ships on voyages of exploration down the Arabian coast and the name of <u>Tylos</u> appears to be the name given by the Greeks to the island.

0056

18. It seems that the importance of Bahrain dwindled with the rise of the Roman Empire when trade from India was transferred from the Arabian Gulf to the Red Sea. It would appear that Bahrain was under the domination of Arab tribes from the mainland of Arabia until the fourth century B.C., when Shapur II, the Sassanian monarch of Persia, captured the islands, and much of the Arabian coast. Thereafter and for a thousand years Bahrain was known as Awal. The Sassanians exercised indirect rule until the time of the Prophet Mohamed, when the Arab rule of Bahrain and his followers embraced Islam.

19. In the second half of the ninth century, the country was under Carmathian rule and was used both as naval base and a penal settlement. A popular rising dislodged the Carmathians in the eleventh century and until the sixteenth century and the coming of Portuguese, the island was ruled by different Arab dynasties.

20. Portuguese voyages toward the end of the fifteenth and beginning of the sixteenth centuries opened up the Arabian Gulf to European ships, although Portuguese rule in Bahrain lasted only some eighty years. From 1602 until the end of the century, a series of Persian governors ruled Bahrain but at the turn of the century, the Omanis invaded Bahrain. Omani rule ended with the sale of Bahrain to the Persians. A period of anarchy followed and Bahrain once more changed hands several times.

21. The first contact between the British and the Khalifa family, who had triumphed over the Persians in the latter half of the eighteenth century, occurred in 1814. The khalifas had then reigned for some 40 years. With the proclamation of Shaikh Isa as the ruler by the local notables, a more stable period of Bahrain's history began. Treaties were signed with the British and a convention was signed in 1913 recognizing Bahrain's independence and control of a number of nearby islands.

22. The story of modern Bahrain begins with the accession of Shaikh Hamed in 1935 when conditions in the pearl industry were reformed, municipalities, education and other public services were developed. In May 1970, at the 1536th meeting of the Security Council, by unanimous vote, the Council passed a resolution based on the report submitted to the United Nations Secretary-General by his personal delegate to Bahrain declaring that the people of Bahrain "were virtually unanimous in wanting a fully independent sovereign State. The great majority added that this should be an Arab State". The declaration of the state's independent status was proclaimed in August 1971. Bahrain is a member of the Arab League and it became a member of the United Nations on 21 September 1971.

0057

ECONOMY

23.   Bahrain's geographical position at the centre of the Middle East oil producing region helped to establish the island as a business centre for the whole Gulf.   However, the importance of oil as a mainstay of the economy is lessening - natural oil supplies, never vast are diminishing.   During recent years, the government has been seriously committed to a policy of economic diversification.

24.   The airport on Muharraq Island, linked by causeway to mainland Bahrain, handles more than 16 million kilograms of freight each year.   Mina Salman, the main harbour, has been undergoing a major extension and re-development; traditionally the port also handles transit cargo for neighbouring Gulf countries.

25.   Sitra oil jetty handles a continuous flow of oil tankers delivering products from Bahrain's refinery to more than 55 countries.   The Aluminium Bahrain (ALBA) jetty receives over 240,000 of alumina annually from Australia and the 110,000 tons of finished aluminium ingot exported each year go as far afield as Japan, North America and Europe.

26.   The opening of the Arab Shipbuilding and Repair Yard (ASRY), constitutes a major development in Bahrain's industry.   The giant complex includes a sophisticated network of repair shops and tank cleaning facilities, as well as the actual dry dock with the capacity to handle ships up to 500,000 dead-weight ton.

27.   Recently Bahrain encouraged the formation of offshore banking Units (OBUs).   Presently there are over 76 offshore banks, 22 investment companies, foreign exchange and money brokers as well as 18 commercial banks and 62 representative offices of financial institutions.   Bahrain also has long been a home for the fishing fleets of the Gulf, catching the tasteful local fish and prawns for which the country is famous.   Pearl-diving industry, which flourished in the past, has steadily declined, mainly due to the large scale cultured pearl production in the Far East which, in turn led to a reduction in demand for natural pearls.

28.   In 1984, imports in Bahrain were valued at BD 590 million and exports at BD 91.5 million.   The figure for crude oil production in 1984 was put at 15 million barrels and gas

0058

production was 145 billion cu. ft. The value of oil export was BD 53 million.

29. The Government of Bahrain is aware that oil reserves will not last much longer than the year 2,000 and, as a result, they attach a great importance to the development of alternative industries. Policy initiatives have thus been taken over the past years to develop the island as a regional business service centre.

30. There are 28 tourist hotels of different categories with 6,219 beds. There are 48 government hospitals and health centres in the country and the number of hospital beds/1000 inhabitants was put at 2.7. There are 459 physicians, making it 1 physician per 872 inhabitants.

31. The Gross National Product (GNP) per capita for 1983 in Bahrain was BD 3,952 (US$10,510), whereas GNP per capita for 1986 has decreased to BD 3,200 equivalent to US$8.510.

TRAVEL TO THE COUNTRY

32. Bahrain's position as a stopover and refuelling point provides frequent direct flights by major airlines (such as UTA, Singapore Airlines, Lufthansa, British Airways, Swiss Air, Qantas and of course Gulf Air) which link it with many countries in Europe, Asia, Africa, the Middle East and Australia. The airport is situated on the island of Muharraq linked to Manama by a 3 km causeway. An airport tax of BD 3 has been imposed on all out-bound passengers since May 1986.

33. All visitors to Bahrain should ensure that their passports are valid and will not expire during their stay. Visas are available at the airport. British passport holders born and resident in UK do not require a visa to come to Bahrain. However, British passport holders born outside the United Kingdom and other nationalities from European countries will need a visa in order to enter the country. No visa is required by nationals of the Gulf Cooperation Council (GCC) countries, i.e. - Kuwait, Oman, Qatar, Saudi Arabia and the United Arab Emirates. Whereas other nationals with valid Residence Permits from GCC countries, can obtain 72-hour visas upon arrival at immigration point.

0059

TRAVEL WITHIN THE COUNTRY AND LOCAL TRANSPORT

34. Bahrain has an efficient public transport system which provides regular bus services to most of the towns and villages. Fares are 100 fils.

35. Taxis are always available including a 24-hour on-call taxi service. Taxis can easily be recognized by their overhead signs and yellow & white license plates. The cost for an average trip is BD 2. More than one hour, the fare will be decided by the consent of both parties, and will be increased if it is from the airport to any other place due to waiting. Fares are subject to 50% increase between midnight and 5 a.m. A street taxi usually costs less. The average taxi fare from the airport to the centre of the city, i.e., hotels' locations, costs about BD 4.

36. Cost of petrol is now BD 0.080 per litre for high octane and BD 0.100 for the super octane.

MAIL SERVICES

37. Bahrain has an efficient postal system, and air-mail service to and from Bahrain is fast and reliable. Overseas courier companies offer fast mail delivery to over 20 countries in the world.

38. Post offices: Central Manama, Government Road near Bab Al-Bahrain. This is the island's main post office. Open from 0700 to 1900 hrs. Adliya's post office is off the intersection of Shaikh Isa Road and near the Al-Jazeera Supermarket and is open from 0700 to 1415 hrs.

39. Airmail postal charges for letters and printed-matters of 10 grams each are as follows:

Zones	Letter*	Postcard*	Printed Matter*
Zone 'A' (Arabian Gulf States) Saudi Arabia, Kuwait, Qatar, Emirates, Oman and Iraq.	50 Fils	40 Fils	25 Fils

0060

Zone 'B'
Other Arab countries
Member of Arab Postal Union   80 Fils   60 Fils   40 Fils

Zone 'C'
Europe, India, Pakistan,
Afghanistan, Iran, Bangladesh,
Sri Lanka, Maldives Islands   150 Fils   120 Fils   75 Fils

Zone 'D'
South & North America, Canada,
Japan, South East Asia,
Australia, New Zealand and
Africa   200 Fils   150 Fils   100 Fils

*   **Tax stamp of 5 Fils is to be added to the charges above.**

Airletters (Aerogrammes):   125 Files each.

Local Mails: Letters 50 Fils each 20 grams
                Printed matters 25 File each 20 grams.

Other Charges: Registration   300 Fils
                Advice of Delivery   200 Fils
                Enquiry   200 Fils

TELEPHONE SERVICE

40. The international telephone system incorporates subscriber dialling between Bahrain and all neighbouring countries and to most countries in Asia, Africa, Western Europe, Australia and the Americas.

41. There are a total of 124 coin-operated telephones taking 100 fils coins. Some 35 are in public booths in the main towns and the rest are in hotels, restaurants and shops.

0061

TELEX/FAX

42.   Bahrain is reputed to have more telex machines per head population than any other country in the world.

CURRENCY

43.   The unit of currency is the Bahraini Dinar (BD) which is divided into 1,000 fils. Coins are issued in denominations of 5 fils (bronze); 10 fils (bronze); 25 fils (small metallic silver); 50 fils (medium metallic silver); 100 fils (large metallic silver). Notes are issued in denominations of 500 fils (purple); BD 1 (red); BD 5 (blue); BD 10 (green) and BD 20 (brownish pink).

44.   The present rate of exchange is approximately US$1.00 - BD 0.376 (i.e. one Bahraini Dinar equals US$2.66). However, since exchange rates are subject to fluctuation, the latest rate of exchange should be consulted.

EXCHANGE CONTROLS AND BANKING FACILITIES

45.   There are no restrictions on the inflow and outflow of local and foreign currency. Bahraini Dinar is itself convertible. Traveller's cheques and drafts are easily obtainable from commercial banks. One can easily change currency at exchange offices in town. Banking hours: 0730 to 1200 Saturday through Wednesday; 0730 to 1100 Thursday. Friday closed.

The following commercial banks have branches in Bahrain:

		Telephone
-	Al-Ahli Commercial Bank B.S.C.	244333
-	Algemene Bank Nederland N.V.	255420
-	Arab Banking Limited	255988
-	Bahrain Islamic Bank	231402
-	Bank of Bahrain and Kuwait B.S.C.	253388
-	Bank Saderat Iran	250809
-	Banque du Caire	254454
-	Banque Paribas	253119
-	British Bank of the Middle East	255933
-	Standard Chartered Bank	255946
-	Chase Manhattan Bank N.A.	251401
-	Citi Bank N.A.	257124
-	Grindlays Bank Limited	250805

0062

–	Habib Bank Limited	255062
–	National Bank of Abu Dhabi	250824
–	National Bank of Bahrain B.S.C.	258800
–	Rafidain Bank	255389
–	United Bank Limited	254032

ELECTRICITY

46. Electric current throughout the country is 220 volts AC, 50 cycles. Wall points and plugs are of the English type (three-point) with either round or flat pins.

IMMUNIZATION REQUIREMENTS

47. Vaccination certificates against yellow fever are required from travellers coming from infected areas. Visitors are advised to check if any emergency vaccinations have been implemented. Vaccinations are available 24 hours at Bahrain International Airport. Typhoid and tetanus inoculations are recommended.

HEALTH CONDITIONS

48. General health conditions are good and sanitary conditions are reasonably satisfactory. The best prevention is to ensure that fruit and vegetables are thoroughly washed in detergent. Irritation to eyes and ears is however caused by the use of fans and A/C units or by dust and wind-carried sand. In the summer time good health is best maintained by taking plenty of liquid and enough sleep. Exposure to the sun during the hot summer months should be avoided. Occasional stomach upsets are not uncommon as in most hot countries. Discretion is needed in the choice of public eating places.

MEDICAL FACILITIES

49. Medical and dental services are reasonably good. For serious cases, however, treatment abroad may sometimes be necessary. There is in Bahrain one major government hospital - Salmaniya Medical Centre (SMC). There are also numerous government primary health care centres situated throughout the towns and villages of Bahrain providing paediatrics, ante-natal, dental and general medical services. A number of private hospitals, private clinics, private doctors and dentists are available with reasonable charges.

0063

50. The hospital most commonly used by the expatriates are the government-run Salmaniya Medical Centre, the International Hospital, the American Mission Hospital, Bahrain Defense Force Hospital and Awali Hospital.

51. Salmaniya Medical Centre (SMC), is the largest hospital in Bahrain, recently expanded and modernized. It has chest, psychiatric, maternity and general wings, a 24-hour accident and emergency department, very good radiology, laboratory and physiotherapy facilities and several operating theatres. There are both public wards and private rooms.

52. International Hospital of Bahrain is a luxurious private hospital opened in 1978 and located in a beautiful surrounding. There are two operation theatres, a laboratory and very good X-ray and physiotherapy departments with the latest equipment. However, charges are relatively high.

53. American Mission Hospital is a private and general hospital with X-ray and laboratory facilities, operating theatre and maternity and out-patient departments, but no emergency or casualty departments.

54. Some medicines are provided free of charge by the government hospitals and health care centres on consultation or admittance. However, there are many private pharmacies which are well stocked and almost every kind of drugs are available.

FOOD

55. Except for certain sea food items, nearly all other food supplies are imported from Europe, the Americas, Australia, New Zealand, India, Asia, the Far East and Middle East countries. Imported fresh meat (lamb, beef, pork) is available in all supermarkets. Locally slaughtered sheep, goat and beef is also available at the Central Markets at subsidized prices.

56. Imported fresh fruits and vegetables are also available. Occasionally, during the winter season, there are some local vegetables and fruits. Variety of palm dates are also available during summer season.

0064

57.   Fresh fish is found all year round at the Central Markets. The prawns of Bahrain are very popular in season. Most supermarkets stock frozen fish including lobster, cod etc. There are many large supermarkets for those who prefer to do their weekly shopping under one roof.

58.   Supermarkets are well stocked with a wide variety of canned food, cheese, biscuits, chocolates, baby food, cosmetics, kitchen ware, cigarettes, cigars, pipe tobacco, bread, spices, pickles, soft drinks etc. There are also special shops that sell only beer, liquor and wine. In fact, there is practically everything in town of internationally known food supplies at all times. Supermarkets are a good source of fresh eggs. However, prices in supermarkets are generally very high compared to Europe.

RESTAURANTS

59.   All hotel restaurants offer European, Eastern, Indian and American food. There are now quite a number of good Indian, Chinese and Lebanese restaurants. There are also several smaller Pakistani, Indian and Lebanese restaurants that are located in popular areas of the capital at cheaper prices. Discretion is advised in eating salads and raw vegetables in these small restaurants, especially during summer.

60.   All hotels have coffee-shops. Fast food places including Kentucky Fried Chicken, Dairy Queen, Burger Land, Hardees, Magnumberger and Pizza Hut are also available.

CLOTHING

61.   In winter, sometimes it is necessary to wear woollen sweaters and jackets. In summer, light-weight clothing is recommended. Ready-made clothing is available for both men and women and a number of boutiques offer European fashions. Prices are comparatively high in boutiques and it is recommended that clothing and shoes be brought into the country. Fabric is available and there are some tailoring shops of high standard. All reasonable styles of women's wear are acceptable.

62.   A contrasting variety of clothing is seen in the streets of the capital. It ranges from the traditional long dress of Arab men and women to the Indian sarees and fashioned summer European dresses.

0065

63. There are many small stores which sell much cheaper qualities of clothing from Asian countries. The market also offers a wide range of shoes/sandals.

MISCELLANEOUS

64. Toilet goods and cosmetics are in good supply. Hairdressing and beauty salons for ladies, barber shops, laundry and dry-cleaning services are available. There are several toy shops. Cameras, related accessories and films are in good supply. Black and white and colour films may be processed locally. It is more expensive compared to Europe and North America.

NATIONAL AND PUBLIC HOLIDAYS

65. Following is a list of national and public holidays observed in Bahrain.

New Year	1 Jan
Eid Al-Fitr	
Eid Al-Adha	
Islamic New Year	
Ashora	
Prophet's Birthday	
National Day	16 Dec

With the exception of the New Year and National Day holidays, all the other public holidays depend upon the actual start of the lunar months.

SOCIAL LIFE

66. Bahrain is known as the Gulf leisure centre. Entertainment is concentrated at the major hotels, most of which feature one or more live bands with considerable variation and frequency. Dining out at these hotels to the sound of music by foreign or local music groups is a common pastime in Bahrain. In addition to hotels, there are many clubs, associations and other social groups of foreign communities in Bahrain and of big employers, which have numerous social functions.

67. As to public leisure, the country is relatively rich with park and sport facilities. There are many festivals and public holidays which are well celebrated.

0066

ENTERTAINMENT

68.   Bahrain introduced colour television in 1973, the first country in the Gulf to do so. Three channels broadcast daily channel 4 (VHF) and channel 44 (UHF), show Arabic and English language programmes, while channel 55 (UHF) carries English programmes only. Broadcasts can also be received from other transmitters in the region, Abu Dhabi, Aramco Station (Dhahran), Dammam (Saudi Arabia), Dubai, Abu Dhabi, Kuwait, Oman and Qatar.

69.   Radio Bahrain broadcasts through a few AM stations in Arabic and English every day from 0600 to 2400. There are two English FM stations which feature modern music, variety programmes, news programmes and regular classical and jazz music programmes. AM radio programmes can also be received from other countries and from Aramco.

70.   Details of television and radio programmes are published in the Gulf Daily News, the Arabic Khaleej Times and the Gulf News.

71.   Music cassettes and records of a wide variety are locally available in many shops. Video has become the top form of home entertainment and there are many video rental shops.

72.   A few years back, there were discos all over the island, but now only a few hotels offer dancing facilities. The programme of the night-clubs is published in the Gulf Mirror's Time Out magazine.

73.   The Bahrain national museum, as well as the New Heritage Centre though small, is well laid out and extremely interesting. It covers the fascinating archaeology and history of the island as well as providing information on customs, trades and crafts traditional to the island.

BOOKS, PERIODICALS AND NEWSPAPERS

74.   The local bookshops are well stocked with a good selection of books in Arabic and English, i.e. Family Bookshop, Al-Hilal Bookshop, M. Mubeen & Bros. and Jashanmal & Sons. In addition, the public library (Arabic and English) has branches in Manama, Muharraq, Isa Town and a Mobile unit to reach smaller towns. BAPCO Club and British Council also have libraries.

0067

75.   Arabic books are available in a number of small bookshops, as are a very limited choice of books in German and French.

76.   Bahrain has its own English language tabloid newspaper, the Gulf Daily News, which is published seven days a week. In addition, the UAE based Khaleej Times and Gulf News are available seven days a week. There is one independent Arabic language daily Akbar Al-khaleej and one weekly newspaper appears on Saturdays Al-Adwaa, published by the owners of the Gulf Daily News, while the Information Ministry publishes a daily news-sheet Akhbar Al-bahrain (Bahrain News) in both Arabic and English. There are several Arabic weekly magazines and government announcements appear in the weekly Al-Jarida Al-Rasmiya (The Official Gazette).

77.   All major magazines from Europe, the US, Australia, the Far East, India and the Arab countries are available. Most of the major British dailies are available while other European daily papers are not regularly available. Some Arabic newspapers from neighbouring countries are also available.

OUTDOOR PASTIMES

78.   The most popular and easily available outdoor pastimes is swimming and there are various beaches where the water is shallow and comparatively clean and very clear. Fishing and jogging are also other favourite outdoor pastimes.

79.   Bahrain has a very active sporting community. Most sports facilities are owned either by the large companies, under whose auspices sports clubs are formed, or by independent groups. By joining clubs, one can practise a good variety of sports such as athletics, basketball, badminton, cricket, football, golf, hockey, tennis, cross-country running, motor-racing, squash, sailing, water-skiing, bowling, rugby, soccer etc. Horse-riding is another popular pastime.

80.   There are five major clubs with extensive club premises and a range of social and sporting activities in Bahrain. These are the BAPCO Club, Marina Club, British Club, Dilmun Club, American Club. Membership is often limited and the admission and annual fee extremely high.

0068

81. Besides clubs, there are interest groups like, Bahrain
Artists' Association, Bahrain Historical and Archaeological
Society and Bahrain Garden Club.

82. One of the most delightful ways of spending a summer Friday
is to hire a dhow and sail in a group of 20 to 30 persons to one
of the small islands nearby. Dhows can be hired at the Dhow port
in Muharraq or via a travel agency.

HISTORIC SITES AND PLACES OF INTEREST

83. There are in Bahrain a number of sites worth visiting, many
of them evoking the centuries-old traditions of Arabia.
Particularly noteworthy are Khamis Mosque (Two Minarets' Mosque),
which dates as far back as the 7th century, making it one of the
oldest mosques in the Gulf; the 16th century Portuguese fort near
Budaiya; the burial mounds (mainly between Hamala and Awali) are
impressive sights; weavers at Bani Jamra; basket makers at
Karbabad; potters at A'Ali and the old Adhari Pool which is
supplied by fresh water springs. Jabel El-DuKhan, the "mountain
of smoke" is the highest point in Bahrain overlooking the west
and east coasts of the island.

84. A recent addition to the visiting list is the Al-Areen
Wildlife Park and Reserve. Al-Areen is situated southeast of
Zellaque. It consists of a private reserve for breeding rare and
endangered species and a park where animals can be viewed and
photographed. The park is officially open for public visitors.

. . . . .

0069

IRAQ

GEOGRAPHY

1.   Iraq, covering an area of 438,446 square kilometres, is
bordered to the south by Kuwait and Saudi Arabia, to the west by
Jordan and Syria, and to the north and east by Turkey and Iran.
It has access to the Arabian Gulf at Basrah in the southeast.
The country is in the form of a basin, lying between the great
Syrian Desert to the west and south of the Zagros Mountains along
the Iranian frontier to the north. The land descends from the
mountains to the desert in a series of hills and steppes
intersected by rivers and wadis which carry the winter rainfall
and melted snow to the rivers Tigris and Euphrates.

2.   The geographical regions can be distinguished as follows:
The Mesopotamian Valley, a broad fertile plain between the twin
rivers; the mountain area comprising the imposing Kurdistan chain
which extended over some 92,000 sq km with peaks reaching 3,500
metres; the terrace lands which cover about 42,500 sq km between
the Mesopotamian Valley and the mountains; the plains (including
marshes and lakes) covering about 132,500 sq km and deserts,
approximately 167,000 sq km stretching from the Euphrates to the
western frontier.

CLIMATE

3.   The climate of Iraq is typical of an inland subtropical
region. The Mesopotamian Valley area may be described as semi-
arid, with its six-inch average rainfall occurring almost
exclusively in the three winter months. Temperatures vary widely
between winter and summer. Dust storms are common. In the
coldest months, December, January and February, the mean daily
temperature in Baghdad and the plains area is around 11°C (52°f),
although the actual day-time temperatures during this period
range from freezing point to 29°C (84°F). This is also the rainy
seasons, but there are extensive sunny periods.

4.   Temperatures rise gradually from March or April onwards,
until June, July and August, which are the hottest months.
Sunshine is virtually continuous from May to September. During
July and August, the average daily maximum is about 43°C (109°F)
and the average minimum about 27°C (81°F). The highest recorded

0070

shade temperature for Baghdad is 50°C (122°F), although the
temperature at night may occasionally drop as low as 20°C (68°F).
The air, except near the coast at Basrah, is very dry and these
high temperatures are quite tolerable provided one avoids the
mid-day sun and wears light clothing. There are generally only a
few days during the summer when southeast winds, bringing
humidity from the Gulf, make the heat less tolerable. About mid-
September, the temperature begins to fall gradually. March,
April, October and November are generally pleasant in Baghdad.

5.   In the Basrah areas, the temperatures are less extreme, but
humidity is high and this, during the hot summer months of May
through October, can make living and working conditions
uncomfortable. Dust storms are also common.

6.   The climate in the northern mountain areas is more temperate
with an average rainfall of about 650 mm (25 inches) and average
maximum temperatures of about 35°C (95°F). Winters are more
severe, with some snow and hail.

HUMAN GEOGRAPHY

7.   The estimated population of Iraq is about 15 million.
Nearly 70% of the population live in urban areas, concentrated
mainly in Baghdad, the capital, and three other cities, Basrah
(Iraq's only seaport) in the south, Mosul and Kirkuk in the
north.

8.   Most of the people are Arabs. The inhabitants of the
northern provinces (Sulaimaniyah, Arbil and Dohuk) are, however,
predominantly Kurds, ethnically and linguistically related to the
Indo-European peoples. Kurdish is the general language of these
areas, having equal status with Arabic as an official language.
Armenians, Assyrians, Chaldeans and Turkomans form smaller
groups, which have generally retained their own language, in
addition to speaking Arabic. English is the most widely spoken
foreign language.

9.   About half of the people earn their living from agriculture.
The irrigated central plain is the most densely populated region
and accounts for the great part of agricultural production. For
administrative purposes, the country is grouped into 245 Mahias,
99 Qadhas and 18 Muhafadhas. There are industrial centres around
Baghdad, Basrah and Mosul, while petroleum industries are
concentrated mostly in the Kirkuk and Basrah areas.

0071

RELIGION

10.   The official religion of Iraq is Islam and the major part of the population is Moslem. Shias and Sunnis represent the two major sects in almost equal numbers. According to the official census taken in 1965, there were 232,406 Christians, 69,653 Yazidis in the north who have a religion of their own, and 14,262 Sabeans, followers of St. John the Baptist.

11.   In Baghdad, services for all Protestant denominations are held every Sunday at 6.00pm, in English, at the George's Memorial Church of England. Roman Catholic services in Arabic, English and French are conducted at the Presentation Sisters' Convent, and in French by the Franciscan Fathers at St Joseph's Cathedral. There are several other Catholic churches in Baghdad. There a number of other churches in Baghdad of various other Christian denominations.

HISTORY

12.   Iraq, site of one of the earliest known civilizations and, according to legend, of the Garden of Eden, has witnessed the coming of many cultures, empires and races, including Sumerians, Semites, Babylonians, Assyrians, Persians, Greeks, Romans, Arbas, Ottomans and British.

13.   The Sumerian City States began to flourish around 3500 B.C. Less than 700 years later, Sagron of Akkad created an empire out of the land between the Tigris and Euphrates and extended its boundaries to the Mediterranean. There followed a period of Sumerian ascendency during which the City of Ur, the biblical home of Abraham, was most powerful. Gradually, the Semites (who had begun to move into the land before 2300 B.C.), and the Sumerians intermixed. About 1750 B.C., they were all brought under the rule of the celebrated Hammurabi the law giver, a Semitic King who established his capital in Babylon.

14.   The next group to gain power in the north was the Assyrians; the Kassites, an Indo-European group, took control in the south. The zenith of the Assyrian Empire (911 to 612 B.C.) saw the cities of Nineveh, Nimrud and Khorsabad rise to new heights of splendour. With the downfall of Assyria, the city of Babylon rose again briefly, under a dynasty whose best known figure is Nebuchadnezzar. The downfall of the Neo-Babylonian Empire saw the shifting of the centre of power away from Iraq. The Achemenian Persians ruled Mesopotamia and much of the Middle East

0072

from 539 B.C. until their defeat by the Macedonians under Alexander the Great some 2000 years later. Following his death at Babylon in 323 B.C., Iraq was ruled by his successor, Seleucus, who moved the capital to Seleucia on the Tigris. The Seleucids were followed by the Parthian Persians (135 B.C. - 226 A.D.), another Persian dynasty, and later by the Sassanids who ruled until the Arab conquest in 637 A.D.

15. More than 100 years after the Arab conquests, Baghdad was founded by the Abbasid Caliph, Al-Mansour. The "Round City" and its suburbs were served by elaborate networks of waterways, radiating from major canals. Then followed one of the most brilliant periods in the history of Iraq, a period that reached a peak in the time of Haroun Al-Rashid (787-809 A.D.), the celebrated Caliph of "The Thousand and One Nights". Baghdad became one of the world's most renowned cities, the capital of a great empire, famous for its buildings, its learning, its university and libraries and its luxury. The destruction of its culture by the Mongols in the late 13th century was so complete and ruthless that it took Iraq centuries to recover.

16. From the 16th century until the end of the First World War, Iraq was part of the Ottoman Empire. After World War I, Iraq was established as a separate political entity with its present boundaries and came under British Mandate. In 1932, the country became an independent kingdom under the Hashemite King, Faisal Ibu Hussein of Mecca, who had been reigning since 1921.

POLITICS

17. Following the 14 July 1956 Revolution, Iraq was declared a Republic. A number of changes of government have since occurred, but from 1968, the Arab Ba'ath Socialist Party has been in power. The Revolutionary Command Council headed by the President, Field Marshal Saddam Hussein, is the supreme body of the national government and is responsible for electing the President, the Cabinet, and supervising the command of the Armed Forces. It is also vested with power to ratify or reject all legislation.

18. The Constitution defines the State as a Popular Socialist Republic. The President is the head of the Revolutionary Command Council.

0073

ADMINISTRATION

19.   Iraq is governed through some twenty ministries. A number of autonomous and semi-autonomous organizations are allocated special budgets and control the most important agricultural, industrial, commercial, banking and insurance activities. Regional administration is carried on through 18 provinces (known as Governorates or Muhafadhas); each with a Governor. Within the Governorates, there are some 99 districts (Qadhas), which are divided into 245 sub-districts (Nahiyahs).

20.   Iraq became a Member State of the United Nations on 21 November 1945.

ECONOMY

21.   Iraq is predominantly an agricultural country with about 2.5 million hectares under cultivation. This is about 6% of the total land area and about half of the cultivable area. The area under forests is small, about 18,000 hectares. The rest is mountain, desert or marsh, containing some sparse pasture land.

22.   Iraq provides about 30% of the total world supply of dates, with some 22 million palm trees yielding an annual average of 697,190 tons with an average yield of about 35-40 kg per tree. Other crops are wheat, barley, lentils, chick-peas and linseed in winter; rice, cotton, tobacco, millet and a wide variety of vegetables in summer. Barley, wheat and rice at present account for almost 95% of the field crops. Efforts are being made to increase the cultivation of rice and wheat so that the country may gain self-sufficiency in food. Amongst the commercial crops, the emphasis is on sugar-beet, sugar-cane, cotton and oilseeds so that these raw materials become available to the industrial projects for local processing. The main fruit crops, other than dates, are citrus fruits, melons, grapes, pomegranates, apricots, apples, peaches, plums and olives.

23.   Sheep production, largely in the western plains, is the main form of animal husbandry. The Government is making major efforts to develop livestock and poultry on a large scale so that the requirements of red and white meat may be met locally.

24.   The country's main resource is petroleum (including natural gas). Geological surveys have uncovered the presence of ceramic clay, glass sand, phosphates and iron and copper ores. Another

0074

natural resource, sulphur, is playing an important role in Iraq's industrial development and export trade where it ranks as the second most important hard currency earner. Mining and quarrying account for about 58% of the Gross Domestic Product.

25. Up to 1950, development was left largely to private initiative. Industrial activity was confined to extraction of petroleum by foreign-owned companies mainly for export and to a number of consumer and construction goods industries operated by the private sector. With the increase in oil revenues, the Government has assumed a much more active role to ensure proper utilization of these funds for development purposes. Iraq is one of the important oil-producing countries which is investing the bulk of its oil revenues in national development in all sectors, but particularly in the industrial and agricultural sectors. The results of this national effort are plainly visible. The country is bustling with development activity, new industries, and construction projects while large-scale irrigation and agricultural projects are being implemented. In 1964, key industries were nationalized and today the great majority of industrial enterprises are operated by the public sector and a number of organizations have been established for this purpose.

TAXIS

26. Taxis are numerous. It is essential to agree on the fare before engaging a taxi without a taxi meter. Tipping is optional.

CURRENCY

27. The unit of currency is the Iraqi Dinar (I.D.) divided into 1,000 fils.

WEIGHTS AND MEASURES

28. The official system of weights and measures is metric. Agricultural land is measured in donums (d donums = 1 hectare).

ELECTRICITY

29. The electricity supply in Iraq is 220 volts AC, 50 cycles (electric clocks, tape-recorders and record-players designed for

0075

60-cycle operation will not function properly on 50 cycles, even if the voltage is 220). Most of the fittings are of the British type of two and three round-pin outlets and bayonet-type light bulbs.

HEALTH

30. On the whole, Iraq is a healthy place to live in provided normal standards of hygiene are observed. Malaria is diminishing but has not yet been eradicated from certain areas in northern Iraq. If posted in these areas, it is necessary to adhere to the recommendations of the Directorate, Malaria Eradication Programme.

31. Protection against parasitic and food-borne diseases includes thorough washing of raw fruits and vegetables, preventing children from playing barefoot outdoors and the avoidance of bathing or paddling in irrigation water.

32. During the hot season, adequate amounts of fluids and salt must be taken to replace those lost by perspiration, in order to avoid dehydration.

FOOD

33. A range of local and imported foods is available and locally-grown fruits and vegetables are found seasonally throughout the year.

34. Lamb is the most popular meat and is usually of better quality than beef or veal. Since Moslems do not eat pork or pork products, local supplies should be relied upon. Good local chicken and turkeys are sold. Supplies of imported frozen chickens, meat, lamb and beef are sometime available.

35. Fresh fish (local river fish of the carp family) is available but somewhat expensive; supplies of frozen flat fish from the gulf are also occasionally available at reasonable prices.

36. Pasteurized milk and milk products are normally available in Baghdad and are very good. Local and a limited selection of imported cheese is usually obtainable.

0076

37. Rice, lentils, barley, chick-peas, etc., are available. The local flour is rather coarse but satisfactory for most types of cooking. Bread is of good quality. Local factories produce macaroni, spaghetti, vermicelli, cornflour, custard powder, icing sugar, jams, jellies, dried fruits, biscuits, sweets and chocolates, etc. Tea and imported ground and instant coffee are readily available.

38. There is a variety of locally-bottled carbonated beverages at reasonable prices (soda water, lemonade, colas, etc.) as well as lemon and orange squash.

39. There are several varieties of locally-brewed beer and lager, all of which are good. Imported brands are available at the Duty-Free Shop. Very little wine is consumed. A variety of imported spirits and dessert wines can be purchased in the larger grocery stores.

RESTAURANTS

40. All the better Baghdad hotels have restaurants open to non-residents. There are also a number of other restaurants, usually serving a choice of European or Iraqi dishes. Tips, if not included as a service charge on the bill, should be approximately 10%-15%.

CLOTHING

41. The wide temperature range between winter and summer in Iraq demands a considerable variety of clothing.

42. Woollen suits, overcoats and sweaters are worn by men during the winter months, and loose-fitting tropical-weight suits in summer. Cotton or cotton mixture shirts are preferable for summer wear to synthetic fibres. Dark suits, collar and tie, are standard office attire throughout the year. Dress on social occasions tends to be rather formal, although full evening dress and dinner-jackets are almost never worn. Shorts are not worn in public except for sports. Most clubs insist on white outfits for tennis, etc.

43. Clothing for women should include woollen suits, dresses, cardigans and blouses suitable for winter wear, since houses and

0077

offices are not centrally heated. An overcoat is essential. All summer wear should be light, porous and easily laundered, cotton being the most suitable material. Although sleeveless dresses are worn, the conventions of the country do not favour bare shoulders, low-cut dresses or very short skirts. Nylon dresses and underwear should be avoided during the hot weather. Hats are seldom worn except for church attendance but a large shady hat is useful for summer wear.

44. A limited selection and quantity of locally manufactured and imported ready-to-wear clothing (dresses, suits, blouses, shirts, pants, etc.) is available, but prices and quality vary. Ladies' good quality lingerie is difficult to find. Imported shoes are not always available. Locally manufactured shoes of reasonable good quality are always available.

45. A variety of imported and locally manufactured suit and dress fabrics is available. Tailoring and dress-making services are good but highly-priced.

MISCELLANEOUS

46. Laundry and dry-cleaning services are adequate. Shoe repairs are reasonable. It is advisable to store winter clothes in nepthalene during the summer months to avoid damage by termite and moth. Imported and locally manufactured cosmetics and toilet articles are available, but selection is somewhat limited. There are good barbers and hairdressers in Baghdad.

NATIONAL AND PUBLIC HOLIDAYS

47. The following is a list of national and public holidays in Iraq. Those marked with an asterisk are dependent on the lunar phase. For Eids lasting more than one day, only the first working day is observed as an official holiday:

New Year's Day   1 January

Army Day   6 January

8 February Revolution   8 February

Eid Al-Fitr*

Labour Day   1 May

0078

Republic Day	14 July
17 July Revolution	17 July
Eid Al-Adha*	
Islamic New Year*	
Ashoura	3 September
Prophet's Birthday*	

48.   There are two major Moslem "Eids" (festivals): Eid Al-Fitr (Ramadhan), which lasts three days following the holy month of Ramadhan, and Eid Al-Adha, for the pilgrimage to Mecca, which lasts four days. During these periods, greeting cards and visits are exchanged and festivities take place.

ENTERTAINMENT

49.   There are a number of modern air-conditioned cinemas in Baghdad and the main towns where films from a number of countries are shown with sub-titles in both Arabic and either French or English. Baghdad has a 1000-seat National Theatre which has a revolving stage and two halls fitted for cinematic projections. Concerts, plays, musical performances and film shows are presented regularly by local and visiting groups. The Baghdad Symphony Orchestra, under the direction of expatriate conductors performs from time to time. An Iraqi folk-lore troupe with an interesting repertoire of traditional songs and dances performs quite frequently also.

50.   Iraq has many talented artists, including painters, sculptors, and ceramic artists, who put on frequent exhibitions of their work. The Iraqi National Museum contains an outstanding display of archaeological exhibits and has an excellent library.

51.   Cultural centres of various countries as well as the Iraqi National Museum provide films and other documentary material and occasional exhibitions, lectures and performances.

52.   Radio programmes in Baghdad are almost entirely in Arabic or Kurdish. The FM Broadcasting Station also provides broadcasting services of 8 hours daily. The state-owned television station in

0079

Baghdad has programmes mainly in Arabic. There are daily newscasts in English and foreign films are shown several times a week.

53. The Al-Mansour Melia an Al-Ishtar Sheraton Hotels offer good entertainment and a discotheque.

OUTDOOR PASTIMES

54 Swimming is the most popular pastime in the summer. The various clubs offer swimming, tennis, squash, billiards, table tennis, etc. A limited choice of sports equipment is available in Baghdad. There are frequent football matches and athletic events and a new sports indoor (gymnasium) stadium (Saddam Stadium) has been built. Important matches are often televised. Stables exist which provide horses for hire and for sale and riding lessons are given at reasonable rates.

55. Fishing is a popular sport and boating on the Tigris is a most pleasant pastime, provided that a permit is obtained.

56. In Iraq, there are many centres of attractions, for tourists, including the Tourist Village in Bahhaniya, Tharthar Lake, Razaza Lake, Tajiyt Island, Abu Nawas Tourist Complex, Ctesiphon, New Baghdad Island.

HISTORIC SITES

57. Baghdad offers many places of interest such as Abbasid Place, Al-Mustansiriyah, Marjan Mosque, Khan Marjan, Bab Al-Wastani (the last of Baghdad's remaining gates) and Zubaida's Tomb. The huge magnificent gold-domed Mosque of Kadhimain, with its four golden minarets, provides an impressive landmark for visitors.

58. Iraq is so rich in historical sites that it is possible to name but a few here.

59. The visitor to Babylon can still see the site of the famous Hanging Gardens, the Lion of Babylon and the reconstructed Ishtar Gate with its beautiful bas-reliefs. It lies approximately one and a half hours by car from Baghdad along a good road.

0080

60. The most ancient university known in the world (about 4,000 years old), Tel-Harmel, is about 9.6 km from Baghdad. Some of the earliest mathematical calculations known were discovered here, one proving the knowledge of a principle which was hitherto thought to have originated with Euclid 17 centuries later.

61. The great Arch of Ctesiphone, believed to be the largest unsupported brick arch in the world, is only half an hour's drive from Baghdad. The arch dates back to the time of the Sassanian Persians who ruled Iraq in the third century A.D.

62. Visitors to Ctesiphone should not miss the Qadissiyah Panorama, which shows the great battle of Qaddissiyah in graphic detail with very striking light and sound effects, almost bringing to life the din of warriors, neighing of horses and the sound of the swords.

63. Also close to Baghdad is Agargouf, an ancient city built on a Sumero-Babylonian plan in the 15th century B.C. by King Kurigalzu, where there are the remains of an impressive ziggurat or staged tower.

64. The remains of the great city of Nineeh lie just east of Mosul. This city flourished around the 7th century B.C. and became exceedingly powerful at the time of King Sannacherib. One gate with two winged bulls still stands as a reminder of its past grandeur. The Mosque of Nabi Younis, built on a small hill a few hundred metres from the ruins of Nineveh, is said to contain the tomb of the Prophet Ionah.

65. Also near Mosul is Nimrud, the first inhabited place mentioned in the Old Testament. Here, one may see a ziggurat, the ruins of a great temple, where two huge stone lions were among the many discoveries, as well as the remains of the Palace of the ancient Assyrian King Assurnasirpal.

66. Ur, which lies in close proximity to Nasiriyah, was a brilliant centre of Sumerian civilization and the capital of three dynasties of kings. The great temple tower built in 2000 B.C., a shrine, and the famous tombs in which kings and members of the royal households were buried 4,500 years ago can still be seen.

67. The mounds of Ashur, earliest capital of the Assyrians, and the ruins of Hatra, the ancient city which became important

0081

during the 2nd century after Christ, can be visited. The former
lies near Sherqat (350 km of good metalled road from Baghdad) on
the River Tigris and the latter about one and a half hours by car
over a desert track to the west of Sherqat. The ruins of Hatra,
most impressive and worth a visit, are at present being excavated
and restored. There is a rest-house at Hatra.

68.   Other important sites include Warka, Nippur, Borsippa,
Khorosabad, Eridu, Seleucia, etc.

69.   The most outstanding monument of the 8th century is the
fortress Palace of Ukaidir, 48 km from Kerbala; its isolation and
dry desert climate make it one of the best preserved antiquities
in Iraq.

70.   The Iraqi Government enforces strict laws prohibiting the
possession of archaeological antiquities and their removal from
the country.

. . . . .

0082

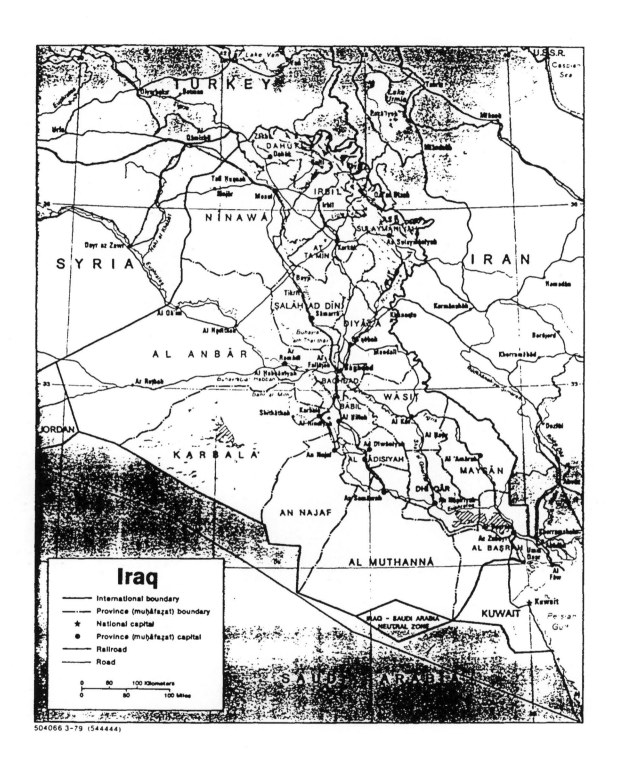

Iraq

— International boundary
—·— Province (muḥāfaẓat) boundary
★ National capital
● Province (muḥāfaẓat) capital
— Railroad
— Road

0   50   100 Kilometers
0   50   100 Miles

504066 3-79 (544444)

0083

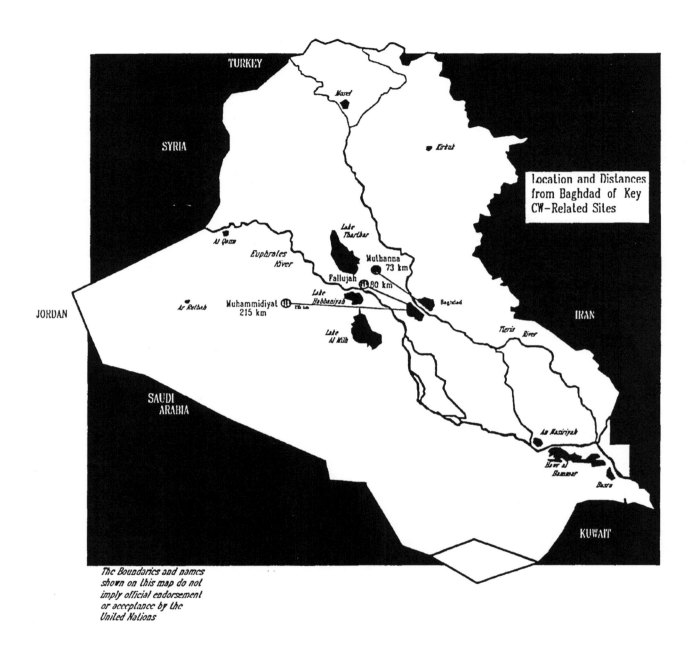

Location and Distances from Baghdad of Key CW-Related Sites

The Boundaries and names
shown on this map do not
imply official endorsement
or acceptance by the
United Nations

0084

PERSONAL CLOTHING, EQUIPMENT AND DOCUMENTATION

GENERAL

1.   This annex does not constitute a comprehensive list of what clothing and equipment CDG personnel will require in Iraq but is intended to assist in individual preparation.

2.   Military uniforms and insignia are not to be worn.

3.   It should be remembered that any excess baggage requirements should be approved by UNSCOM NY before embarkation.

CLOTHING

4.   a.   Shirts, cotton, long and short sleeved.
      b.   Trousers.
      c.   Underwear, cotton.
      d.   Pullover.
      e.   Socks.
      f.   Shoes, boots with ankle support.
      g.   Handkerchiefs.
      h.   Jacket and tie. For those likely to be involved in formal talks - analysts, shift leaders, deputy shift leaders; optional for others.
      i.   Sun hat.
      j.   Shorts.
      k.   Tee shirts
      l.   Trainers.
      m.   Waterproof jacket.
      n.   Coveralls, useful for wearing under IPE.

EQUIPMENT

5.   a.   Toilet gear.
      b.   Towel (for Muthanna).
      c.   Sunblock, minimum of #15.
      d.   Personal medications.
      e.   Sunglasses, minimum of 80% UV, A & B protection, very dark green/grey lenses.
      f.   Respirator with canisters.

0085

```
g.   IPE (NBC suit) x 2.
h.   Walkman + tapes (tapes are inexpensive in Bahrain).
i.   Money belt or pouch.
j.   Small backpack.
k.   Small torch.
l.   Pocket knife.
m.   Hearing protectors.
n.   Compass.
```

DOCUMENTATION

```
6.   a.   Passport.
     b.   Passport photographs x 10.
     c.   UN certificate (collected in Bahrain).
     d.   Driving licence, international.
```

. . . . .

0086

공 란

공   란

공   란

공   란

공   란

공   란

관리 92
번호 -703

원 본

외 무 부

종 별 :

번 호 : UNW-1712

일 시 : 92 0616 1940

수 신 : 장 관(연일)

발 신 : 주 유엔 대사

제 목 : 이락 화학무기 폐기 작업단

연: 주국련 2031-653

1. 이락 화학무기 폐기작업단 참여와 관련, UNSCOM 은 6.11 자 서한으로 재작성된 안내서를 송부하여 왔는바, 동 안내서를 별첨 송부하니 서약서, 신상자료, 유엔 신분증 신청서, 건강진단서는 조속 송부바람

2. 상기 제출 서류는 연호 송부자료에 포함된 서식과 동일하나 건강진단서는 상이하니, 별첨 서식을 사용하기 바람

(대사 유종하-국장)

예고:1992.12.31 에 일반고문에
의거 일반문서로 재분류

첨부:UNW(F)-0544

검 토 필 (1992.6.30.)

국기국

유엔이라크대량살상무기폐기특별위원회(UNSCOM)의 화학무기폐기작업단 참여 요청, 1992. 전2권 (V.2 6.10-12월) 99

UN W(5)-0544 X0616 1940   *#전방외*

OFFICE OF THE SPECIAL COMMISSION

JUNE 1992

INFORMATION FOR UNSCOM INSPECTORS

UNITED NATIONS STATUS

1.   While on duty with the United Nations Special Commission
(UNSCOM), personnel will enjoy the privileges and immunities
accorded to experts performing missions for the United Nations
under article VI of the Convention on the Privileges and
Immunities of the United Nations of 13 February 1946. To be
covered under this Convention, personnel will be requested to
sign a group Special Service Agreement, a type of UN contract,
which identifies them as experts on mission as well as making
them eligible for cover under UN provided special insurances.
Further special arrangements regarding facilities, privileges and
immunities for UNSCOM operations have been negotiated with
Bahrain and with Iraq. The Chief Inspector will be furnished
with copies of the arrangements.

CONDUCT AND PERFORMANCE

2.   UNSCOM personnel shall, during the term of their
appointment, discharge their functions and regulate their conduct
with the interests of the United Nations only in view and shall
not seek or accept instructions in respect of the performance of
their duties from their own government or from any other
authority external to the United Nations.

3.   UNSCOM personnel must always be completely impartial and
objective, and should avoid any action that might give rise to
doubts about their ability to remain so.

4.   UNSCOM personnel are to exercise the utmost discretion in
respect of all matters of official business. They must not
communicate to any person any information known to them by reason
of their official position which has not been made public, except
in the course of their duties or with the authorization of the

544-20-1

0094

2

Chief Inspector. In addition, they must not use such information
to private advantage. On taking up their assignment, UNSCOM
personnel are required to sign an undertaking, the text of which
is attached. These obligations shall not cease after the term of
their appointment with UNSCOM.

PRIVILEGES AND IMMUNITIES

5.   The privileges and immunities of UNSCOM personnel are
defined under article VI, "Experts on missions for the United
Nations", of the Convention on the Privileges and Immunities of
the United Nations, which have been acceded to by Bahrain and
Iraq.

6.   These privileges and immunities are granted in the interests
of the United Nations and not for the personal benefit of
individuals. The United Nations or a national authority may take
whatever legal or disciplinary action may be warranted against
UNSCOM personnel, in accordance with his country's laws and
regulations.

FINANCIAL LIABILITIES

7.   UNSCOM personnel may be required to reimburse the United
Nations either partially or in full for any financial loss
suffered by the United Nations as a result of their negligence or
of their having violated any regulation, rule or administrative
instruction. This may be done by withholding the mission
subsistence allowance.

TRAINING

8.   Members of inspection teams will receive mission training in
Bahrain and in Iraq, as required.

BRIEFING

9.   In addition to information provided to nominated
individuals, personnel will receive detailed briefings on all
aspects of their employment in Bahrain and Baghdad.

0095

TRAVEL

10.   a.   <u>Bahrain</u>. The United Nations, in accordance with
           existing United Nations rules and regulations, will
           provide round-trip transportation on a recognised
           public carrier, at the most economical rate, via the
           shortest, most direct route from country of residence
           to Bahrain. For flights under nine hours duration,
           travel accommodation will be in economy class; when the
           duration of a flight exceeds nine hours, accommodation
           will be in business class. UNSCOM's NY Administrative
           Office will contact personnel, normally by fax, with
           information on where to pick up the prepaid ticket,
           which must be used. Standard time in Bahrain is GMT +
           3. Travel to Bahrain, will require, at this time, a
           national passport and an entry visa for nationals of
           all countries other than countries which are members of
           the Gulf Cooperation Council (Saudi Arabia, Kuwait,
           Oman, Qatar and the United Arab Emirates) and British
           nationals. Personnel will be met at the airport by an
           UNSCOM representative and the entry visa will be issued
           upon arrival in Bahrain. Should you be unable to
           locate the UNSCOM representative, please telephone as
           follows:

                      UNSCOM Office - 33-6898
                      Chief Field Operations - 45-9273
                      Movement Control Assistant; - 45-9656.

      NOTE: Personnel will be denied entry into Bahrain
              if their national passport contains an
              entry/exit stamp from Israel. If this is the
              case, personnel should obtain a new passport
              before leaving for Bahrain.

      b.   <u>Iraq</u>. Standard time in Iraq is GMT + 3. Personnel
           will fly on a UN aircraft from Bahrain to Iraq and
           back. Normally, members of inspection teams will enter
           Iraq on the UN Certificate, a form of "passport"
           identifying them as a UN expert on mission. These
           certificates will be given to each inspector in
           Bahrain. Upon completion of the mission, the
           certificate will be collected and maintained in Bahrain
           and be available for any subsequent deployment. UN
           certificates which have expired will be extended in
           Bahrain. Thus, if personnel already have a
           certificate, it should be taken to Bahrain even if
           expired.

11. In order to obtain this essential travel document for the
first time, it is imperative that personnel fill out <u>all</u>

0096

4

information required on the UN Certificate application form (a blue original card or a facsimile thereof, as attached), <u>sign the card or the facsimile</u>, attach 8 passport-size photos and return immediately by the most expeditious way (DHL or other express mail if necessary) to:

> Ms. Alice Hecht
> United Nations Special Commission
> Room S-3120D
> United Nations
> New York, N.Y. 10017
> U.S.A.
>
> Telephone: (international access code + 1-212-963-5545)

12. <u>**NO NEW CERTIFICATES WILL BE ISSUED IN BAHRAIN.**</u> New certificates are issued only at UN Headquarters in New York.

13. **IF THE INFORMATION IS NOT RECEIVED AT LEAST 7 DAYS PRIOR TO THE TEAM'S ASSEMBLY DATE IN BAHRAIN, IT MAY NOT BE POSSIBLE TO OBTAIN THE UN CERTIFICATE IN TIME.**

ACCOMMODATION

14. UNSCOM will book hotel accommodation for personnel in Bahrain and Baghdad.

ALLOWANCES

15. In addition to roundtrip transportation to and from Baghdad, the United Nations will provide personnel with a per diem allowance for their stay in Bahrain and in Baghdad. At this time, the allowance, which is subject to change, for Bahrain is US$154.00, and for long-term Baghdad-based personnel (over 30 days) it is US$250.00. Personnel selected for a short-duration mission, less than 30 days, will be entitled to a per diem of US$335.00. Personnel will receive a cash advance on arrival in Bahrain. UNSCOM personnel are fully responsible for expenses, including paying hotel bills before check out, meals, telephone calls, etc.

16. The exchange rate is very unfavourable making simple amenities expensive.

17. Final settlement of all entitlements and claims will take place before departure from Bahrain for the return trip home.

0097

INSURANCE

18. Personnel are fully responsible for arranging, at their own expense, such ordinary life, health and other forms of insurance cover for the period of their service for the United Nations as they consider appropriate. The responsibility of the United Nations is limited solely to the payment of compensation, if appropriate, under the following 2 schemes:

    (1) Compensation coverage in the event of death, injury or illness attributable to the performance of official duties on behalf of the United Nations.

       The death, injury or illness of personnel is deemed to be attributable to the performance of official duties on behalf of the United Nations in the absence of any wilful misconduct or wilful intent when:

          a. the death, injury or illness was the result of a natural incident when performing official duties in the course of a United Nations assignment;

          b. the death, injury or illness was a direct result of the presence of personnel in accordance with a United Nations assignment in an area involving special hazards to the staff member's health or security, and occurred as a result of such hazards; or

          c. the death, injury or illness occurred as a direct result of travelling by means of transportation furnished by, or at the expense of, the United Nations in connection with the performance of official duties only. This provision shall not extend to motor-vehicle transportation provided by the staff member or sanctioned or authorized by the United Nations solely at the request of and for the convenience of personnel.

       The compensation payable under the United Nations rules governing entitlement will be the sole compensation payable by the United Nations in respect of death, injury or illness which is not covered by the hazardous duty and malicious acts insurance.

    (2) A hazardous duty and malicious acts personal accident insurance coverage for civilian personnel exclusively is related only to malicious acts, i.e. for death or disability caused directly or indirectly by war, invasion, acts of foreign enemies, hostilities, civil war, revolution, rebellion, military or usurped power, explosion of war weapons, terrorist activities, etc.

0098

6

Coverage begins when the staff member boards the
aircraft for the last leg of the flight to the
designated duty station, in this case Iraq, and ceases
when the staff member deplanes from a flight departing
from the designated duty station.

COMPENSATION

19. **Compensation Claims.** A claim for compensation by or on
behalf of UNSCOM personnel should be submitted through the
Executive Office of UNSCOM within four months of death, injury or
onset of illness. In exceptional circumstances, the Secretary-
General may accept for consideration a claim made at a later
date. The determination of the injury or illness and the type
and degree of incapacity and of the relevant award will be
decided on the basis of the documentary evidence and in
accordance with the provisions established by the Secretary-
General.

20. Except for payment of reasonable medical and hospital
expenses, and in case of death, payment of transportation or
reasonable burial expenses of the remains, the United Nations
will not be responsible and will not pay compensation for death,
injury or illness not attributable to the performance of official
duties.

21. **Disability Payments.** In the event of disability deemed by
the Secretary-General to be attributable to United Nations
service, the total compensation awarded by the United Nations
will be payable to UNSCOM Personnel under the rules governing
entitlement.

22. **Beneficiary.** UNSCOM personnel should provide the name of
their beneficiary. For this purpose, personnel are required to
complete, in triplicate, a designation of beneficiary form upon
arrival in Bahrain.

23. **Death.** In the event of death in the service of the United
Nations, the award of compensation will follow a similar
procedure, but the payment will be made to the duly designated
beneficiary, subject to the requirements of the laws of the
individual's own country. If no beneficiary has been named, the
payment will be made to the deceased's estate. In either case,
payment will be made by the United Nations through the individual
Governments.

HL4-20-8

0099

Compensation for Loss of Personal Effects

24. **Entitlement**. Administrative instruction ST/AI/149/Rev.3 sets out the provisions concerning compensation for loss or theft of personal effects incurred in the course of duty in the mission area. This instruction will be available at UNSCOM Headquarters.

25. **Limitations**. UNSCOM personnel are advised not only to take all possible precautions against loss or theft of their personal property, but to avoid having with them expensive cameras, watches, radios or similar items, or large amounts of cash or traveller's cheques. In cases of loss or theft which qualify for compensation under the terms of ST/AI/149/Rev.3, the maximum payment will not exceed the amount indicated for each of the following items:

		$US
(a)	Camera (still or movie and accessories)	350
(b)	Radio, record player, tape recorder or watch	350
(c)	Binoculars or typewriter	175
(d)	Video camera	600
(e)	Electronic typewriter	300
(f)	Personal computer	1000
(g)	Cash	400

26. These figures are revised periodically in the light of prevailing circumstances. No compensation will be paid for loss of or damage to more than one of each of the articles mentioned.

27. UNSCOM personnel should not encumber themselves with personal household effects, especially in view of the need for mobility in the execution of duties. Moreover, UNSCOM personnel are compensated by receiving a mission subsistence allowance during their entire tour of duty which should be sufficient to cover the cost of accommodation from which personnel can move at short notice. However, long-term personnel (6 months) may be entitled to a baggage allowance of up to 100 kgs., provided prior authorization is obtained from the UNSCOM Administrative Office.

HEALTH/MEDICAL

28. Healthy personnel are essential to the success of the inspection process. Inspection activities will take their toll on everyone, more so in hot weather and on individuals who are not fit. For Bahrain and Iraq, the United Nations recommends immunizations for typhoid, tetanus, and also recommends gamma

8

globulin. Although there have been cases of cholera reported, it does not appear to be a significant danger in the areas to which UNSCOM personnel will travel.

29. <u>Initial Medical Examination Before Departure</u>. UNSCOM Personnel should ensure that, prior to their departure for the mission area, the appropriate authorities of their country forward the appropriate medical form to the Chief Administrative Officer, UNSCOM, at the address listed on page 11, either by DHL or fax, depending upon time constraints. These will be used by the Medical Director of the United Nations for verification of physical fitness and as a record of physical condition upon assignment:

     (a) <u>For missions less than 3 months</u> - a Health Certificate signed by a physician that the expert is in good health and fit to travel, copy attached.

     (b) <u>For missions over 3 months</u> - their medical history and the result of their latest medical examination along with the interpretation of the chest X-rays (do not send original X-rays) using United Nations form MS.2, copy attached.

30. Medical, hospital and dental facilities in Iraq are inadequate by UN standards. Emergency medical services will be provided to UNSCOM personnel by a medical support team, which will be provided at United Nations expense. An UNSCOM doctor or medical assistant will accompany each team. Should an individual require hospitalisation outside Iraq, he will normally be evacuated from Iraq into the country appropriate to his condition and the Medical Support Plan.

31. Personnel should bring with them an adequate supply of <u>all</u> personal medications, as re-filling prescriptions may not be possible. They should also bring spare spectacles, as well as sunglasses which are at least 80% UV, A&B protection, with lenses preferrably very dark green or grey. Sunblock (at least #15 waterproof to be reapplied every 2 hours), chapstick, and salves for rashes are advised. Rashes, stomach aches, and diarrhoea are likely ailments. Personnel will be given a complete medical briefing while in Bahrain.

<u>CLOTHING</u>

32. Personnel are responsible for their own personal clothing. Prudent selection of clothing will contribute significantly to comfortable working conditions and should be adapted to the weather. Temperatures in summer are up to 54 degrees Celsius, in

0101

9

winter, temperatures will drop to zero. In January/March, light-
weight daytime clothing with warm sweaters or jackets for the
evening will be required. Outerwear providing warmth and rain
protection is strongly recommended. It is also recommended that
personnel who will be engaged in official meetings with Iraqis
bring suitable attire.

33. Natural fibre materials such as cotton are cooler and easier
to launder; long-sleeve shirts will afford protection against
sunburn and flying insects. A laundry service is available in
the hotel in Baghdad. Shoes are a most critical item of
clothing. Lightweight, over-the-ankle shoes/boots are advised.
Shoes or boots with steel in the sole or toe conduct extremes of
cold and heat and can become very uncomfortable. New footwear
should be broken in prior to arriving in Bahrain.

34. Personnel may wear/use military items such as boots and
canteens, but should not wear military uniforms or insignia. The
UN will provide identifying floppy-brimmed hats and armbands.

INDIVIDUAL PROTECTION EQUIPMENT

35. Chemical inspectors only must bring their own individual
protection equipment. They must also bring a respirator with two
spare canisters/sets of filters and optical inserts if required.

MEDIA

36. Media interest in the activities of the Special Commission
continues to be high. The authorised spokesman for the team is
the Chief Inspector. Operations will be considered confidential
until authorised for release by the Special Commission.

GOVERNMENT REPORTS

37. Team members should not make personal reports to their
government prior to the completion of the official mission.

444-20-9

PHOTOGRAPHS

38.   The use of personal cameras in Iraq is normally permitted
during leisure activities in civilian areas. However, on the
inspection site itself, or going to and from the inspection site,
photographs will be taken only by the official team photographers
or by individuals specifically designated by the Chief Inspector.
These official photographs will be released only with the
specific authority of the Special Commission. Further details on
the rules relating to the taking of photographs will be provided
during the initial briefing in Bahrain.

MAIL TO UNSCOM PERSONNEL

39.   Mail to UNSCOM personnel in Iraq should be addressed as
follows:

> Ms./Mr. _____
> UNSCOM #_____
> United Nations Special Commission
> c/o UNDP Bahrain
> P.O. Box 26814
> Manama, Bahrain

40.   Mail from UNSCOM personnel out of Iraq will be collected at
the Baghdad office and will be periodically flown out of Iraq to
the Bahrain office, where it will be dispatched. Appropriate
stamps will be made available.

EMERGENCY NOTIFICATION

41.   UNSCOM must have on record an individual or institution,
personal designate as an emergency point of contact. Please
ensure the information provided on the attached Inspector Data
Sheet is accurate. Family members or designated points of
contact may pass urgent messages to personnel through UNSCOM
Headquarters New York (international access code + 1-212-963-
9044/9041) or Field Office Bahrain (international access code +
973-320-936).

POINT OF CONTACT

42. Queries relating to administrative matters should be
directed to:

            Ms. Alice Hecht
            Chief Administrative Officer
            United Nations Special Commission
            United Nations Secretariat, Room 3120D
            New York, New York

            Telephone - + 1-212-963-5545
            Fax - + 1-212-963-3922

Attachments:

1.   UNSCOM Undertaking (Attachment I)
2.   Inspector Data Sheet (Attachment II)
3.   UN Certificate (Attachment III)
4.   UN Medical Form (MS.2) (Attachment IV)
5.   UN Health Certificate (Attachment V)

0104

TEXT OF THE UNDERTAKING TO BE SIGNED BY
UNITED NATIONS SPECIAL COMMISSION (UNSCOM) PERSONNEL

I, the undersigned, undertake to avoid any action which may adversely reflect on my status as UNSCOM Personnel assigned to the United Nations Special Commission in Iraq or on the integrity, independence and impartiality which are required by that status.

I undertake to observe the following rules:

(a) Publication of any material or information, whether or not protected by copyright, is forbidden during an UNSCOM assignment, except by the express authorization of the UNSCOM Chief Inspector;

(b) Unless specifically authorised by the UNSCOM Chief Inspector, I shall not accept speaking engagements or make statements to, or grant interviews with the press, radio, television or other agencies of public information during my assignment with UNSCOM;

(c) I shall exercise the utmost discretion in regard to the handling of documents, cables, maps or other UNSCOM papers, and shall follow detailed instructions issued by UNSCOM concerning such documentation. In particular, documents, cables, maps or other papers, copies thereof or notes on their contents will not be taken away from the mission, published or otherwise handled or communicated to others, except with the prior approval of the UNSCOM Chief Inspector in each case;

(d) Without the prior approval of the UNSCOM Chief Inspector in each case, I shall not accept any invitation to visit military or industrial installations or to participate in or be present at official ceremonies sponsored by Iraq;

(e) I shall follow specific regulations issued by UNSCOM regarding the taking of private photographs and the carrying of private photographic equipment. In particular, I shall not photograph restricted subjects;

(f) I shall follow specific regulations issued by UNSCOM regarding the purchase, import and disposal of duty-free merchandise and shall co-operate with measures taken by UNSCOM to prevent the occurrence of any abuse of privileges or facilities accorded to UNSCOM Personnel.

0105

I understand that non-compliance on my part with any of the above rules during my UNSCOM assignment may result in my immediate repatriation.

I further recognise that the following rules may apply after completion of assignment to UNSCOM and undertake to observe them:

(a) Publication of any material or information whether or not protected by copyright, is forbidden after completion of the Iraq assignment, except with the prior approval of the Executive Chairman of UNSCOM in each case;

(b) I, after my UNSCOM assignment, shall not divulge the contents of documents, cables, maps or other papers of UNSCOM except with the prior approval of the Executive Chairman of UNSCOM in each case.

Signature: _____

Name printed in block letters: _____

Date: _____

0106

INSPECTOR DATA SHEET

NAME: _____

ADDRESS: _____

_____

_____

TELEPHONE NUMBERS: OFFICE: _____

FAX: _____   HOME: _____

NATIONALITY: _____   DATE OF BIRTH: _____

PLACE OF BIRTH: _____   SEX: _____   BLOOD TYPE: _____

EMERGENCY NOTIFICATION: NAME: _____

ADDRESS: _____

_____

TELEPHONE NO.: _____

LANGUAGES: _____

PASSPORT: TYPE: _____   NUMBER: _____

DATE OF ISSUE: _____   DATE OF EXPIRATION _____

PLACE OF ISSUE: _____   CURRENT VISAS: _____

PRIMARY AREA OF EXPERTISE: CW, BW, NUCLEAR, BALLISTIC MISSILE

SPECIALITY: _____

PREVIOUS INSPECTION EXPERIENCE: _____

DATES OF AVAILABILITY: _____

UN CERTIFICATE NUMBER (When available): _____

PLEASE FORWARD BY MOST EXPEDITIOUS MEANS THIS DATA SHEET AND
EIGHT PASSPORT SIZE PHOTOS FOR UN CERTIFICATE:

Ms. Alice Hecht
United Nations Special Commission
Room 3120-D
United Nations
New York, New York   10017
(212) 963-5545

544-20-10

0107

PT.64.12-701 - E.

APPLICATION FOR UNITED NATIONS CERTIFICATE

INSTRUCTIONS.

1. Please *TYPE* or *PRINT* all information requested.
2. Attach two front view (shoulder and above) passport photographs (2 x 2½), printed on thin photographic paper and taken within six months of the date of this application.
3. Print full name on the reverse of each photograph.
4. Submit this form through the appropriate U.N. Office.

NAME: _____
Last   First   Middle

ADDRESS: _____
(Local)
_____

Tel. No. _____

DURATION of CONTRACT: _____

PURPOSE of TRAVEL:

Activities pursuant to SCR 687 (1991) UNSCOM.

TITLE: __Adviser to Special Commission__

NATIONALITY: _____

PASSPORT No.: _____

ISSUED BY (Country): _____

DATE of EXPIRY: _____

TRAVELLING on BEHALF of:

United Nations
(Name of Organization)

UNSCOM
(Division or Section)

I certify that the above statements are true to the best of my knowledge.

_____   _____
Date   Signature of Applicant

Certified that the applicant is entitled to a United Nations Certificate. Please issue valid until

_____
(Not exceeding one year)

Date: _____   Certifying Officer:

Name: __Alice Hecht__   Office: __UNSCOM__

Do not write below this line

DATE of ISSUE: _____   EXPIRES on: _____   CERT. No.: _____

REVALIDATED: _____   EXPIRES on: _____

544-20-15

0108

FAO	GATT	IAEA	ILO	ITC	ITU	UN	UNDP	UNESCO	UNICEF	UNIDO	WHO	WIPO	WMO

CONFIDENTIAL	ENTRY MEDICAL EXAMINATION		UNITED NATIONS AND SPECIALIZED AGENCIES

I hereby authorize any of the doctors, hospitals or clinics mentioned in this form to provide the United Nations Medical Service with copies of all my medical records so that the Organization can take action upon my application for employment.

I certify that the statements made by me in answer to the questions below are, to the best of my knowledge, true, complete and correct. I realize that any incorrect statement or material omission in the medical information form or in any other document required by the Organization renders a staff member liable to termination or dismissal.

Date: . . . . Signature: . . . .

Pages 1 and 2 are to be completed by the candidate

FAMILY NAME (IN BLOCK CAPITALS)	GIVEN NAMES	MAIDEN NAME (FOR WOMEN ONLY)	SEX □ M □ F

ADDRESS (STREET, TOWN, DISTRICT OR PROVINCE, COUNTRY)	DATE OF BIRTH
. . . .	
. . . .	NATIONALITY
. . . .	

POSITION APPLIED FOR (DESCRIBE NATURE OF WORK)	TELEPHONE	BIRTHPLACE
. . . .		
. . . .	PRESENT MARITAL STATUS	

Married □ DATE . . . .   Single □

Separated □ DATE . . . .   Divorced □ DATE: . . . .

DUTY STATION   Widowed □ DATE: . . . .

Have you ever undergone a medical examination for the United Nations or one of its agencies? . . . .

Have you ever been employed by the United Nations or one of its agencies? . . . .

If so, please state when, where and for which Organization: . . . .

FAMILY HISTORY

Relative	Age (if still alive)	State of Health (If still alive, present state; If deceased, cause of death)	Age at death	Have members of your family had the following illnesses or disorders?	Yes	No	Who?
Father				High Blood Pressure			
Mother				Heart Disease			
Brothers				Diabetes			
Sisters				Tuberculosis			
Spouse				Asthma			
Children				Cancer			
				Epilepsy			
				Mental Disorders			
				Paralysis			

TO BE COMPLETED BY THE OFFICIAL REQUESTING THE MEDICAL EXAMINATION	TO BE COMPLETED BY THE DIRECTOR OF THE MEDICAL SERVICE
Name of Official:	Medical Classification: □ 1a □ 1b □ 2a □ 2b
Department or Unit:	Comments: . . . .
Date:	Date: Signature:

VERY IMPORTANT: Please indicate the recruiting Agency or Organization:

544-20-16

0109

MS.2 (1-85) - E.

- 2 -

Each question requires a specific answer (yes, no, date, etc.); to leave a blank or draw a line is not sufficient. If the questionnaire is not fully completed and enquiries are therefore needed, time may be lost.

1. Have you suffered from any of the following diseases or disorders? Check yes or no. If yes, state the year.

	YES Date	NO		YES Date	NO		YES Date	NO		YES Date	NO
Frequent sore throats			Heart and blood vessel disease			Urinary disorder			Fainting spells		
Hay fever			Pains in the heart region			Kidney trouble			Epilepsy		
Asthma			Varicose veins			Kidney stones			Diabetes		
Tuberculosis			Frequent indigestion			Back pain			Gonorrhoea		
Pneumonia			Ulcer of stomach or duodenum			Joint problems			Any other sexually transmitted disease		
Pleurisy			Jaundice			Skin disease			Tropical disease		
Repeated bronchitis			Gall stones			Sleeplessness			Amoebic dysentery		
Rheumatic fever			Hernia			Any nervous or mental disorder			Malaria		
High blood pressure			Haemorrhoids			Frequent headache					

2. Are you being treated for any condition now?_____ Describe: _____

3. Have you ever coughed up blood? _____

4. Have you ever noticed blood in your stools?_____ In your urine?_____ Give details: _____

5. Have you ever been hospitalized (hospital, clinic, etc.)? _____
    Why, where and when? _____

6. Have you ever been absent from work for longer than one month through illness?_____ If so, when? _____
    And for what illness? _____

7. Have you had any accidents as a result of which you are partially disabled?_____ If so, what and when? _____
    Do you have any other disability? _____

8. Have you ever consulted a neurologist, a psychiatrist or a psychoanalyst? _____
    If so, please give his/her name and address: _____
    For what reason? _____ Date of the consultation: _____

9. Are you taking any medicine regularly?_____ If so, which? _____

10. Have you gained or lost weight during the last three years? _____ If so, how much? _____

11. Have you ever been refused life insurance?_____ If so, state reason: _____

12. Have you ever been refused employment on health grounds?_____ If so, state reason: _____

13. Have you ever received or applied for a pension or compensation for any permanent disability?_____ Degree? _____
    Please give details: _____

14. Have you ever stayed in a tropical country?_____ If so, for how long? _____

15. Have you in the past suffered from any condition which prevented travel by air? _____

16. Do you consider yourself to be in good health?_____ Do you have full work capacity? _____

17. Do you smoke regularly? ☐ Yes ☐ No   If so, what do you smoke? ☐ Cigarettes ☐ Pipe ☐ Cigars
    For how many years have you smoked? _____ How much per day? _____

18. Daily consumption of alcoholic beverages: _____

19. Has any doctor or dentist advised you to undergo medical or surgical treatment in the foreseeable future? _____
    Give details: _____

20. Give any other significant information concerning your health: _____
    _____

21. What is your occupation? _____ Indicate the last three posts you have occupied: _____

22. List any occupational or other hazards to which you have been exposed: _____
    _____

23. Have you been rejected for military service for medical reasons? _____

24. **FOR WOMEN** Are your periods regular? ☐ Yes ☐ No   Do you take contraceptive pills? ☐ Yes ☐ No If so, for
                 Are they painful? ☐ Yes ☐ No   how many years have you been doing so?_____ Have you ever
    Do you have to stay in bed when they come? ☐ Yes ☐ No   been treated for a gynaecological complaint? ☐ Yes ☐ No
If so, for how long? _____ Date of your last period: _____   If so, which? _____

E44-20-11

0110

– 3 –

TO BE COMPLETED BY THE EXAMINING PHYSICIAN

GENERAL APPEARANCE   Height: cm. _____   Weight: kg. _____

Skin: _____   Scalp : _____

SIGHT, MEASURED VISUAL ACUITY

Gross vision   : Right _____ Left _____   Pupils: Equal? _____ Regular? _____

Vision with spectacles : Right _____ Left _____   Fundi (if necessary): _____

Near vision   : Right _____ Left _____   Colour vision: _____

With correction   : Right _____ Left _____

HEARING (test by whispering)	Right : Normal: _____	Sufficient: _____	Insufficient: _____
	Left : Normal: _____	Sufficient: _____	Insufficient: _____
	Ear drum : Right: _____	Left: _____	–

NOSE · MOUTH · NECK	Nose : _____	Pharynx: _____	Teeth : _____
	Tongue: _____	Tonsils: _____	Thyroid: _____

CARDIOVASCULAR SYSTEM

                                                   Peripheral arteries

Pulse rate   : _____   Auscultation   : _____   –carotid   : _____

Rhythm   : _____   Blood pressure : _____   –posterior tibialis _____

Apex beat   : _____   Varicose veins : _____   –dorsalis pedes: _____

/ Electrocardiogram (if indicated or after age of 45) – Please attach tracing.

RESPIRATORY SYSTEM

                                                    Breasts

Thorax:

DIGESTIVE SYSTEM

                                                    Spleen: _____

Abdomen: _____   Hernia: _____

Liver   : _____   Rectal examination: _____

NERVOUS SYSTEM

                                                    Plantar reflexes : _____

Pupillary reflexes: { – To light: _____   Motor functions : _____

                 { – On accommodation: _____   Sensory functions : _____

Patellar reflexes : _____   Muscular tonus : _____

Achilles reflexes : _____   Romberg's sign : _____

MENTAL STATE

Appearance: Behaviour:

GENITO–URINARY SYSTEM

Kidneys: Genitals:

SKELETAL SYSTEM

Skull : _____   Upper extremities: _____

Spine: _____   Lower extremities: _____

LYMPHATIC SYSTEM

CHEST X-RAY (Full size film – Please send film itself, the radiologist's report is not sufficient. Lateral film not necessary unless indicated medically.)

tull 70-18

0111

- 4 -

LABORATORY

The results of <u>all</u> the following investigations must be included except where marked "if indicated".

Except by prior agreement, only the investigations mentioned are done at the Organization's expense.

<u>Urine</u> :   Albumin _____   Sugar _____   Microscopic _____

<u>Blood</u> :   Haemoglobin : _____ % _____ grams/l   Leucocytes: _____

                Haematocrit : _____ % _____   Differential count (if indicated) : _____

                Erythrocytes : _____   Blood sedimentation rate : _____

<u>Blood chemistry</u> (if these tests can be carried out on the spot):

                Sugar   : _____   Urea or creatinine : _____

                Cholesterol : _____   Uric acid   : _____

<u>Serological test for syphilis</u>: Please attach laboratory report

<u>Stool examination</u> (if indicated):

COMMENTS (Please comment on all the positive answers given by the candidate and summarize the abnormal findings)

CONCLUSIONS (Please state your opinion on the physical and mental health of the candidate and fitness for the proposed post)

The examining doctor is requested before sending this report to verify that the questionnaire, pages 1 and 2 of this form, has been fully completed by the candidate and that all the results of the investigations required are given on the report. Incomplete reports are a major source of delay in recruitment.

Name of the examining physician (in block capitals):

_____

Address: _____

_____

Signature: _____

Date: _____

HEALTH CERTIFICATE

_____ is in good health and is
physically fit to travel to Bahrain and Iraq to carry
out inspection activities as required by the United
Nations. All required inoculations for the travel area
have been administered.

_____
Physician

_____
Date

544-70-70

0113

외 무 부

110-760 서울 종로구 세종로 77번지   /   (02) 720-2334   /   (02) 723-3505

문서번호 연일 2031-1605

시행일자 1992. 6. 17.

(경유)

수신   주유엔대사

참조

취급		장 관
보존		
국 장	전 결	
심의관		
과 장	김ㅇㅇ	
기 안	황준국	협조

제목   이라크 화학무기 폐기반

───────────────────────────────

대 : 주국련 2031-119(92.6.1)

표제 참여 아국장교 2명의 유엔 제출서류를 별첨 송부합니다.

첨 부 : 양인의 Data Sheet, UN Certificate 신청서,
         Health Certificate 각 1매.

0114

공   란

공   란

공   란

공   란

공   란

공   란

<table>
<tr><td>관리
번호</td><td>92
-120</td></tr>
</table>

외 무 부

원 본

종 별 :

번 호 : UNW-1726

일 시 : 92 0618 1900

수 신 : 장 관(연일)

발 신 : 주 유엔 대사

제 목 : 이락무기 폐기작업단

연:UNW-1712

유엔측은 연호 이락 무기폐기 작업단 요원의 서류(여권 사진 8 매포함)를
지급제출하여 줄것을 요청하고 있의 최단 파편 송부바람

(대사 유종하-국장)

예고: 98.12.31 일반
의거 인반 시

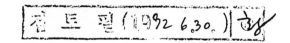

전 토 필 (1992. 6.30.)

___

국기국

PAGE 1

110-760 서울 종로구 세종로 77번지 / (02) 720-2334 / (02) 723-3505

문서번호 연일 2031-(63)

시행일자 1992. 6. 22.

(경유)

수신 주유엔대사

참조

취급		장 관		
보존				
국 장	전 결			
심의관				
과 장				
기안	황준국			협조

제목 이라크 화학무기 폐기반

　　　　대 : UNW-1712

　　　　연 : 연일 2031-1605(92.6.17)

　　　　표제참여 아국장교 2명의 유엔 제출서류를 별첨 송부합니다.

　　첨 부 : 양인의 서약서, 건강진단서.

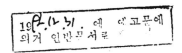

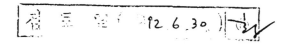

0122

공   란

공   란

| 판리
번호 | 72
-592 | | 외　무　부 | | | 원　본 |

종　별 :

번　호 : UNW-1758　　　　　　　　　　　일　시 : 92 0623 1700

수　신 : 장 관(연일)

발　신 : 주 유엔 대사

제　목 : 이락무기 폐기작업단

　　대:연일 2031-1605

　　연:UNW-1712

　　1. 이락무기 폐기작업단 참여와 관련, UNSCOM 은 아국 장교 2 인의 파견 기간을 3 개월로 단축함에 동의함을 구두 통보하여 왔으며 파견일은 7 월중이 될것이나 구체적 파견일은 결정되는대로 통보해주겠다함

　　2. 또한 유엔측은 신체적 적정여부를 판단하여야 하므로 대호 송부자료에 포함되지 않은 연호 진단서와 서약서를 금주중 제출하여 줄것을 요청하여 왔으니당관에 지급 FAX 송부하고 원본은 파편 송부바람

　　(대사 유종하-국장)

　　예고:92.12.31 까지

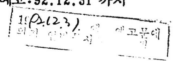

검 토 필 (1992. 6.30.)

국기국　　　장관　　　차관　　　1차보　　　분석관　　　청와대　　　안기부

PAGE 1　　　　　　　　　　　　　　　　　　　　　　92.06.24　　06:48

　　　　　　　　　　　　　　　　　　　　　　　　　외신 2과　통제관 BX

　　　　　　　　　　　　　　　　　　　　　　　　　　　　0125

공   란

관리	92
번호	-810

외 무 부

종 별 :

번 호 : UNW-1896

수 신 : 장 관(연일)

발 신 : 주 유엔 대사

제 목 : 이락무기 폐기작업단

일 시 : 92 0710 1740

연:UNW-1758

연호 아국인의 이락무기 폐기작업단 파견시기를 UNSCOM 에 문의한바, UN 측은 이락 현지 사정상 파견일이 늦어져 8 월중순에서 9 월초 사이에 소집될 것으로 예상된다 하며 구체적 일자는 기보고한 바와 같이 소집 7 일전 통보할 것이라함

(대사 유종하-국장)

예고 : 92. 12. 31. 일반문에 의거 일반 자료로 재분류 됨

국기국

| 관리
번호 | 92
~890 |

원 본

외 무 부

종 별 :

번 호 : UNW-2025

일 시 : 92 0724 2130

수 신 : 장 관(연일,중동일,기정,국방부)

발 신 : 주 유엔 대사

제 목 : 이락화학 무기 폐기작업단

연:UNW-1896

1. 아국의 이락화학무기 폐기작업단 참여와 관련, 금 7.24 당관 이수혁 참사관이 UNSCOM 아그네스 보좌관에 확인한바에 의하면 이락농무성 사찰 거부사건에도 불구하고 돌발적 사태가 없는한 화학무기 폐기작업단의 8 월중순-9 월초 파견계획은 아무런 변동이 없다하며 8 월초 동파견 계획에 관해 해당국 대표부에 설명 예정이라함.

2. 동보좌관에 의하면 이락 농무성 사찰 실패후 UNSCOM 사찰단의 이락철수 보도는 사실이 아니며 이락 외무성앞에서 주야 교대 근무하여온 사찰단원중 5 명이 과로로 이락에서 철수하였고 화학무기 폐기작업단등 65 명의 사찰인원은 계속 이락내에서 근무중이라 함.끝.

(대사 유종하-국장)

| 국기국 | 장관 | 차관 | 1차보 | 중아국 | 분석관 | 청와대 | 안기부 | 국방부 |

92.07.25   11:38
외신 2과   통제관 BS

0128

외 무 부

종 별 :

번 호 : UNW-2114

일 시 : 92 0805 2030

수 신 : 장관(연일,중동일,국방부,기정)

발 신 : 주 유엔 대사

제 목 : 이라크 화학무기 폐기 작업반

1. 금 8.5. UNSCOM (이라크 무기폐기 유엔특위)은 이라크 화학무기 폐기 유엔 작업반 참여국을 초치하여 브리핑을 실시하였는바, UNSCOM 는 아국 장교 2 인을 포함한 작업반원 21 명의 바레인 도착일을 8.25, 이라크 향발일을 8.28 로 결정하였음을 설명하고 바레인 도착 7 일전까지 구체적 사항을 개인별로 통보하여 줄 예정이라함.

2. UNSCOM 측은 농무성 사찰 거부사건등으로 동 작업반의 작업개시가 지연되어 해당 요원들에 많은 불편을 주었음에 대하여 양해를 구하고 금번 작업반의 명단은 관례에 따라 공개치 않는다함. 또한 UNSCOM 은 이라크측이 안보리 결의에의한 무기 신고나 정보제공등에는 비협조적이나 화학무기 폐기 자체에 대하여는 자국의 이익을 위해서도 안전한 폐기가 절실함을 인식하여 유엔에 협조적임을설명하고 화학무기의 권위자들이 유엔 자문관으로 근무중이므로 작업의 안전도에는 아무런 문제가 없다고 언급함.

3. 작업반 요원의 항공표는 출국시 공항 항공사에서 찾을 수 있도록 준비할것 이라하며, 바레인에서 배포할 유엔신분증으로 이라크에 입국하므로 개인별 이라크 입국비자는 불필요하다함. 또한 유엔측이 기요청한 여가 선용을 위한 VTR 등의 기증이 정부차원에서 어려울 경우 현지사정이 매우 어려움을 감안 하여 개인별로라도 서적, 비데오 테이프등을 휴대할 것을 권유하였음을 참고 바람. 끝

(대사 유종하 - 국장)

예고 : 92. 12.31 일반

국기국	장관	차관	1차보	중아국	분석관	정와대	안기부	국방부

외신 2과 통제관 BX

0129

분류번호	보존기간

발 신 전 보

번 호 : WUN-2019 920818 1023 WH 종별 : _____

수 신 : 주 유엔 대사. ♣♣♣♣

발 신 : 장 관 (연일)

제 목 : 이라크 화학무기 폐기 작업반

．．．．．．．．．

대 : UNW-2114

1. 8.18(화)자 한겨레신문은 표제관련 별전(Fax) 기사를 게재함.

     따로방부

2. 본부는 동 보도와 관련, 우리의 작업반 참여계획을 확인해 주고
   유엔이 대외보안을 요청하고 있음에 비추어 보도는 자제해 주도록
   협조 요청하였음.

3. 본건관련 5.26자 Ekeus 의장 서한은 at this time 보도자제를
   요청하고 있고 UNSCOM측은 작업반의 명단을 관례에 따라 공개하지
   않는다(대호 2항)고 하였는바, 본건 보도관례(상기 at this time의
   의미등)를 확인, 보고바람. 끝.

(국제기구국장   김재섭)

예 고   19 92.12.31 일반 고문에
        의거 일반문서로 재분됨

보안통제	2

앙 고 재	92년 8월 18일	유엔1 과	기안자 성명		과 장	심의관	국 장		차 관	장 관	
			황준국								외신과통제

외 무 부

WUNF-0090 920818 1035 WH

번 호 :   년월일 :   시간 :

수 신 : 주 UN   대사(총영사)

발 신 : 외무부장관(UN)

제 목 : 이라크 화학무기 폐기작업반

총 2 매(표지포함)

보안 통제	√√
외신과 통제	

0131

한겨레신문 92·8·18·

정부, 이라크사찰 참여
화학무기 전문가 이달말 유엔 파견방침

정부는 이라크의 대량 살상무기 폐기를 위한 유엔 사찰활동에 적극 참여하기로 결정하고, 군의 화학무기 전문가 2명을 이달 하순께 유엔 무기사찰단에 파견할 방침이다.

이들 전문가 2명은 앞으로 3개월 동안 유엔 사찰단에 참여해 다른 13개국의 파견자들과 함께 이라크에서 무기사찰 활동을 벌이게 된다. 정부가 유엔 결의 이행을 위한 군사적 사찰활동 참여를 결정하기는 이번이 처음이다.

정부의 한 고위소식통은 17일 "유엔 안보리 산하의 '이라크 대량 파괴무기 폐기 특별위원회'가 우리나라에 유엔 사찰단 참여를 요청해왔다"면서 "외무부·국방부 등 관계부처에서 검토한 결과 유엔 회원국으로서 참여하는 게 좋다는 결론을 내리고 화학무기 전문가를 이달 하순께 파견하겠다고 유엔쪽에 공식 통보했다"고 밝혔다.

유엔 무기사찰단은 91년초 걸프전이 끝난 뒤 유엔 안보리 결의에 따라 구성돼 이라크의 핵무기, 화학무기, 생물학무기, 사정거리 150km 이상의 탄도미사일을 수색하고 파기하는 임무를 맡고 있는데 지금까지 이라크를 40여차례 방문해 사찰활동을 벌였다.

미국과 이라크는 현재 유엔 사찰단의 이라크 농무부 사찰에 이어 방위산업부와 국방부 청사 추가사찰 실시를 둘러싸고 마찰을 빚고 있으며, 미국의 〈뉴욕타임스〉는 부시 행정부가 이라크의 '대량살상 무기 개발관련 시설들'에 대한 추가사찰을 요구해 거부되면 바그다드를 공습할 계획이라고 보도해 세계적으로 큰 관심을 모으고 있다.

0132

외 무 부

원 본

종 별 :

번 호 : UNW-2235   일 시 : 92 0818 1740

수 신 : 장 관(연일,중동일,기정,국방부)

발 신 : 주 유엔 대사

제 목 : 이라크 화학무기 작업반

　　　대 : WUN-2019

　　　연 : UNW-2114

　　1. UNSCOM 측에 확인결과, 연호 이라크 화학무기 작업반원의 8.25 바레인 도착을 위하여 여행사를 통하여 항공표 발권 업무를 진행중이므로 근일중 항공표를 서울에서 찾을 수 있을 것이라함. 관련사항을 통보 받는대로 재보고 위계임.

　　2. 대호 보도와 관련, UNSCOM 측은 무기폐기 사찰반 또는 작업반의 명단을 공개치 않음이 관례인바 이는 동 사찰반원은 국가대표로서가 아니라 유엔이 필요한 전문가를 모집하여 유엔직원의 신분으로 파견하는 점과 신변안전문제 및 특별히 파견국가와 이라크와의 양자관계등을 감안한 조치라는 설명임.

　　3. 특히 최근 이라크 농무성 사찰과 관련, 이라크 요청으로 사찰반원에 미국인이 제외되었다는 보도에 대하여 UNSCOM 측은 매우 강한 불만을 가지고 있는바, UNSCOM 측으로서는 구성국이 여하하든 사찰 목적을 달성할 수 있는 전문가들로서 구성만되면 아무런 문제가 없다는것이 일관된 입장이나 일부 언론이 구성국에 너무 민감한 반응을 보이고 있음에 유감과 우려를 표명함. 다만 그간 대이라크 무기사찰반에 미국인이 많이 포함된 것은 사실이나 이는 미국이 다른 나라에 비해 상대적으로 높은 수준의 무기 전문가를 보유하고 있기 때문이며 앞으로도 UNSCOM 은 구성국가보다는 자질을 고려하여 요원을 선발할 계획이라고 설명함

　　4. 상기 UNSCOM 측의 입장등을 고려하여 아국 장교의 작업반 참여를 보도아니 하도록 요청함이 바람직할것으로 사료됨 (8.7 UNSCOM 측은 유엔 대변인을 통하여 8.7-17 간 파견된 사찰반의 사찰장소와 명단을 공개치 않을 것임을 밝힌바 있음).끝.

　　　(대사 유종하-국장)

예고:92.12.31 일반 문서로 재분류됨

국기국	장관	차관	1차보	중아국	분석관	정와대	안기부	국방부

92.08.19   14:16

외신 2과 통제관 BS

0133

외 무 부

관리
번호 92-814

종 별 :

번 호 : UNW-2241

일 시 : 92 0818 1900

수 신 : 장 관 (연일,중동일,미일,기정)

발 신 : 주 유엔 대사

제 목 : 대 이라크 사찰

1. 유엔 특별위원회 (UNSCOM)의 대 이라크 무기사찰과 관련, 금 8.18 자 NYT는 유엔사찰반의 8.17 이라크 국방성 사찰계획이 마지막 순간에 취소되었다고 보도 하였는바, TIM TREVAN UNSCOM 대변인이 작 8.17 기자회견에서 언급한 내용을 아래 보고함.

0 (이라크 정부부처 사찰계획 유무에 대하여) 사찰반의 활동에 관한 정보는 공개할 수 없음. 유엔사찰반은 이라크내 어느 장소든지 UNSCOM 에 위임된 사항과 관련된 정보가 있을 수 있다고 믿을만한 이유가 있으면 언제든지 사찰 할수있음

0 (이락 정부부처를 사찰하는데 이라크측으로부터 아무문제가 없다는 보장을받았느냐는 질문에 대하여) 이라크측이 그와같이 시사한바 없음. 사찰 장소를 선택하는것은 이라크 정부가 아님. UNSCOM 의 권한은 유엔 안보리가 부여한 것이므로 이러한 권한을 변경할 수 있는것은 이라크나 UNSCOM 이 아니라 안보리임.

0 (농무성사찰 불허사건의 재발방지를 이라크로부터 확약받았느냐는 질문에 대하여) 이라크 정부와의 논의된 내용을 구체적으로 밝힐 수 없으나 정부부처건물 사찰과 관련하여 두개의 선례가 있음. 즉 지난 2 월 산업 및 광업성 방문과 7 월 농업성 방문임. 유엔의 사찰권리는 부인될 수 없음

0 (금번 사찰반의 이라크 정부부처 사찰여부에 대하여) 금번 사찰반은 정부 부처를 방문한바 없음. 동사찰반이 사찰을 계획하였던 모든 장소에 대하여 성공적인 사찰을 수행하였음. 어느장소도 동사찰반의 사찰이 거부된 바 없음. UNSCOM 은 이라크의 무기계획에 대해 보다 잘 파악하게 되어 사찰 빈도가 줄어들 것임.

0 (사찰반 활동 공개와 관련) 지난번 농무성 사찰때에는 대치상태로 긴장이 고조 되어 사찰반의 활동이 공개되었으나 통상 UNSCOM 은 사찰반의 파견일등 활동에 관한 정보는 공개하지 않음이 원칙임. 금번사찰반은 한장소에서 미사일계획에 관한 정보를

국기국 　　 장관 　　 차관 　　 1차보 　　 미주국 　　 중아국 　　 분석관 　　 정와대 　　 안기부

PAGE 1

92.08.19 　 08:59

외신 2과 통제관 FS

0134

발견한후 동건과 관련하여 이라크 당국과 대화를 가진바 있음.

0 (미국 정부로부터 산업성 사찰을 요청받았느냐는 질문에 대하여) 사찰장소와 관련한 정보와 제의는 개인, 기관, 정부등 다양한 소스로부터 제공되고 있음. 미국정부가 유엔사찰반의 활동에 주요 지원자임은 비밀이 아님. 그러나 정보를 분석하고 사찰 여부와 장소, 일자를 결정하는 것은 UNSCOM 의 책임임.

0 (금번 사찰반의 사찰 계획변경 여부에 대하여) 사찰반은 사찰 목표 (TARGETS)가 있으나 그 일정은 융통성이 있음. 예정대로 사찰이 실시되지 못할 수도있으나 이는 이라크 사정때문일 수도있고 사찰반의 형편상 실시되지 못할 수도있음. 금번 사찰반은 계획했던 모든 장소를 성공적으로 사찰했음.

2. 지난 주말이후 대이라크 사찰을 위요한 미국언론의 보도에도 불구하고 안보리 및 UNSCOM 은 이에 관한 특이동향 없음. UNSCOM 의 EKEUS 위원장은 현재 휴가중임

(대사 유종하 - 국장)
예고 : 92.12.31 일반
첨부 : UNW(F)-0675

UNいた万-0675 20818 1900   #첨부요

U.N. Calls Off Inspection Of Iraqi Military Ministry

Confrontation Postponed, but Reason Is Unclear

By ERIC SCHMITT
Special to The New York Times

WASHINGTON, Aug. 17 — Acting at the last minute, United Nations inspectors in Baghdad canceled a visit today to a military ministry considered off-limits by Iraq, apparently abandoning for now a United States plan to demand access to sensitive sites.

American officials had said over the weekend that Washington and its allies might renew bombing raids on Baghdad if inspections were blocked.

The United Nations team, which made one inspection today but did not disclose where, plans to leave Iraq Tuesday. The next round of inspections has not yet been scheduled, leaving uncertain when the United Nations might test Iraq's threat to bar access to military ministries.

Reasons Unclear

It was not immediately clear why the planned inspection of an Iraqi military ministry this morning was postponed. Some Bush Administration officials said the inspectors abandoned the plans out of concern they would appear to be pawns in Washington's effort to confront Saddam Hussein.

Other Administration officials said the White House itself had second thoughts after a report Sunday in The New York Times that described a plan to force inspections. The Times also reported that some officials had said the timing appeared calculated to give President Bush a boost during the Republican National Convention. Mr. Bush and others have angrily denied any political motivations.

The 'No Fly' Zone

As the possibility of a confrontation over the inspections seemed to recede, Washington continued discussions with Britain, France, Saudi Arabia and Kuwait on creating new safeguards to protect Shiite Muslims in southern Iraq from Iraqi air attacks.

Under the plan, the United States and its allies would declare a "no fly" zone, roughly below the 32d parallel in Iraq, from which Iraqi aircraft would be barred. The proposal came as intelligence reports indicated that President Hussein's Government is preparing to renew an air and ground offensive against the Shiites, Administration officials said today. [Page A6.]

Regarding the inspection today in Baghdad, which was supposed to include the Ministry of Military Industrialization, it was not clear whether any last-minute misgivings originated with the inspectors in Baghdad, at higher levels of the United Nations or among the members of the Security Council.

"After the publicity, they decided it wouldn't be good to continue on," a Defense Department official said. "The publicity killed the idea of any confrontation."

'We Retain the Right'

Defense Secretary Dick Cheney today sharply criticized the New York Times article on forcing inspections. "I think it's a new low in political reporting," he said in an interview on "The MacNeil-Lehrer Newshour" on PBS. "I'm outraged by it."

Tim Trevan, a spokesman for the United Nations special commission in charge of destroying Iraq's major weapons, said at a news conference at the United Nations headquarters in New York that the 22-member team did not visit a ministry "because this time round we didn't have the need to."

"Of course, we retain the right to designate any location in Iraq," Mr. Trevan said. "And when we have the need to, we shall visit any location."

Administration officials said again today that Washington was not calling the shots for the inspectors, although

Continued on Page A6, Column 1

675-2-1

0136

U.N. Team Cancels Inspection Of a Military Ministry in Iraq

Continued From Page A1

many sites visited were selected based on tips from United States intelligence sources.

"What they elect to inspect and when they do these inspections is strictly for their decision," said Richard A. Boucher, a State Department spokesman.

Trying to Protect Shiites

The plan to protect the Shiites in southern Iraq could lead to allied air patrols over the area with authority to shoot down Iraqi aircraft. Iraqi helicopters and, in at least one instance, fixed-wing aircraft have attacked the Shiite areas, Administration officials said.

In an interview today with the Cable News Network, President Bush referred to the Iraqi flights, saying of President Hussein: "He has been using air power to go after the Shiites in the

The question is, Who's in charge? The answer is still in doubt.

south and regrettably the Kurds in the north, both regrettable. And so if there is some edict that keeps him from flying, clearly that would deny him one way of harassing his own people."

At the State Department, Mr. Boucher elaborated, saying, "The situation is that over the past several days there's been a significant amount of fixed-wing aircraft and helicopter activity in the south.

"The Iraqi army's pressure against the people in the marshes continues," he continued. "There have been skirmishes that continue to occur. So the military pressure on the population in the south has continued."

If Shiites Get Stronger

In London today, British military officials told reporters that after a special meeting of military and foreign policy advisors that Prime Minister John Major is to convene on Tuesday, British air forces would be put on alert, ready to participate in any patrols over southern Iraq.

The proposal to support and protect the Shiites was adopted only after some sharp disagreement among allied military planners. Some Administration officials, for example, have voiced concern since the gulf war that a resurgent fundamentalist Shiite force in southern Iraq, backed by Iran, could destabilize the region.

Countering this argument, Western officials said that creating a security zone in the south, as the coalition did in the Kurdish area in northern Iraq after the gulf war, would hurt Mr. Hussein politically without significantly strengthening the military hand of the Shiites.

With the focus of attention shifting to the protection of the Shiites, the end of a 10-day inspection by the United Nations weapons experts became a bit of an anticlimax.

Lesser Facility Visited

The team's leader, Nikita Smidovich of Russia, declined to identify the site visited today or to describe the mission's findings. But he said Iraq had not interfered. Senior Defense Department officials said the building inspected today was a "military facility, but not one of any great consequence."

Mr. Trevan, the United Nations spokesman, said that during the 10 days of inspections, the team "found significant additional information concerning the ballistic missiles programs."

"We have learned things that will be very useful and very helpful now in future inspections," Mr. Smidovich said in Baghdad.

The main drama, however, had been reserved for the visits to places identified by officials earlier as Baghdad's most closely guarded ministry buildings. A Defense Department official said today that the principal aim of those visits was to re-establish "who's in charge."

A Question of Precedent

After the three-week standoff at the Agriculture Ministry last month, which ended when the United Nations agreed not to include experts from countries that had attacked Iraq in the gulf war, diplomats and Administration officials said the United Nations teams had to reaffirm their right to go anywhere they wanted in Iraq and to select team members without Baghdad's veto.

"Re-establishing that precedent was the main goal," the Defense Department official said. "Whatever they found inside the buildings was secondary."

Indeed, the genesis for several Administration decisions in recent weeks was the standoff at the Agriculture Ministry, Administration officials said.

Days after the Administration was widely criticized for allowing Baghdad a say in the makeup of the inspection teams, Washington began pursuing three options.

One included having the United Nations speed up inspections to show that Iraq had to submit to the will of the international organization. Administration officials also said they would press Iraq to end attacks against the

The possibility of a confrontation over U.N. inspections in Baghdad seems to have receded.

Shiites. Finally, Washington began taking steps to elevate the status of opposition groups inside and outside of Iraq.

British Consider Bombing

Special to The New York Times

LONDON, Aug. 17 — The British Government said today that it was discussing with the United States and other allies whether to resort to force, including bombing missions, to protect the Shiites in southern Iraq.

In what appeared to be a sharp change in the tone of public statements, the Foreign Office characterized the situation in southern Iraq as "shocking" and "intolerable," and said it might be necessary once again to force Iraq to comply with the cease-fire imposed by the United Nations at the end of the Persian Gulf war.

British officials referred specifically to Iraq's use of aircraft against the Shiites. The Foreign Office spokesman said President Hussein's Government appeared to have embarked on a military campaign in recent weeks "to systematically wipe out" civilian opposition in southern Iraq.

'Have Not Ruled Out' Planes

A senior British official, describing options to enforce the cease-fire, said Britain and its allies "have not ruled out the use of British aircraft."

The Foreign Office said the Iraqi assault on the Shiites was the most recent instance of what it described as a pattern of systematic defiance of the cease-fire, which was imposed after Baghdad's forces were defeated in March 1991.

That includes the obstruction of aid shipments to Iraqi civilians, the refusal to take part in talks about the disputed border with Kuwait and the refusal to allow inspections of buildings in which Iraq is believed to be maintaining records or research on weapons of mass destruction.

615-1-2

0137

원 본

외 무 부

종 별 :

번 호 : UNW-2263

일 시 : 92 0820 1840

수 신 : 장관 (연일, 국방부, 기정)

발 신 : 주 유엔 대사

제 목 : 이라크 화학무기 폐기 작업반

연 : UNW-2235

1. 이라크 화학무기 폐기작업반 참여와 관련, 금 8.20 UNSCOM 측에 확인 결과 우리 장교 2 인의 서울 - 바레인간 항공표 (KE-801 편 8.24 (월) 21:00 서울출발, 8.25(화) 01:30AM 바레인 착)를 김포공항 대한항공 사무소에서 찾도록 여행사를 통해 명 8.21 까지 조치 예정이라함.

2. UNSCOM 측은 동인들의 바레인 도착이후 일정은 기송부한 안내서에 따르도록 요청하였음

(대사 유종하 - 국장)

예고 : 92.12.31 일반문서로 재분류
의거 인반문서로 재분류

국기국   안기부   국방부

이라크 화학무기 폐기반 참여

92. 8. 21.
유엔 1과

O 유엔의 이라크 화학무기폐기 작업반에 참여하는 우리 장교 8.24(월)
   출국 예정

   - 참여 장교는 소령 1명, 대위 1명이며 이들은 8.28(금) 바레인 경유
     하여 이라크 향발 예정

   - 3개월간 바그다드 교외에서 화학무기폐기 감독

※ 금번 작업반은 「유엔 이라크무기 폐기 특별위원회」(UNSCOM)가 구성한
   화학무기관련 13번째 작업반이며 39명으로 구성됨.

0139

분류번호	보존기간

발 신 전 보

번   호 :　WJO-0282　　920821 1802 WG　종별 :

수　신 : 주 요르단, 바레인 대사. 총영사　　　　WBH -0139
　　　　　　　(연일)

발　신 : 장 관

제　목 : 이라크 화학무기폐기 작업반

1. 유엔의 대이라크 제재조치의 일환으로 UNSCOM(유엔 이라크무기 폐기특위)이
   설치하는 화학무기 폐기 작업반에 우리 장교 2인이 참여할 예정임. 이들은 8.25
   (화) 01:30 KE-801편으로 바레인 도착하여 UNSCOM 측의 주선으로 바레인에서
   2-3일 체류후 다른 작업반원과 함께 바그다드로 향발하게 될 것임.

2. 이들의 인적사항 및 동 작업반 참여 경위등을 아래 통보하니 참고바라며
   이들이 귀관에 협조를 요청해 올 경우 적의 지원해 주기바람.

/ 계 속 /

중동아국장 :

보안 통제	74

앙 고 재	92 년 8 월 21 일	유엔 1 과	기안자 성명 황준국	과 장	심의관	국 장		차 관	장 관	외신과통제

0140

（2） 관련 참고사항

　　　o 92.4. 유엔측 요청에 따라 국방부등 관계부처와 협의 상기 2명 선발

　　　o 임   무 : 이라크의 화학무기 폐기를 감독·지휘

　　　o 기   간 : 우리 장교 2명의 경우 3개월

　　　o 작업반 규모 : 39명

　　　o 작업장소 : Muthanna State Establishment

　　　　　　　　　　 (바그다드에서 북서쪽 70km)

　　　o 근무조건 : 유엔에서 항공료 및 생활비 지급

3. 작업반원의 신변안전 및 이라크와 파견국의 양자관계등을 고려하여 작업
　　반원의 명단을 공개치 않는 UNSCOM의 관례에 따라서 본부도 본건관련
　　대외보안을 유지하고 있음을 유의바람.   끝.

　　　　　　　　　　　　　　　　　（국제기구국장　　　김재섭 ）

예 고　　1992.12.31. 일반문서에
　　　　의거 인영문서

3. 우리將校, 이라크 化學武器 廢棄班 參與

　o 유엔의 이라크 化學武器 廢棄 作業班에 參與하는 우리 將校團
　　(소령1명, 대위1명)이 8.24 出國, 바레인 경유하여 이라크
　　향발 예정임.

　　- 3개월간 바그다드 교외에서 化學武器廢棄 監督 예정
　　　* 금번 作業班은 '유엔 이라크무기 廢棄 特別委員會'(UNSCOM)가 構成한
　　　　化學武器 관련 13번째 作業班이며 39명으로 構成됨.　　　　끝.

0142

공   란

공   란

공   란

공   란

공   란

UNSCOM #38 - CHEMICAL DESTRUCTION GROUP

PERSONNEL/CARGO ROLL/MANIFEST

DATE: 11 November 1992

ROLL	NAME	CALLSIGN	LOCATION MUTHANNA
	HEADQUARTERS		
X	Garth Whitty	FOXTROT 1	영(뉴)
X	Peter Bruce	FOXTROT 2	호주
✗	Jurgen Mihm	FOXTROT 3	독일
X	▇▇▇▇▇▇▇	FOXTROT 4	한국
✗	Wayne Evans	FOXTROT 5	뉴질랜드
X	Steve Noon	FOXTROT 6	"
X	Samih Abou Faress	FOXTROT TANGO 2	팔레스타인 (통역관)
	TEAM 1		
X	Patrick Dewez 1	FOXTROT 21	프랑스
)	Pavel Castulik 2	FOXTROT 22	체코
✗	Carl Winger 3	FOXTROT 23	미국
X	Jacob Moerland 2	FOXTROT 24	덴마크
✗	Gabor Nagy 2	FOXTROT 25A	1305 헝가리
X	Darrel Connick 1	FOXTROT 25B	카나다
X	▇▇▇▇▇▇▇	FOXTROT 26A	10.13 · 한국
✗	Paul Papalia	FOXTROT 26B	로마
X	David Kellogg 2	FOXTROT 27A	미국

```
Total Seats Available              =  32
Total Seats (Extended Range Tank)  =  20

Total Pax                          =
Total Cargo (M')                   =
```

Note:
1. Total seats assumes 3 Iraqi escorts.
2. Qty of cargo will effect seat availability.

0148

ROLL	NAME	CALLSIGN	LOCATION MUTHANNA
	TEAM 2		
	Cees Wolterbeek	FOXTROT 31	덴마크
	Roger Noble	FOXTROT 32	호주
	Dominique Anelli	FOXTROT 33	프랑스
	John Wood 2	FOXTROT 34	영국
	Roland Steck	FOXTROT 35A	스위스
	Botond Bognar	FOXTROT 35B	헝가리
	Neil Pitts	FOXTROT 36A	카나다
	Lutz Hecker	FOXTROT 36B	독일
	Tibor Mikes ∧	FOXTROT 37A	체코
	MEDICAL TEAM		
	David Le Page	MIKE (의사)	
	John Hobbs	MIKE 1	
✕	Harawera Downs	MIKE 2	
✕	Frank Prendergast	MIKE 3	뉴질랜드
	Andrew Boykett	MIKE 4	
✕	Bill Coker	MIKE 5 (의사)	
	Tony Brown	MIKE 6	영국
✕	Adrian West	MIKE 7	

0149

ROLL	NAME	CALLSIGN	LOCATION MUTHANNA
	COMMUNICATORS		
✗	Tim Sopp	ZERO	
	Kent Burstrom	OSCAR 1	
	Catherina Terling	OSCAR 2	흥신반산 유민상주요해
	Tim Norris	OSCAR 3	
	Vernon Woolford	ROMEO	
✗	Richard Harkett	KILO	
	ATTACHED		
	Basil Tabbah	TANGO	홍덕만 열레느라인
	MSE PERSONNEL		
✗	Dr Ghazi Feisal	이사크	
✗	Dr Ala'a Al-Saeed		

0150

CARGO DESCRIPTION	ESTIMATED WT(KG)/VOL(M³)	NO. OF PIECES

0151

UNSCOM #38 - CDG

PROPOSED DESTRUCTION TASKS

15 October 1992

TASK		X	
122 mm Rockets			
122 mm Warheads	Setup Pits	X	A + EOD ①
122 mm Rocket Motor			
122 mm Propellant Grain			
155 mm Artillery Projectile Test Drill			
155 mm Artillery Projectile Test Explosive			
Al Hussein Warhead			
R400 Aerial Bomb		X	B
250 Gauge Polymerised Partial Fill		X	A + EOD
500 Gauge Polymerised Partial Fill			
250 Gauge Polymerised Complete			
500 Gauge Polymerised Complete			
Nerve Agent Sample Taking			
Mustard Agent Sample Taking			
Nerve Agent Hydrolysis		X	B
D4 Hydrolysis			
Mustard Incineration			
DF Neutralisation			
Bulk Agent Tank Decontamination/Destruction		X	A
250/500 Gauge - Agent Decanting		X	A

A Patrick   B Gabor   EOD Paul.
   Carl   David.
   Darrel   Roger
   Kim   Lutz

0152

공   란

공   란

공　　　　란

공 란

공 란

報 告 事 項

報 告 畢

1992. 12. 9.
國 際 機 構 局
國際聯合1課(46)

題 目 : 이라크 化學武器廢棄班 參與要員 歸國

> 유엔 이라크 化學武器廢棄班에 參與한 우리將校 2명이 3개월간의
> 任務를 마치고 12.4(金) 歸國하였는 바, 이들의 活動槪要等을 아래
> 報告합니다.

1. 廢棄班 活動槪要

　ㅇ 13개국(미, 영, 불, 독, 카나다, 호주, 체코, 헝가리등) 39명으로 構成

　ㅇ 바그다드 외곽의 「알 무타나」化學武器廢棄場을 중심으로 이라크
　　　要員들의 化學彈 廢棄作業 監督 및 安全節次 主管

　ㅇ 이라크 政府는 化學武器의 안전한 廢棄를 위해 유엔 廢棄班 活動에
　　　協調的
　　　- 유엔 査察班에 대한 態度와는 對照的

　ㅇ 廢棄班은 93.12月까지 繼續活動 豫定

2. 成 果

　ㅇ 우리의 平和이미지 高揚

　ㅇ 化學武器 廢棄關聯 經驗蓄積으로 향후 化學武器禁止協約 및 對北韓査察
　　　對備等에 有益

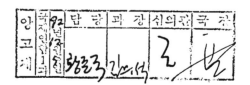

0158

3. 特記事項

  ㅇ 參與國들은 대부분 自國人으로 後任者를 계속 派遣하는데 반해, 우리의
    경우 러시아인 2명이 後任으로 대체되었음.
    - 우리의 경우 이같은 활동참여가 처음이므로 우리요원의 活動結果
      評價後에 후임자 계속 파견문제를 검토키로 했었음.

4. 後續措置(아래사항 檢討後 追後 報告)

  ㅇ 상기 化學武器廢棄班에 다시 參與하는 問題
    - 유엔 이라크武器廢棄特委(UNSCOM)측과 協調
    ※ 國防部에 의하면 適格者는 상당수 있다고 함.
  ㅇ 우리의 參與活動相을 일정한 範圍內에서 弘報하는 問題(UNSCOM측은
    당초 대외보안을 요청)
    - 본 廢棄班活動이 미 CNN TV에 放映되는 등 이미 言論에 公開되었고
      이라크측도 우리의 參與事實을 알고 있을 것임을 고려
    ※ 國防部는 軍 新聞等을 통해 弘報할 것을 希望

5. 言論對策 : 弘報問題에 관한 上記 檢討後 施行

                                              - 끝 -

0159

報 告 事 項

報 告 畢

1992. 12. 9.
國 際 機 構 局
國際聯合1課(46)

題 目 : 이라크 化學武器廢棄班 參與要員 歸國

　　　유엔 이라크 化學武器廢棄班에 參與한 우리將校 2명이 3개월간의
任務를 마치고 12.4(金) 歸國하였는 바, 이들의 活動槪要等을 아래
報告합니다.

1.　廢棄班 活動槪要

　ㅇ　13개국(미, 영, 불, 독, 캐나다, 호주, 체코, 헝가리등) 39명으로 構成

　ㅇ　바그다드 외곽의 「알 무타나」 化學武器廢棄場을 중심으로 이라크
　　　要員들의 化學彈 廢棄作業 監督 및 安全節次 主管

　ㅇ　이라크 政府는 化學武器의 안전한 廢棄를 위해 유엔 廢棄班 活動에
　　　協調的
　　　- 유엔 査察班에 대한 態度와는 對照的

　ㅇ　廢棄班은 93.12月까지 繼續活動 豫定

2.　成　果

　ㅇ　우리의 平和이미지 高揚

　ㅇ　化學武器 廢棄關聯 經驗蓄積으로 향후 化學武器禁止協約 및 對北韓査察
　　　對備等에 有益

0160

3. **特記事項**

     o   參與國들은 대부분 自國人으로 後任者를 계속 派遣하는데 반해, 우리의
          경우 러시아인 2명이 後任으로 대체되었음.

        - 우리의 경우 이같은 활동참여가 처음이므로 우리요원의 活動結果
          評價後에 후임자 계속 파견문제를 검토키로 했었음.

4. **後續措置**(아래사항 檢討後 追後 報告)

     o   상기 化學武器廢棄班에 다시 參與하는 問題
        - 유엔 이라크武器廢棄特委(UNSCOM)측과 協調
        ※   國防部에 의하면 適格者는 상당수 있다고 함.

     o   우리의 參與活動相을 일정한 範圍內에서 弘報하는 問題(UNSCOM측은
          당초 대외보안을 요청)
        - 본 廢棄班活動이 미 CNN TV에 放映되는 등 이미 言論에 公開되었고
          이라크측도 우리의 參與事實을 알고 있을 것임을 고려
        ※   國防部는 軍 新聞等을 통해 弘報할 것을 希望

5. **言論對策** :   弘報問題에 관한 上記 檢討後 施行

                                          - 끝 -

발 신 전 보

번   호 : **WUN-3536**   921210 1047 WH   종별 : _____

수   신 : 주   유엔   대사. ~~동경대사~~

발   신 : 장 관 (연일)

제   목 : 이라크 화학무기 폐기작업반

대 : UNW-2235

1. 표제작업반에 참여한 우리장교 2명이 3개월간의 임무를 마치고 12.4(금)
   귀국하였음.

2. 본부는 금번 참여활동이 유익했다고 평가하고 우리 화학무기 전문가가
   동 작업반(93.12까지 계속 활동예상)에 다시 참여하는 문제를 검토코자
   하는 바 UNSCOM측의 견해를 타진, 보고바람.
   - 참여국들은 대부분 자국인으로 후임자를 계속 파견하는데 반해 우리의
     경우 러시아인 2명이 후임으로 대체되었음. 이는 우리의 경우 처음
     참여이므로 우리요원의 활동결과 평가후에 후임자 선발문제를 검토키로
     했었기 때문임. (국방부에 의하면 적격자는 상당수 있다고 함)

3. 국방부측은 금번 우리의 참여활동상을 군신문 등을 통해 홍보할 것을 희망
   하고 있는 바, 당초 UNSCOM측의 대외보안 요청이 지금도 유효한지 UNSCOM측
   견해를 보고바람. 본 폐기반 활동은 미 CNN TV에 방영되는등 이미 언론에
   공개되었고 이라크측도 우리의 참여사실을 알고 있으리라는 점을 참고바람. 끝.

(국제기구국장   김재섭)

예 고 : 193. 6. 30. 일반   고 에
         의거 인반문서로

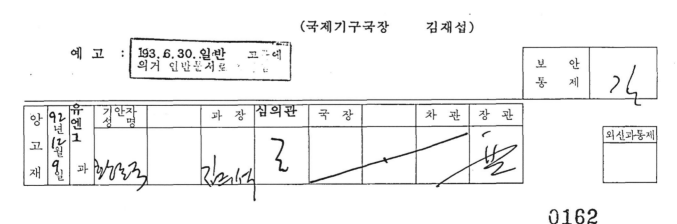

0162

관리 번호	92-1713

외 무 부

종 별 :

번 호 : UNW-3748

일 시 : 92 1211 1700

수 신 : 장 관(연일)

발 신 : 주 유엔 대사

제 목 : 이라크 화학무기 폐기 작업반

대:WUN-3536

대호건 UNSCOM 관계 담당관 사정상 12.14 접촉 보고위계임

(대사 유종하-국장)

여공:1993.6.30 일반
의거 인반문서

국기국

PAGE 1

이라크 최항해
도에개반 왔어 *file*

동아. 92.12.13. 일, 6면

유엔査察 협조중단

이라크, 협조자 처벌 위협

[유엔본부=연합] 이라크 당국은 더이상 유엔의 이라크 무기사찰단에 협조하지 않을것이며 앞으로 협력자는 처벌하겠다는 위협을 사찰단에 전달한것으로 11일 공개된 유엔사찰단의 보고서가 밝혔다.

이 보고서는 이라크 군 자산업위원회의 아메르 라시드 장군이 「이라크는 사찰단을 신뢰했으나 기만당했다. 유엔은 이라크 당국으로부터 더이상 얻을것이

없다. 모든것이 끝났다」고 말하고 사찰단에 협력하는 이라크人들은 처벌받을 것이라고 강조했다고 전했다.

보고서는 또 아메르 장군의 이같은 발언은 이라크 당국의 對유엔 협조상태가 심각하게 악화됐음을 반영하는것이라고 말하고 실제로 최근 이라크당국은 유엔사찰단 헬리콥터의 바그다드상공비행을 금지하는 등 비협조적 태도를 보였다고 밝혔다.

0164

외　무　부

원　본

종　별 :

번　호 : UNW-3770

일　시 : 92 1214 2000

수　신 : 장 관(연일,중동일,기정)

발　신 : 주 유엔 대사

제　목 : 이라크 화학무기 폐기 작업반

　　　대:WUN-3536

　　　연:UNW-2235

　　금 12.4 당관 강참사관은 UNSCOM 의 AGNES 화학무기 폐기 담당관과 접촉, 대호관련 사항 협의한바 동결과 아래보고함

　　1. 대호 2 항관련, AGNES 담당관은 지난 11 월 이락 방문시 표제 작업반에 참여했던 우리장교들과 면담할 기회를 갖고 이때에 동장교들로부터도 우리의 향후 재참여 희망을 들은 적이 있다고 하면서, UNSCOM 으로서는 가능하면 많은 나라들에게 공평한 참여기회를 준다는 의미에서 동일국에서의 연속적인 참여는 가능한한 피하고 일정 기간 경과후에 재참여를 유도하고 있다고 하고 만약 우리나라가 재참여를 희망한다면 93.3.1 자로 임무가 완료되는 화학무기 폐기작업반의 일부 인원 교체시 재참여가 가능할 것으로 보며 이경우 파견 기간은 사정에 따라4-6 개월이 될것으로 본다고 하면서 93.1 월에 파견될 신규 폐기 작업반 구성이완료되는대로 참여를 희망하는 국가에 대해 공식적인 통보를 해줄수 있을것이라고 말하바, 재참여 여부에 관한 우리의 입장을 조속 확정 통보바람

　　2. 대호 3 항관련, 동인은 동 폐기 작업반 참여국가 및 참여인원 명단, 제재위 활동에 관한 이락 정부측 협조태도, 대이락 SANCTION 에 대한 COMMENT, 이락정정상황등 정치적으로 민감함 문제에 대한 대외보안 요청은 지금도 유효하나 신문, 세미나, 논문등을 통해 화학무기의 구체적 폐기내용에 관한 기술적 측면을널리 알리는 것은 화학무기 폐기로 인해 생길수도 있는 환경피해에 관한 오해를불식시킨다는 측면에서도 이는 환영하는 바 이라고 말하면서 그러나, 어느경우에도 동인들은 특정국가를 대표한것이 아니고 유엔 작업반의 일원으로서 활동했던점을 고려하며 COMMON SENSE 선에서 대처해 주되 TECHNICAL ASPECT 의

국기국　　장관　　차관　　1차보　　중아국　　분석관　　중아국　　정와대　　안기부

범주를 넘지 않도록 유념해 주는것이 좋겠다는 의견을 피력함

3. 상기 2 항관련, 우리나라가 표제 작업반 활동에 참여했다는 사실이 비록외부에 알려져 있다하더라도 우리의 참여 활동상에 대해 의도적으로 홍보활동을 전개할 경우, 불필요하게 이락을 자극할 비판내용이 포함될수 있는 가능성도 있을 것인바, 장기적 관점에서의 이락과의 양자관계등을 고려 좀더 신중하게 대처함이 좋을 것으로 생각됨

(대사 유종하-국장)

예규:93.6.30。일반 고문에 의거 인반문서로 ○○됨

공   란

공 란

공　　　　란

공　　　　란

공   란

공   란

공   란

공   란

공   란

공   란

공 란

공   란

공   란

공   란

정 리 보 존 문 서 목 록					
기록물종류	일반공문서철	등록번호	21927	등록일자	1996-05-15
분류번호	731.33	국가코드	IQ	보존기간	30년
명 칭	유엔안전보장위원회 이라크 배상위원회, 1991~92. 전6권				
생 산 과	중동1과/국제연합1과	생산년도	1991~1992	담당그룹	
권 차 명	V.1 1991.3-7월				
내용목차	* 1991.5.20 걸프전 배상위원회 설치 결의안 채택 (안보리 결의 692호) 　　　7.23-8.2 제1차 집행위원회 * 유엔 배상위원회: UN compensation commission * 한국의 대이라크 배상(피해보상) 청구 포함				

0001

걸프전후 피해 배상 청구문제

1991. 3.

외   무   부

0002

걸프전후 피해배상 청구문제

1. 각국 사례

   가. 쿠웨이트

   ○ 주유엔 쿠웨이트 대표부가 각 유엔 회원국중 관계 국가대표부에
      신청 안내문을 배포하였으며, 이는 이라크 정부에 청구하기 위한
      것이라함.

   나. 유 엔

   ○ 유엔 사무국측은 안보리 결의 674, 686호가 국제법상 이라크의
      배상책임을 재확인하고, 특히 674호는 각국에게 자국의 배상
      청구사항을 수집토록 권유하는 사항임을 설명.
      (단, 동결의가 사무국에 권한 및 임무를 부여치 않아 현재 사무국
       측의 조치는 없음)

   ○ 유엔주재 쿠웨이트 대표부는 어떤 주도적 역할을 취하지 않고,
      관련국 각자가 조치할 문제라고 주장
      (그러나 실제 피해 배상청구 관련절차 문제는 추후 유엔에서 토의가
       있을 것으로 보고 있음)

   ○ 유엔주재 영국 대표부는 자국이 청구할 것이 적지 않으나, 현재
      구체적 조치는 취하지 않고 있으며, 앞으로 적절한 시기에 유엔(안보리)
      에서 청구절차에 관한 후속 논의가 있을 것으로 보고 있음

   ○ 불,독등 서구 및 인도등의 유엔 주재 대표부는 자국의 배상청구 관련
      자료를 나름대로 정리중 이라함.

   다. 카나다

   ○ 외무·무역부내 피해 신고처를 설치하고 카나다 국민 및 기업의 재산적,
      신체적 피해에 대해 이라크 정부 당국에 손해 배상을 청구하기 위해
      조속 신고(외무부 조약국 경제통상법과)하도록 2.28 자로 공고하고
      피해내용 접수중

0003

o 배상 청구범위로서 쿠웨이트 및 이라크내에 약 800여명의 카나다
  석유분야 기술자가 체제하였는바, 이들의 직접 피해에 대한 배상청구가
  주가 될것임 (건설공사는 없었으며, 수출업체 피해는 카나다 수출
  개발공사등에 보험 가입되어있어 배상청구에서 제외)

o 청구 방법은 유엔 안보리 결의에 의거, 유엔이 이라크 정부에 대해
  피해 배상 청구시 이에 따르되, 그렇지 않을 경우 카나다 정부가
  이라크 정부에 직접 청구 예정
  (카나다내 동결 이라크 자산 압류, 사용하는 방법 고려중이며,
  이와 유사한 미국과 보조를 맞춰 처리할 방침)

라. 독일

o 쿠웨이트 주재 공관건물 및 자국국민과 업체등이 입은 피해에 대한
  손해 배상을 청구 하여야 한다는 입장에 따라 대사관 건물 피해
  유무, 기타 독일 국민 재산피해 내용 조사중

o 세부방침은 현지파견 주쿠웨이트 대사관 요원 보고접수후 검토예정

마. 불란서

o 배상문제가 제기 되고 있으나, 쿠웨이트와는 달리 이라크는 복구
  사업과 배상 재원이 고갈된 상태인바, 우선 경제 봉쇄 특히 석유수출
  금지 조치가 해제된 이후 구체적 거론이 가능할 것으로 보고 있음.

o 이라크의 원유 수출 금지가 해제되면 국제 금융 기구가 원유를
  담보로 차관공여, 전후 복구 및 배상등 현실화 조치가 있을 것으로
  전망

바. 일본

o 이라크 정부에 대한 손해 배상 청구가 국제법상 가능 여부 검토중

o 피해를 당한 자국민이나 기업이 이라크 정부에 직접 손해 배상
  청구하는 것은 가능하다고 보고 있으나, 일정부가 개인이나 기업의
  피해 신고를 받아 이라크 정부에 일괄 청구 할지 여부는 미검토

0004

2. 우리나라의 입장

　　ㅇ 주 쿠웨이트 대사 보고에 의하면, 유엔 주재 쿠웨이트 대표부가 유엔주재
　　　 회원국중 관계 국가 대표부에 피해배상 신청 안내문을 배포하였다는바,
　　　 주 유엔 아국 대표부를 통해 동 안내문 입수 검토.

　　ㅇ 이와 병행하여 추후 걸프전쟁으로 인한 피해 배상 청구 절차, 범위,
　　　 방법등에 관한 유엔에서의 논의에 대비, 조속히 아국 교민, 기업체 등의
　　　 손해액을 추계(가능한한 증빙 문건 구비), 정리 완료함.

　　ㅇ 피해조사 방법은 우선 쿠웨이트 교민 회장과 진출업체등에 대해 서울에서
　　　 추계 가능한 손해를 집계, 가능한데로 증빙문건 구비케하고, 추가로
　　　 현장 조사 필요 부분에 대하여는 일단 쿠웨이트에 귀환하여 조사한후
　　　 대사관을 창구로 쿠웨이트 관계 기관과 협의 진행토록 하여야 할 것임.

0005

관리 번호 91/1244

외 무 부

종 별 :

번 호 : UNW-0532　　　　　　　　　일 시 : 91 0308 1200

수 신 : 장관 (중동일,법규,국연,기정)

발 신 : 주 유엔 대사

제 목 : 걸프사태 (손해배상 청구)

대: WUN-0434, 0468

대호 손해배상 청구문제 관련 당관에서 유엔사무국 및 관련 대표부들에 탐문한바,
동 반응을 아래 보고함.

1. 사무국 (B.BLENMAN 안보리 담당관, N.SCHRIJVER 법률담당관)

　가. 안보리 결의 674, 686 호는 국제법상의 이락의 배상책임을 재확인하고 있고,
특히 674 호는 (본문 9 항) 각국에게 자국의 청구사항을 수집토록 권유 (INVITE) 하고
있음.

　나. 그러나 동 결의는 본건 관련 사무국에 어떤 권한이나 임무를 부여하고 있지
않은바, 사무국측이 현재 취하고 있거나 검토중인 조치는 없음.

　다. 본건은 안보리 제재위원회 (661 호 결의에 의거 설치) 에서도 ~~누84타. 본건은 안보리 재재위원화 (661 호 결의에 의거 설치) 에서도~~ 다루어지고 있지
않으며 각 관련국이 개별적으로 자국의 청구사항을 수집하고 있다고 듣고 있음. (미,
영, 쿠웨이트 예시)

2. 관련국 대표부

가. 쿠웨이트 (M.AL SALLAL 참사관)

　1) 현 단계에서 자국 청구사항 수집은 관련국들이 각자 조치할 문제이며,
쿠웨이트가 어떤 주도적인 역할을 하고있지 않음. (대호 배상 신청 안내문 배부사실
부인)

　2) 실제적인 청구와 관련한 절차문제는 추후 유엔에서 토의가 있을것으로 봄.

나. 영국 (I.CLIFF 서기관)

　1) 본국에서 자국의 청구내용을 정리중에 있으나, 추후의 청구절차 (안보리의장,
사무총장을 통한 방법 또는 이락에 대한 직접 청구방법)에 관해서는 영국으로서나
중요 관련국간에 방침이 아직 섬일지 않은것으로 알구있음.

<table>
<tr><td>중아국</td><td>장관</td><td>차관</td><td>1차보</td><td>2차보</td><td>북기국</td><td>국기국</td><td>청와대</td><td>안기부</td></tr>
</table>

2) 불, 독을 비롯한 서구제국, 안도등도 자국의 배상청구 관련 자료를 정리중이며 미국의 경우 정리작업이 완료되었다고 들었음.

　다. 미국 (D.RUSSEL 담당관)

　1) 미국도 청구할것이 적지않으나 현단계에서 구체적인 조치를 취하고 있지는 않음.

　2)앞으로 적절한 시기에 유엔 (안보리)에서 청구 절차에 관한 후속 논의가 있을것으로 봄.

　라. 일본 (S.SUMI 서기관)

　1) 개별적으로 자국의 청구내용을 수집하고 있는 나라들 (카나다 예시) 이 있다고 듣고있으나, 일본으로서는 아직 구체적 조치를 취하고 있지 않음.

　2) 향후 안보리에서 청구절차 문제에 관한 토의가 있을것으로 기대하나, 현재로서는 본건 청구문제에 관한 어떤 전망을 하기에는 이른감이 있음. 우선은 유엔 조사단 쿠웨이트 방문 (UNW-0526) 결과, 대 이락 경제제재조치 해제문제 추이를 지켜보아야 할것으로 봄. 끝 (대사대리 신기복-국장)

　예고:91.6.30. 일반

91. 6. 30. 예고문에기 일어거해

PAGE 2

0007

건 설 부

해외 30600-10152   (503-7396)   1991. 4. 12
                                                (1년)

수신 외무부 장관

참조 국제경제국장, 중동아국장

제목 대이라크 미회수 채권 회수방안 협의

　　　1. Gulf전 발생에 따라 이라크에서 시공중이던 공사 중단으로 발생한
아국업체의 피해 내역은 10억불에 이르고 있습니다.

　　　2. '91. 4. 6 이라크측이 수락한 UN 안보리 결의안 (687호 제 16~19항)
에는 향후 이라크의 원유수출대금중 일부를 참전국의 피해보상을 위한 기금으로
할당할 것이라고 하는바, 이와 관련하여 동기금 할당시 한국업체의 대이라크
미회수 채권도 가급적 수령하는 방안이 강구되도록 UN 대표부등에서 추진하여
주시기를 협조 요청합니다.

　　　첨부 : 아국업체의 대이라크 미회수 채권내역 1부. 끝.

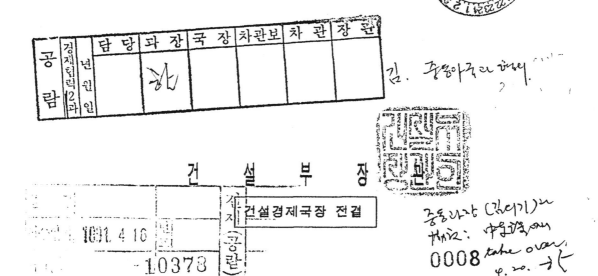

건설경제국장 전결

건 설 부 장

대이라크 미회수 채권현황

단위 : 천불

구 분	금 액	비 고
총 계	1,059,134	
공사 미수금	49,662	
기성 유보금	145,227	
어음 미결제분	583,995	
미수령 원유대금	204,419	
예 치 금	4,550	계약보증금, 하자보증금 등 예치
클레임 제기금액	52,388	
은행예금	18,893	

0009

외 무 부

종 별 :

번 호 : UNW-0954   일 시 : 91 0417 2000

수 신 : 장 관(국연,중동일,기정)

발 신 : 주 유엔 대사

제 목 : 걸프사태(안보리)

연: UNW-0937

1. 4.16 이락은 식량을 비롯한 필수품 긴급수입 (4개월분)을 위해 약 10억불 상당의 석유수출을 허가해 줄것을 안보리 제재위원회에 요청하여 온바, 동 위원회 의장 (오지리대사)은 이사국들과의 개별협의를 거쳐 4.19 경 위원회소집 예정인 것으로 알려짐.

2. 유엔 S.KHAN 대표일행은 이락 당국과 쿠르드족, 쉬아교파 난민보호소 (RECEPTION CENTERS)설치문제를 협의해온바, 금명간 동협의결과가 발표될것으로 관측되고있음. 한편 이락 북부지역에 미, 영, 불 병력이 관할하는 난민수용소 (5-6 개소)를 설치하는 문제에 대한 유엔사무총장 반응은 별첨 총장대변인 발표내용 참조바람.

3. 안보리 휴전결의 (687호) 후속조치 문제와 관련하여 다음사항 참고바람.

가. 무기폐기 관련 특별위원회

동 위원회 (위원:20-25 명)는 5가지분야 (화학무기, 미사일, 핵무기, 검증, 지원업무)로 나누어 분임반 (UNITS)을 두며, 상당수지원인력 (수백명)을 갖게될 것으로알려짐. 위원회 의장국으로 스칸디나비아 국가도 거론되고 있음.

나. 배상기금

동 기금 적립을 위한 이락 석유수출수입 공제분은 10-15 프로 수준이 보도되고있음. (4.17자 NYT 지)

첨부:사무총장 대변인 발표내용: UNW(F)-172

끝

(대사 노창희-국장)

국기국   1차보   정문국   정와대   안기부

PAGE 1   91.04.18 10:39 WG

외신 1과 통제관

0010

Asked if the intention of the United States, the United Kingdom and France to provide military protection for the Kurds had been discussed, the Secretary-General said that it was an aspect "on which we have to reflect; because we would first of all like to be in touch with the Iraqis to see what their reaction would be to this military presence on their territory." Did a military presence constitute a problem, he was asked? "It depends", the Secretary-General replied. "If it is a military presence under the UN flag, of course I must obtain the consent, so to speak, of the Security Council. If it is up to countries which do not request the UN flag, the situation is completely different."

Did this mean, the Secretary-General was asked further, that a resolution would be needed before action was taken? The Secretary-General replied "not necessarily. But in any case, we are studying the situation with a great deal of attention so that Iraq's sovereignty shall be respected, and we hope that the Iraqis will understand that the objective of the three countries is quite simply humanitarian, as also is that of the UN. The Iraqi government received my team, Sadruddin Aga Khan and Ambassador Suy, and I shall see them in Paris on Saturday when they will inform me of what they heard and then we shall take decisions."

Asked whether he was hostile to a military presence in Iraq, the Secretary-General said "the word 'military' is awkward. If the objective is humanitarian, I do not see a difficulty, I mean a difficulty from the moral point of view. But from the legal point of view, of course it is a problem."

The Secretary-General was then asked what he thought about the possibility of establishing enclaves in Iraqi territory. He replied "the word 'enclave' has never been used. The term that is used is 'reception centre'. The word 'enclave' has, of course, a connotation which affects the sovereignty of Iraq. I still have good hopes that the Iraqis will accept the reception centres. Whether these centres will have a kind of military observation or not, that is another story."

Asked whether the military presence could be established in Iraq before a reply from the Iraqi government, the Secretary-General replied "No, no, no. For me, we have in any case first of all to be in touch with the Iraqis - it is a question of sovereignty."

0011

통화기록

1. 일 시 : 4.25(목) 14:45 - 14:50

2. 송화자 : AFP 특파원 Michael Gonzales (전화 : 737-7354)

3. 수화자 : 중동 1과 조태용

4. 통화내용

Gonzales : 주 쿠웨이트 소병용 대사의 기자회견 내용중 피해
보상문제와 관련한 한국 정부 입장은 ?

조 : background briefing으로 말씀드리면, 소대사의
언급내용 처럼 우리는 걸프전으로 인한 한국교민 및
회사의 피해를 조사중이며 아직 결정은 안됐으나,
유엔측에 피해목록을 제출할 것을 검토중임. 이는
유엔 안보리 결의 687호에 따른 것이며, 이미 20여개국이
피해액을 유엔측에 통보한 바 있음. 동 유엔 결의에
의하면 이라크의 원유수입등을 재원으로 피해 보상기금이
설립될 계획인데, 상세한 관련 절차가 이미 마련되어
있는지는 확실치 않음.

Gonzales : 언론 보도에는 제소(suit)라고 되어 있는데 ?

조 : 유엔 결의 내에서 보상청구를 하는 것을 검토중이며,
법적 제소와는 성격이 다름.

0012

Seoul ready to file damage suit against Iraq: Amb. Soh

By Kim Hyeh-won
Staff reporter

Korean Ambassador to Kuwait Soh Byung-yong has said he would soon claim damage against Iraq for the material losses inflicted to Korean residents and firms in Kuwait by the Iraqi invasion of the small emirate and the subsequent Gulf war.

He said he would file complaints with the United Nations as soon as he completes gathering reports on the losses.

Amb. Soh

The ambassador expected the hundreds of Koreans who had left Kuwait after the outbreak of the Gulf conflict to be able to return to the Middle East country by the end of next month.

There were over 600 Koreans living in Kuwait before the Iraqi invasion of the oil-rich kingdom. Most of them left the country soon after and are staying in Red Cross facilities and with relatives in Seoul.

Amb. Soh said their return to Kuwait has been delayed mainly because they have failed to make contact with their "sponsors" yet.

He said that under Kuwait law, foreigners can enter and stay in the country only when they have sponsors with Kuwaiti nationality.

Many of the Kuwaitis have still failed to return home for security reasons, and therefore, are difficult to contact by the Koreans, he said.

The Kuwaiti government also does not want foreigners to return to the kingdom for the moment.

Amb. Soh expected the biddings for reconstruction projects in Kuwait to begin in full in May, after the Kuwaiti government finishes its survey of the war damages.

He painted a bright picture for Korea's participation in the projects. Kuwaiti officials including emir Shaikh al-Sabah, pledged their full support for Korea's participation when Soh met them at the government-in-exile in Taif, Saudi Arabia in February, he said.

"The government has done what it can politically to help Korean businesses and what is left to do now is mostly up to the businessmen," said Soh who was staying in Seoul for the annual meeting of the Korean diplomatic mission chiefs. He left Seoul for Kuwait yesterday.

The ambassador had left his post since the temporary closure of the Korean Embassy in Kuwait last summer and returned to the post in March soon after Iraq's withdrawal.

He said several Korean firms, including Hyundai, have already begun contacting Kuwaitis for resumption of their suspended projects in Kuwait or are exploring new possibilities.

The ambassador recommended reconstruction of interior facilities in big buildings as a most prominent field for Korean firms. He also suggested reconstruction of electricity-supplying, communications and port facilities as good fields.

Surprisingly he said, the Iraqi invasion and the Gulf war did not destroy many buildings in Kuwait. Most structures remain intact, but their inside have been seriously damaged by fires the Iraqis set while withdrawing from the country.

4.25 Korea Herald.

1991.

Korea Sees Many Ways to Help Postwar Kuwait Reconstruction

South Korean Ambassador to Kuwait Soh Byung-yong eyed brighter prospects for export of goods and equipment to the Middle East emirate for rehabilitation works rather than participation in large-scale construction projects there.

Amb. Soh

"The most urgent works for the post-war recovery in Kuwait is rehabilitation of electric and communications facilities," Amb. Soh said in an interview yesterday.

He said that the Kuwaiti government is devoting itself to rehabilitating communications, utility facilities and equipment, and other infrastructure under its 3-month emergency recovery program, which is entering a final stage.

"The assessment of war damages has yet to be reported by the U.S. Army Corps of Engineering. As a result, the Kuwaiti government is still not ready to issue large-scale construction projects," Amb. Soh said.

He then called upon Korean companies to prepare for exports of communications and utility facilities and equipment to the war-ravaged country.

Amb. Soh and embassy officials evacuated from Kuwait immediately after the Iraqi occupation of the emirate and resumed their duty at the embassy in Kuwait on Mar. 9.

He is in Seoul for the annual meeting of Korean diplomatic mission chiefs which ended on Monday. Because of the retarded resumption of air flights to and from Kuwait City, it took three days to arrive in Seoul from Kuwait, Amb. Soh said.

Some $80 billion is estimated to be needed for the recovery and rehabilitation of war damage but this calculation is rather inflated, Amb. Soh said, quoting ranking Kuwaiti government officials.

He said that the damages of roads, buildings and other infrastructure are lower than originally expected. Instead, the Kuwaiti people are suffering from shortage in piped water, communications facilities and equipment and power.

As a result, the Kuwaiti government will allow 60,000 citizens to return home per week, beginning May 4.

Some 602 Korean people evacuated from Kuwait following the outbreak of war and will be able to return to the country from late next month. Ten Korean people already got approval for return from the Kuwaiti government, he said.

Amb. Soh made it clear that the government and Korean citizens will go through due procedures for reparation for war damages under the United Nations resolutions.

Asked about the possibility for South Korea to participate in recovery projects there, Amb. Soh said, "I confirmed through the meetings with the Kuwaiti emir and ranking government officials that South Korean companies' participation in recovery works will be welcomed. The remaining question is up to the capability of our business firms."

4. 25 Korea Times

外務部 걸프事態 非常對策 本部

題 目: 1991.

쿠웨이트 교민피해
이라크에 배상청구
蔡乘用대사 밝혀

제임스 주장의참석차 일

시귀국한 蔡乘用駐쿠웨이
트대사는 23일 기자들과 만
나 「오는 5월말까지 교민들이
쿠웨이트로복귀하는대로 교
민피해행위을 접수, 이라크에
손해배상을청구하기위해 최

종집계작업을 유엔에 제출할
예정」이라고 밝혔다.
蔡대사는 또 「서독에 와
있는 쿠웨이트교민들은 5
월말까지 모두 복귀할 수
있을 것」이라고 전망했다.

4.24 韓國

外務部 걸프事態 非常對策 本部

題 目: 1991.

第21456號

인터뷰

일시 귀국한 駐쿠웨이트 蘇秉用대사

"僑民피해 이라크에 보상청구"

「6백여 교민들의 재산, 費用 駐쿠웨이트 대사 蘇秉用(55)는 27일 걸프戰 종 피해에 대한 조사가… 난 대로 유엔 안보리를 전후 현지를 둘러본 결 통해 이라크에 정 사관 복구작업에 매달 식으로 피해보상을 청구 왔는데 지금은 모든 대사 할 방침입니다」 과 現代건설을 비롯한

교민들의 피해가 적지않 았다면서 이같이 밝혔 다.

蘇대사는 지난 3월9 일 쿠웨이트에 복귀 피해를 「現代건설은 물론 큰 교민들을 보았고 급박에 교민들은 이라크의 약

...

...

「4·2·7 東亞

政府綜合廳舍 810號   電話:730-8283/5, 730-2941.6.7.9, (구내)2331/4, 2337/8   Fax:730-8209

0016

외 무 부

종   별 :

번   호 : UNW-1096   일   시 : 91 0430 2210

수   신 : 장 관(국연,중동일,기정)

발   신 : 주 유엔 대사

제   목 : 안보리동향(걸프사태,엘살바돌)

1. 안보리 제재위원회는 지난 4.19 회의에 이어 금 4.30 회의를갖고 이락측의 석유수출 (약 10억불)허가 요청을 토의하였으나 진전이 없었던 것으로 알려짐.

2. 걸프사태관련 ZAKHO 다국적군 관할 난민수용소의 유엔접수 교섭이 진행중인바, 동접수후 난민안전보호문제, 특히 유엔민간경찰 (CIVILIAN POLICE UNIT) 파견, 이를 위한 안보리 승인필요 여부가 주요현안이 되고있다고함.

3. 한편 엘살바돌문제관련 안보리는 금일 비공식 협의에서 사무총장의 유엔옵서버단 배치계획을 토의한바, 곧 공식회의에서 승인절차를 밟을 것으로 관측됨.

첨부: 이락난민문제관련 NYT 기자: UNW(F)-188끝

(대사 노창희-국장)

대책반 보고돼 장님

국기국   1차보   중아국   정문국   정와대   안기부

PAGE 1   91.05.01   11:14 WG
                                              외신 1과 통제관

                                                0017

UNW.(FI)-188 10(7)0 2210
(국연. 중동일. 기2b)   총104

U.N. SEEKS ACCORD ON A POLICE FORCE IN NORTHERN IRAQ

TO REPLACE U.S. TROOPS

Security Council Would Avoid New Debate and Provide Protection for Kurds

By PATRICK E. TYLER
Special to The New York Times

WASHINGTON, April 29 — The five permanent members of the Security Council are seeking agreement on establishing a United Nations police force in the Kurdish region of northern Iraq. The force would take over from American and allied military units, which have set up a refugee zone in the area.

The idea of sending United Nations policemen into northern Iraq, as opposed to a full-fledged peacekeeping force, is intended to avoid a debate in the Security Council over whether such an intervention in Iraq's affairs can be authorized without a request from the Baghdad Government.

Replacing American Soldiers

Sending in a United Nations police force to take over the military security role now being performed by the United States and its allies would save Washington from having large numbers of American soldiers indefinitely committed in northern Iraq.

Those soldiers are there for the time being to provide security against Iraqi forces so that Kurdish families will feel confident enough to come down from the mountains, where they have fled from the army of President Saddam Hussein.

The idea for a police force, as detailed today at the United Nations by the British, who originated it, would be a logical extension of an agreement signed with Iraq on April 18 by the United Nations Secretary General's special refugee envoy, Prince Sadruddin Aga Khan. That agreement authorizes United Nations forces to take over refugee assistance operations in Iraq.

Avoiding a Special Resolution

Since the authorization of a police force for the area flows from this United Nations action, its advocates argue that it would not need any special resolution. From the point of view of the Western allies, this is crucial since it is thought very unlikely that either China or the Soviet Union would allow the adoption of any resolution that sanctioned the presence in Iraq of uninvited foreign military forces.

After the late-afternoon deliberations broke up, a second meeting began tonight in the office of Secretary General Javier Pérez de Cuéllar. It included only representatives from the United States, Britain and France, the nations that now have forces in Iraq.

United Nations peacekeeping forces consist of uniformed soldiers from the military units of member countries. They have automatic weapons, armored vehicles and artillery. The United Nations police are drawn from civilian forces, carry sidearms and wear armbands. They are quicker to deploy but do not use heavy weapons.

Any new security arrangement deemed satisfactory to Washington and its allies would bring about the hoped-for next step — American and allied withdrawal from the northern refugee zone, where commanders worry that they are being drawn into an open-ended regional occupation to protect the Kurds from further retribution by Baghdad.

But any assumption of a security role by a United Nations force would raise questions of air support and other military backstopping from the allies, who came to the region prepared for confrontations both with the estimated 30,000 Iraqi troops in the north and with thousands of Kurdish guerrillas fighting for autonomy.

Some Official U.S. Views

Today, the White House spokesman, Marlin Fitzwater, suggested that a new assessment would have to be made of the danger in northern Iraq.

At the Pentagon, a senior official said the long-term safety of the Kurds would probably have to be secured politically before a military withdrawal. And such political steps would presumably involve the Iraqi Government and either some agency of the United Nations or representatives of the Kurdish nationalist movements. The Kurdish nationalists are expected to resume talks with Mr. Hussein on greater autonomy.

The official also said he believed that American forces would not be involved in a United Nations police force if one is established in Iraq.

"But whether we would be over the horizon" with back-up forces, "I don't know," he said. "Whether we would continue to have a quick-reaction force or combat air patrols, I don't know."

Mr. Pérez de Cuéllar, commenting in New York today on the concept of a United Nations force said, "Perhaps the Security Council is not needed; that is a possibility."

The American representative to the United Nations, Thomas R. Pickering, said today that Washington is taking "a very positive look" at the idea, adding that such a force is "potentially a very effective way to provide security and to provide protection" for the Kurds.

The first convoys of United Nations relief trucks were scheduled to arrive Tuesday in Zakho "to begin the process of taking over" the Kurdish relief operation, Mr. Fitzwater said. He added that administration of the camps could be turned over in weeks if the security issue was resolved.

Refugee Zone Extended

United States officials announced today that they had extended the refugee security zone well to the east of Zakho to Amadiya, another Kurdish city in ... the ... camp, ... a second refugee center, capable of accommodating 25,000 people, will be built near Amadiya.

Mr. Fitzwater, reflecting the trouble that the American forces have encountered in understanding tribal differences among the Kurds and among their guerrilla movements, said, "Their guerrillas are part of their people, so it's a very difficult situation to sort out, but we are trying as best we can — to get the guerrillas to stop any activities that would thwart the humanitarian relief efforts."

Several hundred Kurdish refugees entered the Zakho area in recent days, and the first families took up residence in the tent city today. United States officials said a major transport effort would begin in a few days to bring 25,000 Kurds down from the mountains to the Zakho site. The total allied relief effort has delivered 10,000 tons of supplies by airdrop and truck.

At a news conference in Baghdad today, a United Nations official said Iraqi Kurdish refugees who fled to the border regions with Turkey and Iran are returning to their homes at the rate of 20,000 a day, a figure that could not be confirmed in Washington.

#UNW-1096
첨부물

0018

외 무 부

종 별 :

번 호 : UNW-1117　　　　　　　　　일 시 : 91 0502 1900

수 신 : 장 관(국연,중동일,기정)

발 신 : 주 유엔 대사

제 목 : 걸프사태(안보리)

1. 안보리 휴전결의에 앞서 사무총장은 이락.쿠웨이트 국경획정안 (동결의 본문3항), 배상기금 설치안 (본문 17항)을 안보리에 금명간 제출예정임. 5.2.자 NYT지 보도에 의하면 동기금충당을 위한 이락 석유수출 수입공제 비율에 대해서는 10프로이하 (인도, 쿠바, 예멘), 25-30프로 (영국), 40-50프로 (미국)수준이 거론되고 있다함.

2. 이락의 특정무기 폐기업무를 관장할 특별위는 5.6-10 간 유엔본부에서 회의를 갖고, 향후 작업계획을 수립할 예정임.

3. 다국적군 관할 난민수용소의 유엔이관 교섭과관련, S.KHAN 대표가 바그다드를 곧방문할 예정인 것으로 관측되고 있음.

첨부:1.5.2.자 N.Y.T. 지 기사

2. 상기 특별위명단:UNW(F)-190

끝

(대사 노창희-국장)

국기국　　1차보　　중아국　　정문국　　안기부

91.05.03　　09:48 WG

외신 1과 통제관

0019

분류기호 문서번호	중동일 720- **15963**		기안용지 (720-2327)		시 행 상 특별취급	
보존기간	영구:준영구 10. 5. 3. 1		장 관			
수 신 처 보존기간						
시행일자	1991. 5. 6.					

<table>
<tr><td rowspan="3">보조기관</td><td>국 장</td><td>전결</td><td rowspan="4">협
조
기
관</td><td></td><td></td><td>문 서 통 제</td></tr>
<tr><td>심의관</td><td>과장</td><td></td><td></td><td>검열
1991. 5. 06
통제관</td></tr>
<tr><td>과 장</td><td>7h</td><td></td><td></td><td rowspan="2">발송상
1991. 5. 06
의무부</td></tr>
<tr><td colspan="2">기안책임자</td><td>박종순</td><td></td><td></td></tr>
<tr><td>경 유
수 신
참 조</td><td colspan="3">주쿠웨이트 대사</td><td>발
신
명
의</td><td></td></tr>
<tr><td>제 목</td><td colspan="6">이라크 배상책임 이행시안 제출</td></tr>
</table>

유엔 안보리 휴전결의(제687호)중 유엔 사무총장의 배상기금

운용 계획 제출(19항) 지시와 관련, 지난 5.2. 사무총장은 이라크 배상

책임 이행시안(S/22559)을 안보리에 제출한바, 주유엔 대표부를 통하여

입수한 동 이행안을 별첨 송부하니 ~~아국 진출업체 및 교민들을 위한~~

~~손해 배상청구~~ ~~준비에~~ 참고하시기 바랍니다.

　　　첨　부 : 동 배상책임 이행 시안　　끝.

0020

외 무 부

종 별 :

번 호 : UNW-1125

일 시 : 91 0503 1530

수 신 : 장 관 (국연,법규,중동일,기정)

발 신 : 주 유엔 대사

제 목 : 걸프사태 (안보리)

1. 안보리 휴전결의에 의거 사무총장은 5.2. 이락 배상책임 이행시안 (S/22559) 을 안보리에 제출한바, 동요지는 다음과같음. (상세별첨참조)

　가. 배상기금 (UNITED NATIONS COMPENSATION FUND) 설립

　나. 배상위원회 (UNITED NATIONS COMPENSATIONCOMMISSION) 운영

　1) 집행부 (GOVERNING COUNCIL): 안보리 15개국대표참여

　2) 전문위원 (COMMISSIONERS): 사무총장추천,집행부임명

　3) 사무처 (SECRETARIAT)

　다. 기금재원 확보

　1) 이락 석유수출 수입에서 공제 (동 공제수준은 추후결정)단, 초기단계에서 동수입외의 재원마련 문제제기

　2) 공제방식:5개 대안제시

　라. 청구절차

　1) 각국정부가 일괄봉합 청구 (CONSOLIDATED CLAIMS)원칙

　2) 청구제출 시한(안):제출절차 (FILING GUIDELINES)확정후 2년후 제출

2. 또한 상기 휴전결의 후속조치관련 사무총장은 이락.쿠웨이트 국경획정안 (S/22558) 을 동일자로 안보리에 제출한바, 동요지는 다음과같음. (상세설명참조)

　가. 국경획정위원회 (IRAQ-KUWAIT BOUNDARY DEMARCATION COMMISSION 설치:이락, 쿠웨이트 대표 각1인, 사무총장이 지명하는 전문가 3인 (총 5명)

　나. 동위원회의 획정 결정 최종적:다수결로결정

3. 한편, 이락측은 안보리 휴전결의 (본문 7항)에 의거 72년 세균무기 관련 협약비준서 (4.8.자)를 기탁한것으로 알려짐. (기탁국:소련)

　첨부:1. 이락배상책임 이행안

국기국　　1차보　　중아국　　국기국　　정문국　　안기부

91.05.04　　08:55 WG

외신 1과　통제관

0021

2. 이락.쿠웨이트국경획정안
3.5.3.자 WP 지 관련기사:UNW(F)-191
끝
(대사 노창희-국장)

UNITED
NATIONS   ⨆ᴺᵂ⁽ꜰ⁾-0191   10503 1530   총13매.

청우 UNW-1125

Security Council

Distr.
GENERAL

S/22559
2 May 1991

ORIGINAL: ENGLISH

REPORT OF THE SECRETARY-GENERAL PURSUANT TO PARAGRAPH 19 OF
SECURITY COUNCIL RESOLUTION 687 (1991)

INTRODUCTION

1.   The present report is submitted pursuant to paragraph 19 of Security
Council resolution 687 (1991) of 3 April 1991. In paragraph 16 of that
resolution, the Council reaffirmed that Iraq "is liable, under international
law, for any direct loss, damage, including environmental damage and the
depletion of natural resources, or injury to foreign Governments, nationals
and corporations, as a result of Iraq's unlawful invasion and occupation of
Kuwait". In paragraph 17 of the resolution, the Council decided "that all
Iraqi statements made since 2 August 1990 repudiating its foreign debt are
null and void", and demanded that "Iraq adhere scrupulously to all of its
obligations concerning servicing and repayment of its foreign debt". The
Council also decided, in paragraph 18 of the resolution, "to create a fund to
pay compensation for claims that fall within the scope of paragraph 16 ... and
to establish a Commission that will administer the fund".

2.   In paragraph 19 of the resolution, the Security Council directed the
Secretary-General "to develop and present to the Security Council for
decision, no later than 30 days following the adoption of the present
resolution, recommendations for the fund to meet the requirement for the
payment of claims established in accordance with paragraph 18 ..., and for a
programme to implement the decisions in paragraphs 16, 17 and 18 ...,
including: administration of the fund; mechanisms for determining the
appropriate level of Iraq's contribution to the fund based on a percentage of
the value of the exports of petroleum and petroleum products from Iraq not to
exceed a figure to be suggested to the Council by the Secretary-General,
taking into account the requirements of the people of Iraq, Iraq's payment
capacity as assessed in conjunction with the international financial
institutions taking into consideration external debt service, and the needs of
the Iraqi economy; arrangements for ensuring that payments are made to the
fund; the process by which funds will be allocated and claims paid;
appropriate procedures for evaluating losses, listing claims and verifying
their validity and resolving disputed claims in respect of Iraq's liability as
specified in paragraph 16 ...; and the composition of the Commission

91-14225 2316f (E)   /...

13 - 1

0023

S/22559
English
Page 2

designated [in paragraph 18]". In making the following recommendations, I
have borne in mind the need for maximum transparency, efficiency, flexibility
and economy in the institutional framework that will be required for the
implementation of the decisions contained in paragraphs 16, 17 and 18 of the
resolution.

I. INSTITUTIONAL FRAMEWORK

A. The Fund

3.   The Fund created by paragraph 18 of Security Council resolution
687 (1991) will be established by the Secretary-General as a special account
of the United Nations. The Fund will be known as the United Nations
Compensation Fund (hereinafter referred to as "the Fund"). The Fund will be
operated in accordance with the United Nations Financial Regulations and
Rules. As a special account of the United Nations, the Fund, therefore, will
enjoy, in accordance with Article 105 of the Charter and the Convention on the
Privileges and Immunities of the United Nations of 13 February 1946, 1/ the
status, facilities, privileges and immunities accorded to the United Nations.
The Fund will be used to pay compensation for "any direct loss, damage,
including environmental damage and the depletion of natural resources, or
injury to foreign Governments, nationals and corporations, as a result of
Iraq's unlawful invasion and occupation of Kuwait" as provided for in
paragraph 16 of resolution 687 (1991).

B. The Commission

4.   The Fund is to be administered by the Commission established by the
Security Council in paragraph 18 of resolution 687 (1991). The Commission,
which is to be known as the United Nations Compensation Commission
(hereinafter referred to as "the Commission"), will function under the
authority of the Security Council and be a subsidiary organ thereof. In
accordance with the terms of paragraph 19 of resolution 687 (1991), in
carrying out its functions, the Commission will be required to address a
variety of complex administrative, financial, legal and policy issues,
including the mechanism for determining the level of contribution to the Fund;
the allocation of funds and payments of claims; the procedures for evaluating
losses, listing claims and verifying their validity; and resolving disputed
claims. In the light of the multifarious nature of the tasks to be performed
by the Commission, it will, in my view, be necessary to distinguish between
questions of policy and the functional aspects of the Commission's work. The
Commission should, therefore, operate at a policy-making level and a
functional level. A secretariat will be necessary for servicing the work of
the Commission at both the policy-making and the functional levels.

/3-2

/...

0024

C.   Structure and composition of the Commission

5.   The principal organ of the Commission will be a 15-member Governing Council composed of the representatives of the current members of the Security Council at any given time.   The Governing Council will be assisted by a number of commissioners who will perform the tasks assigned to them by the Governing Council.   The precise number of commissioners will be determined by the Governing Council in the light of the tasks to be performed.   The commissioners will be experts in fields such as finance, law, accountancy, insurance and environmental damage assessment, who will act in their personal capacity.   They will be nominated by the Secretary-General and appointed by the Governing Council for specific tasks and terms.   In nominating the commissioners, the Secretary-General will pay due regard to the need for geographical representation, professional qualifications, experience and integrity.   The Secretary-General will establish a register of experts which might be drawn upon when commissioners are to be appointed.

6.   A secretariat, composed of an Executive Secretary and the necessary staff, will be established to service the Commission.   The Executive Secretary's primary responsibility will be the technical administration of the Fund and the servicing of the Commission.   He will be appointed by the Secretary-General after consultation with the Governing Council.   The staff of the secretariat will be appointed by the Secretary-General.   The Executive Secretary and staff will serve under the United Nations Staff Regulations and Rules.

D.   Status, privileges and immunities of the Commission

7.   The Convention on the Privileges and Immunities of the United Nations of 13 February 1946 1/ will apply to the Commission and its secretariat.   The members of the Governing Council will have the status of representatives of States, the commissioners will have the status of experts on missions within the meaning of article VI of the Convention and the Executive Secretary and the staff of the secretariat will have the status of officials within the meaning of articles V and VII of the Convention.

E.   Expenses of the Commission

8.   The expenses of the Commission will be borne by the Fund.   More detailed recommendations regarding the budgetary administration of the Commission are set out in paragraph 29 below.

F.   Headquarters of the Commission

9.   For reasons of economy and practicality, particularly in the secretariat servicing of the Governing Council and the commissioners, the headquarters of the Commission should be in New York.   Alternatively, it might be located at the site of one of the two Offices of the United Nations in Europe, i.e.

/...

13-3

S/22559
English
Page 4

Geneva or Vienna. The Governing Council may decide whether some of the activities of the Commission should be carried out elsewhere.

G. Functions of the Commission

1. The Governing Council

10. As the policy-making organ of the Commission, the Governing Council will have the responsibility for establishing guidelines on all policy matters, in particular, those relating to the administration and financing of the Fund, the organization of the work of the Commission and the procedures to be applied to the processing of claims and to the settlement of disputed claims, as well as to the payments to be made from the Fund. In addition to its policy-making role, the Governing Council will perform important functional tasks with respect to claims presented to the Commission. Except with regard to the method of ensuring that payments are made to the Fund, which should be decided upon by consensus, the decisions of the Governing Council should be taken by a majority of at least nine of its members. No veto will apply in the Governing Council. If consensus is not achieved on any matter for which it is required, the question will be referred to the Security Council on the request of any member of the Governing Council. The Governing Council may invite States that it considers to have particular interest in its work to participate without a vote in its discussions. It may also invite members of the United Nations Secretariat or other persons to supply it with information or to give other assistance in examining matters within its competence. The Governing Council will, on behalf of the Commission, report periodically to the Security Council.

2. The commissioners

11. The commissioners will, under the guidelines established by the Governing Council, carry out such tasks and responsibilities as may be assigned to them by the Governing Council.

3. The secretariat

12. Under the direction of the Executive Secretary, the secretariat will carry out such tasks as may be assigned to it by the Governing Council and the commissioners, in particular the technical administration of the Fund, and the provision of secretariat services to the Governing Council and the commissioners.

13-4

/...

0026

II.   THE IMPLEMENTATION OF THE DECISIONS CONTAINED IN PARAGRAPHS 16, 17 AND 18 OF RESOLUTION 687 (1991)

A.   Mechanisms for determining the appropriate level of Iraq's contribution to the Fund

13.   In accordance with the institutional framework outlined in section I above, it would be for the Governing Council to establish the mechanisms for determining the appropriate level of Iraq's contribution to the Fund in accordance with the criteria laid down in paragraph 19 of Security Council resolution 687 (1991). In carrying out this task, the Governing Council should consider the probable levels of future oil export revenues of Iraq, the amounts of military spending and arms imports in the past, the service of Iraq's foreign debt and the needs for reconstruction and development in the country. The objective should be to settle compensation claims within a reasonable period of time. The Governing Council will, of course, be free to draw upon expert advice as it sees fit. It might wish to be assisted by one or more commissioners who, under the guidance of and within the terms of reference provided by the Governing Council, might give advice with regard to the appropriate level of Iraq's contribution to the Fund as well as to the periodic monitoring of that level of contribution. Simultaneously with the establishment of the Governing Council, I will undertake the appropriate consultations as required by paragraph 19 of resolution 687 (1991) so that, as soon as possible, I will be in a position to suggest the figure not to be exceeded by the Iraqi contribution.

B.   Arrangements for ensuring that payments are made to the Fund

14.   The arrangements for ensuring payments to the Fund are among the most technical and difficult of the tasks that have been entrusted to the Commission. The decisions taken in this regard will determine, _inter alia_, the financial viability of the Fund and its capacity to meet the compensation claims decided upon by the Commission as well as the size and organization of the secretariat.

15.   In addressing the question of the possible arrangements for ensuring payments to the Fund, there is an obvious necessity for securing constant and reliable financing of the Fund, without which the essential purpose of the Fund will be defeated. It is also desirable to seek modalities for the financing of the Fund that avoid the necessity of legal and other proceedings in a multiplicity of third countries and jurisdictions.

16.   The legal basis for the payments by Iraq to the Fund is to be found in paragraph 19 of resolution 687 (1991). Iraq has officially notified the United Nations of its acceptance of the provisions of the resolution, including paragraph 19, in accordance with paragraph 33 of the resolution. It follows from paragraph 19 of resolution 687 (1991) that the method envisaged by the Security Council for the financing of the Fund is a contribution by Iraq based on a percentage of the value of its exports determined in

/...

13-5

0027

accordance with the mechanism referred to in paragraph 13 above. It also follows from the resolution that the Security Council did not envisage using "frozen assets" of Iraq held in third countries for the financing of the Fund.

17. Under these circumstances, there are several options for ensuring that Iraq makes payments to the Fund. These options include the following:

     (a) Iraq would pay to the Fund the established percentage of the market value of its exports of petroleum and petroleum products; the market value to be calculated on the day of the export. The payment would be effected in United States dollars and made within 30 days of the export from Iraq;

     (b) An escrow account would be opened into which Iraq would deposit advance payments of lump sums equivalent to the estimated quarterly or semi-annual contribution required of it. These lump-sum payments would be re-evaluated periodically;

     (c) A physical share of the exports would be taken and sold on the market on behalf of the Fund;

     (d) The Fund would be designated as either the sole or co-beneficiary on the bill of lading or other title document and any letter of credit issued. The Fund, in turn, would retain its share and remit the remainder to Iraq;

     (e) An escrow account provided with the appropriate privileges and immunities (e.g. at a central bank or an appropriate international institution) would be designated as beneficiary on the bill of lading or other title document and any letter of credit issued. The escrow agent would remit to the Fund the sum designated to be used to satisfy claims and the remainder to Iraq.

It would be for the Governing Council to decide among these various options.

18. All of these methods presuppose cooperation by Iraq and strict supervision of the exports of petroleum and petroleum products from Iraq. To this end, the Commission should arrange for appropriate monitoring. Whatever approach is adopted, should Iraq fail to meet its payment obligation, the Governing Council would report the matter to the Security Council.

19. It must be recognized that, in all probability, it may be some time before Iraq is able to resume oil exports. In the short term, the Fund is therefore unlikely to receive revenues, and some consideration will have to be given to the financing of the work of the Commission, a problem which is addressed in paragraph 29 below, but more particularly to the financing of the Fund in the near term from assets other than resumed oil exports by Iraq.

C. Claims procedure

20. The process by which funds will be allocated and claims paid, the appropriate procedures for evaluating losses, the listing of claims and the

/...

13-6

0028

verification of their validity and the resolution of disputed claims as set
out in paragraph 19 of resolution 687 (1991) - the claims procedure - is the
central purpose and object of paragraphs 16 to 19 of resolution 687 (1991).
It is in this area of the Commission's work that the distinction between
policy-making and function is most important. The Commission is not a court
or an arbitral tribunal before which the parties appear; it is a political
organ that performs an essentially fact-finding function of examining claims,
verifying their validity, evaluating losses, assessing payments and resolving
disputed claims. It is only in this last respect that a quasi-judicial
function may be involved. Given the nature of the Commission, it is all the
more important that some element of due process be built into the procedure.
It will be the function of the commissioners to provide this element. As the
policy-making organ of the Commission, it will fall to the Governing Council
to establish the guidelines regarding the claims procedure. The commissioners
will implement the guidelines in respect of claims that are presented and in
resolving disputed claims. They will make the appropriate recommendations to
the Governing Council, which in turn will make the final determination. The
recommendations that follow have been divided for the sake of convenience
under three main headings: the filing of claims; the processing of claims;
and the payments of claims.

1. Filing of claims

21. With regard to the filing of claims, the Governing Council must first
decide in what manner the claims of foreign Governments, nationals and
corporations are to be filed with the Commission. It is recommended that the
Commission should entertain, as a general rule, only consolidated claims filed
by individual Governments on their own behalf or on behalf of their nationals
and corporations. The filing of individual claims would entail tens of
thousands of claims to be processed by the Commission, a task which could take
a decade or more and could lead to inequalities in the filing of claims
disadvantaging small claimants. It will be for each individual Government to
decide on the procedures to be followed internally in respect of the
consolidation of the claim having regard to its own legal system, practice and
procedures. The Governing Council may, in addition, consider whether, in
exceptional circumstances involving very large and complex claims, a somewhat
different procedure could apply. The question might be considered whether
such claims, the character of which, of course, would have to be defined by
the Governing Council, could be filed individually with the Commission by
Governments, nationals or corporations and whether the individual Government,
national or corporation could be authorized to present these claims.

22. In this context, there is another matter that requires consideration by
the Commission and regarding which the Governing Council should establish
guidelines, namely the question of the exclusivity or non-exclusivity of the
claims procedure foreseen in paragraph 19 of the resolution. It is clear from
paragraph 16 of the resolution that the debts and obligations of Iraq arising
prior to 2 August 1990 are an entirely separate issue and will be addressed
"through the normal mechanisms". It is also clear from paragraph 16 that the

/...

13-7

0029

S/22559
English
Page 8

resolution and the procedure foreseen in paragraph 19 relate to liability under international law. Resolution 687 (1991) could not, and does not, establish the Commission as an organ with exclusive competence to consider claims arising from Iraq's unlawful invasion and occupation of Kuwait. In other words, it is entirely possible, indeed probable, that individual claimants will proceed with claims against Iraq in their domestic legal systems. The likelihood of parallel actions taking place on the international level in the Commission and on the domestic level in national courts cannot be ignored. It is, therefore, recommended that the Governing Council establish guidelines regarding the non-exclusivity of claims and the appropriate mechanisms for coordination of actions at the international and domestic levels in order to ensure that the aggregate of compensation awarded by the Commission and a national court or commission does not exceed the amount of the loss. A particular problem might arise in this regard concerning default judgements obtained in national courts.

23. In addition to deciding on the consolidation of claims, the Governing Council may also wish to establish a categorization of claims according to both type and size. The categorization of claims according to type might, for example, distinguish between claims for loss of life or personal injury and property damage, environmental damage or damage due to the depletion of natural resources. The categorization of claims by size might for example, differentiate between small-, medium- and large-sized claims. A further categorization might be to distinguish between losses incurred by Governments, on the one hand, and losses incurred by nationals and corporations, on the other hand.

24. Governments could be requested by the Governing Council to use these categorizations when filing their consolidated claims. The Governing Council should also establish guidelines regarding the formal requirements for the presentation of claims such as the type of documentation to be presented in support of the claim and the time-delays for the filing of claims. The time-delays should be of sufficient length to permit Governments to establish and implement an internal procedure for the assembling and consolidation of claims. It is recommended that a fixed time period be established for the filing of all claims. A period of two years from the adoption of the filing guidelines would appear to be adequate. Alternatively, the Governing Council could set different filing periods for different types of claims in order to ensure that priority is given to certain claims, for example, loss of life or personal injury. In this respect, I am of the opinion that there would be some merit in providing for a priority consideration of small claims relating to losses by individuals so that these are disposed of before the consideration of claims relating to losses by foreign Governments and by corporations.

2. Processing of claims

25. The processing of claims will entail the verification of claims and evaluation of losses and the resolution of any disputed claims. The major

13-8

/...

0030

part of this task is not of a judicial nature; the resolution of disputed claims would, however, be quasi-judicial. It is envisaged that the processing of claims would be carried out principally by the commissioners. Before proceeding to the verification of claims and evaluation of losses, however, a determination will have to be made as to whether the losses for which claims are presented fall within the meaning of paragraph 16 of resolution 687 (1991), that is to say, whether the loss, damage or injury is direct and as a result of Iraq's unlawful invasion and occupation of Kuwait. It is recommended that the Governing Council establish detailed guidelines regarding what constitutes such direct loss for the guidance of all claimants as well as the commissioners.

26. Claims will be addressed to the Commission. The Commission will make a preliminary assessment of the claims, which will be carried out by the Secretariat, to determine whether they meet the formal requirements established by the Governing Council. The claims would then be submitted to verification and evaluation by panels normally comprised of three commissioners for this purpose. In carrying out these tasks, it is recommended that the commissioners be given the necessary powers to request additional evidence, to hold hearings in which individual Governments, nationals and corporations can present their views and to hear expert testimony. The Governing Council might wish to address the question of possible assistance to ensure the adequacy of the representation of countries of limited financial means. Iraq will be informed of all claims and will have the right to present its comments to the commissioners within time-delays to be fixed by the Governing Council or the Panel dealing with the individual claim. Recommendations of the commissioners regarding the verification and evaluation of claims will be final and subject only to the approval of the Governing Council, which shall make the final determination. The Governing Council should have the power to return claims to the commissioners for further revision if it so decides.

27. Where a dispute arises out of the allegation made by a claimant that the Panel of Commissioners, in dealing with its claims, has made an error, whether on a point of law and procedure or on a point of fact, such disputes will be dealt with by a board of commissioners who for this purpose should be guided by such guidelines as have been established by the Governing Council and the Arbitration Rules of the United Nations Commission on International Trade Law (UNCITRAL). The UNCITRAL Arbitration Rules will be modified as necessary. The final decision will be made by the Governing Council.

3. Payment of claims

28. It is to be anticipated that the value of claims approved by the Commission will at any given time far exceed the resources of the Fund. It will, therefore, be incumbent upon the Commission to decide on an allocation of funds and a procedure for the payment of claims. It is recommended that the Governing Council establish criteria for the allocation of funds, taking into account the size of claims, the scope of the losses sustained by the

/...

13-9

S/22559
English
Page 10

country concerned and any other relevant factors. In this connection, it
might be necessary to distinguish between Kuwait, on the one hand, and other
countries on the other hand. As far as the payment of claims is concerned, it
follows from the consolidation of the claims and their filing by individual
Governments that payments will be made exclusively to Governments. Individual
Governments will be responsible for the appropriate distribution to individual
claimants. The Governing Council should establish further guidelines
regarding the payment of claims, for example, whether claims should be paid in
full or whether percentages should be paid. In the latter case, the
unsatisfied portions of the claims will remain as outstanding obligations.

29. The expenses of the Commission, including those of the Governing Council,
the commissioners and the secretariat, should in principle be paid from the
Fund. However, as some time will elapse before the Fund is adequately
financed, consideration must be given to the financial implications of the
programme outlined. It is recommended that urgent consideration be given to
the means by which the initial costs of the Commission will be met

Notes

1/   General Assembly resolution 22 A (I).

13-10

0032

UNITED NATIONS

Security Council

Distr.
GENERAL

S/22558
2 May 1991

ORIGINAL: ENGLISH

REPORT OF THE SECRETARY-GENERAL REGARDING PARAGRAPH 3
OF SECURITY COUNCIL RESOLUTION 687 (1991)

1.   The present report is submitted pursuant to Security Council resolution 687 (1991) of 3 April 1991. In paragraph 3 of the resolution, the Security Council called upon me to lend assistance to make arrangements with Iraq and Kuwait to demarcate the boundary between Iraq and Kuwait, drawing on appropriate material, including the map transmitted by Security Council document S/22412, and to report back to the Security Council within one month.

2.   In lending my assistance to Iraq and Kuwait with a view to making the arrangements to demarcate the boundary between them, I have borne in mind that, in paragraph 2 of Security Council resolution 687 (1991), the Council demanded "that Iraq and Kuwait respect the inviolability of the international boundary and the allocation of islands set out in the 'Agreed Minutes between the State of Kuwait and the Republic of Iraq regarding the Restoration of Friendly Relations, Recognition and Related Matters', signed by them in the exercise of their sovereignty at Baghdad on 4 October 1963 and registered with the United Nations and published by the United Nations in document 7063, United Nations, Treaty Series, 1964". I have also taken into account that, in a letter dated 4 April 1991 addressed to me by the Deputy Prime Minister and Minister for Foreign Affairs of Kuwait, Kuwait has expressed its intention to scrupulously comply with all the provisions of resolution 687 (1991) and to cooperate with me with a view to ensuring its implementation (S/22457, annex) and that, in accordance with paragraph 33 of Security Council resolution 687 (1991), the Minister for Foreign Affairs of Iraq in the penultimate paragraph of a letter dated 6 April 1991 (S/22456) has notified the Security Council and the Secretary-General of Iraq's acceptance of the provisions of that resolution. The text of the Agreed Minutes referred to in paragraph 2 of Security Council resolution 687 (1991) is contained in Security Council document S/22432.

3.   After consultations with the Governments of Iraq and Kuwait, I will now establish an Iraq-Kuwait Boundary Demarcation Commission, to be composed of one representative each of Iraq and Kuwait and three independent experts who will be appointed by me, one of whom will serve as the Chairman. The Council will be informed as soon as the Commission is established. The terms of reference of the Commission will be to demarcate in geographical coordinates of latitude and longitude the international boundary set out in the Agreed

91-13804   2331e (E)

/...

13 - 11

S/22558
English
Page 2

Minutes between Kuwait and Iraq referred to above. In view of the fact that one of the main purposes of the demarcation of the boundary between Kuwait and Iraq is to promote stability and peace and security along the border, the Commission will also make arrangements for the physical representation of the boundary. The coordinates established by the Commission will constitute the final demarcation of the international boundary between Iraq and Kuwait in accordance with the Agreed Minutes of 4 October 1963. They will be lodged in the archives of both Governments and a certified copy will also be submitted to me, which I will communicate to the Security Council and will retain for safe-keeping in the archives of the United Nations.

4.   The demarcation of the boundary between Iraq and Kuwait will be accomplished by drawing upon appropriate material, including the map transmitted by Security Council document S/22412, and by utilizing appropriate technology. The physical representation of the boundary will be carried out through the erection of an appropriate number and type of boundary pillars or monuments. The Commission will provide for arrangements for maintenance on a continuing basis and locational accuracy (including repositioning, if necessary) of the surficial boundary representation.

5.   As soon as the Commission is constituted and after an initial assessment of the resources required for the demarcation of the boundary has been made, the Commission will transmit to me an estimate of costs, which I will communicate to the Security Council; simultaneously, I will make a proposal that all costs, including the initial costs of the Commission, should be shared between the two interested parties.

6.   The Commission will be assisted by a small staff that will adopt its own rules of procedure and working methods and make the necessary arrangements for the identification and examination of appropriate material relevant to the demarcation of the boundary. The Commission will be responsible to me in the conduct of its work and will report regularly to me on the progress of its work with a view to the earliest possible finalization of the demarcation of the boundary. The Commission will take its decisions by majority. Its decisions regarding the demarcation of the boundary will be final.

7.   The Commission shall enjoy unimpeded freedom of movement in the area of the demarcation of the international boundary as well as all necessary privileges and immunities for the fulfilment of its task. The three independent experts shall enjoy the status of experts on missions within the meaning of article VI of the Convention on Privileges and Immunities of the United Nations of 1946. 1/

8.   In the exercise of its task of demarcating the boundary, with respect to physical security and clearance of mines the Commission will rely on the relevant arrangements made for the United Nations Iraq-Kuwait Observer Mission (UNIKOM).

<u>Notes</u>

1/   General Assembly resolution 22 A (I).

/...

13-12

0034

U.N. Ducks Key Issues On Reparations by Iraq

Draft Report Sets General Rules on Claims

By Trevor Rowe
Special to The Washington Post

UNITED NATIONS, May 2—A draft report on Iraqi reparations by U.N. Secretary General Javier Perez de Cuellar lays out general guidelines for seeking compensation for war damages, but it leaves many key issues about the claims process unresolved.

The study had been expected, for example, to set a limit on the percentage of Iraq's oil revenues that could be used for settling claims. But the report ducks this issue, leaving it until the establishment of a governing council made up of 15 members representing the current Security Council. The governing council will ultimately determine the precise percentage of Iraqi oil revenues to be used for compensation within the limit set by Perez de Cuellar.

However, the draft report, a copy of which was obtained by The Washington Post, does lay out a variety of options for securing payment from Iraq as well as for the collection of claims against Baghdad.

The study recommends that individual governments, rather than individuals or corporations, be in charge of seeking compensation for the losses suffered by each country as a result of Iraq's invasion of Kuwait.

The secretary general says that in determining the precise percentage of Iraq's oil revenues to be used, the governing council should consider the probable levels of future oil exports, the amounts of military spending and arms imports in the past, the service of Iraq's foreign debts and the needs for reconstruction and development in the war-ravaged country.

The secretary general says that he favors giving priority to small claims for losses by individuals and that these should be disposed of before consideration of claims by governments and corporations. He also recommends that a period of two years from the adoption of filing guidelines be given for the filing of all claims.

The secretary general suggests that claims be categorized according to type and to size to distinguish claims for loss of life and personal injury from those for property damage, environmental damage or depletion of natural resources. He also suggests guidelines to differentiate between losses resulting directly and indirectly from Iraq's invasion of Kuwait.

The report says the market value of Iraq's oil exports to be "credited to the Fund" would be calculated on the day of export and payment would be in U.S. dollars and be made within 30 days of export from Iraq. It also suggests some alternatives such as taking a percentage of the physical product or being designated as a sole or co-beneficiary of each bill of exchange.

Another option would be for the governing council to establish a schedule for quarterly or annual payments that would be based on Iraq's arms purchases over the past years and take into account its debt servicing needs. Britain has suggested that the amount be based on Iraq's arms purchases over the last decade.

The report also recommends that Iraq's overseas "frozen" assets not be used for compensation.

The secretary general recommends that nations "consolidate" their claims because "individual claims would entail tens of thousands of claims to be processed," a task he says that could take a decade or more as well as lead to inequalities that would disadvantage small claimants.

The recommendations come one day after a U.N. report by Abdul Farah, a former undersecretary general, saying that while initial estimates of the damage caused to Kuwait by the Iraqi invasion are in the tens of billions of dollars, overall damage to that country's economy is "almost incalculable."

13-13

0035

외 무 부

종 별 :

번 호 : UNW-1203
일 시 : 91 0509 1920

수 신 : 장관(국연,중동일,기정)

발 신 : 주유엔대사

제 목 : 걸프사태(안보리)

연: UNW-1106,1125

1. 연호 사무총장의 이락배상 책임이행 계획안(S/22559) 제출에 따라 안보리상임 이사국들간에 동계획승인 결의안 교섭이 진행중인바, 당관에서 입수한 동결의안초안요지는 다음과같음.

가. 배상기금 및 위원회 설치는 상기 사무총장제출안에 따름

나. 사무총장에게 이락석유수출수입 공제 상한선을조속 건의토록 요망

다. 배상위원회 집행부 (GC: 유엔제네바사무소에 위치)는 사무총장 제출안을 기초로제반조치 추진

라. 동 집행부(GC) 는 이락 석유 수출수입의적정 공제수준 결정을 위한 장치(MECHANISMS),기금재원 보장방안을 조기 마련하여 안보리에 보고

마. 이락이 동집행부(GC) 결정 불이행시,이락석유 금수조치 유지 내지 재실시

2. 한편 안보리제재위는 지난 5.3. 에 이어 금 5.9.회의를 개최코 연호 이락측 요청을 토의하였으나,진전이 없었던 것으로 알려짐.끝.

(대사노창희-국장)

국기국	장관	차관	1차보	2차보	미주국	중아국	정와대	안기부

PAGE 1

0036

21759

분류기호 문서번호	중동일 720-	기안용지 (720-2327)	시 행 상 특별취급	
보존기간	영구.준영구 10. 5. 3. 1	장 관		
수 신 처 보존기간				
시행일자	1991. 5. 10.			

<table>
<tr><td rowspan="3">보조
기관</td><td>국 장</td><td>전 결</td><td rowspan="3">협
조
기
관</td><td></td><td>문 서 통 제
1991. 5. 13</td></tr>
<tr><td>심의관</td><td></td><td></td></tr>
<tr><td>과 장</td><td></td><td></td></tr>
<tr><td>기안책임자</td><td colspan="2">조 태 용</td><td></td><td>발 송 인</td></tr>
</table>

경 유 수 신 참 조	수신처 참조	발 신 명 의		반 송 1991. 5. 13
제 목	걸프사태 관련 대이라크 피해보상 청구절차			

유엔 안전보장 이사회의 걸프전 종전 결의 687호(91.4.3)에

의거 유엔 사무총장은 이라크의 쿠웨이트 침공으로 야기된 피해보상을

위한 보상기금 설치 및 보상청구 절차에 관한 건의서를 5.2 안보리에

제출한바, 관련 내용을 별첨 통보하니 앞으로 아국의 피해보상 청구서

제출에 대비, 참고하시기 바랍니다.

    첨 부 : 1. 장관보고사항 사본 1부.

           2. 유엔 사무총장 건의서 및 국문요약 각 1부.   끝.

    수신처 : 재무부장관, 상공부장관, 건설부장관

0037

더맑은 마음을, 더밝은 사회를, 더넓은 미래를

분류기호 문서번호	중동일 720- **16549**	기안용지 (720-2327)	시 행 상 특별취급	
보존기간	영구,준영구 10. 5. 3. 1	장 관		
수 신 처 보존기간				
시행일자	1991. 5. 10.			

<table>
<tr><td rowspan="3">보조
기관</td><td>국 장</td><td>전 결</td><td rowspan="3">협
조
기
관</td><td></td><td rowspan="2">문 서 특 전 제
1991. 5. 13</td></tr>
<tr><td>심의관</td><td></td><td></td></tr>
<tr><td>과 장</td><td>가</td><td></td><td></td></tr>
</table>

기안책임자	조 태 용		발 송 인
경 유		발신명의	발 송 1991. 5. 13
수 신	수신처 참조		
참 조			
제 목	걸프사태 관련 대이라크 피해보상 청구절차		

유엔 안전보장 이사회의 걸프전 종전 결의 687호(91.4.3)에

의거 유엔 사무총장은 이라크의 쿠웨이트 침공으로 야기된 피해보상을

위한 보상기금 설치 및 보상청구 절차에 관한 건의서를 5.2 안보리에

제출한바, 관련 내용을 별첨 통보하니 귀 업무에 참고하시기 바랍니다.

첨 부 : 1. 장관보고사항 사본 1부.

　　　　　 2. 유엔 사무총장 건의서 및 국문요약 각 1부.　　끝.

수신처 : 주미, 사우디, 쿠웨이트, UAE, 바레인, 카타르, 오만,

　　　　 요르단 대사관 (사본:주 유엔 대표부)

더맑은 마음을, 더밝은 사회를, 더넓은 미래를　　　　0038

長官報告事項

1991. 5. 10.
中東 1 課

題 目 : 걸프事態關聯 對이라크 被害報償 請求節次

> 유엔 事務總長은 安保理의 걸프戰 終戰 決議 687號에 의거 이라크의 쿠웨이트
> 侵攻으로 惹起된 被害 報償을 위한 報償基金 設置 및 報償請求 節次等에 관한
> 建議案을 5.2. 安保理에 提出한바, 關聯事項을 아래 報告드립니다.

1. 根 據
   o 유엔 安保理는 4.3 자 걸프전 正式 休戰 決議(687號)에서 이라크의 쿠웨이트
     侵攻으로 인해 惹起된 被害 報償을 위해 이라크의 石油 輸入中 一部를 控除,
     報償基金을 設置키로 하고, 유엔 사무총장으로 하여금 同 報償基金 設置.
     運用 方案을 立案, 30일 이내에 安保理에 建議토록 要請하였는바, 이에
     따라 유엔 事務總長은 關聯 建議案을 5.2. 安保理에 提出함.

2. 報償 請求 節次 및 基金 造成
   o 報償 請求는 개인이나 기업 단위의 個別的 請求는 原則的으로 不許하고
     各國 政府가 國別 被害額을 取合, 앞으로 구성될 「유엔 報償 委員會」에
     一括 提出하되, 提出期間은 安保理의 報償請求 節次確定後 2年間으로 함.
   o 報償 請求 範圍는 '이라크의 쿠웨이트 侵攻, 占領으로 惹起된 直接的 損失,
     被害'에 한하며, 90.8.2. 以前에 發生된 이라크의 債務는 포함되지 않음.
   o 報償 請求 處理 節次는 各國 政府의 請求 內容을 報償 委員會에서 審查,
     確定하게 되며, 再審 要請도 可能함.
   o 補償額은 個別 政府에 一括 支撥하며 實被害者(個人, 企業等)에 대한 支給은
     該當 政府가 施行키로 하고, 報償基金 造成을 위한 이라크 石油 輸出代金의
     控除 比率 및 方式은 追後 決定키로 함.

3. 關聯 措置 事項
   o 我國 僑民 및 企業이 입은 被害 報償 請求를 위해 安保理에서 具體的 節次가
     確定되는대로 被害現況 調査等 準備 作業을 施行할 計劃임.   끝.

0039

유엔의 걸프事態關聯 被害報償 請求 및 處理 節次
(91.5.2자 유엔事務總長의 建議內容)

① 관계공관 통보
② 관계복지
③ 안내의 Ⅱ

1. 報償 請求(Filing of claims)

    o 各國別로 企業, 個人등 모든 被害報償 請求를 取合, 政府 單位로 유엔 報償
       委員會(UN Compensation Commission)에 提出 (原則的으로 企業, 個人別
       報償請求는 不許)

    o 報償請求 提出期間은 유엔의 請求節次 確定後 2년간으로 하며, 被害類型에
       따라 提出期間을 다르게 하는 方案도 檢討

    o 證憑書類등 請求提出에 따른 詳細 形式要件은 追後 決定

       * 報償請求의 範圍는 '이라크의 쿠웨이트 侵攻, 占領으로 惹起된 直接的
          損失, 被害'에 한하며 詳細 基準은 유엔 報償委員會 執行理事會(Governing
          Council)에서 決定. 단, 90.8.2이전에 發生된 이라크의 債務는 不包含

2. 報償 請求 處理(Processing of claims)

> 各國 政府가 유엔報償委員會에 請求 提出

↓

> 유엔報償委員會 事務局에서 豫備 審査
> - 形式 要件 具備 與否

↓

> 3명의 專門家(commissioner)로 構成된
> Panel에서 實質內容 審査
> - verification & evaluation

↓ * Panel, 필요시 補充證據 提出要求 또는
      聽聞會 開催
      審査過程에서 이라크측의 意見 開陳 可能

> Panel의 審査 結果 執行理事會에 建議

↓

> 執行理事會, 建議承認 또는 Panel의 再審要請

* 報償請求者側이 再審要請時는 專門家團
  (board of commissioners)에서 再審

0040

3. 報償 支拂(Payment of claims)

　　o　報償 所要額이 유엔報償基金(UN Compensation Fund) 財源을 超過할 可能性이
　　　　많으므로 報償의 優先 順位 및 方法 決定 必要 (一時拂 또는 分割 支拂등)

　　o　報償額은 個別 政府에 支拂하며, 各政府가 企業 및 個人에 支給

┌─────────┐
│ 參　考 │　　　　1. 유엔 報償基金의 制度的 裝置
└─────────┘

┌───┐
│ 유엔報償基金(UN Compensation Fund)   │
└───┘
　　　　　　　　　　　　　↕
┌───┐
│ 유엔報償委員會(UN Compensation Commission) │　* 本部 : 뉴욕
└───┘
　　　　　　├── 執行理事會(Governing Council) : 最高決定機關, 15개
　　　　　　│　　　　　　　　　　　　　　　　安保理事國 代表로 構成
　　　　　　├── 專門家(commissioner) : 實務擔當, 유엔事務總長의 推薦으로
　　　　　　│　　　　　　　　　　　　　執行理事會에서 任命
　　　　　　└── 事務局(Secretariat) : Executive Secretary 및 事務要員

　　　　2. 유엔報償基金의 財源 調達
- 이라크의 石油輸出代金에서 一定比率 控除, 基金財源으로 充當
- 控除 比率 및 具體方式은 追後 決定

3. 래
　　- 유엔안보리겵의 687호(P1. 4. 3)ʳ 16, 18, 19항
　　┌
　　└

0041

長 官 報 告 事 項

報 告 畢

1991. 8. 13.
中 東 1 課

題 目 : 걸프事態 關聯 被害 賠償

유엔 安保理는 걸프전 終戰 決議에 의거 「유엔 賠償委員會」(UN Compensation Commission) 設立등 被害賠償 處理를 위한 措置를 취하고 있는바, 이와 關聯 7.23-8.2간 제네바에서 開催된 第1次 「執行 理事會」(Governing Council) 會議 結果와 我國의 被害賠償 請求에 對備한 措置 計劃을 아래 報告드립니다.

---

1. 유엔의 關聯 措置

가. 安保理 決議

  ○ 687號 (91.4.3) : 걸프戰 正式 休戰 決議로서 賠償 問題의 根據 決議 (제16-19조 및 29조)

  ○ 692號 (91.5.20) : 유엔 事務總長의 이라크 賠償 履行計劃 (91.5.2) 承認

나. 유엔의 被害賠償 節次 (槪要)

  ○ 請求主體 : 各國 政府(個人, 企業 單位의 個別請求는 原則的으로 不許하며 例外的인 경우 可能하다고 되어 있으나 詳細는 追後 決定 豫定)

  ○ 請求期間 : 細部節次 確定後 2年 以內

  ○ 請求範圍 : 이라크의 쿠웨이트 侵攻 占領으로 惹起된 直接的 損失 및 被害(90.8.2.이전 發生된 이라크의 償務는 不包含)

  ○ 審議節次 : 各國政府의 請求內容을 유엔 賠償委員會에서 審議하며, 再審 要請도 可能

  ○ 賠償金 支給 : 個別政府에 一括 支拂하며, 實被害者 (個人, 企業等)에 대한 支給은 該當政府가 施行

  ○ 賠償基金 : 이라크의 石油收入 一定 比率 控除(사무총장 30%로 건의)

0042

2. UN 賠償委員會 執行 理事會 第1次 會議 主要 決定事項

　　가. 國家 및 企業에 대한 被害賠償은 그 內容의 複雜性으로 追後 檢討
　　　　(10月中 第2次 會議 開催 豫定)

　　나. 于先 個人에 대한 賠償 基準 및 請求 節次 採擇

　　　　① 定額支拂(2,500 미불) 對象者는 간단한 事實 證明으로 請求 可能

　　　　② 上限線 10만미불 까지의 請求는 證據 資料 提出 必要

　　　　③ 모든 請求는 各國 政府가 主體가 되며 同 賠償委 事務局이 申請書를
　　　　　　配布하는 날로부터 6個月 以內에 請求書 提出 要望

　　다. 賠償基金 財源 確保 方案은 具體的 資料의 未備로 9月中 實務者會議 開催
　　　　및 10月 第2次 會議에서 決定

3. 措置 計劃(建議)

　　가. 걸프事態 被害賠償 對策 委員會(假稱) 構成

　　　　○ 構　成 : 委員長　外務部 第2次官補

　　　　　　　　　　委　員　靑瓦臺, 經企院, 外務部, 建設部, 商工部, 財務部等
　　　　　　　　　　　　　　關係部處 局長級

　　　　○ 機　能 : 我側 被害 賠償 申請 및 賠償金 支給等 細部節次 樹立, 施行

　　나. 유엔 賠償 委員會 專門委員(Commissioner) 推薦

　　　　○ 유엔側은 我國에 대해서도 專門委員 推薦을 要請해 왔는바, 關係部處를
　　　　　통해 候補者 先發 旣要請 (6.21)

　　　　○ 被害賠償 査定에 있어 同 專門委員들의 役割이 重要할것으로 보이는바,
　　　　　我國도 可及的 많은 專門委員 推薦 바람직함.

　　┌─────┐
　　│ 添　附 │　유엔 賠償委員會의 制度的 裝置 및 請求處理 節次
　　└─────┘

0043

報告畢

1991 . 4 .10 .
國際機構條約局
國際法規課(15)

長 官 報 告 事 項

題目 : 유엔안보리 결의 제687호의 전쟁배상 관련조항 검토

> 걸프전 정식휴전에 관한 안보리 결의 내용중 아국의 주요관심사항인
> 전쟁배상 관련조항에 대한 검토내용을 아래와 같이 보고드립니다.

Ⅰ. 문제의 제기

1. 유엔안보리는 1991.4.3. 미·불·영·루마니아·벨지움·자이르가
   공동제안한 걸프전 정식휴전결의안을 결의 제687호로 채택함.

2. 상기 결의의 내용중 특히 아국과 실질적 이해관계가 있는 전쟁손해
   배상청구와 관련된 조항에 대하여 검토함.

Ⅱ. 검토의견

1. 안보리결의 제687호상의 전쟁배상 관련내용

   가. 국제법상 배상책임의 확인(제16항)

   ° 이라크는 자국이 쿠웨이트에 대하여 행한 불법적 침공 및
     점령의 결과로 인해 발생한 외국의 정부, 국민과 기업에
     대한 손상에 대하여 국제법상 배상책임을 짐.

   - 환경에 대한 손해 및 천연자원고갈에 대한 배상책임도 포함.

0044

나. 배상지급을 위한 기금의 창설과 동 기금관리위원회 설치 결정
(제18항)

    ㅇ 이라크의 쿠웨이트 침공으로 인해 발생한 모든 손해에 대하여
각 국가가 직접 이라크와 평화조약을 체결, 배상지급을
요구하게 하는 대신, <u>유엔 주관하에 배상기금을 창설하고
동 기금을 관리할 위원회를 설치하기로 결정.</u>

다. 유엔사무총장의 배상기금운용 계획 제출지시(제19항)

    (1) 제출기한

        ㅇ 유엔사무총장은 본결의 채택후 <u>30일 이내에</u> (1991.5.3.
까지) 동 운용계획에 관한 권고안을 안보리에 제출
해야 함.

    (2) 유엔사무총장의 주요권고 대상사항

        i) 기금의 관리

        ii) 이라크 부담금의 수준 결정 방안

            - 이라크가 수출하는 석유 및 석유제품 수출가액의
일정비율을 공제하며 그 비율의 상한선을 안보리에
제시

        iii) 기금확보에 관한 보장장치의 마련

        iv) 기금의 할당 및 청구된 손해에 대한 지급 절차

        v) 전쟁손해평가를 위한 적절한 절차

            - 청구의 목록 작성과 그 유효성의 확인 및 청구에
관한 분쟁을 해결하는 절차 포함.

        vi) 기금관리위원회의 구성

0045

2. 아국의 대책

　가. 현황

　　o 상기 전쟁배상 관련규정에 비추어 볼때, 현재로서는
　　　이라크의 석유류 수출수입의 일정부분을 공제하여
　　　유엔주관하에 기금을 조성하고, 이를 통해 피해국의
　　　전쟁배상문제를 해결해 나간다는 원칙만 정해졌을 뿐,
　　　그 구체적인 실현과정 및 절차는 확정되어 있지 않음.

　　o 상세한 절차 및 내용은 91.5.3.까지 제출하기로 되어 있는
　　　유엔사무총장의 권고를 토대로 안보리가 결정할 예정임.

　나. 향후 대책

　　o 아국으로서는 전쟁배상기금규모와 운영절차의 구체화
　　　과정과 관련한 동향을 계속 예의주시할 필요가 있음.

　　o 따라서 동 권고안 확정후 신속하고 효율적인 청구요청이
　　　가능하도록 아국의 피해상황에 관한 종합적인 조사 및
　　　구체적인 자료작성 등 동 기금을 통한 배상청구 실현에
　　　대비한 사전준비를 조용한 가운데 해둘 필요성이 있음.

0046

1. 유엔 賠償委員會의 制度的 裝置

> 유엔賠償委員會(UN Compensation Commission)
>
> ├─ 執行理事會(Governing Council)
> │　- 最高決定機關, 15개 安保理理事國 代表로 構成
> │　　(제네바 소재)
> │
> ├─ 專門家(commissioner)
> │　- 實務擔當, 유엔事務總長의 推薦으로 執行理事會
> │　　에서 任命 (아국도 추천 예정)
> │
> └─ 事務局(Secretariat)
> 　　- 사무국장(Executive Secretary) 및 事務要員

2. 賠償 請求 處理(Processing of claims)

> ┌─────────────────────────────┐
> │ 各國 政府가 「유엔賠償委員會」에 請求 提出 │
> └─────────────────────────────┘
> 　　　　　　　　↓
> ┌─────────────────────────────┐
> │ 「유엔賠償委員會 事務局」에서 豫備 審査 │
> │ 　　　　(形式 要件 具備 與否) │
> └─────────────────────────────┘
> 　　　　　　　　↓
> ┌─────────────────────────────┐
> │ 3명의 專門家(commissioner)로 構成된 │
> │ Panel에서 實質內容 審査 (verification & │
> │ evaluation) │
> └─────────────────────────────┘
> 　　↓　* Panel, 필요시 補充證據 提出要求 또는
> 　　　　　聽聞會 開催
> 　　　　　審査過程에서 이라크側의 意見 開陳 可能
> ┌─────────────────────────────┐
> │ Panel의 審査 結果 「執行理事會」에 建議 │
> └─────────────────────────────┘
> 　　　　　　　　↓
> ┌─────────────────────────────┐
> │ 執行理事會, 建議承認 또는 Panel의 再審要請 │
> └─────────────────────────────┘
> 　　　　* 賠償請求者側이 再審要請時는 집행위가
> 　　　　　정하는 지침과 「국제무역법에 관한 유엔
> 　　　　　위원회 중재원칙」(UNCITRAL)에 따라
> 　　　　　專門家團(board of commissioners)에서
> 　　　　　再審査

0047

외 무 부

종 별 :

번 호 : UNW-1255   일 시 : 91 0515 1920

수 신 : 장 관(국연,중동일,기정)

발 신 : 주 유엔 대사

제 목 : 걸프사태(유엔동향)

   1. 안보리 휴전결의 (687호) 에 의거 지난 5.2.사무총장이 이락-쿠웨이트 국경획정안 (S/22558)을 제출한것과 관련 안보리 의장은 안보리 이사국들과의 협의를 거쳐 5.13 자 사무총장 앞서한을 통해 동사무총장안의 접수를 확인 (TAKENOTE) 하는 한편 사무총장의 관련 노력에 지지를 표명한바, 이로써 본건 사무총장안대로 추진케됨. (안보리의 별도 승인 절차는 불요)

   2. 한편 사무총장의 이락 배상 책임 이행안 (S/22559) 과 관련 안보리는 곧 결의안을 채택할것으로 알려지고있음. (동결의안 요지는 UNW-1203 참조), 특히, 휴전결의에 의거 사무총장이 이락 석유 수입 공제상한선을 안보리에 권고토록 되어있는바, 5.15.자 NYT 는 상임이사국들간에 25-30 퍼센트선 (연간 약 5억불수준)에서 합의가 이루어졌다고 보도함.

   금 5.15. 정오브리핑시 사무총장 대변인은 사무총장의 동 공제상한선 권고는 다음주 이후에나 가능할 것으로 본다고 언급함. 동일자 WP지는 쿠웨이트의 대 이락 청구액이 450 억불에 이를것으로 추정 (여타국들의 배상 청구를 포함하는 경우 1,000 억불 예상)된다고 보도함.

   첨부:상기 이락 배상관련 NYT,WP 지 기사:UNW(F)-210

   끝

   (대사 노창희-국장)

국기국   1차보   중아국   정문국   안기부

BY PAUL LEWIS
Special to The New York Times

UNITED NATIONS, May 14 — The United States and the four other permanent members of the Security Council have drawn up a plan under which Iraq could be compelled to pay as much as 25 to 30 percent of its $20 billion annual oil revenue as reparations for the invasion and looting of Kuwait and as repayment of its debts to foreign governments.

Such a limit on reparations would mean that the most Iraq could be asked to pay in any year would be roughly equivalent to the $5 billion or so it spent annually buying foreign weapons before the Persian Gulf war. And the Security Council might set the payment at a lower level than the maximum. The total reparations to be demanded of Iraq could run as high as $50 billion.

A major question is when the Baghdad Government will be permitted to resume selling its oil on the world market. This is dependent on Iraq's compliance with previous orders to turn over and destroy its missiles and chemical weapons, and submit its nuclear material to inspection.

Approval Thought Likely

The proposal on reparations, which has the backing of Britain, France, the Soviet Union and China as well as the United States — is expected to be adopted by the entire Council later this week without major changes, diplomats say.

The proposal itself does not set any figures for the level of Iraqi payments,

---

Reparations to Kuwait and payment of debt.

---

saying it is up to the United Nations Secretary General, Javier Pérez de Cuéllar, to propose a maximum figure to the Council for approval.

Despite the wide expectation of a 25 to 30 percent ceiling, the American Assistant Secretary of State in charge of United Nations affairs, John R. Bolton, recently proposed a ceiling up to 50 percent of Iraq's oil revenue. Other permanent members of the Council, the five nations with veto power, regard this as unrealistic.

Some countries friendly to Iraq have suggested that the Government of President Saddam Hussein be asked to allocate no more than 10 percent of its oil revenue for reparations.

Earlier, Iraq had asked for a five-year delay on reparations payments to allow it to rebuild its shattered economy.

Way of Increasing Oil Flow

The purpose of establishing an annual ceiling on payments, diplomats say, is to encourage Baghdad to produce maximum quantities of oil after sanctions are lifted by insuring that it will always get a portion of any increase in its market share.

In calling for a ceiling, diplomats say the Council also wanted to avoid a disastrous mistake like the Treaty of Versailles of 1919, when the victorious Allies imposed draconian compensation payments on a defeated Germany, threatening it with impoverishment and contributing to the rise of Nazism.

Under previous resolutions, the Security Council has declared Baghdad liable for "any direct loss, damage, including environmental damage and the depletion of natural resources, or injury to foreign governments, nationals and corporations as a result of Iraq's unlawful invasion and occupation of Kuwait."

How Iraqis Can Help Themselves

Diplomats say the payment level demanded may also be influenced by political factors, like the composition of the government in power in Baghdad, and by Saudi Arabia's and Kuwait's demands for repayment of the roughly $50 billion they are believed to have lent Iraq during its eight-year war against Iran.

If Mr. Hussein's Government falls and is replaced by a more acceptable leadership, these diplomats believe that Kuwait and other gulf nations would urge the Council to treat Iraq more leniently and offer to forgive some debts. Iraq also owes $25 billion to the Western industrial nations and the Soviet Union.

In deciding how much Iraq should pay in reparations, the Security Council, working through a new subsidiary to be called the United Nations Compensation Fund, is required to take into account the cost of repaying its foreign debts as well as its economic-development needs.

Security Council approval of the proposed resolution setting up the reparations-payment mechanism fulfills one of two conditions the Council has established for lifting its worldwide ban on the Iraqi oil trade.

The other condition will be met when the Council is satisfied that Iraq has complied with a plan the Secretary General will present on May 18 — for a special commission to take possession of Iraq's chemical and other weapons of mass destruction within 45 days and start destroying them.

NW-1255
첨부특

U.N. Studying War-Damage Assessment

Iraq to Pay Bulk From Oil Revenues

By Trevor Rowe
Special to The Washington Post

UNITED NATIONS—Security Council members and U.N officials say they are studying formulas by which Iraq can begin paying its damage assessment from the Persian Gulf War, with a focus on using Iraq's oil revenues as the chief source of payment.

The process of arriving at an exact damage assessment is a complex one and involves dealing with difficult issues such as how much can Iraq afford to pay. Under the terms of Security Council Resolution 687, the needs of the Iraqi people "and, in particular, humanitarian needs" must be taken into account.

In dollar terms, the assessment is expected to be the highest ever made as a result of a war. But hanging over the process is the memory of the Treaty of Versailles, whose harsh terms for ending World War I were blamed for fueling German resentment and helping spur the outbreak of World War II.

This time, the allies are taking pains to be seen as acting fairly. For instance, they have directed the secretary general to suggest a limit on the amount of Iraqi oil revenue that can be used for compensation to countries, corporations or third-country citizens in Kuwait who suffered as a result of the Aug. 2 invasion.

"To avoid the idea of attempting to bleed Iraq dry ... it was suggested the secretary general come up with a maximum figure" or percentage of Iraq's annual oil revenues, said a Western diplomat closely involved in the process.

"The idea of this is not reparations, ... of saying, 'We beat you and are going to slam you for it.' This is like compensation for a car collision and paying for the damage done," the diplomat said.

U.S. officials estimate that Kuwait's claims alone will amount to $45 billion. This does not include damages claimed by foreign governments, their nationals or corporations. Some estimates forecast the total amount of claims at $100 billion.

It will be up to a Security Council committee to determine the final percentage of Iraq's oil revenues to be used in compensation. The committee members, who have yet to be named, will be guided by the ceiling suggested by Secretary General Javier Perez de Cuellar.

Sources close to de Cuellar suggest he would first like the five permanent members of the Security Council—Britain, France, China, the United States and Soviet Union—to agree on the percentage they believe would be fair for Iraq to pay from its oil revenues.

"There's no point in him [the Secretary General] suggesting a figure the council won't take, and it would overstate the matter to say we [the permanent members] will give him a figure," said a U.S. official. "The truth is somewhere in between."

However, some officials have already suggested figures that their governments would like to see imposed on Iraq. John Bolton, the U.S. assistant secretary of state for international organizations, has suggested that as much as 50 percent of Iraqi oil revenues be allocated for compensation.

An Iraqi diplomat, when told of the U.S. proposal, dismissed it as "the bazaar mentality." Iraq has proposed a five-year moratorium on any payment so it can first rebuild its shattered economy and infrastructure.

Western diplomats say a sliding payment scale has been proposed that would be determined on an annual basis. This would permit a lower percentage to be fixed in the early stages, later to be increased.

Britain and France have both suggested that a reasonable ceiling would be between 25 percent to 30 percent—the portion of Iraq's prewar budget devoted to military expenditures.

2—2

0050

관리 번호	91 /1044

외 무 부

종 별 : 지 급

번 호 : KUW-0206

일 시 : 91 0519 1100

수 신 : 장관(중동일)

발 신 : 주 쿠웨이트 대사

제 목 : 걸프전 손해배상청구

연:JDW-75

대:WJD-124,125

1. 철수 피난간 교민들이 점차 복귀함에따라 손해배상 문제가 구체적으로
제기될것이 예상됨.

2. 유엔에서 배포된 관련자료와 함께 신청요령차등 당관이 이일을 처리하는데
필요한 자세한 정보를 주시기 바람.끝

(대사-국장)

예고:91.12.31.까지

지난번 자료(영보고서, 유엔결의,
사무총장 보고서등) 보냈는지
확인, 보고하십니오.

91. 6. 30. 전포함
91. 12. 31. 인내

중아국

분류번호	보존기간

발 신 전 보

WKU-0160   910520 1642 FL

번 호 :   종별 :

수 신 : 주 쿠웨이트 대사 . 총영사////

발 신 : 장 관 (중동일)

제 목 : 걸프사태 관련 피해 보상 청구

대 : KUW-0206

연 : 중동일 720-16549 (91.5.13)

1. 대호, 연호로 송부한 유엔 사무총장의 표제 관련 건의서 내용을 참조 바람.

2. 주유엔 대사 보고에 의하면, 유엔 안보리는 상기 사무총장 건의서에 관한
   결정을 곧 내릴 예정이라 하는바 관련 내용 추보 하겠음. 끝.

(중동아국장 이 해 순)

예고 : 91.12.31 까지

91. 6. 30. 건도완
91. 12. 31. 여서

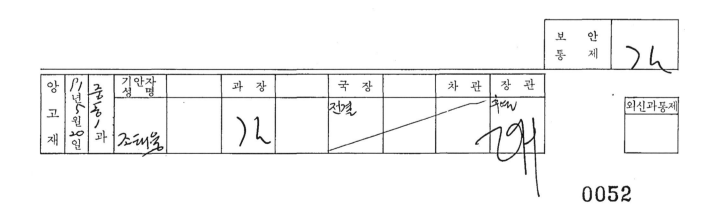

보 안 통 제	74

앙 고 재	91 년 월 20 일	중동1 과	기안자 성명 조태용		과 장 72	국 장 전결		차 관	장 관		외신과통제

외 무 부

종 별 :

번 호 : UNW-1302 일 시 : 91 0520 2010

수 신 : 장 관(국연,중동일,기정)

발 신 : 주 유엔 대사

제 목 : 안보리회의(이락 배상문제)

연: UNW-1125,1203

1. 안보리는 금 5.20 공식회의 (2987차)를 개최코 연호 유엔사무총장의 이락 배상 이행안을 승인하는 결의안을 채택한바 (결의 692호) 동회의 중요경과를 아래보고함.

　가. 의제채택

　0. 이락, 쿠웨이트대표 토의참가 초청 (안보리 의사규칙37조)

　0. 결의안, 공동제안국추가: 원제안국 (미, 영)에 벨지움, 프랑스, 루마니, 소련, 자이르 추가 (총 7개국공동제안)

　나. 표결

　0. 찬 14, 반 0. 기권 1 (쿠바)

　0. 표결전및 표결후 발언국 없었음.

2. 금일 채택된 상기 안보리 결의안은 본건 배상기금 충당을 위한 이락 석유수입의 공제상한 선을 정하지 않은바, 추후 사무총장의 건의를 받아 안보리가 결정예정임.

　첨부: 상기 안보리 결의안: UNW(F)-218

　끝

　(대사 노창희-국장)

국기국　1차보　중아국　정문국　안기부

UNITED NATIONS

UNW(F)-21 10520

(국연 중동일 기획)

총2에

Security Council

PROVISIONAL

S/22613
17 May 1991

692호

ORIGINAL: ENGLISH

United Kingdom of Great Britain and Northern Ireland
and United States of America: draft resolution

The Security Council,

Recalling its resolutions 674 (1990), 686 (1991) and 687 (1991), concerning the liability of Iraq, without prejudice to its debts and obligations arising prior to 2 August 1990, for any direct loss, damage, including environmental damage and the depletion of natural resources, or injury to foreign Governments, nationals and corporations, as a result of Iraq's unlawful invasion and occupation of Kuwait,

Noting the Secretary-General's report of 2 May 1991 (S/22559), submitted in accordance with paragraph 19 of resolution 687 (1991),

Acting under Chapter VII of the Charter,

1. Expresses its appreciation to the Secretary-General for his report of 2 May 1991 (S/22559);

2. Welcomes the fact that the Secretary-General will now undertake the appropriate consultations requested by paragraph 19 of 687 so that he will be in a position to recommend to the Security Council for decision as soon as possible the figure which the level of Iraq's contribution to the Fund will not exceed;

3. Decides to establish the Fund and Commission referred to in paragraph 18 of resolution 687 (1991) in accordance with Part I of the Secretary-General's report and that the Governing Council shall be located at the offices of the United Nations in Geneva and that the Governing Council may decide whether some of the activities of the Commission should be carried out elsewhere;

4. Requests the Secretary-General to take the actions necessary to implement paragraphs 2 and 3 above in consultation with the members of the Governing Council;

5. Directs the Governing Council to proceed in an expeditious manner to implement the provisions of Section E of resolution 687 (1991), taking into account the recommendations in Part II of the Secretary-General's report;

32328 (E)

#UNW-1302   2-1

청부특

/...

6.   <u>Decides</u> that the requirement for Iraqi contributions shall apply in the manner to be prescribed by the Governing Council with respect to all Iraqi petroleum and petroleum products exported from Iraq after 3 April 1991 as well as such petroleum and petroleum products exported earlier but not delivered or not paid for as a specific result of the prohibitions contained in resolution 661 (1990);

7.   <u>Requests</u> the Governing Council to report as soon as possible on the actions it has taken with regard to the mechanisms for determining the appropriate level of Iraq's contribution to the Fund and the arrangements for ensuring that payments are made to the Fund, so that the Security Council can give its approval in accordance with paragraph 22 of resolution 687 (1991);

8.   <u>Requests</u> that all States and international organizations cooperate with the decisions of the Governing Council taken pursuant to paragraph 5 of this resolution and further requests that the Governing Council keep the Security Council informed on this matter;

9.   <u>Decides</u> that if the Governing Council notifies the Security Council that Iraq has failed to carry out decisions of the Governing Council taken pursuant to paragraph 5 of this resolution, the Security Council intends to retain or to take action to reimpose the prohibition against the import of petroleum and petroleum products originating in Iraq and financial transactions related thereto;

10. <u>Decides</u> to remain seized of this matter and that the Governing Council will submit periodic reports to the Secretary-General and the Security Council.

2-2

FROM: A1UNITNA

23220-05

I HAVE THE HONOUR TO TRANSMIT HERE WITH THE TEXT OF RESOLUTION
692 (1991) ADOPTED BY THE SECURITY COUNCIL AT ITS 2987TH MEETING ON
20 MAY 1991.

QUOTE

THE SECURITY COUNCIL,

RECALLING ITS RESOLUTIONS 674 (1990) OF 29 OCTOBER 1990, 686
(1991) OF 2 MARCH 1991 AND 687 (1991) OF 3 APRIL 1991, CONCERNING
LIABILITY OF IRAQ, WITHOUT PREJUDICE TO ITS DEBTS AND OBLIGATIONS
ARISING PRIOR TO 2 AUGUST 1990, FOR ANY DIRECT LODAMAGE,
INCLUDING ENVIRONMENTAL DAMAGE AND THE DEPLETION OF NATURAL
RESOURCES, OR INJURY TO FOREIGN GOVERNMENTS, NATIONALS AND
CORPORATIONS, AS A RESULT OF IRAQ'S UNLAWFUL INVASION AND OCCUPATION
OF KUWAIT;

TAKING NOTE OF THE SECRETARY-GENERAL'S REPORT OF 2 MAY 1991
(S/22559), SUBMITTED IN ACCORDANCE WITH PARAGRAPH 19 OF RESOLUTION
687 (1991);

ACTING UNDER CHAPTER VII OF THE CHARTER OF THE UNITED NATIONS,

1. EXPRESSES ITS APPRECIATION TO THE SECRETARY-GENERAL FOR HIS
REPORT OF 2 MAY 1991: 1/

2. WELCOMES THE FACT THAT THE SECRETARY-GENERAL WILL NOW
UNDERTAKE THE APPROPRIATE CONSULTATIONS REQUESTED BY PARAGRAPH 19 OF
RESOLUTION 687 (1991) SO THAT HE WILL BE IN A POSITION TO RECOMMEND
TO THE SECURITY COUNCIL FOR DECISION AS SOON AS POSSIBLE THE FIGURE
WHICH THE LEVEL OF IRAQ'S CONTRIBUTION TO THE FUND WILL NOT EXCEED:

3. DECIDES TO ESTABLISH THE FUND AND THE COMMISSION REFERRED TO

IN PARAGRAPH 18 OF RESOLUTION 687 (1991) IN ACCORDANCE WITH SECTION I
OF THE SECRETARY-GENERAL'S REPORT, AND THAT THE GOVERNING COUNCIL
WILL BE LOCATED AT THE UNITED NATIONS OFFICE AT GENEVA AND THAT THE
GOVERNING COUNCIL MAY DECIDE WHETHER SOME OF THE ACTIVITIES OF THE
COMMISSION SHOULD BE CARRIED OUT ELSEWHERE:

0056

THE MEMBERS OF THE GOVERNING COUNCIL:

5.   DIRECTS THE GOVERNING COUNCIL TO PROCEED IN AN EXPEDITIOUS MANNER TO IMPLEMENT THE PROVISIONS OF SECTION E   RESOLUTION 687 (1991), TAKING INTO ACCOUNT THE RECOMMENDATIONS IN SECTION II OF THE SECRETARY-GENERAL'S REPORT;

6.   DECIDES THAT THE REQUIREMENT FOR IRAQI CONTRIBUTIONS WILL APPLY IN THE MANNER TO BE PRESCRIBED BY THE GOVERNING COUNCIL WITH RESPECT TO ALL IRAQI PETROLEUM AND PETROLEUM PRODUCTS EXPORTED FROM IRAQ AFTER 3 APRIL 1991 AS WELL AS SUCH PETROLEUM AND PETROLEUM PRODUCTS EXPORTED EARLIER BUT NOT DELIVERED OR NOT PAID FOR AS A SPECIFIC RESULT OF THE PROHIBITIONS CONTAINED IN SECURITY COUNCIL RESOLUTION 661 (1990);

7.   REQUESTS THE GOVERNING COUNCIL TO REPORT AS SOON AS POSSIBLE ON THE ACTIONS IT HAS TAKEN WITH REGARD TO THE MECHANISMS FOR DETERMINING THE APPROPRIATE LEVEL OF IRAQ'S CONTRIBUTION TO THE FUND AND THE ARRANGEMENTS FOR ENSURING THAT PAYMENTS ARE MAD TO THE FUND, SO THAT THE SECURITY COUNCIL CAN GIVE ITS APPROVAL IN ACCORDANCE WITH PARAGRAPH 22 OF RESOLUTION 687 (1991);

8.   REQUESTS THAT ALL STATES AND INTERNATIONAL ORGANIZATIONS COOPERATE WITH THE DECISIONS OF THE GOVERNING COUNCIL TAKEN PURSUANT TO PARAGRAPH 5 OF THE PRESENT RESOLUTION, AND ALSO REQUESTS THAT THE GOVERNING COUNCIL KEEP THE SECURITY COUNCIL INFORMED ON THIS MATTER;

9.   DECIDES THAT, IF THE GOVERNING COUNCIL NOTIFIES THE SECURITY COUNCIL THAT IRAQ HAS FAILED TO CARRY OUT DECISIONS OF THE GOVERNING COUNCIL TAKEN PURSUANT TO PARAGRAPH 5 OF THE PRESENT RESOLUTION, THE SECURIOTY COUNCIL INTENDS TO RETAIN OR TO TAKE ACITON TO REIMPOSE THE PROHIBITION AGAINST THE IMPORT OF PETROLEUM AND PETROLEUM PRODUCTS ORIGINATING IN IRAQ AND FINANCIAL TRANSACTIONS RELATED THERETO;

10.   DECIDES ALSO TO REMAIN SEIZED OF THIS MATTER AND THAT THE GOVERNING COUNCIL WILL SUBMIT PERIODIC REPORTS TO THE SECRETARY-GENERAL AND THE SECURITY COUNCIL.
UNQUOTE.

HIGHEST CONSIDERATION.

JAVIER PEREZ DE CUELLAR
KMO ㅍ - ㄴ ㅠ .5,34-)

:9) :(0 .4759
SCHLITTLER 3520A NAK

UN, 걸프戰 被害賠償委員會 設置 決議案 採擇

1. UN安保理는 5.20 걸프戰 피해배상처리를 전담하는 賠償委員會(본부 : 제네바)設置 決議案 (692號)을 贊成 14, 棄權 1 (쿠바)로 채택했음.

2. 걸프戰 被害賠償 問題는

   가. 지난 4.3 採擇된 걸프戰 停戰 決議案 (687號)에서

   ○ 이락의 石油 收入중 一定比率로 배상기금을 설치하고 동 賠償基金 운영을 위한 特別委員會 創設을 명시하는 한편

   ○ 「케야르」UN事務總長에게 30이내 賠償金 지불방식에 관한 勸告案을 제출토록 함에 따라

   나. 5.3 「케야르」UN事務總長이

   ○ 장래 石油販賣額, 과거 軍事費 支出 및 武器 輸入額, 戰後復舊 費用 등을 고려하여 이락의 賠償金額을 결정할 것과

   ○ 石油收入중 일정비율을 被害賠償 基金에 충당하고 남을 경우 나머지를 이락에 返還토록하는 方式을 제안했으나

   다. 이락政府는 戰後復舊資金 및 對外債務 支拂 등으로 年間 300億弗의 赤字가 불가피하다고 強調하면서 戰爭賠償金 支拂時期를 최소한 5년간 延期해 줄 것을 요청 (5.3 「안바리」UN대사)한 바 있음.

3. 이번 UN安保理의 戰爭被害 賠償委員會 설치 決議案은

　가. UN決議案 687號가 규정하고 있는 전쟁배상조항 이행을 위한 追加決議
　　案으로서

　나. 이락 石油收入에 대한 배상기금 염출 比率 결정 및 各國의 被害賠償
　　청구심사 등 걸프戰 피해배상관련 모든 權限을 同 賠償委員會에 부여
　　하고 있는 점이 特徵的인 바

　다. 安保理 15개 理事國 대표로 구성된 同 賠償委員會의 일방적인 걸프戰
　　피해국 배상활동이 본격화 될 경우 이락政府에 대한 經濟的 壓力加重
　　과 함께 「후세인」의 立地를 더욱 弱化시키는 要因으로 작용할 것으로
　　豫想됨.

36-36

0059

외 무 부

종   별 :

번   호 : UNW-1338   일   시 : 91 0523 1900

수   신 : 장 관(국연,중동일,기정)

발   신 : 주 유엔 대사

제   목 : 걸프사태(유엔동향)

1. 지난 5.20 안보리가 이락배상 책임이행안을 승인함에 따라 배상기금 조성을 위한 이락 석유수입 공제의 상한선 설정문제가 큰 관심사가 되고있는바, 금 5.23 케야르 유엔사무총장은 구체적 수치를 안보리에 수일내로 제시할 것임을 시사하였음.

2. 한편 이락측은 금일 배포된 안보리문서 (S/22629) 에서 안보리의 상기 이락 배상 책임 이행안 승인을 다음 요지로 비난하였음.

    가. 안보리의 월권:배상청구 문제는 ICJ 관할사항

    나. 이락의 청구심사권 박탈

    다. 미국을 비롯한 다국적군측의 배상 책임은 불거론

    라. 이락의 석유증산을 강요, 결과적으로 국제 석유수급영향, OPEC 자율권 상실

    마. 이락국민의 고통:이락측의 배상 유예 (5년)요청불고려

3. 이락의 군비통제를 위한 특별위 (SC) R.EKEUS의장실에 문의한바, 유엔 제 2차 조사단 (화학무기전문가 7개국 30 여명)이 6월 초반 이락방문 예정이라고함.

    첨부:1. 사무총장 기자문답

    2. 유엔이락난민구호현황

    3. WP 지 표제관련사설 및 기사: UNW(F)-224

    끝

    (대사 노창희-국장)

국기국   1차보   중아국   정문국   안기부

UNW(R)-224 1052= 19∞
(국연. 중동원. 기자)   총5매

Secretary-General's remarks after Security Council consultations at
    approximately 1.15 pm on Thursday, 23 May 1991

Q: Are you happy with the Security Council support you are getting
        on all the reports you have submitted?

SG: Oh yes, of course, so far everything looks alright.

Q: Have you any idea how much the percentage of Iraqi oil income
        is to be allocated for compensation??

SG: I am working on it. As you know, it is a very difficult question.
        I have been given a very difficult task. I am working on it
        because I have to present a figure, something which requires
          careful reflection.

Q: Kuwait is asking for the Chernobyl-style compensation
        for its damages.

Sg: Yes, the Ambassador has told me something about it, and well,
        he has a point and I am going to consider his request.

Q: When will you be ready to present the figures?

SG: I hope tomorrow or perhaps very early next week.

Q: You'll be away next week.

SG: I don't have to do it personally.

Q: Are you looking forward to your trip that you are going to
        make now?

SG: It is a very hectic one. I am looking forward to visiting the
        countries, but not to the trip as a whole. It is a very, very
        hectic one; seven countries which I have to visit in a rather
        short period of time.

Q: Will you be meeting with Dr. Al-Qaysi of the Iraqi Foreign
        Ministry?

SG: I have no time because I am leaving tomorrow.

                        *****

#UNW-1338
천부욱   5-1

                                                    0061

UNHCR UPDATE

ON OPERATIONS WITHIN
THE REGIONAL HUMANITARIAN
PLAN OF ACTION

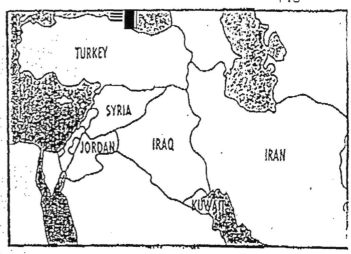

23 May 1991

The United Nations High Commissioner for Refugees dispatched 45 Scandinavian field officers to Baghdad Thursday to strengthen its humanitarian operations across three northern Iraqi provinces.

A senior UNHCR delegation left Thursday for Diyabakir where it will discuss with Coalition officials the handover of all humanitarian activities in northern Iraq to UNHCR.

The delegation, led by Kamal Morjane, Director of UNHCR's Regional Bureau, will consult with Coalition officers on the timetable and logistics of UNHCR's plan to assume full responsibility for all humanitarian relief operations, including food and medical assistance, and voluntary repatriation programs in the area.

A chartered plane carrying the 45 UNHCR officers, funded by the Danish and Norwegian Refugee Councils, departed from Geneva and increased the size of UNHCR's international staff in Iraq to more than 70.

The Scandinavians will expand UNHCR's outreach capacity from its three sub-offices in D'huk, Arbil and Suleimaniya and its eight field offices. They will establish relay stations on returnee routes to distribute relief supplies and organize transport.

The new officers will also help man UNHCR's 21 mobile units which are being deployed to monitor the well-being and safety of the returnees. The work of the mobile teams will be enhanced by 36 four-wheel drive vehicles expected to arrive in Iraq by the end of the week.

According to UNHCR field reports, more than 320,000 Iraqis have left encampments along the mountainous frontier with Turkey and are headed for home. Some 55,600 returnees currently are awaiting developments at the three Zakho transit centres.

5—2

0062

The spontaneous return movement has reduced the number of Iraqis on the Iraq-Turkey border to 123,583, UNHCR field workers said.

The spontaneous repatriation movement from Iran is also gaining momentum and UNHCR field workers estimate that more than 200,000 refugees have gone home. Field reports say about 8,000 people are returning to Suleimaniya each day from Iran, which is still host to an estimated 1.3 million refugees.

UNHCR is closely monitoring the well-being of some 150,000 Iraqis clustered around a make-shift encampment outside Suleimaniya. The site holds displaced persons who were unable to make the trek across the Iranian border and many who returned from Iran but are reluctant to return to their homes as yet.

5-3

0063

Sanctions: The Many Missions

IT BECOMES pressing to sort out the separate tasks that the United Nations' sanctions on Iraq are being asked to perform. The first is to ensure the U.N.'s discovery and destruction of Baghdad's missiles and nuclear, chemical and biological arms. Saddam Hussein's assurances of cooperation with the U.N. in this matter remain suspect and untested. This project badly needs to be expedited while some allied forces are still on the ground in Iraq and usable as additional leverage against him.

The second task of sanctions is to keep the pressure on while the U.N. works out a formula and method for compensating Iraq's victims from its future oil revenues. This will require the world body to permit resumption of some oil exports. The United States seems firmly in support of the U.N. stance on this mission, as on the first.

On a third task, however, some differences are developing between the United States and the U.N. A major American goal has been to protect the Kurds. Sanctions have served this purpose and so have the military forces that Washington and eight other nations belatedly sent to the north—without specific U.N. authorization. But now Baghdad is negotiating an autonomy agreement with the Kurds, and over the weekend it skirted the allies and agreed directly with the U.N. to replace these forces with a small, lightly armed U.N. guard contingent. There is only an informal U.N. understanding, not a resolution, to use sanctions to protect the Kurds. Without deeper consultation between Washington and the U.N., Saddam Hussein could be tempted to try to drive a wedge on this issue.

On a fourth task of sanctions, meanwhile, a real U.S.-U.N. split has already developed. The U.N. is working with Saddam Hussein—on relief and a police contingent in the north, on a peace-keeping force in the south, on oil exports and compensation and on disarmament. Unquestionably, these dealings help legitimize his rule. But President Bush has now put his personal stamp on an American strategy intended to drive Saddam Hussein from power by economic pressure. Earlier he had insisted that his differences were with the Iraqi leader, not the people. Now the White House underlines that sanctions will stay on and "the Iraqis will pay the price while [Saddam Hussein] remains in power." This strategy is entirely justified by Saddam Hussein's record of treachery. We think Mr. Bush is right. But only Britain seems to support him. If Iraq meets U.N. demands on weapons and compensation, then Mr. Bush will have to make the case to restive allies that within a reasonable time sanctions can force out Saddam Hussein.

5 — 4

0064

5-5

Inspectors Find Iraq's Nuclear Material

Chemical Weapons Sites to Be Next in Search

By R. Jeffrey Smith
Washington Post Staff Writer

Inspectors for the International Atomic Energy Agency, concluding a five-week visit to Iraq yesterday, have located all of the highly enriched uranium believed to be in Iraq's possession, according to senior diplomats and U.S. officials.

The inspection marked the first stage of a massive, U.N.-ordered effort to track down, collect and force the disposal of Iraq's arsenal of nuclear weapons-grade materials, ballistic missiles and chemical and biological laboratories.

The second stage begins in two weeks when another U.N. team plans to travel to Iraq from a newly established headquarters in Bahrain to inspect chemical weapons storage and production sites. Those inspections are expected to take weeks, and the actual disposal of the mass destruction weapons in Iraq that survived the Persian Gulf War could take more than a year, according to officials.

The U.N. Security Council has made Iraq's cooperation in eliminating the weapons a condition for lift-

ing economic sanctions. Rolf Ekeus, a Swedish ambassador who chairs the U.N. Special Commission on Iraq, said yesterday the commission may need another three months or more before it can certify Iraqi compliance.

Ekeus said in a meeting with Washington Post reporters and editors that he favors withholding certification until all Iraqi weapons of mass destruction have been placed under the commission's control and some destruction has begun.

The visit to Iraqi storage sites for highly enriched uranium, a key component of primitive nuclear arms, had been delayed four weeks by Iraqi opposition to a draft protocol giving the commission wide access to weapon sites, Ekeus said.

Ekeus threatened to withdraw the 34-member inspection team from Baghdad and obtain a U.N. Security Council vote citing Iraq for not meeting its obligations, unless Iraq agreed to the protocol by 5 p.m. last Friday. At 4:10 p.m. that day, Iraq's ambassador to the United Nations delivered to Ekeus a copy of the protocol signed by the country's foreign minister.

Officials said Iraq had also dropped its refusal to disclose the

location of all nuclear materials until the United Nations guaranteed the sites would not be destroyed by new allied air raids.

During a visit to the main Iraqi nuclear research facility at Tuwaitha, investigators located what officials believe is the country's entire stockpile of weapons-grade uranium—roughly 98 pounds.

A separate inspection of another site that had been suspected of involvement in nuclear research occurred without hindrance and turned up no additional nuclear material, officials said. But various samples of materials possibly related to nuclear research were removed for analysis, and a senior U.S. official said discoveries of hidden Iraqi nuclear materials—other than highly enriched uranium—remained possible.

An IAEA statement, expected to be released today at the group's Vienna headquarters, praised Iraq's full cooperation and compliance "with all the requests of the agency team."

The international effort to find and destroy Iraq's mass destruction weapons is a challenging assignment for a U.N. group that several weeks ago lacked office space, telephones or staff, Ekeus said. He has since hired more than 20 weapons experts from as many countries, but without knowing how the United

Nations will pay their expenses or fund a chemical weapons destruction facility that will likely have to be constructed inside Iraq.

Iraq has provided the United Nations with a detailed accounting of its remaining weaponry. "They have told us of everything they believe we will detect," Ekeus said, as well as some additional information as a "safety margin" against embarrassing discoveries of secret stockpiles. He said he does not rule out such a discovery, particularly since Iraq has denied having the biological warfare materials they were believed to have developed before the war.

Ekeus said that if facilities for production of such materials are uncovered, "my intention is to destroy the whole laboratory."

Several officials said that Iraq this week provided new details about its stocks of chemical arms and ballistic missiles. But the commission, to protect itself from possible Iraqi deception, has also solicited intelligence information from several Middle East countries, including Israel, as well as those countries believed to have provided military-related equipment to Iraq before the war, such as Germany and the Soviet Union.

Ekeus described as "absurd" a claim by a Soviet representative that his country had no information about Iraq's chemical arsenal and said he hoped the Soviets would eventually be more forthcoming.

분류기호 문서번호	중동일 720- 1356	기 안 용 지 (720-2327)		시 행 상 특별취급	
보존기간	영구·준영구 10. 5. 3. 1	장 관			
수 신 처 보존기간					
시행일자	1991. 5. 23.		예		
보조 기관	국 장	전결	협 조 기 관		문 서 통 제 1991. 5. 27
	심의관				
	과 장				
기안책임자		조 태 용			발 송 인 반 송 1991. 5. 27 의무부
경 유 수 신 사 본		주쿠웨이트대사	발 신 명 의		
제 목		걸프사태 관련 피해보상 청구			피해 보상청구 규제정 조리 (특별보고) 예

대 : KUW-0206

연 : WKU-0160(1), 중동일 720-16549(2)

1. 유엔 안전보장 이사회는 5.20. 연호(2) 유엔 사무총장의 표제 관련

건의서를 승인하는 결의(692호)를 찬성 14, 반대 0, 기권 1(쿠바)로

채택하였는바, 관련 문서를 별첨 송부하니 아국의 피해 보상 청구를

위한 기초 자료 수집에 참고하시기 바랍니다. 91. 12. 31. 242

/ 계속 ...

더맑은 마음을, 더밝은 사회를, 더넓은 미래를

0066

2. 상기와 관련, 귀주재국 정부가 유엔에 제출한 피해 현황 보고서를
   참고로 송부 합니다.

   첨 부 : 1. 주유엔 대사 보고 전문 및 안보리 결의 692호 1부

           2. 안보리 정전 결의 687호 1부

           3. 쿠웨이트 정부의 피해 보고서 1부. 끝.

더맑은 마음을, 더밝은 사회를, 더넓은 미래를

0067

외 무 부

종 별 :

번 호 : UNW-1302   일 시 : 91 0520 2010

수 신 : 장 관(국연,중동일,기정)

발 신 : 주 유엔 대사

제 목 : 안보리회의(이락 배상문제)

연: UNW-1125,1203

1. 안보리는 금 5.20 공식회의 (2987차)를 개최코 연호 유엔사무총장의 이락 배상 이행안을 승인하는 결의안을 채택한바 (결의 692호) 동회의 중요경과를 아래보고함.

가.의제채택

0.이락, 쿠웨이트대표 토의참가 초청 (안보리 의사규칙37조)

0.결의안, 공동제안국추가: 원제안국 (미)(영)에 (벨지움), (뜨랑스), (루마니), (소련) (자이르) 추가 (총 7개국공동제안)

나.표결

0. 찬 14,반 0, 기권 1 (쿠바)

0.표결전및 표결후 발언국 없었음.

2.금일 채택된 상기 안보리 결의안은 본건 배상기금 충당을 위한 이락 석유수입의 공제상한 선율 정하지 않은바, 추후 사무총장의 건의를 받아 안보리가 결정예정임.

첨부:상기 안보리 결의안: UNW(F)-218

끝

(대사 노창회-국장)

**UNITED
NATIONS**

Security Council

PROVISIONAL

S/22613
17 May 1991

ORIGINAL: ENGLISH

United Kingdom of Great Britain and Northern Ireland
and United States of America: draft resolution

The Security Council,

Recalling its resolutions 674 (1990), 686 (1991) and 687 (1991),
concerning the liability of Iraq, without prejudice to its debts and
obligations arising prior to 2 August 1990, for any direct loss, damage,
including environmental damage and the depletion of natural resources, or
injury to foreign Governments, nationals and corporations, as a result of
Iraq's unlawful invasion and occupation of Kuwait,

Noting the Secretary-General's report of 2 May 1991 (S/22559), submitted
in accordance with paragraph 19 of resolution 687 (1991),

Acting under Chapter VII of the Charter,

1.   Expresses its appreciation to the Secretary-General for his report
of 2 May 1991 (S/22559);

2.   Welcomes the fact that the Secretary-General will now undertake the
appropriate consultations requested by paragraph 19 of 687 so that he will be
in a position to recommend to the Security Council for decision as soon as
possible the figure which the level of Iraq's contribution to the Fund will
not exceed;

3.   Decides to establish the Fund and Commission referred to in
paragraph 18 of resolution 687 (1991) in accordance with Part I of the
Secretary-General's report and that the Governing Council shall be located at
the Offices of the United Nations in Geneva and that the Governing Council may
decide whether some of the activities of the Commission should be carried out
elsewhere;

4.   Requests the Secretary-General to take the actions necessary to
implement paragraphs 2 and 3 above in consultation with the members of the
Governing Council;

5.   Directs the Governing Council to proceed in an expeditious manner to
implement the provisions of Section E of resolution 687 (1991), taking into
account the recommendations in Part II of the Secretary-General's report;

32328 (E)   /...

#UNW-1302   2-1

청부목

6.   Decides that the requirement for Iraqi contributions shall apply in the manner to be prescribed by the Governing Council with respect to all Iraqi petroleum and petroleum products exported from Iraq after 3 April 1991 as well as such petroleum and petroleum products exported earlier but not delivered or not paid for as a specific result of the prohibitions contained in resolution 661 (1990);

7.   Requests the Governing Council to report as soon as possible on the actions it has taken with regard to the mechanisms for determining the appropriate level of Iraq's contribution to the Fund and the arrangements for ensuring that payments are made to the Fund, so that the Security Council can give its approval in accordance with paragraph 22 of resolution 687 (1991);

8.   Requests that all States and international organizations cooperate with the decisions of the Governing Council taken pursuant to paragraph 5 of this resolution and further requests that the Governing Council keep the Security Council informed on this matter;

9.   Decides that if the Governing Council notifies the Security Council that Iraq has failed to carry out decisions of the Governing Council taken pursuant to paragraph 5 of this resolution, the Security Council intends to retain or to take action to reimpose the prohibition against the import of petroleum and petroleum products originating in Iraq and financial transactions related thereto;

10.   Decides to remain seized of this matter and that the Governing Council will submit periodic reports to the Secretary-General and the Security Council.

2-2

0070

외 무 부

종   별 :

번   호 : UNW-1445   일   시 : 91 0603 1800

수   신 : 장 관(국연,중동일,법규,기정)

발   신 : 주 유엔 대사

제   목 : 걸프사태(안보리)

1. 안보리 휴전결의에 의거 케야르 사무총장은 이락배상기금 조성을 위한 동국 석유수입공제상한 선으로 30 프로를 안보리에 5.31 자로 제시한바 (S/22661), 주요 산출 근거는 다음과 같음.

　　가. 이락 연간 석유 수출수입: 약 210 억불 (93년기준)

　　나. 동 수입사용 배분

　　1) 대외수입: 48 프로

　　2) 외채상환: 22 프로

　　3) 본건 배상기금 공제: 30 프로 (상한선)

2. 미측은 금 6.3. 상기 30 프로안에 반대의견을 표명 (미측안 50 프로)한바, 미대표부로 부터 입수한 별첨 미국무부 대변인 언급내용 참조바람.

3. 사무총장은 난민 구호관련 유엔-이락간에 체결된 유엔경비대 (UN GUARDS CONTINGENT)배치에 관한 합의서 내용을 5.31.자로 안보리에 통보한바 (S/22663), 지난 4.18 자 양해각서 (MOU) 부속서 형식을 취하고 있는 동합의서의 특기사항은 다음과 같음.

　　가. 동 경비대는 전체 500 명을 초과하지 못함. (배치지역당은 150 명을 초과하지 못함.)

　　나. 이동 (차량,헬기), 봉신및 병참수단 주선

　　다. 이락측이 제공하는 권총류 휴대

3. 한편 영국은 휴전 결의에 의거 대이락 금수조치에 관한 안보리 정기 (매 60 일) 심사시 이락정부의 정책과 재반 행태를 고려토록 되어있는것과 관련, 이락당국의 하기 영국민 처리문제를 안보리문서 (S/22664) 로 제기하였음.

　　가. D. BRAND: 걸프사태후 인질억류, 간첩죄목으로 종신형 선고

국기국　　1차보　　중아국　　국기국　　외정실　　안기부

나. I.RICHTER: 87 년 종신형선고 (부패관련죄목)

4.쿠웨이트는 이락 TAHA YASIN RAMADAN 부통령이 요르단 (5.27) 이집트 (5.28) 일간지와의 회견에서 '쿠웨이트는 이락의 일부'운운 발언을 하였다고 이락을 비난하는 안보리문서 (S/22655) 를 5.30 자로 배포하였음.

첨부 FAX:UNW(F)-241: 1. 사무총장의 안보리앞 이락배상기금 관련통보

2.이락 배상 기금관련미국무부 대변인 언급내용

3.유엔-이락간유엔경비대 관련 합의서. (발췌)

끝

(대사 노창희-국장)

PAGE 2

0072

헤(W(F)-241 10603 (ㅁㅁㄲ
(국연·중동월·법규·기정) 총7대

Annex

30 May 1991

Note of the Secretary-General pursuant to paragraph 13 of his report of 2 May 1991 (S/22559)

1.   On 2 May 1991 I presented to the Council, in compliance with Security Council resolution 687, a report (S/22559) pursuant to paragraph 19 of Security Council resolution 687 (1991). In the same paragraph 19 it was stipulated that Iraq's contribution to the fund based on a percentage of the value of the exports of petroleum and petroleum products from Iraq should not exceed a figure to be suggested to the Council by me. In paragraph 13 of the report, I informed the Council that I will undertake the appropriate consultations as required so that, as soon as possible, I will be in a position to suggest this figure.

2.   Authoritative data necessary for the preparation of this communication to the Security Council is not readily available. However, given that Iraq derives almost its entire exports earnings from the export of one single commodity (oil) and that the unit price and export volume of Iraqi oil are monitored by OPEC, it is possible to estimate the size and functioning of its economy in general and of its external trade and payments structure in particular. Data available for this exercise have been taken from various sources including the Government of Iraq, the International Monetary Fund, ESCWA, OPEC, and the United Nations Statistical Office.

3.   Paragraph 16 of resolution 687, in defining the extent of Iraq's liability, states that it is "liable under international law for any direct loss, damage, including environmental damage and the depletion of natural resources, or injury to foreign government, national and corporations, as a result of Iraq's unlawful invasion and occupation of Kuwait". As paragraph 16 states, this liability is "without prejudice to the debts and obligations of Iraq arising prior to 2 August 1990, which will be addressed through the normal mechanisms". Thus, this communication has to limit itself to dealing with the economic and financial possibilities and constraints of Iraq to compensate for the damage defined in paragraph 16.

4.   Iraq's oil production quota, as agreed to within OPEC in July 1990, is of 3.14 million barrels per day. With an estimated internal consumption of about 300,000 barrels per day, the Iraqi Government intends to reach its most recent 1989 level of exports of 2.85 million barrels per day in 1993, as communicated by the Permanent Representative to the United Nations to me in his letter of 29 April 1991. If the reference price of $21 per barrel agreed to by OPEC in July 1990 were to be used during 1993, which after adjustment for quality would result in a price of $20.04 for Iraqi crude, total Iraqi export earnings for 1993 can be expected to reach $21 billion, surpassing its 1989 export revenue. Such earnings could conceivably be higher, given that global demand for oil increases by 2 per cent annually, that production in large industrial countries has been declining over the last four years, and that only a few

/...

#UNW-1445
첨부문
7-1

countries have the reserves and even fewer the production capacity to offset the resulting shortfall. These calculations also assume that all OPEC member countries would return to roughly similar production quotas as those agreed to in July 1990, thus allowing Iraq to reach this level of exports without causing a price collapse.

5.   Estimates for foreign exchange expenditures of the Iraqi economy for strictly civilian purposes during the 1980s vary. By taking account of historical relationships of consumption and investment to GDP and their import intensity, and data on net service imports as provided by Iraq, it is estimated that about $8 billion may be required to sustain a level of civilian imports in 1991 consistent with the needs of the Iraqi economy.

6.   Iraq's total external debt and obligations have been reported by the Government of Iraq at $42,097 million as of 31 December 1990. However, the exact figure of Iraq's external indebtedness can only be ascertained following discussions between Iraq and its creditors. To estimate debt servicing requirements it is assumed that Iraq reschedules its debts at standard Paris Club terms.

7.   With oil exports expected to reach about $21 billion by 1993 imports should absorb about 48 per cent of export earnings and debt servicing approximately 22 per cent. I suggest, therefore, that compensation to be paid by Iraq (as arising from section E of resolution 687) should not exceed 30 per cent of the annual value of the exports of petroleum and petroleum products from Iraq.

8.   The above calculations are based on data and a number of assumptions that have to be kept under review.

7-2

0074

Q   A slightly change of focus.

Q   What does the State Department --

MS. TUTWILER: Wait. Alan was asking -- I think a real question.

Q   A very slight change of focus. The Secretary General of the U.N. made an announcement last Friday saying that there would be a 30 percent limit on the percentage of oil revenues that Iraq could be required to pay in compensation.

MS. TUTWILER: Right.

Q   The United States -- U.S. officials had previously been talking of a figure in the range of 40 to 50 percent. Do you have any reaction?

MS. TUTWILER: Yes. Today, I can confirm for you what our percentage is and what our position has been. As you know, I've been unable to do so up until this date.

Concerning the 30 percent level that was recommended by the Secretary General, we do not think that the 30 percent level suggested is adequate to compensate on a timely basis Kuwaitis and the others who have suffered so grievously at Iraq's hand. As a result of the damages incurred, and Iraq's continued repressive policies, we believe the figure suggested is too long.

We are in consultation with the other members of the Security Council concerning our belief that the ceiling should be 50 percent.

The Secretary General makes a recommendation on the ceiling. The Security Council makes the ultimate decision. The Security Council is not obligated to approve the Secretary General's recommendation, although certainly his recommendation will carry great weight.

There is no date set for consideration of this issue by the Security Council as of this briefing.

Q   Margaret, some people in this building have been talking about an additional 10 or 20 percent, or even more, on top of the 50 to pay for, I guess, environmental damage as opposed to war damages. Is that still an option?

MS. TUTWILER: Let me check, Alan. I don't know if the 50 percent that we've now made public encompasses the environmental or not. I'll just have to ask.

Wait a minute. Jim Anderson had a question.

Q   On that same subject. On such a vote, where the

1

7-3

Security Cou____ is approving a recomme_____n by the Secretary General, does the veto rule apply? In ____r words, if the United States votes no, does that scrap that motion?

MS. TUTWILER: I would assume that it does, Jim, but let me ask. On something that's procedural like this, let me just check for you. I don't know.

Q   One small point. Are you talking about 50 percent of profits or 50 percent of revenues?

MS. TUTWILER: My understanding is -- correct me, Richard (Boucher), if I'm wrong. This was -- what? Revenue, I believe, isn't it?

MR. BOUCHER: We'll have to check the resolution.

MS. TUTWILER: That's what I think it is, Alan, but let's check the resolution.

Q   Margaret --

MS. TUTWILER: Yes, Mark.

Q   It's still United States policy, isn't it, that there should be no relaxation of sanctions at all as long as Saddam Husayn is in power?

MS. TUTWILER: That is how the President has, basically, without using your exact words, expressed our policy and his views.

Q   Isn't any discussion of either of these percentages academic?

MS. TUTWILER: We went through this, I think, last Tuesday before I left. This is the United States' view, but the United States is operating within the United Nations and within the coalition. So that is the United States' view, but we have been, throughout this, operating in an international body. So I would have to assume if the vast majority of the international body feels very, very strongly another way, I don't know what decision the President would make at that particular point. He's expressed our point of view.

Just like, for instance, on this percentage. I'm not going to go through what percentage the other members of the Security Council are advocating, but they're not all at 50 percent. It's all over the globe. Where it will come out, I don't know.

Q   Margaret, just a point of clarification.

MS. TUTWILER: Sure, John.

2

7-4

0076

Q   When the President spoke to the press with Chancellor Kohl of Germany, he was asked this question and, basically, to paraphrase him, what he said was, yes, we are against relaxation of sanctions as long as Saddam Husayn remains but he could see positions whereby in order to make urgent necessary reconstruction, to pay sanctions, that it might be necessary to have some relaxation. That still holds, too?

MS. TUTWILER: Yes. I don't believe he used the word "relaxation." You're correct, the President has a full statement. I'm having a hard time remembering the exact phrase, but I believe he addressed himself to food. As you remember, medicine has always been totally exempt from the sanctions. He did have one particular phrase in there, and I just didn't bring it with me. Do you have it, Richard? But, John, you're absolutely correct.

Q   Did Baker explain the U.S. position on this when he met Perez de Cuellar in Lisbon?

MS. TUTWILER: To be honest with you, I attended that meeting with the Secretary. The subject never came up.

Q   Also on Iraq. Has the State Department seen the report that a former high ranking Iraqi nuclear official had turned himself in to U.S. authorities and said that a lot of the nuclear installations in Iraq had been missed by the raids?

MS. TUTWILER: Yes, we've seen the report. I don't have any comment on the specifics of the NPR report, the one that we have seen, since they clearly involve intelligence matters of some sensitivity.

As you all will recall, we've previously said that the Iraqi disclosures on their nuclear facilities -- the first report they sent to the United Nations, we said, fell well short of reality. You'll remember they then sent in a lengthier report and we characterized that as more in line with reality.

The International Atomic Energy Agency sent a team to Iraq in May, as called for by Resolution 687. The team was able to visit the sites they wanted to see. We provided recommendations to the IAEA team and will continue to do so.

With the assistance of the special commission, the IAEA made its own decisions on what sites to visit. We see this as the first of what will likely be many inspections of Iraq's nuclear, chemical, biological, and missile capabilities in order to ensure their destruction. We expect to continue working with the IAEA and other inspection teams to ensure that they have complete and accurate information as they proceed with their work.

3

7-5

Annex

1.   Following the agreement in principle for the deployment of a United Nations Guards Contingent, discussions were held on 17 and 18 May 1991 to clarify the principal elements associated with the deployment of such guard units, within the framework of the existing Memorandum of Understanding, signed on 18 April 1991 in Baghdad by H.E. Mr. Ahmed Hussein, Minister of Foreign Affairs of the Republic of Iraq and Prince Sadruddin Aga Khan, Executive Delegate of the Secretary-General of the United Nations for the Humanitarian Programme for Iraq, Kuwait and the Iraq-Iran and Iraq-Turkey border areas.

2.   As a first step, ten United Nations Guards have been dispatched to Dohuk, on 19 May 1991, in order to establish a United Nations presence at the sub-office and depots in the town. This unit also liaises with the transit camps in the Zakho plain, with a view to enabling the United Nations to assume control thereof. In addition, the unit collaborates with the local civilian administration which is stepping up the rehabilitation of services in the town. The Dohuk/Zakho-based unit of the Contingent will be built to a strength of 50-60 Guards as soon as possible.

3.   In addition to transit camps in the Zakho plain, transit centres/zones (which can best be described as strengthened and enlarged humanitarian centres) will be established along communications routes in other areas of Iraq, wherever such presence may be needed, in agreement with the Government of Iraq. United Nations Guards will be assigned as needed to any transit centres, United Nations sub-offices and Humanitarian Centres (UNHUCs) which may be established by the United Nations in Iraq.

4.   The number of Guards in the Contingent will be kept under review as further units are dispatched, but will not exceed a total strength of 500. In order to ensure their mobility, special arrangements will be made to import the required number of suitable vehicles. Arrangements will be made to ensure that United Nations-marked helicopter(s) will be allowed to land in Dohuk, Zakho and Mosul, as well as in the other areas, for the movement of United Nations personnel. Necessary arrangements will also be made to provide the Contingent with the required means of communication and the necessary logistical back-up.

5.   The number of Guards assigned to the various regions will be decided in consultation with the Government authorities concerned, but would not exceed 150 in any one region. They will move freely, as their duties require, between humanitarian reception points, transit centres and relay stations, as well as sub-offices, using appropriate existing accommodation facilities in the provincial capitals, other towns and villages, or ad hoc field accommodation at transit centres.

6.   United Nations Guards will be authorized to carry side-arms (pistols/revolvers), which will be provided by the Iraqi authorities (subject

/...

7-6

0078

to the approval of the United Nations with respect to make, model, calibre and munitions). While it is not anticipated that all Guards will be so armed, United Nations guidelines and practices will be followed in this regard.

7. The Iraqi authorities will appoint a Chief Liaison Officer to facilitate the Contingent's operations and a liaison officer at each centre to facilitate their work with the Iraqi authorities. The Iraqi authorities will grant appropriate facilities in Baghdad and elsewhere, including office space, maintenance and repair support, maps, etc.

8. This annex shall be an integral part of the Memorandum of Understanding signed on 18 April 1991. It shall be governed by the terms of that Memorandum; it shall be implemented in cooperation and coordination with the Iraq authorities and expire at the end of the period stated therein (31 December 1991).

7-7

0079

분류번호	보존기간

발 신 전 보

WUN-1615   910605 1848 FO

번   호 :   종별 :

WGV -0740   WKU -0194

수   신 : 주 유엔   대사. 총영사//// (사본 : 주 제네바 대사) 쿠웨이트)

발   신 : 장관 (중동일)

제   목 : 걸프사태 관련 피해보상

대 : UNW-1445

    대호 관련, 아국은 쿠웨이트내 건설업체 장비 유실, 교민 재산피해등
걸프사태로 인한 피해가 적지 않으므로 피해보상 청구를 위한 자료 수집등 준비
작업을 조속 개시코자 하는바, 안보리 결의 692호에 따른 보상기금 및 보상위원회
(COMMISSION) 설치 동향과 보상위원회 GOVERNING COUNCIL에서 마련할 피해보상
청구 관련 세부 지침(보상청구자격등), 그리고 타국의 피해보상 청구동향등에
관하여 수시 보고 바람. 끝. 개시일

(중동아국장   이 해 순)

예 고 : 91.12.31. 까지

91. 6. 30. 건의일
91. 12. 31. 일반

보 안 통 제	74

앙 고 재	91 년 6 월 5 일 중동1 과	기안자 성명		과 장	심의관	국 장 전결		차 관	장 관		외신과통제
				74							

0080

외　무　부

관리번호 9/1126

종　별 :

번　호 : UNW-1465

수　신 : 장관(중동일,국연)

발　신 : 주 유엔 대사

제　목 : 걸프사태관련 피해보상

일　시 : 91 0605 1830

대:WUN-1615

1. 당관에서 탐문한바에 의하면, 표제관련 현재 안보리 의장(코트디브와르)이 각 이사국들과 보상기금을 위한 이락 석유수입공제 상한선문제를 주로 협의중(개별협의방식)이라고 함.

2. 보상위원회 집행이사회(GC)와 관련한 조직및 절차문제에 관해서도 곧 안보리 내부협의가 있을것으로 보인다고 하며, 동집행이사회 첫회의는 7 월이후에나 개채(제네바)가 가능할 것으로 관측되고있음.

3. 관련사항 수시보고위게임.끝

(대사 노창희-국장)

예고:91.12.31. 까지

91. 6. 30. 건조필
91. 12. 31. 반구

중아국　　국기국

91.06.06　09:49
외신 2과　통제관 DO

외 무 부

종 별 :

번 호 : UNW-1512   일 시 : 91 0610 1800

수 신 : 장 관(국연,중동일,기정)

발 신 : 주 유 엔 대사

제 목 : 걸프사태(유엔동향)

연: UNW-1445

1. 이락보상 기금문제

가. 이락 유엔대사는 안보리 휴전결의에 의거한 보상기금을 위한 동국 석유수입 공제문제와관련, 6.7 자 사무총장앞 서한(S/22681) 을 통해 사무총장의 연호공제 상한선(30 프로)의 제반산출기초에 이의를 제기하면서 ,5년간의공제유예 (A GRACE PERIOD OF FIVE YEARS) 를 다시 주장하였음.

나. 한편 금 6.10 자 WSJ 지는 지난주 OPEC석유장관 회의에서 종전의 이락 생산할당량(일 310 만 배럴)이 그대로 인정되었으며,오는 9월 차기 OPEC 회의 개최전에 이락 석유수출이 재개될 가능성이 있다고 보는 일부관측도 있음을 보도하였음.

2. 이락 군비통제

6.10 사무총장 대변인에 의하면, 지난 5월 유엔1차 조사단(핵관련 사찰) 의 이락방문에 이어 2차조사단(화학무기 전문가 28 명)이 이락에 도착하였다고함.

첨부:1.사무총장앞 이락측서한 2. 별침 기사:UNW(F)-251

끝

(대사 노창희-국장)

국기국   중아국   안기부   1차보

**UNITED
NATIONS**

UNW(F)-—1 10610 ...
(국연.중동별.기업)   총4매

 Security Council

Distr.
GENERAL

S/22681
7 June 1991
ENGLISH
ORIGINAL: ARABIC

LETTER DATED 7 JUNE 1991 FROM THE PERMANENT REPRESENTATIVE
OF IRAQ TO THE UNITED NATIONS ADDRESSED TO THE
SECRETARY-GENERAL

On instructions from my Government, and with reference to your note of
30 May 1991 (document S/22661), I have the honour to state below the points
which my Government wishes to be taken into account in setting a ceiling for
the deductions envisaged in your aforementioned report:

1.   In setting the maximum ceiling for deductions from Iraq's earnings, i.e.,
30 per cent, the Secretary-General of the United Nations used the economic
data and figures which are supposed to be attained in 1993 and thereafter in
order to assess what is due from Iraq in 1991 and 1992. These years reflect a
very serious deficit in all Iraq's trade balances, by virtue of the
substantial and broad deficit incurred in Iraq's revenue sectors, as well as
the economic situation, which basically does not allow for any deduction from
its expected modest earnings. These earnings are sufficient only to cover a
tiny portion of the basic needs it has to meet, as referred to in Security
Council resolution 687 (1991) and in the report of Under-Secretary-General
Martti Ahtisaari.

It must be concluded from the above comments that, in accordance with the
premises of the Secretary-General himself, the years 1991 and 1992, at the
very least, should be considered a grace period. Iraq, meanwhile, had
already, given the established facts of its economic situation, requested a
grace period of five years.

2.   We have reservations as to the assertion in the Secretary-General's note
that Iraq's annual requirements for civilian imports amount to $8 billion.
Estimated oil revenue, based on current production capacity rather than on
Iraq's share of OPEC oil, amounts to approximately $13 billion for the years
1991 and 1992. This means that Iraq's total oil revenue for those two years
will amount to less than the Secretary-General's estimates for the
requirements to cover basic civilian imports alone, i.e. $16 billion for the
two-year period.

91-18574 2435e (E)   /...

#UNW-1512
첨부떡   4 —1

S/22681
English
Page 2

3.   The following additional facts make it even more vital to grant Iraq the
grace period to which we referred above and not to deduct any percentage
during that period: firstly, this year's poor harvest; secondly, the
depletion of stocks of food, medicines, vaccines and water purification
materials, together with the destruction of power stations, etc., following
the rioting and sabotage which occurred in northern and southern Iraq. As a
result, there are further urgent basic requirements in excess of those
evaluated in the Secretary-General's report. There are, besides, the facts
that, in mid-1991, it is still not possible to export oil or petroleum
products, the severe economic embargo remains in place and Iraqi funds abroad
remain frozen, despite the decision of the sanctions committee and the letter
of that committee's Chairman, which effectively lifted the ban on those funds.

4.   The Secretary-General's note is full of optimism with respect to world
demand, Iraq's share thereof and what he refers to as the unit price of oil as
monitored by OPEC. This assumption does not accord with the reality of the
oil market, which is suffering from surplus production and frenzied
competition between producers to win the largest shares of that market by
...., ...
to the sea and its net earnings from the price of each barrel exported is
actually less than the export price because it has to bear the costs of
transit and operation of pipelines across Turkey and Saudi Arabia.

5.   With regard to Iraq's foreign debts, the estimate contained in the
Secretary-General's note is lower than the true debts incurred by Iraq.
Additionally, the figure quoted in the note does not include the interest
charged on these debts since the beginning of 1990, which was not and has not
yet been paid: it is estimated that such interest will amount to
approximately $3.4 billion as of the beginning of 1993. The suggested level
for debt servicing should therefore be set higher than 22 per cent of Iraq's
earnings and the level of deductions reduced accordingly.

6.   The Secretary-General has estimated Iraq's civilian requirements at
$8 billion, but those requirements are estimated on the basis of data for
1989, a year of severe austerity due to the circumstances of the eight-year
war imposed on Iraq. Iraq's normal civilian requirements are far in excess of
that, its requirements for food, medicine, vital consumer goods and purely
basic services alone amounting to some $10 billion. Iraq also needs to import
vital production goods at a cost of some $2.6 billion, together with essential
imports for the repair of basic facilities destroyed during the war such as
water, power and sewage systems, bridges, communications, roads, railways and
food and medicine factories, costs of which are estimated at $7 billion, in
addition to the costs of repairs to oil installations destroyed during the
war, estimated at $3.5 billion.

7.   Although it is now mid-1991, the economic embargo against Iraq remains
comprehensive and severe and Iraq's foreign currency reserve funds abroad
remain frozen, as we noted in paragraph 3 above. This has caused yet further
confusion and disorder in the operations of civilian production facilities,
and many have come to a halt. It will therefore be necessary to increase the
current pressing requirement for foreign currency during 1991 and 1992.

4 — 2   /...

0084

270   걸프 사태 유엔안전보장이사회 동향 8

8.   In the light of all the facts set out above, which any fair party is perfectly free to verify, Iraq once again requests that a five-year grace period be set, during which no sum shall be deducted from its oil export earnings, in order that it may address the major problems strangling its economy and threatening the Iraqi people with hunger and disease. It also requests that objective account be taken of economic facts, without any political prejudice, when a percentage begins to be deducted after the grace period.

    I should be grateful if you would have this letter circulated as a document of the Security Council.

(Signed) Abdul Amir A. AL-ANBARI
              Ambassador
         Permanent Representative

-----

4 - 3

0085

Iraq Regains Important Niche in OPEC Even if Nation Can't Yet Export Its Oil

By James Tanner

Staff Reporter of The Wall Street Journal

Iraq can't yet export its oil, but it has regained an important niche among the oil exporters.

That is one of the chief results of last week's brief meeting of the Organization of Petroleum Exporting Countries, industry analysts suggested in the wake of the oil ministers' conference in Vienna.

"This meeting wasn't about the oil markets," said Vahan Zanoyan, senior director of Washington-based Petroleum Finance Co. "It was to settle some scores in OPEC's internal dynamics."

Iran was among those settling scores. Often treated as an outcast in the Arab-dominated exporters' group, Iran, as predicted, was able to strengthen its new middleman role in OPEC at the meeting. Its neutrality on the issue was the key to thwarting opposing moves by one group—Algeria, Nigeria and Libya—to reduce the OPEC production level and by another—Saudi Arabia and the United Arab Emirates—to raise the ceiling. As previously reported, the oil ministers resolved the output issue by agreeing to maintain it at 22.3 million barrels a day, the current ceiling, through September with the idea of taking a new look at it then.

But Iraq clearly emerged as the surprise of the meeting.

This was the first time Iraq has been represented at an OPEC meeting by an officially named oil minister since the Persian Gulf crisis began last August. The new minister is Osama Abdul Razzak Al-Hiti. He is 46 years old, a petroleum engineer and a graduate of Louisiana Polytechnic University.

Appointed as Iraq's oil minister a week before the meeting, Mr. Al-Hiti operated as a seasoned veteran of OPEC politics. He quickly shocked the others by blocking, if only for a few hours, what was expected to be a shoo-in reappointment of the popular Secretary-General Subroto to a second three-year term.

Mr. Al-Hiti also pressed aggressively for the other ministers to urge the United Nations to lift its sanctions against Iraq's oil exports. Some of the other ministers got the idea he was seeking a quid pro quo for his approval of the Subroto reappointment.

But he finally cast an approving vote for Mr. Subroto. That made the reappointment unanimous although it was delayed from the morning's agenda until late afternoon. Also, the Subroto debate pitted Iraq against Saudi Arabia, its foe in the Persian Gulf War.

Saudi Arabia's Hisham Nazer had nominated Mr. Subroto. And Mr. Al-Hiti's approval vote came only after the Saudi oil minister angrily denounced the Iraqi and threatened to lead a move to oust Ramzi Salman, former head of Iraq's State Oil Marketing Organization, as the recently appointed deputy secretary-general. Some suggested the Iraqi strategy was to keep Mr. Subroto out so that Mr. Salman could become acting secretary-general.

Mr. Salman retains his important spot. But Mr. Al-Hiti didn't succeed in his campaign to get OPEC to intercede in the U.N. on Iraq's behalf. The other ministers flatly refused to get involved. Some were infuriated, in fact. "The Iraqis are still acting like the victims instead of the aggressors" in the Persian Gulf War, said the chief delegate of one OPEC member nation that had been neutral during the crisis.

Still, the Iraqi minister left his mark on OPEC. "He was saying: See Iraq as a credible member," said Petroleum Finance's Mr. Zanoyan, who was in Vienna to observe the meeting.

Others agreed that Mr. Al-Hiti took home several rewards. Most important, he was reassured by the other oil ministers that Iraq's former OPEC quota of 3.1 million barrels a day still rightfully belongs to it. Also, "OPEC isn't excluding the possibility that Iraqi exports could be resumed before its next meeting" in late September, reported the London-based Energy Compass.

4—4

외 무 부

종 별 :

번 호 : UNW-1548

일 시 : 91 0613 1800

수 신 : 장 관(국연,중동일)

발 신 : 주 유엔 대사

제 목 : 유엔이락 보상위원회 전문위원 추천요청

대:중동일 720-16549 (91.5.13)

연: UNW-1125,1302

1. 유엔 사무총장은 안보리결의 (692호)에 의거 설립된 표제 위원회의 전문위원(COMMISSIONERS) 후보 추천을 아국을 포함한 각국에 6.12자 공한으로 요청해온바, 동 공한을 별첨송부함.

2. 상기 전문위원은 재무, 법, 회계, 보험 및 환경피해 평가분야의 전문가로서 사무총장의 추천으로 집행이사회 (GC) 가 임명하며, 개인자격 (PERSONAL CAPACITY) 으로 활동하게됨.

3. 관련참고사항은 수시 추보위게임.

첨부:상기 사무총장 6.12자 공한: UNW(F)-259

끝

(대사 노창희-국장)

국기국   중아국 /차보

PAGE 1

91.06.14   09:33 WG

외신 1과 통제관

0087

UNITED NATIONS ⊕ NATIONS UNIES

POSTAL ADDRESS—ADRESSE POSTALE UNITED NATIONS. N.Y. 10017
CABLE ADDRESS—ADRESSE TELEGRAPHIQUE UNATIONS NEWYORK

REF.: LA 37.4.4 (b)

The Secretary-General of the United Nations presents his compliments to the Permanent Observer of the Republic of Korea to the United Nations and has the honour to refer to operative paragraph 3 of Security Council resolution 692 (1991) of 20 May 1991 by which the Security Council decided to establish the United Nations Compensation Fund and the United Nations Compensation Commission referred to in paragraph 18 of resolution 687 (1991), in accordance with section I of the Secretary-General's report (document S/22559 of 2 May 1991).

In accordance with Section I of the report, the principal organ of the Commission will be a 15-member Governing Council which will be assisted by a number of commissioners who will perform the tasks assigned to them by the Governing Council. The commissioners who will be experts in fields such as finance, law, accountancy, insurance and environmental damage assessment, will act in their personal capacity. They will be nominated by the Secretary-General and appointed by the Governing Council for specific tasks and terms.

In his report, the Secretary-General stated that in nominating the commissioners, due regard will be paid to the need for geographical representation, professional qualifications, experience and integrity. In order to facilitate the task of the Secretary-General in nominating the commissioners it seems advisable to establish a register of experts in various fields of interest for the work of the Commission. While the choice of the Secretary-General would, of course, not be limited to the register, he would certainly be helped if he might draw upon the register when nominating commissioners.

Annexes enclosed

JW-1548

첨부뭑

⊃-/

0088

UNITED NATIONS   NATIONS UNIES

-2-

The Secretary-General therefore invites His/Her Excellency's
Government to submit to him the names of persons having relevant
expertise who might be eligible to serve as commissioners. The
names should be accompanied by a curriculum vitae indicating place
of birth and nationality, the educational and professional
qualifications of the expert, professional experience, knowledge
of languages, and any other information that may be deemed of
particular relevance to the work of the Commission. The information
concerning professional qualifications and experience will be used
by the Secretary-General to establish a categorization within the
register. Experts whose names are placed on the register, should
they be nominated by the Secretary-General, will be required to
disclose any prior or actual relationship with Governments, foreign
corporations or individuals which might constitute a possible
conflict of interest. A copy of Security Council resolution
692 (1991) and of the Secretary-General's report is attached.

12 June 1991.

S. B.

౨-౨

0089

외 무 부

종 별 :

번 호 : UNW-1550   일 시 : 91 0613 1800

수 신 : 장 관(국연,중동일,기정)

발 신 : 주 유엔 대사

제 목 : 걸프사태(안보리)

  연: UNW-1542

  1. 이락의 휴전결의(687호) 이행조치

  가. 이락은 6.8.자 A.HUSSEIN 외상명의 서한을 안보리문서 (S/22689) 로 배포한바, 이락측의 휴전결의 이행과 관련한 제반조치를 설명하고 이러한 자국조치 실적을 안보리의 휴전결의이행 심사과정에서 감안해줄것을 요망하는 요지임.

  나. 또한 휴전결의 본문 32항과 관련 이락측은 자국의 반테러리즘 공약을 안보리에 6.11 자로 통보해옴. (S/22687)

  2. 이락남부사태

  이락은 연호 이란측주장 (이락 남부 무력탄 압임박)을 부인하는 한편, 이란의 대이락 내정 간섭저의를 비난하는 6.12자 안보리 문서를 배포하였음. (S/22699)

  3. 이락보상기금을 위한 이락 석유 수입공제상한선 문제

  안보리는 금 6.13 오후 비공식협의에서 본건토의 예정인바 동 토의동향은 추보위계임.

  첨부:1. 이락측 안보리문서

  2. CSM 기사: UNW(F)-260

  끝

  (대사 노창희-국장)

국기국 1차보 중아국 외정실 분석관 안기부

PAGE 1   91.06.14 09:35 WG

외신 1과 통제관

0090

IHW(FH)-269 10613
(국연.충동원.가점)   충5매

Annex

Identical letters dated 8 June 1991 from the Minister for Foreign Affairs of Iraq addressed respectively to the Secretary-General and the President of the Security Council

As you are well aware, the Iraqi Government accepted Security Council resolution 687 (1991) and gave notice of its acceptance in its letter of 6 April 1991 addressed to both the President of the Security Council and the Secretary-General. I should like on this occasion to confirm to you that the Iraqi Government has complied with the said resolution and adopted a positive attitude towards it ever since its adoption. Allow me to review for you the measures taken in this connection by the Government of Iraq.

1.   In connection with section A of the resolution, concerning demarcation of the boundary between Iraq and Kuwait, the Iraqi Government has appointed its representatives to the Boundary Demarcation Commission, which held its first session of meetings in New York from 23 to 24 May 1991. Iraq's representative participated actively, in a constructive and cooperative spirit, in the work of that session.

2.   In connection with section B of resolution 687 (1991), concerning deployment of the United Nations Iraq-Kuwait Observer Mission, the competent Iraqi authorities have received the Chief Military Observer, Major-General Günther Greindl, on several occasions in Baghdad since his appointment, together with his assistants. Agreement was reached at these meetings on all the requirements for the deployment of the Mission in the demilitarized zone established under the resolution, which came into effect on 9 May 1991.

Cooperation between the competent Iraqi authorities and the Observer Mission continues through the channels designated for that purpose between, respectively, the Iraqi Government, the Mission headquarters and the United Nations Secretariat.

3.   In connection with section C of the resolution, which calls for a series of undertakings to dispense with weapons of mass destruction and neither to use, develop, construct nor acquire any such weapons, Iraq has deposited the instrument whereby the Republic of Iraq ratifies the Convention on the Prohibition of the Development, Production and Stockpiling of Bacteriological (Biological) and Toxin Weapons and on Their Destruction, of 10 April 1972. Iraq has also affirmed its unconditional commitment to its obligations under the Geneva Protocol for the Prohibition of the Use in War of Asphyxiating, Poisonous or Other Gases, and of Bacteriological Methods of Warfare, signed at Geneva on 17 June 1925. In addition, the Iraqi Government has provided details of the locations, amounts and types of items relating to chemical weapons and ballistic missiles specified in the resolution and agreed to an inspection of the sites concerned, as laid down in the resolution.

/...

UNW-1550
첨부물

5-1

Iraq has also unconditionally undertaken not to use, develop, construct or acquire any of the items specified in the resolution. It has affirmed its obligations under the Treaty on the Non-Proliferation of Nuclear Weapons of 1 July 1968 and unconditionally agreed not to acquire or develop nuclear weapons or nuclear-weapons-usable material. Iraq informed the International Atomic Energy Agency (IAEA), in a letter dated 27 April 1991 from the Minister for Foreign Affairs, that it was prepared to cooperate with the Agency in implementing the provisions of the resolution: the letter was accompanied by tables providing information on Iraq's nuclear facilities. Iraq has also provided detailed information on the situation with regard to other weapons covered by the resolution to the Special Commission established to implement section C.

In a letter dated 17 May 1991, Iraq agreed to the proposals contained in the Secretary-General's letter of 6 May 1991 concerning the privileges and immunities of the Special Commission and its visiting teams.

The nuclear weapons inspection team visited Iraq from 14 to 22 May 1991. On 23 May 1991, IAEA issued a statement affirming that Iraq had cooperated fully and responded to all the requests submitted by the inspection team. A chemical weapons inspection team, accompanied by the Chairman of the Special Commission, is to visit Iraq from 9 to 15 June in order to begin its mission. Iraq has made all the necessary arrangements to ensure that the inspection team's mission is a success.

4. In connection with section D of the resolution, which relates to the return of Kuwaiti property, Mr. Richard Foran, Assistant Secretary-General and official responsible for coordinating the return of such property, visited Iraq twice during the month of May 1991. The competent Iraqi authorities expressed their readiness to hand over the Kuwaiti property of which Iraq had already notified the Secretariat of the United Nations. A Kuwaiti civilian aircraft was, in fact, handed over at Amman on 11 May 1991. Mr. Foran also undertook a wide-ranging field visit and saw for himself the gold, coins, banknotes, civilian aircraft, museum antiquities and books that will be returned to Kuwait immediately an agreement is reached establishing a location for the handing over, it being understood that it is this property whose handing over Mr. Foran has determined should have priority at the present stage. The same procedures will doubtless be applied to other Kuwaiti property.

5. In connection with sections E and F, which relate to compensation and the lifting of sanctions, no measures are required on the part of Iraq.

6. In connection with section G of the resolution, the competent Iraqi authorities have taken and are continuing to take measures to repatriate all Kuwaiti and third country nationals, and they have provided lists of their names and have facilitated the access of the delegation of the International Committee of the Red Cross (ICRC) in Baghdad to all such persons wherever detained. It should be mentioned that the number of those freed and repatriated has reached 6,366 (6,289 Kuwaitis, 36 Americans, 5 Italians,

/...

5-2

0092

13 Saudis, 17 Frenchmen, 1 Spaniard, 2 Brazilians, 1 Norwegian, 1 Uruguayan and 1 Irishman). The competent Iraqi authorities are still diligently searching for missing subjects of coalition countries with a view to finding them and repatriating them following registration by the ICRC delegation. The competent Iraqi authorities have directly facilitated all matters relating to the work of the ICRC delegation in the registration of Kuwaiti nationals present in Iraq, thereby enabling the delegation to register more than 3,000 Kuwaitis, and they have endeavoured to return the remains of 15 subjects of the coalition countries.

7.   In connection with section H, which relates to international terrorism, it should be mentioned that Iraq is a party to the international conventions relating to numerous aspects of this matter and that it abides by the obligations set forth therein. Iraq has not supported any terrorist activities.

In providing you with these clarifications, we are prompted by the hope that you will deem it appropriate to take account of the facts set forth above in any review that the Security Council might intend to make of Iraq's position on the implementation of Security Council resolution 687 (1991).

(Signed) Ahmed HUSSEIN
Minister for Foreign Affairs
of the Republic of Iraq

5-3

0093

Iraqis protest demands as Western members complain of lax compliance with cease-fire

By Marion Houk
Special to The Christian Science Monitor

UNITED NATIONS, N.Y.

THE United Nations Security Council kept the pressure on Saddam Hussein's government in its first periodic review of economic sanctions imposed on Iraq.

But several "nonaligned" council members argued in a meeting Tuesday that political and legal positions should be tempered by moral considerations. Particular concern was expressed for Iraq's children.

Yemeni Ambassador Abdullah al-Ashtal said there was "an evolving consensus that something must be done – not lifting the [sanctions altogether ... but] only a limited lifting." He suggested a limited sale of oil would enable Iraq to buy milk powder and other essentials.

But United States and British diplomats linked the sanctions to the tenacity of Iraq's leadership.

"Saddam Hussein is singularly unlikely to comply fully with the [cease-fire] terms of Resolution 687, and that could lead you to the view, therefore, that the lifting of sanctions is a remote matter," Sir David Hannay, Britain's ambassador, told journalists.

In Tuesday's closed-door session, Western diplomats charged that Iraq has still not complied with the UN's cease-fire terms in several ways. They cited:

☐ The continued detention of nearly 3,000 Kuwaitis and holding of billions of dollars of stolen Kuwaiti property.

☐ Inadequate disclosure of Iraq's internally held assets.

☐ Inadequate disclosure of its weapons of mass destruction.

☐ Recent public comments by Iraqi Vice President Taha Yassin Ramadan restating Iraq's claim to Kuwait.

☐ The summary trials and life sentences handed down to two British businessmen. (UN resolutions had ordered Iraq to release all third-country nationals.)

☐ The absence of any commitment to renouncing terrorism. (After Tuesday's meeting, Iraq's UN mission supplied a letter declaring its rejection of terrorism.)

Western delegates also said Baghdad hadn't done much to reassure civilians in the Kurdish north and Shiite south – or to guarantee the return of those who fled the postwar crackdown.

Kamal Kharrazi, the Iranian ambassador to the UN, circulated a letter citing "credible evidence that the Iraqi Army is preparing for a general mopping-up operation in the south and southeast where close to 700,000 Iraqi citizens are contained." It warned that Iran "is absolutely unable, with or without international hu-

manitarian assistance, to attend to the needs of another influx of Iraqi refugees."

French sources cited as positive developments Iraq's cooperation in establishing a six-mile demilitarized zone along the Iraqi-Kuwaiti border, and in nominating a representative to the boundary demarcation commission. Samir al-Nima, Iraq's chargé d'affaires here, said Iraq had "complied fully with whatever was required to meet our obligations as stated by Resolution 687." He contested the right of the US and Britain to decide the sanctions issue, and called on the UN Secretariat to issue an objective report on Iraq's cease-fire compliance.

"We believe Iraq has not been treated fairly," he said, citing recent news-media reports that predict Iraq faces "an imminent disaster unless some step is taken to alleviate the hardship."

UN Secretary-General Javier Pérez de Cuéllar said in late May that no more than 30 percent of Iraq's income should go to the payment of war reparations. The UN chief said he set the figure on the basis of Iraq's estimate that it should be able to resume oil exports at its prewar level by 1993.

Mr. Pérez de Cuéllar projected Iraq's income then would be $21 billion, if oil prices remain steady.

Of that amount, he said, 48 percent would go for necessary imports, and 22 percent to service a foreign debt of $42 billion.

Arab diplomats say that without investment funds, Iraq's economy cannot recover. More important, they say, the proposal does not set a cap on Iraq's liability for war damages – and therefore does not limit the number of years Iraq would be required to pay 30 percent of its oil income.

The US State Department has called for a levy of 50 percent, and British sources say 30 percent is the lowest acceptable figure. But France, the Soviet Union, and China say 30 percent is high.

Rising Demand for Oil May Spell End of Iraq Embargo

By Thomas Stauffer

— VIENNA —

THE United States faces a Catch-22 dilemma: Iraqi oil may be needed by the end of the year to dampen price increases.

Ironically, the healthier the world economy, the more quickly Iraqi exports will be seen as indispensable, and the US lifted Iraqi oil ostensibly to protect oil consumers, the US may have to allow Iraqi exports in order to protect those same oil consumers.

If the Organization of Petroleum Exporting Countries is correct in its newest calculations, consumers should expect higher oil prices again this year – despite the fact that last week's one-day ministerial meeting in Vienna revealed only deepened divisions and failed to address either pricing or production policy.

"We are trusting to the 'invisible hand' this time," explained Gonzalo Plaza, chairman of OPEC's board of governors. "Thanks to the war, the market is very tight, so we don't need to intervene."

Oil prices have sunk back to prewar lows. Nonetheless, consumers must be wary because the oil industry expects prices to bounce back. There is near consensus that a 20 to 25 percent increase is possible – adding $250 million a day to the world's oil bill.

But OPEC's new optimism is born of not weakness, strength. A "hands-on policy" to control production was not even attempted, because efforts to cut back output by lowering quotas founders on irreconcilable political differences, painfully aggravated by the Gulf war.

Saudi Arabia refuses to intervene. The minister of petroleum, Hisham Muhyi al-Din Nazir, stated categorically, albeit disingenuously, that the kingdom believes in market forces and will not "manipulate" supply. Algeria, reflecting broad concerns, protested that it was almost criminal to sell oil at such distress prices, but was ignored.

Ironically, it is the Gulf war that dealt OPEC its trump cards. The war weakened OPEC politically, rendering any effort to cut production to bolster prices very difficult. It also worsened the recessionary trend that trimmed oil demand.

But the war actually bolstered OPEC's bargaining position. World oil supply is now precariously balanced: without Kuwaiti and Iraqi production, there is no spare capacity.

OPEC reckons that a modest economic recovery will add 1 million to 1.5 million barrels per day (b.p.d.) to world demand, sopping up the small surplus and absorbing the modest extra inventories. OPEC's calculations are supported by the latest market assessment from the International Energy Agency in Paris, a fact that is significant because the IEA has long been suspected of forecasts designed to soften prices and weaken OPEC.

Other signs corroborate OPEC's new confidence in the "invisible hand." Con-sumers are holding excess inventories, indicating that they, too, expect prices to firm. Indeed, the real fear is that prices will rise too far. Saudi Arabia has increased output again to rebuild stocks overseas – precisely to ensure against a possible shortage and price speculation.

The wild card is production from Iraq and Kuwait. At best, Kuwait will produce 200,000 b.p.d. by the end of the year, largely from the Japanese-controlled off-shore concession; its brethren in the Gulf Cooperation Council last week categorically refused to advance or "loan" crude oil to Kuwait from their own production, citing the possible shortfall.

While Kuwait's production is limited by war damage, Iraq is politically constrained. It could quickly export up to 1 million b.p.d., in spite of massive damage, but is totally dependent on US willingness to lift the boycott, and then on Saudi Arabia to open the southern pipelines.

■ *Thomas Stauffer is a professorial lecturer, Johns Hopkins University, Baltimore, Md.*

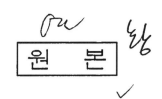

외 무 부

종 별 :

번 호 : UNW-1555　　　　　　　　　　일 시 : 91 0614 1640

수 신 : 장 관 (국연,중동일,기정)

발 신 : 주 유엔 대사

제 목 : 걸프사태 (안보리)

　　　　연: UNW-1550

　　1. 이락 석유수입 공제 상한선 문제

　　안보리는 6.13. 비공식 협의에서 본건 상한선 (사무총장안 30 퍼센트) 문제를 토의한바, 다음과같이 이사국들이 이견을 보임에 따라 이와관련 안보리 의장 (코트디브아르)이 각이사국들과 개별협의를 가질 예정이라고 함.

　　1) 미국 50 퍼센트, 영국, 루마니아 30 퍼센트 이상 (단, 구체적 숫자는 미제시), 불란서 30 퍼센트 이하검토 시사

　　2) 벨지움, 에쿠아돌, 오지리, 짐바붸, 자이르등 30퍼센트

　　3) 소련 25 퍼센트, 중국, 쿠바 30 퍼센트 이하 (숫자미제시)

　　4) 예멘 10 퍼센트

　　2. 이락 남부 사태

　　독일 겐셔 외상은 6.13.자 사무총장앞 서한에서 이락 당국의 남부 주민 탄압으로 난민 대이동 사태위험이 있음을 지적하면서 이와관련 사무총장의 남이락내 유엔인도 지원센타 (HUMANITARIANCENTRES) 설치구상에 지지를 표명하였음.(S/22701)

　　3. 이락의 휴전결의 이행 여부 논의

　　쿠웨이트측은 이락이 안보리의 관련 결의들을 이행하지 않고 있다고 주장하는 안보리문서 (S/22702) 를 배포한바, 특히 포로 및 인질의 계속억류 (3,800명), 쿠웨이트 재산 미반환, 쿠웨이트병합 무효화 의문등의 사례를 제기하였음. 끝

　　(대사 노창희-국장)

국기국　　1차보　　중아국　　외정실　　분석관　　안기부

PAGE 1　　　　　　　　　　　　　　　　　91.06.15　　10:01 WG

　　　　　　　　　　　　　　　　　　　外신 1과 통제관

　　　　　　　　　　　　　　　　　　　0096

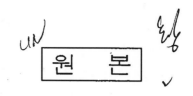

외 무 부

종   별 :

번   호 : UNW-1575 일   시 : 91 0618 1900

수   신 : 장 관(국연,중동일,법규,기정)

발   신 : 주 유엔 대사

제   목 : 안보리협의 (이락보상문제)

1. 안보리는 금 6.18 비공식협의를 갖고, 유엔이락보상위원회 이사회 (GC) 1 차회의 준비문제를 토의한바, 당관에서 파악한 동토의 주요결과는 다음과같음.

가. 이사회 1차회의 (제네바)개최시기: 91.7월(7월상반기 거론)

나. 이사회 의장단 구성: 의장국은 벨지움,부의장2명

다. 1차회의 의제(안)

1) 이사회 작업계획

2) 이사회 의사규칙

3) 국별 청구통합을 위한 요강

4) 이락 석유수입 공제수준 (단, 동 공제상한선은안보리가 결정)

5) 청구범위 기준설정

6) 이락석유 수입 공제절차

7) 전문위원 (COMMISSIONERS) 임명

8) 추진일정

9) 중장기 업무검토

라. 상기외에도 각 안보리이사국의 본건이사회 (GC)대표조기 임명, 이사회 사무국설치 (사무국장임명포함) 문제, 7월1차회의 (비교적 짧은 조직회의)후 9월회의 (실질문제 토의) 개최전망도 거론되었다고함. 반면 이락보상 문제관련 주요현안인 이락석유 수입 공제상한선 문제는 금일 토의되지 않은것으로 알려짐.

2. 안보리는 상기 의제 (안) 문제관련 추후재협의 예정이라고 하는바, 협의동향 추보 위계임.

3. 유엔사무국 R.ZACKLIN 담당관에 문의한바, 각국의 전문위원 (COMMISSIONERS) 후보추천 (UNW-1548) 시한은 없으나, 앞으로 두달안에하는것이 바람직하다는 반응임. (

국기국   1차보   중아국   국기국   외정실   분석관   정와대   안기부

PAGE 1

금일 현재 추천국은 한나라)끝
(대사 노창희-국장)

관리번호 91/1183

외 무 부

종 별 :

번 호 : UNW-1600   일 시 : 91 0620 1840

수 신 : 장관(중동일,법규,국연)

발 신 : 주 유엔 대사

제 목 : 이락보상청구 문제

연:UNW-0557,1575, 주국련 20313-484

1. 금 6.20 당관 원참사관은 연호 J.JANNUZZO 변호사 (COUDERT BROTHERS 법률사무소)와 동인 요청으로 접촉한바, 다음요지 언급함.

가. 이락 보상청구 대행 문제에 관심이 있는 여러 국제법률사무소 관계자들이 지난주 파리에서 회합을 가진바, 앞으로 유엔 이락보상위가 본건 보상대상 청구범위 지침을 정하기에 따라서는 COMMERCIAL CLAIMS (건설, 수출분야 계약예시)포함여부 내지 동 보상범위 전망이 불투명하다는 우려가 제기됨.

나. 보상위의 지침 마련전에 관련국들과 협조하여 상기 COMMERCIAL CLAIMS 를 어느정도 파악(6 월말 SURVEY 마감), 보상위측에 문제를 조기 제기함으로서 동 지침에 반영되도록 추진하는것이 효과적이겠다는 논의가 있었음.

다. 이와관련 가능하다면 아국의 자료협조(관련기업 업종, 동 피해의 규모및 발생시기)요망하며, 아측과 계속 협력희망함.

2. 연호 보고와 같이 보상대상 청구 범위지침(GUIDELINES REGARDING WHAT CONSTITUTES DIRECT LOSS, DAMAGE OR INJURY WITHIN THE MEANING OF PARAGRAPH 16 OF RESOLUTION 687) 문제는 오는 7 월 보상위 집행이사회(GC) 첫회의 의제(안)의 하나라 검토되고있으나 동 지침합의는 상당한 협의와 시일을 요할것으로보이는바, 상기 1 항 사항은 일단 참고로하되 유엔보상위의 향후 동향을 보아가면서 필요시 검토하는것이 좋을것으로 사료됨.

3. 한편 원참사관이 유엔법률국 R.ZACKLIN 국장에게 상기지침 작업전망에 관하여 문의한바, 동인은 7 월 집행이사회 조직회의에서는 담당 전문위원을 지정, 동 위원에게 지침검토 작업을 맡기고 동 작업 결과를 9 월 실질회의에서 토의하는 방안을 상정해 볼수있다고 말함.

중아국	장관	차관	국기국	국기국	분석관	청와대	안기부

PAGE 1

91.06.21   09:00

외신 2과   통제관 FE

0089

③ 당관 참고를위해 아국본건 피해유형및 내용개요, 향후 청구에 대비한 관련조치
현황및 계획을 알려주시기 바람.

4. 표제 관련 미국지방법원 판례(CONSARC 회사)및 이에대한 미행정부 입장에 관한
6.19 자 WSJ, WP 지 기사를 별전 송부함. 끝

(대사 노창희-국장)

예고:91.12.31. 까지

91. 6. 30.

PAGE 2

0100

외 무 부

종 별 :

번 호 : UNW-1603

일 시 : 91 0620 1945

수 신 : 장 관(중동일,법규,국연)

발 신 : 주 유엔 대사

제 목 : 이락 보상청구문제

표제관련 6.19 자 WSJ 및 WP 지 기사를 별첨송부함.

첨부:상기기사: UNW(F)-272

끝

(대사 노창희-국장)

중아국	1차보	국기국	국기국	외정실	안기부

PAGE 1

91.06.21   10:00 WG

외신 1과 통제관

0101

U.S. Seeks to Vacate Ruling on Iraq

Damage Award Said to Conflict With Administration's Plan

By Tracy Thompson
Washington Post Staff Writer

The Justice Department wants to vacate a federal judge's decision awarding $64.1 million in damages from the government of Iraq to a New Jersey firm that sold Iraq several blast furnaces, saying payment would conflict with the Bush administration's plan to process war claims.

The Justice Department made that argument in a brief filed Monday in federal court here in connection with a breach of contract case between Iraq and Consarc Inc. over four blast furnaces that Iraq reportedly planned to use to make nuclear weapons.

Last April, U.S. District Judge Stanley Sporkin awarded Consarc $64.1 million in compensatory and punitive damages after shipment of

the blast furnaces was halted at the docks in Philadelphia on June 27, 1990, by the Department of Defense.

Sporkin based the ruling on his conclusion that Iraq had lied to Consarc about the intended use of the furnaces, telling the firm they would be used for research and manufacture of artificial limbs for veterans of the Iran-Iraq war. Defense Department intelligence, however, indicated Iraq had a more lethal use in mind: melting uranium and zirconium, which are used in nuclear reactors and weapons.

The Justice Department's brief argued that by allowing Consarc to collect on the judge's ruling, the company would in effect go to the head of the line of creditors against Iraq, and this would harm the administration's power to enforce the economic sanctions imposed after

Iraq's invasion of Kuwait last August.

Allowing Consarc to collect the damages, the brief said, "is likely to undermine important foreign policy objectives of the United States concerning the orderly resolution of all U.S. nationals' claims against Iraq in a prompt and equitable manner" through U.S. and U.N. claims proceedings.

Raymon Marks, an attorney for Consarc, said his client had complied with U.S. export control laws in negotiating the sales contract with Iraq and was a victim of the Iraqi government's deception.

"We are very disappointed that the U.S. government has elected to take Iraq's position against a small U.S. company that did everything in its power to further the administration's export control policies," Marks said yesterday.

Consarc Judgment Opposed By the U.S. in Iraqi Case

By a WALL STREET JOURNAL Staff Reporter

WASHINGTON—The Bush administration asked a federal court here to vacate a $64.1 million judgment in favor of a U.S. company, saying the ruling would disrupt administration efforts to settle other U.S. claims against Iraq.

The action snarls Consarc Corp.'s effort to recover $9.1 million in lost business and receive $55 million in punitive damages from Iraq's Ministry of Industry and Minerals. The company says Iraq misrepresented the purpose of its order for industrial furnaces. The U.S. government canceled the order just before Iraq invaded Kuwait last August.

In April, federal Judge Stanley Sporkin in Washington awarded these amounts to the Rancocas, N.J., engineering company in the absence of any opposition from either Iraq or the U.S. However, a Justice Department brief filed this week says the U.S. is contesting the judgment on technical and foreign-policy grounds.

The brief says that the judgment unintentionally contravenes Treasury Department regulations and undermines the U.S. objective of establishing international procedures for settling claims arising from the Persian Gulf War.

Raymond Marks, a lawyer for Consarc, said the company "has acted totally and completely in compliance" with federal regulations and will vigorously oppose the U.S. action. Nevertheless, the action is likely to discourage other potential claimants from going to court at this stage.

0102

28502

분류번호 문서번호	중동일 720-	기안용지 (720-2327)	시 행 상 특별취급	
보존기간	영구.준영구 10. 5. 3. 1	장 관		
수 신 처 보존기간				
시행일자	1991. 6. 21.	예		

보존 기관	국 장	전 결	협 조 기 관	국제기구조약국장	분산통 제
	심의관				1991. 6. 22
	과 장				
기간책임자		조 태 용			발송인 1991. 6. 22 외무부

경 유			
수 신	수신처 참조	발신명의	
참 조			

| 제 목 | 걸프사태 관련 피해 보상 |

연 : 중동일 720-21759(91.5.10)

1. 유엔 사무총장은 91.5.20.자 안전보장 이사회 결의 692호에 의거

    설립된 유엔보상위원회 (UN compensation Commission)의 전문위원

    (commissioner) 후보 추천을 아국을 포함한 각국에 대하여 6.12.

    공한으로 요청하여 왔는바, 아래 사항을 참조, 소관 분야별로 적절

    한 후보자 1,2명을 선정, 7.20.까지 회보하여 주시기 바랍니다.

/ 계 속 . . . .

0103

- 아 래 -
가. 선정분야 : 재정, 법률, 회계, 보험, 환경피해 사정등
※ 재정, 회계, 보험(재무부, 건설부), 환경피해 사정
(환경처)
나. 전문위원 임명 절차 : 각국의 추천을 받아 유엔 사무
총장이 지명하며, ⓑ상위원회 집행 이사회에서 임명
다. 전문위원의 역할 : ⓑ상위원회의 요청을 받아, 3명이
1조로 각국의 피해보상 청구의 실무 검토 담당
라. 구비 서류 : 이력서(생년월일, 출생지, 국적, 학력,
경력, 어학 능력등)
※ 각국정부, 외국회사, 개인을 위해 일한 경험이 있는
경우는 반드시 사전에 밝혀야 함.
마. 추천기한 : 유엔측은 늦어도 8월 중순까지 추천 요망
바. 기타 활동비등 조건 : 아직 확정되지는 않았으나 주로
제네바(보상위원회 소재지)에서 활동하게 될것으로 보이며,
업무가 있을때 제네바로 출장을 가게됨(제네바 상주는
아님.) 고정 보수는 없으나 항공료, 체재비등은 유엔측
에서 지급하게 될것으로 예상됨. ／ 계 속 . . . .

0104

2. 상기와 관련, 아국도 쿠웨이트내 교민과 건설회사 재산피해등 손해

　　보상을 청구할 계획이며, 전문위원의 역할이 중요함을 감안 후보

　　선정시 유의하여 주시기 바랍니다.

3. 손해 보상 청구 범위등 아국의 보상청구에 필요한 세부사항은 7월

　　제네바에서 개최될 유엔 보상위원회 집행이사회에서 결정될 것으로

　　보이는바, 세부사항이 확정되는대로 유관 부처에 통보예정입니다.

첨　부 : 유엔 사무총장 공한 사본 1부.　끝.

수신처 : 재무부, 건설부, 환경처장관 (사본 상공부장관)

0105

관리 번호	91 -651

외 무 부

종 별 :

번 호 : UNW-1625

일 시 : 91 0624 1830

수 신 : 장관(국연,중동일)

발 신 : 주 유엔 대사

제 목 : 이락 보상기금(이락 석유수입공제 상한선문제)

연:UNW-1555

1. 당관에서 탐문한바에 의하면, 본건 상한선 을 사무총장안대로 30 프로로하는 방향으로 다수 이사국들간의 의견이 접근되고 있으며, 당초 50 프로안을 제시해온 미국도 유엔이락 보상위 집행이사회(GC)가 실제 공제수준을 정할때 30 프로에 가깝게 정한다는 양해하에 30 프로 상한선을 받아들이는 방안을 적극 검토하고있는것으로 알려짐.

2. 상기 집행이사회(GC)에서의 제반결정은 단순 9 개국 찬성방식(거부권 부적용)으로 이루어질것이라고 함.(영대표부 A.MILSON 서기관)

3. 관련 동향 추보위계임.끝

(대사 노창희-국장)

예고:1991.12.31.서까지

첨부딜(1991.6.30.)

국기국   1차보   2차보   중아국   외정실   안기부

PAGE 1

91.06.25   08:57

외신 2과 통제관 CH

0106

외 무 부

종   별 :

번   호 : UNW-1692   일   시 : 91 0701 1800

수   신 : 장 관 (중동일,법규,국연)

발   신 : 주 유엔대사

제   목 : 이락 보상문제

연: UNW-1575

1. 안보리 이사국들은 연호 유엔 이락보상위이사회 (GC) 회의 의제에 관해 계속내부협의 중인 바, 당관에서 입수한 동주석의제(안)을 별첨 송부함.

2. 상기 이사회 첫회의는 7월 하반기에나 개최 가능할것 이라는 관측인 바, 관련사항 수시보고위계임. 끝

(대사 노창희-국장)

첨부: FAX (UNW(F)-298)

중아국   1차보   국기국   국기국   외정실   안기부

UNW(가)-29.8 . 1070l 1800   첨부로 UNW-1692
                                                              총 4매

ANNOTATED PROVISIONAL AGENDA FOR THE FIRST MEETING
OF THE GOVERNING COUNCIL
OF THE UNITED NATIONS COMPENSATION COMMISSION

(중동일. 법규. 주연)

1.   Opening of the meeting.

2.   Election of the President.

3.   Adoption of the Agenda.
     [The agenda was provisionally agreed to in informal
     consultations of the Security Council].

4.   Rules of procedure of the Governing Council.
     [By its resolution 692 (1991) the Security Council decided
     to establish the Fund and the Commission referred to in
     paragraph 18 of resolution 687 (1991) in accordance with
     Section I of the Secretary-General's report pursuant to
     paragraph 19 of Security Council resolution 687 (1991)
     (S/22559) (hereafter the Secretary-General's report).
     Paragraph 10 of the Secretary-General's report provides that
     decisions of the Governing Council on the method of ensuring
     that payments are made to the Fund should be taken by
     consensus. Other decisions should be taken by a majority of
     at least nine of its members. No veto will apply in the
     Governing Council. The Governing Council may invite States
     that it considers to have a particular interest in its work
     to participate without a vote in its discussion. The
     Governing Council will, on behalf of the Commission, report
     periodically to the Security Council.
     The Secretariat has received letters by which some Members
     of the Governing Council have communicated the names of
     their representatives.].

5.   Election of the Bureau.
     [It is the normal practice of subsidiary bodies of the
     Security Council to elect two vice-chairpersons].

6.   Organization of work of the Governing Council.

4 - 1

0108

2

[A paper on the organization of work will be prepared by the Secretariat].

7. Recommendations of the Governing Council on the procedures
    to be established at the national level in respect of the
    presentation of claims to the Commission.
    [The Governing Council has been directed by paragraph 5 of
    resolution 692 (1991) to implement the provisions of section
    E of resolution 687 (1991), taking into account the
    recommendations in section II of the Secretary-General's
    report. The Secretary-General's report states, inter alia,
    that the Commission should entertain, as a general rule,
    only consolidated claims filed by individual Governments on
    their own behalf or on behalf of their nationals and
    corporations (paragraph 21 of the Secretary-General's
    report). The Governing Council may also wish to establish a
    categorization of claims according to both type and size
    which States would be requested to use when filing their
    consolidated claims (paragraphs 23 and 24 of the Secretary-
    General's report). Paragraph 24 of the Secretary-General's
    report recommends that the Governing Council establish a
    time period for the filing of claims].

8. Level of Iraq's contribution to the Fund.
    [The Governing Council has been requested by paragraph 7 of
    resolution 692 (1991) to report to the Security Council as
    soon as possible on the actions it has taken with regard to
    the mechanisms for determining the appropriate level of
    Iraq's contribution to the Fund, in order for the Council to
    give its approval in accordance with paragraph 22 of
    resolution 687 (1991). The percentage should not exceed the
    level of ..., as provided for by resolution ...].

9. Establishment of guidelines regarding what constitutes
    direct loss, damage or injury within the meaning of
    paragraph 16 of resolution 687 (1991).

4-2

0109

3

[The Governing Council has been directed by paragraph 5 of resolution 692 (1991) to implement the provisions of section E of resolution 687 (1991), taking into account the recommendations in section II of the Secretary-General's report. The Secretary-General's report recommends, _inter_ _alia_, that the Governing Council establish detailed guidelines regarding what constitutes such direct losses for the guidance of all claimants as well as the commissioners (paragraph 25 of the Secretary-General's report)].

10. Arrangements for ensuring that payments are made to the Fund.

[As the Secretary-General stated in paragraph.16 of the Secretary-General's report, the legal basis for the payments by Iraq to the Fund is to be found in paragraph 19 of resolution 687 (1991). Iraq has officially notified the United Nations of its acceptance of the provisions of the resolution, including paragraph 19.

Paragraph 17 of the Secretary-General's report lists several options for ensuring that Iraq makes payments to the Fund, which include the following:

(a) Iraq would pay to the Fund the established percentage of the market value of its exports of petroleum and petroleum products;

(b) An escrow account would be opened for the deposit by Iraq of advance payments of lump sums;

(c) A physical share of the exports would be taken;

(d) The Fund would be designated as sole or co-beneficiary on title documents and any letter of credit issued;

(e) An escrow account would be designated as beneficiary on title documents and any letter of credit issued].

11. Establishment of the time-frames for the execution of each of these tasks.

12. Overview of other tasks to be dealt with by the Governing Council not immediately, but at a later stage.

4-3

0110

4

13.   Decision whether some of the activities of the Commission
       should be carried out outside of Geneva.
       [Paragraph 3 of resolution 692 (1991) provides that the
       Governing Council may decide whether some of the activities
       of the Commission should take place outside of Geneva].

14.   Other matters.

4-4

외 무 부

종 별 :

번 호 : UNW-1818   일 시 : 91 0712 1830

수 신 : 장 관(국연,중동일,법규)

발 신 : 주 유엔 대사

제 목 : 이락 보상문제

연: UNW-1692

1. 당관 원참사관은 금 7.12 연호 이락 보상위 집행이사회 회의관련 유엔법률국 R.ZACKLIN 국장과 접촉한바, 동인은 7.10 안보리 비공식 협의에서 회의기간이 일단 길게결정 (7.23-8.2.제네바) 되었으나 실질통의를 위한 여건이 충분히 마련되지 않아 실제기간은 단축될 가능성이 있다고 언급함.

2. 본건 보상위 사무국장 (EXECUTIVE SECRETARY)인선을 위해 유엔사무총장은 다음 주안보리 이사국들과 협의를 가질 것으로 보인다고함. (유엔가 주변에서는 G.SCHLITTLER 국장도 동후보로 거명되고 있음.)각국의 보상위전문위원 (COMMISSIONERS) 후보 추천은 부진한 것으로 알려짐.

3. 연호 집행이사회 의제(안)은 현재 그대로임.

4. 관련동향 수시 보고위계임.끝

(대사 노창희-국장)

국기국   1차보   중아국   국기국   외정실   안기부

United Nations

Press Release

Department of Public Information • News Coverage Service • New York

IK/39
24 July 1991

UNITED NATIONS COMPENSATION COMMISSION GOVERNING COUNCIL
OPENS FIRST SESSION AT GENEVA

GENEVA, 23 July (UN Information Service) -- Methods for administering the Fund from which compensation will be made for losses caused by Iraq's unlawful occupation of Kuwait will be determined by the Governing Council of the United Nations Compensation Commission, which held its first meeting at the Palais des Nations this afternoon.

The Council, which is composed of representatives of the current 15 members of the Security Council, is the principal organ of the Commission. It was established under Security Council resolutions 687 and 692 (1991) to determine the appropriate level of Iraq's contribution to the Fund, to establish guidelines regarding what constitutes direct loss, damage or injury and to propose arrangements for ensuring that payments are made to the Fund. The Council will meet, primarily in closed sessions, until 2 August.

In an opening statement, Carl-August Fleischhauer, Under-Secretary-General for Legal Affairs, said the Commission would have to chart new territory in carrying out its tasks. The direct losses and damages arising from Iraq's unlawful invasion and occupation of Kuwait were still occurring and hundreds of thousands of people, as well as Governments and corporations, were suffering.

Also this afternoon, the Council elected Philippe Berg (Belgium) President by consensus and adopted its provisional agenda. Mr. Berg said the creation of the Commission constituted a first in United Nations history. It would set up the mechanism and structures for a path to follow in future.

Governing Council Work Programme

The Governing Council had before it its annotated provisional agenda for the work of its first session. That document recalls Security Council resolution 687 (1991), which had reaffirmed Iraq's liability under international law for any direct loss, damage or injury resulting from its unlawful invasion and occupation of Kuwait. The Council had also decided to create a fund to pay compensation for claims arising from those actions, and to establish a Commission to administer the fund. The resolution further

(more)

3786P

0113

directed the Secretary-General to develop and present to the Council
recommendations for the fund to meet the requirements for the payment of
claims and for a programme to implement the decisions of the resolution,
including administration of the fund and mechanisms for determining the
appropriate level of Iraq's contribution to it.

By its resolution 692 (1991), the Security Council decided to establish
the Fund and the Commission referred to in resolution 687 (1991), which will
be examined by the Governing Council during consideration of its rules of
procedure. The report provides that the Governing Council's decisions on the
method of ensuring that payments are made to the Fund should be taken by
consensus. Other decisions should be taken by a majority of its 15 members.
No veto will apply in the Governing Council.

As to the procedures to be established at the national level for
presenting claims to the Commission, the Commission should as a general rule
entertain only consolidated claims filed by individual Governments on their
own behalf or on behalf of their nationals and corporations, according to a
report of the Secretary-General on the subject. Resolution 687 calls on the
Governing Council to report to the Security Council on action taken to
determine the level of Iraq's contribution to the Fund. In a note, the
Secretary-General suggests that compensation to be paid by Iraq should not
exceed 30 per cent of the annual value of its exports of petroleum and
petroleum products.

In his report, the Secretary-General lists several options for ensuring
that Iraq makes payments to the Fund, including the following: Iraq would pay
to the Fund the established percentage of the market value of its exports of
petroleum and petroleum products; an escrow account would be opened for the
deposit by Iraq of advance payments of lump sums; a physical share of the
exports would be taken; the fund would be designated as sole or co-beneficiary
on title documents and any letter of credit issued; or an escrow account would
be designated as beneficiary.

Statement by Legal Counsel

CARL-AUGUST FLEISCHHAUER, Under-Secretary-General for Legal Affairs and
Representative of the Secretary-General to the Governing Council, said that
the Council was no ordinary body and had no ordinary task. In the history of
the United Nations, there was no precedent for the Security Council
resolutions by which the Governing Council was established. Indeed, those
resolutions had been adopted in the aftermath of the armed enforcement action
authorized by the Security Council with the objective of restoring
international peace and security, but the Charter did not contain specific
provisions on how to do so. The Security Council therefore had to chart new
territory and the United Nations Compensation Commission would in many
respects have to do the same.

He said the principal task of the Commission was to administer the Fund
from which compensation would be made for claims arising out of direct losses,
damage, including environmental damage and the depletion of natural resources,

(more)   0114

3786P

or injury to foreign Governments, nationals and corporations, as a result of
Iraq's unlawful invasion and occupation of Kuwait. Those direct losses and
damages were still occurring; scarce natural resources which were set on fire
were burning, causing immense damage and immeasurable risks to the
environment, as well as accumulating financial losses to the people and State
of Kuwait.

        But it was not, by any means, only Governments and corporations that had
suffered the direct losses and damages resulting from the unlawful occupation
of Kuwait, he continued. Hundreds of thousands of ordinary people had also
been severely victimized -- not only the ordinary people in Kuwait itself, but
also the enormous numbers of foreign workers who had lost their jobs, lodgings
and often all their belongings. Compelled to leave the Gulf area, they
constituted a social and economic burden for their countries of origin, which
had also lost the additional income they once received through the remittances
sent home by their nationals. The Governing Council should bear that
particular humanitarian aspect of its task in mind when setting the priorities
of its work.

                              * *** *

외 무 부

종 별 :

번 호 : UNW-1970　　　　　　　　　　　일 시 : 91 0730 2000

수 신 : 장 관 (국연,중동일,국기,기정)

발 신 : 주 유엔 대사

제 목 : 안보리동향(비공식협의)

연: UNW-1953

　　1. 안보리는 금 7.30 오후 비공식협의를 개최한바, 당관에서 탐문한 금일협의 주요결과를 아래보고함.

　　가. 이락 핵사찰

　　1) H.BLIX IAEA 사무총장, R.EKEUS 이락 군비통제특위의장으로 부터 핵사찰 (제3진 사찰결과) 및 여타 대량 파괴무기 폐기 현황을 청취함.

　　2) 화학무기는 당초 이락이 제출한 현황보다 다량보유한 것으로 나타나고 있으며, 생물무기 조사반을 8월초 이락파견 예정이라고함. 탄도미사일 관련재확인을 위한 조사반은 9월 파견계획중임.

　　3) BLIX 총장은 이락 핵개발이 평화적 목적을 위한 것으로 보기 어렵다는 강한 의구를 표시한 것으로 알려짐.

　　나. 유엔 안보리 평화유지군 (UNIFIL) 임무기간연장

　　1) 7.31 안보리 공식회의에서 동 임무기간 연장을 위한 안보리 결의 채택예정 (동결의와 별도로 레바논 당국의 남부지역 관할권 회복노력을 지지하는 안보리의장 명의 성명도 발표계획)

　　2) 단, UNIFIL 군요원 10 프로 감축문제에 대해서는 여전히 이사국들간에 합의가 이루어지고있지 않은바, 상기 결의안중 관련문안 표현을 놓고 현재 교섭이 진행중인 것으로 알려짐.

　　다. 안보리 운영개선 (TRANSPARECNY 문제)

　　1) 일단 유엔일보 (JOURNAL) 및 구내 방송활용문제를 시행키로 하고 이문제를 사무국에 제기 예정임.

　　2) 총회앞 활동보고 문제등에 관해서는 의견이 일치되고 있지 않은것으로 알려짐

국기국　　1차보　　중아국　　국기국　　외정실　　분석관　　안기부

PAGE 1

91.07.31　　10:23 WG

외신 1과 롱제관

0116

◆ 2. 한편 안보리상임이사국 (PERM-5) 들은 이락석유수출 일부 허용을 위한 안보리결의안을 교섭중이라고 하는바, 당관에서 입수한 동결의안초안 (불란서 초안)주요골자는 다음과 같음.

㉮ 6개월간 이락산 석유일정량 (정확한 수량은추후결정)수출허용

　1)이락산 석유구매시 동구매자가 안보리 대이락제재위 승인요청

　2)동 구매대금은 유엔구좌 (ESCROW ACCOUNT)에 입금되며, 식량등 민수용필수품목 수입대금은 동구좌에서 지불

　3)동 필수품의 이락내 공평한 배급을 위한 유엔감시 절차마련

㉯ 유엔사무총장은 본건 구좌로 부터 이락배상, 대량파괴무기 폐기, 쿠웨이트 재산반환, 이락-쿠웨이트 국경획정에 따른 제반경비 지불

㉰ 사무총장은 상기 사항이행과 관련된 보고서를 안보리에 제출

㉱ 이락은 자국의 금,외화보유고 현황을 매월제출

　첨부:상기 안보리결의안 초안: UNW(F)-371

끝

(대사 노창희-국장)

UN (FH)-371 10730 2005
(국면. 중동일. 축기. 기정)   종 4매

"The Security Council,

A. Recalling its resolutions 660 (1990), 661 (1990), 665 (1990), 666 (1990), 670 (1990), 674 (1990), 687 (1991), 688 (1991), 692 (1991) et 699 (1991),

B. Taking note of the report (S/.....) dated 15 July 1991 of the inter-agency mission headed by the executive delegate of the Secretary Géneral for the United Nations inter-agency humanitarian programme for Iraq, Kuwait and the Iraq/Turkey and Iraq/Iran border areas,

C. Gravely concerned by the nutritional and health situation of the Iraqi civilian population as described in this report, and by the risk of a rapid deterioration of this situation,

D. Taking note of the conclusions of the abovementionned report, and in particular of the proposal for oil sales by Iraq to finance immediate humanitarian relief,

E. Conscious of the need to achieve effective monitoring and transparency in the equitable distribution of humanitarian relief to all segments of the Iraqi civilian population,

F. Recalling and reaffirming in this regard its resolution 688 (1991) and in particular the importance which the Council attaches to Iraq allowing unhindered access by international humanitarian organisations to all those in

uNW-197 0
첨부억

4 -1

0118

need of assistance in all parts of Iraq and making available
all necessary facilities for their operation, and in this
connection stressing the important and continuing role
played by the Memorandum of Understanding between the United
Nations and the Government of Iraq of 18 April 1991
(S/22663),

        G. Recalling that, pursuant to resolutions 687
(1991), 692 (1991) and 699 (1991), Iraq is required to pay
the full costs of the Special Commission and the IAEA in
carrying out the tasks authorised by section C of resolution
687 (1991), and that the Secretary general ~~~~~ in his
report to the Security Council of 15 July 1991 (S/22792),
submitted pursuant to paragraph 4 of resolution 699 (1991),
expressed the view that the most obvious way of obtaining
financial resources from Iraq to meet the costs of the
Special Commission and the IAEA would be to authorise the
sale of some Iraqi petroleum and petroleum products, and
recalling further that Iraq is required to pay the expenses
of the United Nations Compensation Commission, as well as
its contributions to the Compensation Fund and half the
costs of the Iraq-Kuwait Boundary Demarcation Commission,
and recalling further that in its resolutions 686 (1991) and
687 (1991) the Security Council demanded that Iraq return in
the shortest possible time all Kuwaiti property seized by it
and requested the Secretary-General to take steps to
facilitate this,

        H. Acting under chapter VII of the Charter,

        1. Authorizes the import during a period of six
months from the date of passage of this resolution of a
specified quantity of petroleum and petroleum products
originating in Iraq for the purposes set out in this
resolution and subject to the following conditions :

to be specified in accordance with ... as part of the decisions to ... taken under para 3

4-2

.../...

(petroleum and

(a) Notification by the purchaser to and approval of each purchase of Iraqi petroleum products by the Security Council Committee established by resolution 661 (1990),

(b) Payment of the full amount of each of these purchases of Iraqi petroleum and petroleum products directly by the purchaser into a escrow account established by the Secretary General for this purpose,

(c) Payments from this account for the purchase of foodstuffs, medecines and essential civilian needs, as provided in paragraph 20 of resolution 687, to be subject to the joint authorisation of both Iraq and the Committee established by resolution 661 (1990),

(d) Establishment of control procedures within Iraq under United Nations monitoring and supervison to ensure equitable distribution to meet humanitarian needs of these supplies in all regions of Iraq and to all categories of the Iraqi population,

(e) Implementation of the authorisation in 3 tranches by the Security Council Committee established under Security Council resolution 661, only when the Council has taken the decision provided for in paragraph 2. below on the implementation of this resolution.

2. **Decides** in addition, that the Secretary-General is authorised to make payments from this escrow account to finance the obligations of Iraq, including the cost to the United Nations and other humanitarian organizations of monitoring and surveillance and of any other humanitarian expenditures in Iraq, appropriate

4-3

.../...

payments to the United Nations Compensation Fund, the costs
of carrying out the tasks authorised by section C of
resolution 687 (1991), the costs incurred by the United
Nations in facilitating the return of all Kuwaiti property
seized by Iraq and half the costs of the Boundary
Commission.

3. Requests the Secretary General, within 20 days
of the date of adoption of this resolution, to submit a
report to the Security Council for decision on measures to
be taken in order to implement paragraphs 1(a), 1(b), 1(c), and
1(d), and estimates of the humanitarian requirements of Iraq and
the amount of Iraq's financial obligations set out in the
para 2 above, for the period of the authorization in para 1
above.

4. Requires the Government of Iraq to provide to
the Secretary-General and appropriate international
organizations on the first day of the month immediately
following the adoption of the present resolution and on the
first day of each month thereafter until further notice, a
statement of the gold and foreign currency reserves it holds
within Iraq.

5. Calls upon all States to cooperate fully in
the implementation of this resolution.

6. Decides to remain seized of the matter.

4-4

관리번호 91 -800

원 본

외 무 부

종 별 :

번 호 : UNW-1942

일 시 : 91 0726 1800

수 신 : 장 관(국연,중동일,기정)

발 신 : 주 유엔 대사

제 목 : 안보리동향(이락석유수출 일부허용문제)

연:UNW-1926

1. 연호 이락석유수출 일부허용문제와 관련한 안보리 결의안 교섭동향에 대해 당관 원참사관이 금 7.26 미대표부 J.MANSO 담당관에게 탐문한바, 현재 초안형태로 교섭이 진행되고 있지는 않으며 주요골격 (MAIN ELEMENTS) 에 관한 의견을 나누고있는 단계라고함.

2. 동 담당관에 의하면, 상기 결의안은 인도적 분야외에도 여러 현안문제 (UNW-1910) 를 포괄할 가능성이 크며, 예켄데 배상기금 공제 상한선 문제도 다룰가능성이 있다고함. 앞으로 교섭추이를 보아야 하겠지만 상당히 포괄적이고 통합적인 결의안이 될 전망이라고 하며, 이에따라 교섭에 어느정도 시일이 필요할 것이라고함.

첨부:1.NYT, WP 지 기사,2. 유엔사무총장 기자문답:UNW(F)-363

끝.(대사 노창희-국장)

예고:91.12.31. 일반

국기국	차관	1차보	중아국	분석관	청와대	안기부

PAGE 1

91.07.27 07:52

외신 2과 롱제관 BS

0122

외 무 부

종 별 :

번 호 : UNW-1972   일   시 : 91 0730 2000

수 신 : 장 관(중동일,국연,기정)

발 신 : 주 유엔 대사

제 목 : 이락배상문제

　　1.유엔사무총장은 금 7.30 자로 C.ALZAMORA (페루출신, 26년생)를 유엔 이락배상
위원회사무국장 (EXECUTIVE SECRETARY) 으로 임명하였음.

　　2. ALZAMORA 사무국장은 페루 직업 외교관 출신으로 주유엔, 제네바 대사를
역임하였으며, 최근 유엔환경개발회의 (UNCED)사무총장 고문으로 일한바 있음.끝
　　(대사 노창희-국장)

중아국　　　1차보　　　국기국　　　외정실　　　분석관　　　안기부

정 리 보 존 문 서 목 록					
기록물종류	일반공문서철	등록번호	35866	등록일자	2009-09-22
분류번호	731.33	국가코드	IQ	보존기간	30년
명 칭	유엔안전보장위원회 이라크 배상위원회, 1991-92. 전6권				
생 산 과	중동1과/국제연합1과	생산년도	1991~1992	담당그룹	
권 차 명	V.6 각국 동향				
내용목차					

0001

발 신 전 보

번   호 : WUS-0779   910228 1836   FD종별 :

수   신 : 주   수신처 참조 /대사//총영사/

발   신 : 장 관   (중동일)

제   목 : 걸프전후 손해배상 청구 검토

WUK -0383	WFR -0403
WCN -0192	WGE -0336
WJA -0890	WJD -0124

　　　　종전후 각국은 쿠웨이트내 자국민과 업체등이 입은 피해에 대한 손해
배상을 청구하기 위해 기술적 검토를 하고 있다는바, 상세를 파악 보고 바람. 끝.

　　　　　　　　　　　　　　　　　　　　　　(중동아국장   이 해 순)

수신처 : 주 미, 영, 불, 카나다, 독, 일 대사
　　　　　(사본: 주젯다총영사 경유 소병용 주쿠웨이트대사)

미주국장 :
국제경제국장 :

보 안 통 제	

앙고재	91년 2월 28일 중동1과	기안자 성명		과장 출장중	심의관	국장 전결		차관	장관		외신과통제

분류번호	보존기간

발 신 전 보

번   호 : WJD-0125   910228 2058 CT   종별 : _____

수   신 : 주   젯다 ////대사. 총영사 (소병용 주쿠웨이트 대사)

발   신 : 장   관 (중동일)

제   목 : 걸프전후 손해배상 청구 검토

연 : WJD - 0124

1. 쿠웨이트내 아국교민과 업체등이 입은 손실에 대한 손해배상 ~~를~~ 청구 할경우

쿠웨이트 또는 이라크중 어느 정부에 대하여 청구함이 적절한지 귀견 ~~회보 바람~~
~~을 정부시서 안일청구해야하는일위~~ 해야 하는지 쿠정부접촉시 타진 보고바람.

2. 동 손해배상 ~~청구를 위해서는~~ 각교민 및 업체별 구체적 피해액 산정이

필요한바, 효과적인 산정 방법에 대한 귀견도 보고 바람. 끝.   취함

취함

(중동아국장 이 해 순)

예 고 : 90.6.30. 까지

91. 6. 30. 일반재

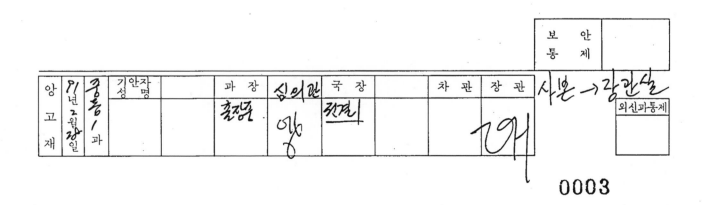

앙 고 재	91 년 2 월 28 일	중동 1 과	기 안 자 성 명		과 장 홍정표	심의관	국 장 전견		차 관	장 관	사인→장관실
											외신과통제

보 안	
통 제	

0003

관리
번호 91/1970

외 무 부

종 별 :

번 호 : JDW-0075

일 시 : 91 0301 1700

수 신 : 장관(중동일,기정)

발 신 : 주쿠웨이트 대사(주 젯다총영사관 경유)

제 목 : 손해보상청구(출장보고 8)

대:WJD-0124,0125

1.SHAIKH SABBA 부총리겸 외무장관의 수석보좌관(DIRECTOR OF THE OFFICE OF-)ABUDULLA 대사는 2.28 에 이 손해보상청구는 관련 유엔결의에 따른 것으로서주 유엔 쿠웨이트대표부가 각 유엔회원국중 관계국가대표부에 신청안내문을 배부했다고 말하면서, 이것은 이라크정부에 청구하기 위한 것이라고 말함(청구절차는 전술한 안내서에 설명되었을 것 같아서 묻지 아니했었음)

2. 절차등에 관하여 추가로 조사 보고하겠음. 다만 이 일은 유엔대표부에서관계문서를 받았는지 확인해볼 필요가 있다고 생각되며 손해조사는 우선 쿠웨이트 교민회장과 관계회사(건설,상사등)에 서울에서 계산(추계)가능한 손해를 가능한대로 증빙문건 구비정리케하고, 추가로 현장조사 평가가 필요한 부분에 대하여는 일단 쿠웨이트에 귀환하여 대사관을 창구로 하여 쿠웨이트정부 관계기관과 협의하면서 진행해가야 할 것으로 생각됨.

3. 우선 이상과 같은 개괄적인 보고를 드리고 더 자세하고 실제적인 것을 조사되는대로 추보하겠으니 일단 이런 사정을 관계인들에게 알려주는 예비적 조치가 필요할 것으로 생각됨. 끝.

(대사-국장)

예고:91.6.30 일반

91.6.30. 예고보다까.

일반

중아국	장관	차관	1차보	2차보	안기부

PAGE 1

91.03.02   02:45
외신 2과 통제관 CE

0004

외　무　부

관리번호 <u>91 1247</u>

종　별 :

번　호 : FRW-0747 　　　　　　　　일　시 : 91 0304 1850

수　신 : 장관(중동일,경일,정일)

발　신 : 주 불 대사

제　목 : 쿠웨이트내 손해 배상 문제

대:WFR-0403K

1. 대호 당관 손서기관이 금 3.4 일 접촉한 주재국 외무성 SASTOURNE 걸프전 전담관에 의하면 대호 배상 문제가 제기되고 있으나, 쿠웨이트와는 달리 복구 사업 및 배상 재원이 고갈된 이락에 대해서는 우선 경제 봉쇄 특히 석유 수출금지 조치가 해제된 이후에야 구체적으로 거론이 가능할것이며, 그경우 전후 복구 사업과의 연계도 고려될수 있을것이라함.

2. 동인은 이어 이락의 경우, <u>원유 수출 금지가 해제되면 국제금융기구(IBRD등) 가 원유를 담보로 차관공여,</u> 전후복구 및 배상등을 현실화 시키는 조치가 장기적으로 있을것으로 전망된다함. 끝

(대사 노영찬-국장)

예고: 91.6.30 까지

91.6.3. 예고문 억기
일어2기

중아국	차관	1차보	2차보	경제국	정문국	청와대	안기부

PAGE 1 　　　　　　　　　　　　　　　　　　91.03.05　　04:30

외신 2과　통제관 CW

외 무 부

종 별 :

번 호 : GEW-0545

일 시 : 91 0304 1800

수 신 : 장 관(중동일, 구일)

발 신 : 주 독 대사대리

제 목 : 걸프전 피해 보상문제

대: WGE-0336

1. 대호 관련 3.4.전참사관이 외무부 DASSEL국장을 방문, 문의한바 주재국으로서는 우선, 쿠웨이트 주재 자국공관 건물에 대한 피해 및 자국민과 업체등이 입은 피해에 대한 손해배상을 청구하여야 한다는 입장에 따라 대사관 건물에 대한 피해유무, 기타 독일국민의 재산피해 내용 상세를 조사키로 하고 있다함

2. 이에 관한 세부방침등은 이미 현지로 파견한 주쿠웨이트 대사관 복귀요원의 보고를 접수한후 검토될 예정이라함

(대사대리 안현원-국장)

중아국 1차보   구주국   정문국   안기부

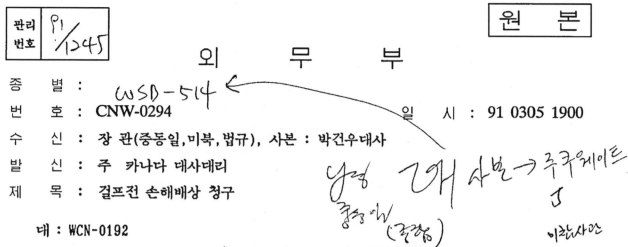

```
관리
번호 91
     1245
```

외 무 부

종   별 : ~~WSB-514~~ ←

번   호 : CNW-0294   일   시 : 91 0305 1900

수   신 : 장 관(중동일,미북,법규), 사본 : 박건우대사

발   신 : 주 카나다 대사대리

제   목 : 걸프전 손해배상 청구

    대 : WCN-0192

1. 안참사관이 3.5.(화) 주재국 외무무역부 경제정책국 HAGE 국제재정부자 과장과 면담, 파악한 내용을 아래 보고함.

    가. 피핵 파악(외무무역부내 피해 신고처 설치)

    0 주재국 정부는 걸프사태 이락의 쿠웨이트 침공으로 카나다 국민 및 기업이 입은 재산상 피해와 신체적 피해(부상)에 대해 이락 정부당국에 손해배상을 청구하기 위해 외무무역부 조약국내의 경제, 봉상법과에 피해자가 구체적 피해 내용을 조속 신고하도록 2.28. 자로 공고하고, 현재 피해 내용을 접수중이며, 피해규모는 아직 미상임.

    나. 손해 배상 청구범위

    0 걸프사태 발생시 쿠웨이트 및 이락내에는 석유분야 기술자 등 약 800 명의 카나다 국민이 체재하고 있었는바, 이들이 입은 손실이 직접 피해로서 주된 손해 배상 청구 대상이며, 카나다의 경우 여타국처럼 수주 건설공사는 없었으므로 공사 중단으로 인한 피해는 없었음.

    0 안보리 결의에 따른 경제제재 조치와 걸프전 수행에 따라 카나다 수출업체가 입은 피해는 당초부터 대중동지역 수출이 잠재적인 위험 부담을 지니고 있었다는 점과 카나다 수출개발공사(EDC) 등에 의해 보험에 가입되어 있었다는 점 등을 감안, 손해배상 청구에서 제외되었음.

    다. 손해배상 청구방법

    0 유엔 안보리 결의에 의거, 유엔이 이락정부에 대해 손해배상 청구 조치를 취할경우 이에 따르되 그렇지 않을 경우에는 이락정부 당국에 직접 청구 예정임.

    라. 손해배상 지불확보

중아국 안기부	장관	차관	1차보	2차보	미주국	미주국	국기국	정와대

0 현재 카나다내에 동결된 이락 자산이 수백만 카붐 이상으로 추정되므로 이 동결 자산을 압류, 사용하는것을 고려중이며, 미국의 경우도 유사한 이락 동결 자산이 있으므로 미측과 보조를 맞춰 처리해 나갈 방침임.

2. 손해배상을 실제 이락으로부터 받아내는 문제는 향후 훗세인 대통령의 거취 등 사태 진전을 보아가면서 신축성있게 대처한다는 것이 카측의 기본 입장임.

(대사대리 조원일 - 국장)

예고문 : 91.12.31. 까지

91. 6. 30. 까쥐곁
91. 12. 31. 있나쥐

관리
번호 91/1971

외 무 부

종 별 :

번 호 : JAW-1341

일 시 : 91 0307 1844

수 신 : 장관(중동일,아일)

발 신 : 주 일 대사(일정)

제 목 : 걸프전후 손해배상청구검토 및 주이라크 대사관 복귀

대 : WJA-0890,0934

표제건, 당관 신현석 서기관이 3.7. 주재국 외무성 중근동 2 과 요시다
사무관으로부터 청취한 내용 아래 보고함.

　　1. 손해배상 청구

　　0 일본정부는 현재 일반론적으로 이라크 정부에 대해 손해배상을 청구하는 것이
국제법적으로 가능한지 여부를 검토하는 단계임.

　　0 다만 피해를 입은 일본국민이나 기업이 이라크 정부에 대해 직접 손해배상을
청구하는 것은 가능하다는 입장이며 정부가 개인이나 기업의 손해를 신고받아 이라크
정부에 일괄 배상을 청구할지 여부는 현단계에서 검토하고 있지 않음.

　　2. 주이라크 대사관 복귀

　　0 현 이라크정세는 반정부 폭동으로 유동적이므로 당분간 사태를 관망하고 있으며
정세가 안정된 단계에서 우선 선발대를 파견할 계획이며 선발대의 대사관 활동재개
준비가 끝난후 대사가 복귀할 예정임.

　　0 주이라크 일본대사관은 폭격으로 인한 외견상 피해는 없음.

　　3. 주쿠웨이트 대사관 복귀

　　0 주쿠웨이트 일본대사는, 3.1. 일본을 출발하여 3.2. 사우디아라비아 리야드에
도착, 쿠웨이트로의 복귀를 준비중에 있으며 쿠웨이트정부로부터의 입국허가가
나오는대로 대사 포함 3 명 정도가 입국할 예정임.

　　4. 본건 계속 추보예정임.끝

　　(대사 이원경-국장)

예고:원본배부처:91.6.30. 일반

사본접수처:91.6.30. 일반

91. 6. 30.

중아국	장관	차관	1차보	2차보	아주국	미주국	청와대	안기부

관리
번호 91/1504

	분류번호	보존기간

발 신 전 보

번 호 : WND-0726   910822 1710 FN   종별 :

수 신 : 주   수신처 참조 대사//총영사/ (사본 : 주 UN제네바대표부대사)
WPA -0543   WBA -0268
WSK제네바대표부 WPH 대사42
WCP -1319   WUN -2294
WGV -1094

발 신 : 장 관   (중동일)

제 목 : 대이라크 피해배상 청구

1. UN은 91.4.3. 안보리 결의안 제687호 채택 이후, 91.8.15. 이라크산 원유 수입
   대금의 30%를 피해배상 기금으로 적립토록 하는 안보리 결의안 제705호채택에
   이르는 일련의 조치를 통하여 대이라크 배상 청구 절차를 협의중에 있음.

2. 상기 절차에 의하면 90.8.2-91.3.2.간 이라크의 불법적 쿠웨이트 침공 및 점령
   으로 인해 입은 직접적 손실 및 피해에 대하여 각국은 UN을 통해 배상을 청구할수
   있게 된바, 이와관련 귀 주재국이 전쟁전 근로자를 이라크와 쿠웨이트에 파견하고
   있었던점을 감안, 현재 귀 주재국 정부가 국가, 기업 및 개인에 입은 피해에
   대한 청구를 위하여 현재 강구중인 방안에 대하여 탐문 보고 바람.   (근로자들이
   입은 리해가 있을시에는
   이에 대한 리해도)

3. 동건 관련 UN 문서집을 파편 송부 하겠음.   끝.

(중동아국장   이 해 순)

수신처 : 주 인도, 파키스탄, 방글라데시, 스리랑카, 필리핀, 한국 대사 및
주 북경 대표부 대사

예 고 : 91.12.31. 까지

91.12.31. 보존

제2차반보 :

앙고재	91년8월21일	중동1과	기안자성명 주		과장 심의관	국장 전결		차관 장관	외신과통제

0010

320 걸프 사태 유엔안전보장이사회 동향 8

발 신 전 보

번 호 : WSB-0920   910822 1713 FN   종별 :

수 신 : 주 수신처 참조   ///대사///총영사사본 : 주 UN, 제네바대표부

WAE -0384	WBH -0325
WCA -0577	WUN -2295
WGV -1095	WBE -0185

발 신 : 장 관 (중동일)

제 목 : 대이라크 피해배상 청구

1. UN은 91.4.3. 안보리 결의안 제687호 채택이후 91.8.15. 이라크산 원유 수입 대금의 30%를 배상 기금으로 적립토록 하는 안보리 결의안 제705호의 채택에 이르는 일련의 조치를 통하여 대이라크 배상청구 절차를 협의중에 있음.

2. 상기 절차에 따라 90.8.2-91.3.2.간 불법적인 이라크의 쿠웨이트 침공 및 점령으로 인해 직접적으로 입은 손실 및 피해에 대하여 각국은 UN을 통해 대이라크 피해배상을 청구할수 있게 되어 있는바, 이와관련 귀 주재국이 국가, 기업 및 개인이 입은 피해에 대한 청구를 위해 현재 강구중인 방안에 대하여 탐문 보고 바람.

3. 동건 관련 UN 문서집을 파편 송부 하겠음.   끝.

(중동아국장   이 해 순)

수신처 : 주 사우디, UAE, 바레인, 카타르, 오만 대사 및 카이로 총영사

예 고 : 91.12.31. 까지

91.12.31. 일반 ~

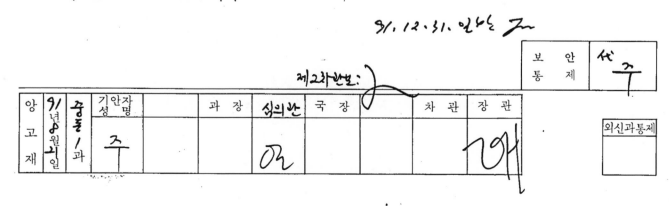

제2과반부:

앙고재	91년8월21일 중동1과	기안자 성명	주	과 장	심의관	국 장	차 관	장 관
					02			

보 안 통 제	代 주

외신과통제

0011

발 신 전 보

번   호 : WJA-3737   910822 1730 FN   종별 :

수   신 : 주 수신처 참조 ///대사//총영사/ (사본 : 주 UN제네바 대표분 대사)

WUS-3806   WCN-1084
WAV-0884   WSD-0450
WUN-2297   WGV-1097

발   신 : 장 관 (중동일)

제   목 : 대이라크 배상 청구

1. UN은 91.4.3. 안보리 결의 제687호 채택이후 91.8.15. 이라크산 원유 수입의
    30%를 배상기금으로 적립토록 하는 안보리 결의안 제705호의 채택에 이르는
    일련의 조치를 통하여, 대이라크 배상청구 절차를 협의중에 있음.

2. 상기 절차에 의하면 90.8.2-91.3.2.간 이라크의 불법적인 쿠웨이트 침공 및
    점령으로 인해 입은 직접적 손실 및 피해에 대하여 각국은 UN을 통해 배상을
    청구할수 있게 되어 있는바, 이와 관련 귀 주재국이 국가, 기업 및 개인이 입은
    피해에 대한 청구를 위하여 현재 강구중인 방안에 대하여 탐문 보고 바람.

3. 또한 귀 주재국은 UN의 대이라크 경제제재 조치에 따라 주재국내에 있는
    이라크의 자산을 동결하고 있는 국가로 파악되고 있는바, 90.8.2. 이전 대이라크
    채무 변제와 관련, 상기 UN의 조치와는 별도로 기업이나 개인의 피해에 대하여
    동 자산을 활용 배상케 해 주려는 움직임이 있는지 여부도 파악 보고 바람.

4. 동건 관련 UN 문서집을 파편 송부 하겠음.   끝.

(중동아국장   이 해 순)

수신처 : 주 일, 미, 카나다, 영, 프랑스, 독일, 이태리, 벨기에, 스위스 오지리,
         스웨덴 대사. 폴두갈 대사.

예 고 : 91.12.31. 까지

제2차 반보 :   91.12.31.
                       인보

보 안 통 제	대 우

앙 고 재	91 년 월 일	중동 1 과	기안자 성 명		과 장	심의관	국 장		차 관	장 관		외신과통제
			주			이 전결						

0012

관리번호 91/1506

외 무 부

종 별 :

번 호 : BBW-0564

수 신 : 장관(중동일)

발 신 : 주 벨기에 대사

제 목 : 대이라크 피해배상청구

일 시 : 91 0822 1900

대:WECM-0040

대호, 주재국 외무부 DELFOSSE 유엔국장을 통해 확인한바, 동인의 언급 내용을 하기 보고함.

1. 피해배상 기금을 활용한 대이라크 배상청구는 현재 동기금 관리위원회(UN 안보리 회원국)에서 아직 구체적 시행절차를 협의중인 상태에 있으므로(금년 10월말경 성안될 것으로 예측), 주재국 정부로서는 아직 피해 청구를위한 구체적 방안을 검토한바 없음.

2. 외무성으로서는 하기 휴가철이 끝나고 또한 상기위원회에서 어느정도 구체적인 시행방식이 결정되면 일차적으로 관보를통해 대국민 홍보를하고, 세부 시행방식이 확정되면 이에따라 벨기에 정부의 시행절차를 확정, 관보공보, 당사자들로부터 피해 청구서 접수등의 절차를 거치는 방안을 생각하고 있음.

3. 대호 3 항, 주재국내 동결 이라크 자산을 활용한 배상 방안은 현재로서 주재국 정부는 전혀 검토한바 없을뿐만 아니라 법률적 정당성에도 문제가 있을것으로 보임.끝.

(대사 정우영-국장)

예고:91.12.31 까지

91.12.31. 일반 (서명)

중아국

PAGE 1

91.08.23   06:30
외신 2과   통제관 DO

0013

발 신 전 보

	분류번호	보존기간

번   호 : WSZ-0343   910823 1420 FH 종별 : 지급 (암호송신)

수   신 : 주 스위스   대사. 총영사 (심경보 참사관)

발   신 : 장 관   (중동아국, 임대택 심의관)

제   목 : UN 배상위 건

      WSZ - 0341 관련, 스위스는 UN의 대이락 배상 청구와는 별관련이 없을
듯하여 다시 업연을 보내오니, 이와 관련 보고는 불요할것 같습니다. 다만 연호
3항과 관련된 정보 있을시 연락 바랍니다.   끝.

앙고재	91년 4월 23일	수출 1과	기안자 성명		과장	신의관	국장			차관	장관		보안통제	
			주										외신과통제	

0014

분류번호 문서번호	중동일 720- **30603**	기안용지 (720-2327)	시 행 상 특별취급	
보존기간	영구.준영구 10. 5. 3. 1	장 관		
수 신 처 보존기간		代 ら		
시행일자	1991. 8. 23.			

보존 기관	국 장	전경	협 조 기 관		문 서 통 제 1991. 8. 26 5 재 건
	심의관	아			
	과 장	씨 시			
기안책임자		주 복 룡			발 송 인

경 유		발 신 명 의	발 송 송 1991. 8. 26 외무부
수 신	수신처 참조		
참 조			
제 목	자료 송부		

     연호, UN 배상위 관련 문서목록을 별첨 송부합니다.

     첨 부 : UN 배상위 관련 문서 목록 1부.   끝.

   수신처 : 주 일대사(WJA-3737)   주 사우디대사(WSB-0920)

          주 미대사(연WUS-3806)   주 UAE대사(WAE-0384)

          주 카나다대사(WCN-1084)   주 바레인대사(WBH 0325)

          주 영대사(WECM 0040)   주 카타르대사(WQT 0497)

                    / 계 속 .... /

0015

주 독대사 (WECM·0040)	주 오만대사 (WOM-0185)
주 이태리대사 (WECM·0040)	주 카이로총영사 (WCA 0577)
주 벨기에대사 (WECM-0040)	주 쿠웨이트대사 (WKU 0310)
주 인도대사 (WND-0726)	주 오지리대사 (WAV 0884)
주 파키스탄대사 (WPA-0543)	주 스웨덴대사 (WSO 0450)
주 방글라데시대사 (WBA-0268)	주 UN대사 (WUN 1297)
주 스리랑카대사 (WSK-0318)	주 제네바대사 (WGV·1097)
주 북경대사 (WCP-1319)	주 필리핀대사 (WPH 0742)

더 맑은 마음을, 더 밝은 사회를, 더 넓은 미래를

0016

UN 배상위원회 관련 문서 목록

1991. 8.

재분류(1991.12.31.)

재분류(1992.6.30.)

예.

外 務 部
中東아프리카局

0017

목   차
==================

1. 유엔 안보리 결의안 제674호 (90.10.29)

   ㅇ 이라크의 쿠웨이트 침공으로 인한 모든 손실은 이라크가 책임져야 함. (8조)

   ㅇ 이에 따라 각국은 자국의 국민, 기업이 입은 손실을 파악토록 권고 (9조)

2. 유엔 안보리 결의안 제687호 (91.4.3)

   ㅇ 걸프전 정식 휴전 결의로서 이라크의 배상 책임 규정 (제16-19조 및 29조)

3. 유엔 사무총장의 안전보장 이사회 앞 건의서 (91.5.2)

   ㅇ 대이라크 배상청구 이행 계획 건의서

4. 유엔 안보리 결의 제692호 (91.5.20)

   ㅇ 상기 유엔 사무총장의 건의서 승인

5. 유엔 사무총장의 안전보장이사회 의장앞 서한 (91.5.30)

   ㅇ 배상기금 조성을 위한 이라크산 석유 수입공제 상한선 설정

     (석유 금수조치 해제시 년간 석유수입액 210억불중 30%)

6. 유엔 안보리 결의 제705호 (91.8.15)

   ㅇ 상기 유엔 사무총장 건의서 승인

7. 유엔 안보리 결의 제706호 (91.8.15)

   ㅇ 이라크내 인도적 수요를 위해 임시로 향후 6개월간 16억불 한도 내에서

     석유수출 허가, 이중 30%는 배상기금으로 적립

0018

Security Council

Distr.
GENERAL

S/RES/674 (1990)
29 October 1990

RESOLUTION 674 (1990)

Adopted by the Security Council at its 2951st meeting,
on 29 October 1990

The Security Council,

Recalling its resolutions 660 (1990), 661 (1990), 662 (1990), 664 (1990),
665 (1990), 666 (1990), 667 (1990) and 670 (1990),

Stressing the urgent need for the immediate and unconditional withdrawal of
all Iraqi forces from Kuwait, for the restoration of Kuwait's sovereignty,
independence and territorial integrity and of the authority of its legitimate
government,

Condemning the actions by the Iraqi authorities and occupying forces to take
third-State nationals hostage and to mistreat and oppress Kuwaiti and third-State
nationals, and the other actions reported to the Security Council, such as the
destruction of Kuwaiti demographic records, the forced departure of Kuwaitis, the
relocation of population in Kuwait and the unlawful destruction and seizure of
public and private property in Kuwait, including hospital supplies and equipment,
in violation of the decisions of the Council, the Charter of the United Nations,
the Fourth Geneva Convention, the Vienna Conventions on Diplomatic and Consular
Relations and international law,

Expressing grave alarm over the situation of nationals of third States in
Kuwait and Iraq, including the personnel of the diplomatic and consular missions of
such States,

Reaffirming that the Fourth Geneva Convention applies to Kuwait and that as a
High Contracting Party to the Convention Iraq is bound to comply fully with all its
terms and in particular is liable under the Convention in respect of the grave
breaches committed by it, as are individuals who commit or order the commission of
grave breaches,

Recalling the efforts of the Secretary-General concerning the safety and
well-being of third-State nationals in Iraq and Kuwait,

90-27986 2526Z (E)

- 1 -

0019

Deeply concerned at the economic cost and at the loss and suffering caused to individuals in Kuwait and Iraq as a result of the invasion and occupation of Kuwait by Iraq,

Acting under Chapter VII of the Charter of the United Nations,

* * *

Reaffirming the goal of the international community of maintaining international peace and security by seeking to resolve international disputes and conflicts through peaceful means,

Recalling the important role that the United Nations and its Secretary-General have played in the peaceful solution of disputes and conflicts in conformity with the provisions of the Charter,

Alarmed by the dangers of the present crisis caused by the Iraqi invasion and occupation of Kuwait, which directly threaten international peace and security, and seeking to avoid any further worsening of the situation,

Calling upon Iraq to comply with the relevant resolutions of the Security Council, in particular its resolutions 660 (1990), 662 (1990) and 664 (1990),

Reaffirming its determination to ensure compliance by Iraq with the Security Council resolutions by maximum use of political and diplomatic means,

A

1. Demands that the Iraqi authorities and occupying forces immediately cease and desist from taking third-State nationals hostage, mistreating and oppressing Kuwaiti and third-State nationals and any other actions, such as those reported to the Security Council and described above, that violate the decisions of this Council, the Charter of the United Nations, the Fourth Geneva Convention, the Vienna Conventions on Diplomatic and Consular Relations and international law;

2. Invites States to collate substantiated information in their possession or submitted to them on the grave breaches by Iraq as per paragraph 1 above and to make this information available to the Security Council;

3. Reaffirms its demand that Iraq immediately fulfil its obligations to third-State nationals in Kuwait and Iraq, including the personnel of diplomatic and consular missions, under the Charter, the Fourth Geneva Convention, the Vienna Conventions on Diplomatic and Consular Relations, general principles of international law and the relevant resolutions of the Council;

4. Also reaffirms its demand that Iraq permit and facilitate the immediate departure from Kuwait and Iraq of those third-State nationals, including diplomatic and consular personnel, who wish to leave;

5. Demands that Iraq ensure the immediate access to food, water and basic services necessary to the protection and well-being of Kuwaiti nationals and of nationals of third States in Kuwait and Iraq, including the personnel of diplomatic and consular missions in Kuwait;

6. Reaffirms its demand that Iraq immediately protect the safety and well-being of diplomatic and consular personnel and premises in Kuwait and in Iraq, take no action to hinder these diplomatic and consular missions in the performance of their functions, including access to their nationals and the protection of their person and interests and rescind its orders for the closure of diplomatic and consular missions in Kuwait and the withdrawal of the immunity of their personnel;

7. Requests the Secretary-General, in the context of the continued exercise of his good offices concerning the safety and well-being of third-State nationals in Iraq and Kuwait, to seek to achieve the objectives of paragraphs 4, 5 and 6

- 2 -

above and in particular the provision of food, water and basic services to Kuwaiti nationals and to the diplomatic and consular missions in Kuwait and the evacuation of third-State nationals;

8.   Reminds Iraq that under international law it is liable for any loss, damage or injury arising in regard to Kuwait and third States, and their nationals and corporations, as a result of the invasion and illegal occupation of Kuwait by Iraq;

9.   Invites States to collect relevant information regarding their claims, and those of their nationals and corporations, for restitution or financial compensation by Iraq with a view to such arrangements as may be established in accordance with international law;

10. Requires that Iraq comply with the provisions of the present resolution and its previous resolutions, failing which the Security Council will need to take further measures under the Charter;

11. Decides to remain actively and permanently seized of the matter until Kuwait has regained its independence and peace has been restored in conformity with the relevant resolutions of the Security Council.

B

12. Reposes its trust in the Secretary-General to make available his good offices and, as he considers appropriate, to pursue them and to undertake diplomatic efforts in order to reach a peaceful solution to the crisis caused by the Iraqi invasion and occupation of Kuwait on the basis of Security Council resolutions 660 (1990), 662 (1990) and 664 (1990), and calls upon all States, both those in the region and others, to pursue on this basis their efforts to this end, in conformity with the Charter, in order to improve the situation and restore peace, security and stability;

13. Requests the Secretary-General to report to the Security Council on the results of his good offices and diplomatic efforts.

Security Council

Distr.
GENERAL

S/RES/687 (1991)*
8 April 1991

RESOLUTION 687 (1991)

Adopted by the Security Council at its 2981st meeting,
on 3 April 1991

The Security Council,

Recalling its resolutions 660 (1990) of 2 August 1990, 661 (1990) of 6 August 1990, 662 (1990) of 9 August 1990, 664 (1990) of 18 August 1990, 665 (1990) of 25 August 1990, 666 (1990) of 13 September 1990, 667 (1990) of 16 September 1990, 669 (1990) of 24 September 1990, 670 (1990) of 25 September 1990, 674 (1990) of 29 October 1990, 677 (1990) of 28 November 1990, 678 (1990) of 29 November 1990 and 686 (1991) of 2 March 1991,

Welcoming the restoration to Kuwait of its sovereignty, independence and territorial integrity and the return of its legitimate Government,

Affirming the commitment of all Member States to the sovereignty, territorial integrity and political independence of Kuwait and Iraq, and noting the intention expressed by the Member States cooperating with Kuwait under paragraph 2 of resolution 678 (1990) to bring their military presence in Iraq to an end as soon as possible consistent with paragraph 8 of resolution 686 (1991),

Reaffirming the need to be assured of Iraq's peaceful intentions in the light of its unlawful invasion and occupation of Kuwait,

Taking note of the letter sent by the Minister for Foreign Affairs of Iraq on 27 February 1991 [1] and those sent pursuant to resolution 686 (1991), [2]

---

* Reissued for technical reasons.

[1] S/22275, annex.

[2] S/22273, S/22276, S/22320, S/22321 and S/22330.

91-11221 3315Z (E)

/...

-4-

0022

Noting that Iraq and Kuwait, as independent sovereign States, signed at Baghdad on 4 October 1963 "Agreed Minutes Between the State of Kuwait and the Republic of Iraq Regarding the Restoration of Friendly Relations, Recognition and Related Matters", thereby recognizing formally the boundary between Iraq and Kuwait and the allocation of islands, which were registered with the United Nations in accordance with Article 102 of the Charter of the United Nations and in which Iraq recognized the independence and complete sovereignty of the State of Kuwait within its borders as specified and accepted in the letter of the Prime Minister of Iraq dated 21 July 1932, and as accepted by the Ruler of Kuwait in his letter dated 10 August 1932,

Conscious of the need for demarcation of the said boundary,

Conscious also of the statements by Iraq threatening to use weapons in violation of its obligations under the Geneva Protocol for the Prohibition of the Use in War of Asphyxiating, Poisonous or Other Gases, and of Bacteriological Methods of Warfare, signed at Geneva on 17 June 1925, 3/ and of its prior use of chemical weapons and affirming that grave consequences would follow any further use by Iraq of such weapons,

Recalling that Iraq has subscribed to the Declaration adopted by all States participating in the Conference of States Parties to the 1925 Geneva Protocol and Other Interested States, held in Paris from 7 to 11 January 1989, establishing the objective of universal elimination of chemical and biological weapons,

Recalling also that Iraq has signed the Convention on the Prohibition of the Development, Production and Stockpiling of Bacteriological (Biological) and Toxin Weapons and on Their Destruction, of 10 April 1972, 4/

Noting the importance of Iraq ratifying this Convention,

Noting moreover the importance of all States adhering to this Convention and encouraging its forthcoming Review Conference to reinforce the authority, efficiency and universal scope of the convention,

Stressing the importance of an early conclusion by the Conference on Disarmament of its work on a Convention on the Universal Prohibition of Chemical Weapons and of universal adherence thereto,

Aware of the use by Iraq of ballistic missiles in unprovoked attacks and therefore of the need to take specific measures in regard to such missiles located in Iraq,

Concerned by the reports in the hands of Member States that Iraq has attempted to acquire materials for a nuclear-weapons programme contrary to its obligations under the Treaty on the Non-Proliferation of Nuclear Weapons of 1 July 1968, 5/

Recalling the objective of the establishment of a nuclear-weapons-free zone in the region of the Middle East,

Conscious of the threat that all weapons of mass destruction pose to peace and security in the area and of the need to work towards the establishment in the Middle East of a zone free of such weapons,

---

3/   League of Nations, Treaty Series, vol. XCIV (1929), No. 2138.

4/   General Assembly resolution 2826 (XXVI), annex.

5/   General Assembly resolution 2373 (XXII).

Conscious also of the objective of achieving balanced and comprehensive control of armaments in the region,

Conscious further of the importance of achieving the objectives noted above using all available means, including a dialogue among the States of the region,

Noting that resolution 686 (1991) marked the lifting of the measures imposed by resolution 661 (1990) in so far as they applied to Kuwait,

Noting that despite the progress being made in fulfilling the obligations of resolution 686 (1991), many Kuwaiti and third country nationals are still not accounted for and property remains unreturned,

Recalling the International Convention against the Taking of Hostages, 6/ opened for signature at New York on 18 December 1979, which categorizes all acts of taking hostages as manifestations of international terrorism,

Deploring threats made by Iraq during the recent conflict to make use of terrorism against targets outside Iraq and the taking of hostages by Iraq,

Taking note with grave concern of the reports of the Secretary-General of 20 March 1991 7/ and 28 March 1991, 8/ and conscious of the necessity to meet urgently the humanitarian needs in Kuwait and Iraq,

Bearing in mind its objective of restoring international peace and security in the area as set out in recent resolutions of the Security Council,

Conscious of the need to take the following measures acting under Chapter VII of the Charter,

1.   Affirms all thirteen resolutions noted above, except as expressly changed below to achieve the goals of this resolution, including a formal cease-fire;

A

2.   Demands that Iraq and Kuwait respect the inviolability of the international boundary and the allocation of islands set out in the "Agreed Minutes Between the State of Kuwait and the Republic of Iraq Regarding the Restoration of Friendly Relations, Recognition and Related Matters", signed by them in the exercise of their sovereignty at Baghdad on 4 October 1963 and registered with the United Nations and published by the United Nations in document 7063, United Nations, Treaty Series, 1964;

3.   Calls upon the Secretary-General to lend his assistance to make arrangements with Iraq and Kuwait to demarcate the boundary between Iraq and Kuwait, drawing on appropriate material, including the map transmitted by Security Council document S/22412 and to report back to the Security Council within one month;

4.   Decides to guarantee the inviolability of the above-mentioned international boundary and to take as appropriate all necessary measures to that end in accordance with the Charter of the United Nations;

6/   General Assembly resolution 34/146.

7/   S/22366.

8/   S/22409.

5. Requests the Secretary-General, after consulting with Iraq and Kuwait, to submit within three days to the Security Council for its approval a plan for the immediate deployment of a United Nations observer unit to monitor the Khor Abdullah and a demilitarized zone, which is hereby established, extending ten kilometres into Iraq and five kilometres into Kuwait from the boundary referred to in the "Agreed Minutes Between the State of Kuwait and the Republic of Iraq Regarding the Restoration of Friendly Relations, Recognition and Related Matters" of 4 October 1963; to deter violations of the boundary through its presence in and surveillance of the demilitarized zone; to observe any hostile or potentially hostile action mounted from the territory of one State to the other; and for the Secretary-General to report regularly to the Security Council on the operations of the unit, and immediately if there are serious violations of the zone or potential threats to peace;

6. Notes that as soon as the Secretary-General notifies the Security Council of the completion of the deployment of the United Nations observer unit, the conditions will be established for the Member States cooperating with Kuwait in accordance with resolution 678 (1990) to bring their military presence in Iraq to an end consistent with resolution 686 (1991);

7. Invites Iraq to reaffirm unconditionally its obligations under the Geneva Protocol for the Prohibition of the Use in War of Asphyxiating, Poisonous or Other Gases, and of Bacteriological Methods of Warfare, signed at Geneva on 17 June 1925, and to ratify the Convention on the Prohibition of the Development, Production and Stockpiling of Bacteriological (Biological) and Toxin Weapons and on Their Destruction, of 10 April 1972;

8. Decides that Iraq shall unconditionally accept the destruction, removal, or rendering harmless, under international supervision, of:

(a) All chemical and biological weapons and all stocks of agents and all related subsystems and components and all research, development, support and manufacturing facilities;

(b) All ballistic missiles with a range greater than 150 kilometres and related major parts, and repair and production facilities;

9. Decides, for the implementation of paragraph 8 above, the following:

(a) Iraq shall submit to the Secretary-General, within fifteen days of the adoption of the present resolution, a declaration of the locations, amounts and types of all items specified in paragraph 8 and agree to urgent, on-site inspection as specified below;

(b) The Secretary-General, in consultation with the appropriate Governments and, where appropriate, with the Director-General of the World Health Organization, within forty-five days of the passage of the present resolution, shall develop, and submit to the Council for approval, a plan calling for the completion of the following acts within forty-five days of such approval:

(i) The forming of a Special Commission, which shall carry out immediate on-site inspection of Iraq's biological, chemical and missile capabilities, based on Iraq's declarations and the designation of any additional locations by the Special Commission itself;

(ii) The yielding by Iraq of possession to the Special Commission for destruction, removal or rendering harmless, taking into account the requirements of public safety, of all items specified under paragraph 8 (a) above, including items at the additional locations designated by the Special Commission under paragraph 9 (b) (i) above and the destruction by Iraq, under the supervision of the Special Commission, of all its missile capabilities, including launchers, as specified under paragraph 8 (b) above;

(iii) The provision by the Special Commission of the assistance and cooperation to the Director-General of the International Atomic Energy Agency required in paragraphs 12 and 13 below;

10. __Decides__ that Iraq shall unconditionally undertake not to use, develop, construct or acquire any of the items specified in paragraphs 8 and 9 above and requests the Secretary-General, in consultation with the Special Commission, to develop a plan for the future ongoing monitoring and verification of Iraq's compliance with this paragraph, to be submitted to the Security Council for approval within one hundred and twenty days of the passage of this resolution;

11. __Invites__ Iraq to reaffirm unconditionally its obligations under the Treaty on the Non-Proliferation of Nuclear Weapons of 1 July 1968;

12. __Decides__ that Iraq shall unconditionally agree not to acquire or develop nuclear weapons or nuclear-weapons-usable material or any subsystems or components or any research, development, support or manufacturing facilities related to the above; to submit to the Secretary-General and the Director-General of the International Atomic Energy Agency within fifteen days of the adoption of the present resolution a declaration of the locations, amounts, and types of all items specified above; to place all of its nuclear-weapons-usable materials under the exclusive control, for custody and removal, of the International Atomic Energy Agency, with the assistance and cooperation of the Special Commission as provided for in the plan of the Secretary-General discussed in paragraph 9 (b) above; to accept, in accordance with the arrangements provided for in paragraph 13 below, urgent on-site inspection and the destruction, removal or rendering harmless as appropriate of all items specified above; and to accept the plan discussed in paragraph 13 below for the future ongoing monitoring and verification of its compliance with these undertakings;

13. __Requests__ the Director-General of the International Atomic Energy Agency, through the Secretary-General, with the assistance and cooperation of the Special Commission as provided for in the plan of the Secretary-General in paragraph 9 (b) above, to carry out immediate on-site inspection of Iraq's nuclear capabilities based on Iraq's declarations and the designation of any additional locations by the Special Commission; to develop a plan for submission to the Security Council within forty-five days calling for the destruction, removal, or rendering harmless as appropriate of all items listed in paragraph 12 above; to carry out the plan within forty-five days following approval by the Security Council; and to develop a plan, taking into account the rights and obligations of Iraq under the Treaty on the Non-Proliferation of Nuclear Weapons of 1 July 1968, for the future ongoing monitoring and verification of Iraq's compliance with paragraph 12 above, including an inventory of all nuclear material in Iraq subject to the Agency's verification and inspections to confirm that Agency safeguards cover all relevant nuclear activities in Iraq, to be submitted to the Security Council for approval within one hundred and twenty days of the passage of the present resolution;

14. __Takes note__ that the actions to be taken by Iraq in paragraphs 8, 9, 10, 11, 12 and 13 of the present resolution represent steps towards the goal of establishing in the Middle East a zone free from weapons of mass destruction and all missiles for their delivery and the objective of a global ban on chemical weapons;

D

15. __Requests__ the Secretary-General to report to the Security Council on the steps taken to facilitate the return of all Kuwaiti property seized by Iraq, including a list of any property that Kuwait claims has not been returned or which has not been returned intact;

- 8 -

0026

16. **Reaffirms** that Iraq, without prejudice to the debts and obligations of Iraq arising prior to 2 August 1990, which will be addressed through the normal mechanisms, is liable under international law for any direct loss, damage, including environmental damage and the depletion of natural resources, or injury to foreign Governments, nationals and corporations, as a result of Iraq's unlawful invasion and occupation of Kuwait;

17. **Decides** that all Iraqi statements made since 2 August 1990 repudiating its foreign debt are null and void, and demands that Iraq adhere scrupulously to all of its obligations concerning servicing and repayment of its foreign debt;

18. **Decides also** to create a fund to pay compensation for claims that fall within paragraph 16 above and to establish a Commission that will administer the fund;

19. **Directs** the Secretary-General to develop and present to the Security Council for decision, no later than thirty days following the adoption of the present resolution, recommendations for the fund to meet the requirement for the payment of claims established in accordance with paragraph 18 above and for a programme to implement the decisions in paragraphs 16, 17 and 18 above, including: administration of the fund; mechanisms for determining the appropriate level of Iraq's contribution to the fund based on a percentage of the value of the exports of petroleum and petroleum products from Iraq not to exceed a figure to be suggested to the Council by the Secretary-General, taking into account the requirements of the people of Iraq, Iraq's payment capacity as assessed in conjunction with the international financial institutions taking into consideration external debt service, and the needs of the Iraqi economy; arrangements for ensuring that payments are made to the fund; the process by which funds will be allocated and claims paid; appropriate procedures for evaluating losses, listing claims and verifying their validity and resolving disputed claims in respect of Iraq's liability as specified in paragraph 16 above; and the composition of the Commission designated above;

20. **Decides**, effective immediately, that the prohibitions against the sale or supply to Iraq of commodities or products, other than medicine and health supplies, and prohibitions against financial transactions related thereto contained in resolution 661 (1990) shall not apply to foodstuffs notified to the Security Council Committee established by resolution 661 (1990) concerning the situation between Iraq and Kuwait or, with the approval of that Committee, under the simplified and accelerated "no-objection" procedure, to materials and supplies for essential civilian needs as identified in the report of the Secretary-General dated 20 March 1991, 9/ and in any further findings of humanitarian need by the Committee;

21. **Decides** that the Security Council shall review the provisions of paragraph 20 above every sixty days in the light of the policies and practices of the Government of Iraq, including the implementation of all relevant resolutions of the Security Council, for the purpose of determining whether to reduce or lift the prohibitions referred to therein;

22. **Decides** that upon the approval by the Security Council of the programme called for in paragraph 19 above and upon Council agreement that Iraq has completed all actions contemplated in paragraphs 8, 9, 10, 11, 12 and 13 above, the prohibitions against the import of commodities and products originating in Iraq and the prohibitions against financial transactions related thereto contained in resolution 661 (1990) shall have no further force or effect;

23. *Decides* that, pending action by the Security Council under paragraph 22 above, the Security Council Committee established by resolution 661 (1990) shall be empowered to approve, when required to assure adequate financial resources on the part of Iraq to carry out the activities under paragraph 20 above, exceptions to the prohibition against the import of commodities and products originating in Iraq;

24. *Decides* that, in accordance with resolution 661 (1990) and subsequent related resolutions and until a further decision is taken by the Security Council, all States shall continue to prevent the sale or supply, or the promotion or facilitation of such sale or supply, to Iraq by their nationals, or from their territories or using their flag vessels or aircraft, of:

(a) Arms and related matériel of all types, specifically including the sale or transfer through other means of all forms of conventional military equipment, including for paramilitary forces, and spare parts and components and their means of production, for such equipment;

(b) Items specified and defined in paragraphs 8 and 12 above not otherwise covered above;

(c) Technology under licensing or other transfer arrangements used in the production, utilization or stockpiling of items specified in subparagraphs (a) and (b) above;

(d) Personnel or materials for training or technical support services relating to the design, development, manufacture, use, maintenance or support of items specified in subparagraphs (a) and (b) above;

25. *Calls upon* all States and international organizations to act strictly in accordance with paragraph 24 above, notwithstanding the existence of any contracts, agreements, licences or any other arrangements;

26. *Requests* the Secretary-General, in consultation with appropriate Governments, to develop within sixty days, for the approval of the Security Council, guidelines to facilitate full international implementation of paragraphs 24 and 25 above and paragraph 27 below, and to make them available to all States and to establish a procedure for updating these guidelines periodically;

27. *Calls upon* all States to maintain such national controls and procedures and to take such other actions consistent with the guidelines to be established by the Security Council under paragraph 26 above as may be necessary to ensure compliance with the terms of paragraph 24 above, and calls upon international organizations to take all appropriate steps to assist in ensuring such full compliance;

28. *Agrees* to review its decisions in paragraphs 22, 23, 24 and 25 above, except for the items specified and defined in paragraphs 8 and 12 above, on a regular basis and in any case one hundred and twenty days following passage of the present resolution, taking into account Iraq's compliance with the resolution and general progress towards the control of armaments in the region;

29. *Decides* that all States, including Iraq, shall take the necessary measures to ensure that no claim shall lie at the instance of the Government of Iraq, or of any person or body in Iraq, or of any person claiming through or for the benefit of any such person or body, in connection with any contract or other transaction where its performance was affected by reason of the measures taken by the Security Council in resolution 661 (1990) and related resolutions;

G

30. *Decides* that, in furtherance of its commitment to facilitate the repatriation of all Kuwaiti and third country nationals, Iraq shall extend all necessary cooperation to the International Committee of the Red Cross, providing

- 10 -

0028

lists of such persons, facilitating the access of the International Committee of the Red Cross to all such persons wherever located or detained and facilitating the search by the International Committee of the Red Cross for those Kuwaiti and third country nationals still unaccounted for;

31. __Invites__ the International Committee of the Red Cross to keep the Secretary-General apprised as appropriate of all activities undertaken in connection with facilitating the repatriation or return of all Kuwaiti and third country nationals or their remains present in Iraq on or after 2 August 1990;

H

32. __Requires__ Iraq to inform the Security Council that it will not commit or support any act of international terrorism or allow any organization directed towards commission of such acts to operate within its territory and to condemn unequivocally and renounce all acts, methods and practices of terrorism;

I

33. __Declares__ that, upon official notification by Iraq to the Secretary-General and to the Security Council of its acceptance of the provisions above, a formal cease-fire is effective between Iraq and Kuwait and the Member States cooperating with Kuwait in accordance with resolution 678 (1990);

34. __Decides__ to remain seized of the matter and to take such further steps as may be required for the implementation of the present resolution and to secure peace and security in the area.

Security Council

Distr.
GENERAL

S/22559
2 May 1991

ORIGINAL: ENGLISH

REPORT OF THE SECRETARY-GENERAL PURSUANT TO PARAGRAPH 19 OF
SECURITY COUNCIL RESOLUTION 687 (1991)

INTRODUCTION

1.   The present report is submitted pursuant to paragraph 19 of Security Council resolution 687 (1991) of 3 April 1991. In paragraph 16 of that resolution, the Council reaffirmed that Iraq "is liable, under international law, for any direct loss, damage, including environmental damage and the depletion of natural resources, or injury to foreign Governments, nationals and corporations, as a result of Iraq's unlawful invasion and occupation of Kuwait". In paragraph 17 of the resolution, the Council decided "that all Iraqi statements made since 2 August 1990 repudiating its foreign debt are null and void", and demanded that "Iraq adhere scrupulously to all of its obligations concerning servicing and repayment of its foreign debt". The Council also decided, in paragraph 18 of the resolution, "to create a fund to pay compensation for claims that fall within the scope of paragraph 16 ... and to establish a Commission that will administer the fund".

2.   In paragraph 19 of the resolution, the Security Council directed the Secretary-General "to develop and present to the Security Council for decision, no later than 30 days following the adoption of the present resolution, recommendations for the fund to meet the requirement for the payment of claims established in accordance with paragraph 18 ..., and for a programme to implement the decisions in paragraphs 16, 17 and 18 ..., including: administration of the fund; mechanisms for determining the appropriate level of Iraq's contribution to the fund based on a percentage of the value of the exports of petroleum and petroleum products from Iraq not to exceed a figure to be suggested to the Council by the Secretary-General, taking into account the requirements of the people of Iraq, Iraq's payment capacity as assessed in conjunction with the international financial institutions taking into consideration external debt service, and the needs of the Iraqi economy; arrangements for ensuring that payments are made to the fund; the process by which funds will be allocated and claims paid; appropriate procedures for evaluating losses, listing claims and verifying their validity and resolving disputed claims in respect of Iraq's liability as specified in paragraph 16 ...; and the composition of the Commission

/...

- 12 -

0030

designated [in paragraph 18]". In making the following recommendations, I
have borne in mind the need for maximum transparency, efficiency, flexibility
and economy in the institutional framework that will be required for the
implementation of the decisions contained in paragraphs 16, 17 and 18 of the
resolution.

I. INSTITUTIONAL FRAMEWORK

A. The Fund

3.   The Fund created by paragraph 18 of Security Council resolution
687 (1991) will be established by the Secretary-General as a special account
of the United Nations. The Fund will be known as the United Nations
Compensation Fund (hereinafter referred to as "the Fund"). The Fund will be
operated in accordance with the United Nations Financial Regulations and
Rules. As a special account of the United Nations, the Fund, therefore, will
enjoy, in accordance with Article 105 of the Charter and the Convention on the
Privileges and Immunities of the United Nations of 13 February 1946, 1/ the
status, facilities, privileges and immunities accorded to the United Nations.
The Fund will be used to pay compensation for "any direct loss, damage,
including environmental damage and the depletion of natural resources, or
injury to foreign Governments, nationals and corporations, as a result of
Iraq's unlawful invasion and occupation of Kuwait" as provided for in
paragraph 16 of resolution 687 (1991).

B. The Commission

4.   The Fund is to be administered by the Commission established by the
Security Council in paragraph 18 of resolution 687 (1991). The Commission,
which is to be known as the United Nations Compensation Commission
(hereinafter referred to as "the Commission"), will function under the
authority of the Security Council and be a subsidiary organ thereof. In
accordance with the terms of paragraph 19 of resolution 687 (1991), in
carrying out its functions, the Commission will be required to address a
variety of complex administrative, financial, legal and policy issues,
including the mechanism for determining the level of contribution to the Fund;
the allocation of funds and payments of claims; the procedures for evaluating
losses, listing claims and verifying their validity; and resolving disputed
claims. In the light of the multifarious nature of the tasks to be performed
by the Commission, it will, in my view, be necessary to distinguish between
questions of policy and the functional aspects of the Commission's work. The
Commission should, therefore, operate at a policy-making level and a
functional level. A secretariat will be necessary for servicing the work of
the Commission at both the policy-making and the functional levels.

- 13 -

0031

C. Structure and composition of the Commission

5. The principal organ of the Commission will be a 15-member Governing Council composed of the representatives of the current members of the Security Council at any given time. The Governing Council will be assisted by a number of commissioners who will perform the tasks assigned to them by the Governing Council. The precise number of commissioners will be determined by the Governing Council in the light of the tasks to be performed. The commissioners will be experts in fields such as finance, law, accountancy, insurance and environmental damage assessment, who will act in their personal capacity. They will be nominated by the Secretary-General and appointed by the Governing Council for specific tasks and terms. In nominating the commissioners, the Secretary-General will pay due regard to the need for geographical representation, professional qualifications, experience and integrity. The Secretary-General will establish a register of experts which might be drawn upon when commissioners are to be appointed.

6. A secretariat, composed of an Executive Secretary and the necessary staff, will be established to service the Commission. The Executive Secretary's primary responsibility will be the technical administration of the Fund and the servicing of the Commission. He will be appointed by the Secretary-General after consultation with the Governing Council. The staff of the secretariat will be appointed by the Secretary-General. The Executive Secretary and staff will serve under the United Nations Staff Regulations and Rules.

D. Status, privileges and immunities of the Commission

7. The Convention on the Privileges and Immunities of the United Nations of 13 February 1946 1/ will apply to the Commission and its secretariat. The members of the Governing Council will have the status of representatives of States, the commissioners will have the status of experts on missions within the meaning of article VI of the Convention and the Executive Secretary and the staff of the secretariat will have the status of officials within the meaning of articles V and VII of the Convention.

E. Expenses of the Commission

8. The expenses of the Commission will be borne by the Fund. More detailed recommendations regarding the budgetary administration of the Commission are set out in paragraph 29 below.

F. Headquarters of the Commission

9. For reasons of economy and practicality, particularly in the secretariat servicing of the Governing Council and the commissioners, the headquarters of the Commission should be in New York. Alternatively, it might be located at the site of one of the two Offices of the United Nations in Europe, i.e.

Geneva or Vienna. The Governing Council may decide whether some of the activities of the Commission should be carried out elsewhere.

G. Functions of the Commission

1. The Governing Council

10. As the policy-making organ of the Commission, the Governing Council will have the responsibility for establishing guidelines on all policy matters, in particular, those relating to the administration and financing of the Fund, the organization of the work of the Commission and the procedures to be applied to the processing of claims and to the settlement of disputed claims, as well as to the payments to be made from the Fund. In addition to its policy-making role, the Governing Council will perform important functional tasks with respect to claims presented to the Commission. Except with regard to the method of ensuring that payments are made to the Fund, which should be decided upon by consensus, the decisions of the Governing Council should be taken by a majority of at least nine of its members. No veto will apply in the Governing Council. If consensus is not achieved on any matter for which it is required, the question will be referred to the Security Council on the request of any member of the Governing Council. The Governing Council may invite States that it considers to have particular interest in its work to participate without a vote in its discussions. It may also invite members of the United Nations Secretariat or other persons to supply it with information or to give other assistance in examining matters within its competence. The Governing Council will, on behalf of the Commission, report periodically to the Security Council.

2. The commissioners

11. The commissioners will, under the guidelines established by the Governing Council, carry out such tasks and responsibilities as may be assigned to them by the Governing Council.

3. The secretariat

12. Under the direction of the Executive Secretary, the secretariat will carry out such tasks as may be assigned to it by the Governing Council and the commissioners, in particular the technical administration of the Fund, and the provision of secretariat services to the Governing Council and the commissioners.

II. THE IMPLEMENTATION OF THE DECISIONS CONTAINED IN PARAGRAPHS 16, 17 AND 18 OF RESOLUTION 687 (1991)

A. Mechanisms for determining the appropriate level of Iraq's contribution to the Fund

13.   In accordance with the institutional framework outlined in section I above, it would be for the Governing Council to establish the mechanisms for determining the appropriate level of Iraq's contribution to the Fund in accordance with the criteria laid down in paragraph 19 of Security Council resolution 687 (1991).   In carrying out this task, the Governing Council should consider the probable levels of future oil export revenues of Iraq, the amounts of military spending and arms imports in the past, the service of Iraq's foreign debt and the needs for reconstruction and development in the country.   The objective should be to settle compensation claims within a reasonable period of time.   The Governing Council will, of course, be free to draw upon expert advice as it sees fit.   It might wish to be assisted by one or more commissioners who, under the guidance of and within the terms of reference provided by the Governing Council, might give advice with regard to the appropriate level of Iraq's contribution to the Fund as well as to the periodic monitoring of that level of contribution.   Simultaneously with the establishment of the Governing Council, I will undertake the appropriate consultations as required by paragraph 19 of resolution 687 (1991) so that, as soon as possible, I will be in a position to suggest the figure not to be exceeded by the Iraqi contribution.

B. Arrangements for ensuring that payments are made to the Fund

14.   The arrangements for ensuring payments to the Fund are among the most technical and difficult of the tasks that have been entrusted to the Commission.   The decisions taken in this regard will determine, _inter alia_, the financial viability of the Fund and its capacity to meet the compensation claims decided upon by the Commission as well as the size and organization of the secretariat.

15.   In addressing the question of the possible arrangements for ensuring payments to the Fund, there is an obvious necessity for securing constant and reliable financing of the Fund, without which the essential purpose of the Fund will be defeated.   It is also desirable to seek modalities for the financing of the Fund that avoid the necessity of legal and other proceedings in a multiplicity of third countries and jurisdictions.

16.   The legal basis for the payments by Iraq to the Fund is to be found in paragraph 19 of resolution 687 (1991).   Iraq has officially notified the United Nations of its acceptance of the provisions of the resolution, including paragraph 19, in accordance with paragraph 33 of the resolution.   It follows from paragraph 19 of resolution 687 (1991) that the method envisaged by the Security Council for the financing of the Fund is a contribution by Iraq based on a percentage of the value of its exports determined in

- 16 -

0034

accordance with the mechanism referred to in paragraph 13 above. It also follows from the resolution that the Security Council did not envisage using "frozen assets" of Iraq held in third countries for the financing of the Fund.

17. Under these circumstances, there are several options for ensuring that Iraq makes payments to the Fund. These options include the following:

(a) Iraq would pay to the Fund the established percentage of the market value of its exports of petroleum and petroleum products; the market value to be calculated on the day of the export. The payment would be effected in United States dollars and made within 30 days of the export from Iraq;

(b) An escrow account would be opened into which Iraq would deposit advance payments of lump sums equivalent to the estimated quarterly or semi-annual contribution required of it. These lump-sum payments would be re-evaluated periodically;

(c) A physical share of the exports would be taken and sold on the market on behalf of the Fund;

(d) The Fund would be designated as either the sole or co-beneficiary on the bill of lading or other title document and any letter of credit issued. The Fund, in turn, would retain its share and remit the remainder to Iraq;

(e) An escrow account provided with the appropriate privileges and immunities (e.g. at a central bank or an appropriate international institution) would be designated as beneficiary on the bill of lading or other title document and any letter of credit issued. The escrow agent would remit to the Fund the sum designated to be used to satisfy claims and the remainder to Iraq.

It would be for the Governing Council to decide among these various options.

18. All of these methods presuppose cooperation by Iraq and strict supervision of the exports of petroleum and petroleum products from Iraq. To this end, the Commission should arrange for appropriate monitoring. Whatever approach is adopted, should Iraq fail to meet its payment obligation, the Governing Council would report the matter to the Security Council.

19. It must be recognized that, in all probability, it may be some time before Iraq is able to resume oil exports. In the short term, the Fund is therefore unlikely to receive revenues, and some consideration will have to be given to the financing of the work of the Commission, a problem which is addressed in paragraph 29 below, but more particularly to the financing of the Fund in the near term from assets other than resumed oil exports by Iraq.

C. Claims procedure

20. The process by which funds will be allocated and claims paid, the appropriate procedures for evaluating losses, the listing of claims and the

verification of their validity and the resolution of disputed claims as set out in paragraph 19 of resolution 687 (1991) - the claims procedure - is the central purpose and object of paragraphs 16 to 19 of resolution 687 (1991). It is in this area of the Commission's work that the distinction between policy-making and function is most important. The Commission is not a court or an arbitral tribunal before which the parties appear; it is a political organ that performs an essentially fact-finding function of examining claims, verifying their validity, evaluating losses, assessing payments and resolving disputed claims. It is only in this last respect that a quasi-judicial function may be involved. Given the nature of the Commission, it is all the more important that some element of due process be built into the procedure. It will be the function of the commissioners to provide this element. As the policy-making organ of the Commission, it will fall to the Governing Council to establish the guidelines regarding the claims procedure. The commissioners will implement the guidelines in respect of claims that are presented and in resolving disputed claims. They will make the appropriate recommendations to the Governing Council, which in turn will make the final determination. The recommendations that follow have been divided for the sake of convenience under three main headings: the filing of claims; the processing of claims; and the payments of claims.

1. Filing of claims

21. With regard to the filing of claims, the Governing Council must first decide in what manner the claims of foreign Governments, nationals and corporations are to be filed with the Commission. It is recommended that the Commission should entertain, as a general rule, only consolidated claims filed by individual Governments on their own behalf or on behalf of their nationals and corporations. The filing of individual claims would entail tens of thousands of claims to be processed by the Commission, a task which could take a decade or more and could lead to inequalities in the filing of claims disadvantaging small claimants. It will be for each individual Government to decide on the procedures to be followed internally in respect of the consolidation of the claim having regard to its own legal system, practice and procedures. The Governing Council may, in addition, consider whether, in exceptional circumstances involving very large and complex claims, a somewhat different procedure could apply. The question might be considered whether such claims, the character of which, of course, would have to be defined by the Governing Council, could be filed individually with the Commission by Governments, nationals or corporations and whether the individual Government, national or corporation could be authorized to present these claims.

22. In this context, there is another matter that requires consideration by the Commission and regarding which the Governing Council should establish guidelines, namely the question of the exclusivity or non-exclusivity of the claims procedure foreseen in paragraph 19 of the resolution. It is clear from paragraph 16 of the resolution that the debts and obligations of Iraq arising prior to 2 August 1990 are an entirely separate issue and will be addressed "through the normal mechanisms". It is also clear from paragraph 16 that the

0036

- 18 -

resolution and the procedure foreseen in paragraph 19 relate to liability under international law. Resolution 687 (1991) could not, and does not, establish the Commission as an organ with exclusive competence to consider claims arising from Iraq's unlawful invasion and occupation of Kuwait. In other words, it is entirely possible, indeed probable, that individual claimants will proceed with claims against Iraq in their domestic legal systems. The likelihood of parallel actions taking place on the international level in the Commission and on the domestic level in national courts cannot be ignored. It is, therefore, recommended that the Governing Council establish guidelines regarding the non-exclusivity of claims and the appropriate mechanisms for coordination of actions at the international and domestic levels in order to ensure that the aggregate of compensation awarded by the Commission and a national court or commission does not exceed the amount of the loss. A particular problem might arise in this regard concerning default judgements obtained in national courts.

23. In addition to deciding on the consolidation of claims, the Governing Council may also wish to establish a categorization of claims according to both type and size. The categorization of claims according to type might, for example, distinguish between claims for loss of life or personal injury and property damage, environmental damage or damage due to the depletion of natural resources. The categorization of claims by size might for example, differentiate between small-, medium- and large-sized claims. A further categorization might be to distinguish between losses incurred by Governments, on the one hand, and losses incurred by nationals and corporations, on the other hand.

24. Governments could be requested by the Governing Council to use these categorizations when filing their consolidated claims. The Governing Council should also establish guidelines regarding the formal requirements for the presentation of claims such as the type of documentation to be presented in support of the claim and the time-delays for the filing of claims. The time-delays should be of sufficient length to permit Governments to establish and implement an internal procedure for the assembling and consolidation of claims. It is recommended that a fixed time period be established for the filing of all claims. A period of two years from the adoption of the filing guidelines would appear to be adequate. Alternatively, the Governing Council could set different filing periods for different types of claims in order to ensure that priority is given to certain claims, for example, loss of life or personal injury. In this respect, I am of the opinion that there would be some merit in providing for a priority consideration of small claims relating to losses by individuals so that these are disposed of before the consideration of claims relating to losses by foreign Governments and by corporations.

2. Processing of claims

25. The processing of claims will entail the verification of claims and evaluation of losses and the resolution of any disputed claims. The major

part of this task is not of a judicial nature; the resolution of disputed claims would, however, be quasi-judicial. It is envisaged that the processing of claims would be carried out principally by the commissioners. Before proceeding to the verification of claims and evaluation of losses, however, a determination will have to be made as to whether the losses for which claims are presented fall within the meaning of paragraph 16 of resolution 687 (1991), that is to say, whether the loss, damage or injury is direct and as a result of Iraq's unlawful invasion and occupation of Kuwait. It is recommended that the Governing Council establish detailed guidelines regarding what constitutes such direct loss for the guidance of all claimants as well as the commissioners.

26. Claims will be addressed to the Commission. The Commission will make a preliminary assessment of the claims, which will be carried out by the Secretariat, to determine whether they meet the formal requirements established by the Governing Council. The claims would then be submitted to verification and evaluation by panels normally comprised of three commissioners for this purpose. In carrying out these tasks, it is recommended that the commissioners be given the necessary powers to request additional evidence, to hold hearings in which individual Governments, nationals and corporations can present their views and to hear expert testimony. The Governing Council might wish to address the question of possible assistance to ensure the adequacy of the representation of countries of limited financial means. Iraq will be informed of all claims and will have the right to present its comments to the commissioners within time-delays to be fixed by the Governing Council or the Panel dealing with the individual claim. Recommendations of the commissioners regarding the verification and evaluation of claims will be final and subject only to the approval of the Governing Council, which shall make the final determination. The Governing Council should have the power to return claims to the commissioners for further revision if it so decides.

27. Where a dispute arises out of the allegation made by a claimant that the Panel of Commissioners, in dealing with its claims, has made an error, whether on a point of law and procedure or on a point of fact, such disputes will be dealt with by a board of commissioners who for this purpose should be guided by such guidelines as have been established by the Governing Council and the Arbitration Rules of the United Nations Commission on International Trade Law (UNCITRAL). The UNCITRAL Arbitration Rules will be modified as necessary. The final decision will be made by the Governing Council.

3. Payment of claims

28. It is to be anticipated that the value of claims approved by the Commission will at any given time far exceed the resources of the Fund. It will, therefore, be incumbent upon the Commission to decide on an allocation of funds and a procedure for the payment of claims. It is recommended that the Governing Council establish criteria for the allocation of funds, taking into account the size of claims, the scope of the losses sustained by the

- 20 -

0038

country concerned and any other relevant factors. In this connection, it might be necessary to distinguish between Kuwait, on the one hand, and other countries on the other hand. As far as the payment of claims is concerned, it follows from the consolidation of the claims and their filing by individual Governments that payments will be made exclusively to Governments. Individual Governments will be responsible for the appropriate distribution to individual claimants. The Governing Council should establish further guidelines regarding the payment of claims, for example, whether claims should be paid in full or whether percentages should be paid. In the latter case, the unsatisfied portions of the claims will remain as outstanding obligations.

D. Expenses of the Commission

29. The expenses of the Commission, including those of the Governing Council, the commissioners and the secretariat, should in principle be paid from the Fund. However, as some time will elapse before the Fund is adequately financed, consideration must be given to the financial implications of the programme outlined. It is recommended that urgent consideration be given to the means by which the initial costs of the Commission will be met.

Notes

1/   General Assembly resolution 22 A (I).

Security Council

Distr.
GENERAL

S/22613
20 May 1991

ORIGINAL: ENGLISH

Belgium, France, Romania, Union of Soviet Socialist Republics,
United Kingdom of Great Britain and Northern Ireland, United
States of America and Zaire: draft resolution

The Security Council,

Recalling its resolutions 674 (1990) of 29 October 1990, 686 (1991) of
2 March 1991 and 687 (1991) of 3 April 1991, concerning the liability of Iraq,
without prejudice to its debts and obligations arising prior to 2 August 1990,
for any direct loss, damage, including environmental damage and the depletion
of natural resources, or injury to foreign Governments, nationals and
corporations, as a result of Iraq's unlawful invasion and occupation of
Kuwait,

Taking note of the Secretary-General's report of 2 May 1991 (S/22559),
submitted in accordance with paragraph 19 of resolution 687 (1991),

Acting under Chapter VII of the Charter of the United Nations,

1. Expresses its appreciation to the Secretary-General for his report
of 2 May 1991 (S/22559);

2. Welcomes the fact that the Secretary-General will now undertake the
appropriate consultations requested by paragraph 19 of resolution 687 (1991)
so that he will be in a position to recommend to the Security Council for
decision as soon as possible the figure which the level of Iraq's contribution
to the Fund will not exceed;

3. Decides to establish the Fund and the Commission referred to in
paragraph 18 of resolution 687 (1991) in accordance with section I of the
Secretary-General's report and that the Governing Council shall be located at
the United Nations Office at Geneva and that the Governing Council may decide
whether some of the activities of the Commission should be carried out
elsewhere;

4. Requests the Secretary-General to take the actions necessary to
implement paragraphs 2 and 3 above in consultation with the members of the
Governing Council;

5.   **Directs** the Governing Council to proceed in an expeditious manner to implement the provisions of section E of resolution 687 (1991), taking into account the recommendations in section II of the Secretary-General's report;

6.   **Decides** that the requirement for Iraqi contributions will apply in the manner to be prescribed by the Governing Council with respect to all Iraqi petroleum and petroleum products exported from Iraq after 3 April 1991 as well as such petroleum and petroleum products exported earlier but not delivered or not paid for as a specific result of the prohibitions contained in Security Council resolution 661 (1990);

7.   **Requests** the Governing Council to report as soon as possible on the actions it has taken with regard to the mechanisms for determining the appropriate level of Iraq's contribution to the Fund and the arrangements for ensuring that payments are made to the Fund, so that the Security Council can give its approval in accordance with paragraph 22 of resolution 687 (1991);

8.   **Requests** that all States and international organizations cooperate with the decisions of the Governing Council taken pursuant to paragraph 5 of the present resolution, and also requests that the Governing Council keep the Security Council informed on this matter;

9.   **Decides** that, if the Governing Council notifies the Security Council that Iraq has failed to carry out decisions of the Governing Council taken pursuant to paragraph 5 of the present resolution, the Security Council intends to retain or to take action to reimpose the prohibition against the import of petroleum and petroleum products originating in Iraq and financial transactions related thereto;

10. **Decides also** to remain seized of this matter and that the Governing Council will submit periodic reports to the Secretary-General and the Security Council.

Security Council

Distr.
GENERAL

S/22661
31 May 1991

ORIGINAL: ENGLISH

LETTER DATED 30 MAY 1991 FROM THE SECRETARY-GENERAL
ADDRESSED TO THE PRESIDENT OF THE SECURITY COUNCIL

As I indicated in paragraph 13 of my report (S/22559) to the Security
Council, pursuant to paragraph 19 of its resolution 687 (1991), I attach
herewith a note suggesting a percentage figure of the value of Iraq's
petroleum exports which should not exceed its contribution to the Fund.

(Signed) Javier PEREZ de CUELLAR

- 24 -

0042

30 May 1991

Note of the Secretary-General pursuant to paragraph 13 of his report of 2 May 1991 (S/22559)

1.   On 2 May 1991 I presented to the Council, in compliance with Security Council resolution 687, a report (S/22559) pursuant to paragraph 19 of Security Council resolution 687 (1991).   In the same paragraph 19 it was stipulated that Iraq's contribution to the fund based on a percentage of the value of the exports of petroleum and petroleum products from Iraq should not exceed a figure to be suggested to the Council by me.   In paragraph 13 of the report, I informed the Council that I will undertake the appropriate consultations as required so that, as soon as possible, I will be in a position to suggest this figure.

2.   Authoritative data necessary for the preparation of this communication to the Security Council is not readily available.   However, given that Iraq derives almost its entire exports earnings from the export of one single commodity (oil) and that the unit price and export volume of Iraqi oil are monitored by OPEC, it is possible to estimate the size and functioning of its economy in general and of its external trade and payments structure in particular.   Data available for this exercise have been taken from various sources including the Government of Iraq, the International Monetary Fund, ESCWA, OPEC, and the United Nations Statistical Office.

3.   Paragraph 16 of resolution 687, in defining the extent of Iraq's liability, states that it is "liable under international law for any direct loss, damage, including environmental damage and the depletion of natural resources, or injury to foreign government, national and corporations, as a result of Iraq's unlawful invasion and occupation of Kuwait".   As paragraph 16 states, this liability is "without prejudice to the debts and obligations of Iraq arising prior to 2 August 1990, which will be addressed through the normal mechanisms".   Thus, this communication has to limit itself to dealing with the economic and financial possibilities and constraints of Iraq to compensate for the damage defined in paragraph 16.

4.   Iraq's oil production quota, as agreed to within OPEC in July 1990, is of 3.14 million barrels per day.   With an estimated internal consumption of about 300,000 barrels per day, the Iraqi Government intends to reach its most recent 1989 level of exports of 2.85 million barrels per day in 1993, as communicated by the Permanent Representative to the United Nations to me in his letter of 29 April 1991.   If the reference price of $21 per barrel agreed to by OPEC in July 1990 were to be used during 1993, which after adjustment for quality would result in a price of $20.04 for Iraqi crude, total Iraqi export earnings for 1993 can be expected to reach $21 billion, surpassing its 1989 export revenue.   Such earnings could conceivably be higher, given that global demand for oil increases by 2 per cent annually, that production in large industrial countries has been declining over the last four years, and that only a few

- 25 -

0043

countries have the reserves and even fewer the production capacity to offset the resulting shortfall. These calculations also assume that all OPEC member countries would return to roughly similar production quotas as those agreed to in July 1990, thus allowing Iraq to reach this level of exports without causing a price collapse.

5.   Estimates for foreign exchange expenditures of the Iraqi economy for strictly civilian purposes during the 1980s vary. By taking account of historical relationships of consumption and investment to GDP and their import intensity, and data on net service imports as provided by Iraq, it is estimated that about $8 billion may be required to sustain a level of civilian imports in 1991 consistent with the needs of the Iraqi economy.

6.   Iraq's total external debt and obligations have been reported by the Government of Iraq at $42,097 million as of 31 December 1990. However, the exact figure of Iraq's external indebtedness can only be ascertained following discussions between Iraq and its creditors. To estimate debt servicing requirements it is assumed that Iraq reschedules its debts at standard Paris Club terms.

7.   With oil exports expected to reach about $21 billion by 1993 imports should absorb about 48 per cent of export earnings and debt servicing approximately 22 per cent. I suggest, therefore, that compensation to be paid by Iraq (as arising from section E of resolution 687) should not exceed 30 per cent of the annual value of the exports of petroleum and petroleum products from Iraq.

8.   The above calculations are based on data and a number of assumptions that have to be kept under review.

Security Council

Distr.
GENERAL

S/RES/705 (1991)
15 August 1991

RESOLUTION 705 (1991)

Adopted by the Security Council at its 3004th meeting,
on 15 August 1991

The Security Council,

Having considered the note of 30 May 1991 of the Secretary-General pursuant to paragraph 13 of his report of 2 May 1991 (S/22559) which was annexed to the Secretary-General's letter of 30 May 1991 to the President of the Security Council (S/22661),

Acting under Chapter VII of the Charter,

1. Expresses its appreciation to the Secretary-General for his note of 30 May 1991 which was annexed to his letter to the President of the Security Council of the same date (S/22661);

2. Decides that in accordance with the suggestion made by the Secretary-General in paragraph 7 of his note of 30 May 1991, compensation to be paid by Iraq (as arising from section E of resolution 687) shall not exceed 30 per cent of the annual value of the exports of petroleum and petroleum products from Iraq;

3. Decides further, in accordance with paragraph 8 of the Secretary-General's note of 30 May 1991, to review the figure established in paragraph 2 above from time to time in light of data and assumptions contained in the letter of the Secretary-General (S/22661) and other relevant developments.

- 27 -

0045

Security Council

Distr.
GENERAL

S/RES/706 (1991)
15 August 1991

RESOLUTION 706 (1991)

Adopted by the Security Council at its 3004th meeting,
on 15 August 1991

The Security Council,

Recalling its previous relevant resolutions and in particular resolutions 661 (1990), 686 (1991), 687 (1991), 688 (1991), 692 (1991), 699 (1991) and 705 (1991),

Taking note of the report (S/22799) dated 15 July 1991 of the inter-agency mission headed by the executive delegate of the Secretary-General for the United Nations inter-agency humanitarian programme for Iraq, Kuwait and the Iraq/Turkey and Iraq/Iran border areas,

Concerned by the serious nutritional and health situation of the Iraqi civilian population as described in this report, and by the risk of a further deterioration of this situation,

Concerned also that the repatriation or return of all Kuwaitis and third country nationals or their remains present in Iraq on or after 2 August 1990, pursuant to paragraph 2 (c) of resolution 686 (1991), and paragraphs 30 and 31 of resolution 687 (1991) has not yet been fully carried out,

Taking note of the conclusions of the above-mentioned report, and in particular of the proposal for oil sales by Iraq to finance the purchase of foodstuffs, medicines and materials and supplies for essential civilian needs for the purpose of providing humanitarian relief,

Taking note also of the letters dated 14 April 1991, 31 May 1991, 6 June 1991, 9 July 1991 and 22 July 1991 from the Minister of Foreign Affairs of Iraq and the Permanent Representative of Iraq to the Chairman of the Committee established by resolution 661 (1990) concerning the export from Iraq of petroleum and petroleum products,

Convinced of the need for equitable distribution of humanitarian relief to all segments of the Iraqi civilian population through effective monitoring and transparency

91-26589   35740   E   - 28 -

0046

Recalling and reaffirming in this regard its resolution 688 (1991) and in particular the importance which the Council attaches to Iraq allowing unhindered access by international humanitarian organizations to all those in need of assistance in all parts of Iraq and making available all necessary facilities for their operation, and in this connection stressing the important and continuing role played by the Memorandum of Understanding between the United Nations and the Government of Iraq of 18 April 1991 (S/22663),

Recalling that, pursuant to resolutions 687 (1991), 692 (1991) and 699 (1991), Iraq is required to pay the full costs of the Special Commission and the IAEA in carrying out the tasks authorized by section C of resolution 687 (1991), and that the Secretary-General in his report to the Security Council of 15 July 1991 (S/22792), submitted pursuant to paragraph 4 of resolution 699 (1991), expressed the view that the most obvious way of obtaining financial resources from Iraq to meet the costs of the Special Commission and the IAEA would be to authorize the sale of some Iraqi petroleum and petroleum products; recalling further that Iraq is required to pay its contributions to the Compensation Fund and half the costs of the Iraq-Kuwait Boundary Demarcation Commission, and recalling further that in its resolutions 686 (1991) and 687 (1991) the Security Council demanded that Iraq return in the shortest possible time all Kuwaiti property seized by it and requested the Secretary-General to take steps to facilitate this,

Acting under Chapter VII of the Charter,

1.   Authorizes all States, subject to the decision to be taken by the Security Council pursuant to paragraph 5 below and notwithstanding the provisions of paragraphs 3 (a), 3 (b) and 4 of resolution 661 (1990), to permit the import, during a period of 6 months from the date of passage of the resolution pursuant to paragraph 5 below, of petroleum and petroleum products originating in Iraq sufficient to produce a sum to be determined by the Council following receipt of the report of the Secretary-General requested in paragraph 5 of this resolution but not to exceed 1.6 billion United States dollars for the purposes set out in this resolution and subject to the following conditions:

(a)   Approval of each purchase of Iraqi petroleum and petroleum products by the Security Council Committee established by resolution 661 (1990) following notification to the Committee by the State concerned;

(b)   Payment of the full amount of each purchase of Iraqi petroleum and petroleum products directly by the purchaser in the State concerned into an escrow account to be established by the United Nations and to be administered by the Secretary-General, exclusively to meet the purposes of this resolution;

(c)   Approval by the Council, following the report of the Secretary-General requested in paragraph 5 of this resolution, of a scheme for the purchase of foodstuffs, medicines and materials and supplies for essential civilian needs as referred to in paragraph 20 of resolution 687 (1991), in particular health related materials, all of which to be labelled to the extent

- 29 -

possible as being supplied under this scheme, and for all feasible and appropriate United Nations monitoring and supervision for the purpose of assuring their equitable distribution to meet humanitarian needs in all regions of Iraq and to all categories of the Iraqi civilian population, as well as all feasible and appropriate management relevant to this purpose, such a United Nations role to be available if desired for humanitarian assistance from other sources;

(d) The sum authorized in this paragraph to be released by successive decisions of the Committee established by resolution 661 (1990) in three equal portions after the Council has taken the decision provided for in paragraph 5 below on the implementation of this resolution, and notwithstanding any other provision of this paragraph, the sum to be subject to review concurrently by the Council on the basis of its ongoing assessment of the needs and requirements;

2. Decides that a part of the sum in the account to be established by the Secretary-General shall be made available by him to finance the purchase of foodstuffs, medicines and materials and supplies for essential civilian needs, as referred to in paragraph 20 of resolution 687, and the cost to the United Nations of its roles under this resolution and of other necessary humanitarian activities in Iraq;

3. Decides further that a part of the sum in the account to be established by the Secretary-General shall be used by him for appropriate payments to the United Nations Compensation Fund, the full costs of carrying out the tasks authorized by Section C of resolution 687 (1991), the full costs incurred by the United Nations in facilitating the return of all Kuwaiti property seized by Iraq, and half the costs of the Boundary Commission;

4. Decides that the percentage of the value of exports of petroleum and petroleum products from Iraq, authorized under this resolution to be paid to the United Nations Compensation Fund, as called for in paragraph 19 of resolution 687 (1991), and as defined in paragraph 6 of resolution 692 (1991), shall be the same as the percentage decided by the Security Council in paragraph 2 of resolution 705 (1991) for payments to the Compensation Fund, until such time as the Governing Council of the Fund decides otherwise;

5. Requests the Secretary-General to submit within 20 days of the date of adoption of this resolution a report to the Security Council for decision on measures to be taken in order to implement paragraphs 1 (a), (b) and (c), estimates of the humanitarian requirements of Iraq set out in paragraph 2 above and of the amount of Iraq's financial obligations set out in paragraph 3 above up to the end of the period of the authorization in paragraph 1 above, as well as the method for taking the necessary legal measures to ensure that the purposes of this resolution are carried out and the method for taking account of the costs of transportation of such Iraqi petroleum and petroleum products;

6.   Further requests the Secretary-General in consultation with the International Committee of the Red Cross to submit within 20 days of the date of adoption of this resolution a report to the Security Council on activities undertaken in accordance with paragraph 31 of resolution 687 (1991) in connection with facilitating the repatriation or return of all Kuwaiti and third country nationals or their remains present in Iraq on or after 2 August 1990;

7.   Requires the Government of Iraq to provide to the Secretary-General and appropriate international organizations on the first day of the month immediately following the adoption of the present resolution and on the first day of each month thereafter until further notice, a statement of the gold and foreign currency reserves it holds whether in Iraq or elsewhere;

8.   Calls upon all States to cooperate fully in the implementation of this resolution;

9.   Decides to remain seized of the matter.

Security Council

Distr.
GENERAL

S/22885
2 August 1991
ENGLISH
ORIGINAL: SPANISH

LETTER DATED 2 AUGUST 1991 FROM THE PRESIDENT OF THE GOVERNING
COUNCIL OF THE UNITED NATIONS COMPENSATION COMMISSION TO THE
PRESIDENT OF THE SECURITY COUNCIL

In accordance with a decision taken by the Governing Council of the
United Nations Compensation Commission, at its tenth meeting, held on
2 August 1991, I have the honour to transmit the following for the information
of the members of the Security Council.

The Governing Council of the United Nations Compensation Commission
established by Security Council resolution 692 (1991), of 20 May 1991, held
its first session at Geneva from 23 July to 2 August 1991.

At its fourth meeting, held on 25 July 1991, the Governing Council
approved Guidelines for the conduct of its work (see annex I), a copy of which
is attached. In accordance with paragraph 5 of its Guidelines, the Governing
Council invited the representatives of Bangladesh, Iraq, Kuwait, Pakistan, the
Philippines and Sri Lanka to address the Council and reply to questions put to
them by the members.

At its ninth meeting, held on 1 August 1991, the Governing Council
decided to hold informal consultations the week beginning 16 September 1991
and to convene its second session the week beginning 14 October 1991.

At its tenth meeting, held today, 2 August 1991, the Governing Council
adopted the attached criteria for expedited processing of urgent claims, a
copy of which is attached (see annex II). The criteria will be issued as a
document of the Governing Council for general distribution (S/AC.26/1991/1).

At the same meeting, the Governing Council approved the proposals
contained in a working paper submitted by the United States of America on
arrangements for ensuring payments to the Compensation Fund

- 32 -

0050

(S/AC.26/1991/WP.4/Rev.1), as orally revised. The text of that decision is
contained in document S/AC.26/1991/2 of the Governing Council, which is being
given general distribution (see annex III).

(Signed) Philippe J. BERG
President of the Governing Council
of the United Nations Compensation
Commission

<u>Annex I</u>

<u>Guidelines for the conduct of the work of the Governing
Council of the United Nations Compensation Commission</u>

(Approved at the 4th meeting, held on 25 July 1991)

1.   The mandate of the Governing Council is defined in the report of the
Secretary-General pursuant to paragraph 19 of Security Council resolution
687 (1991) (S/22559). By paragraphs 3 and 5 of its resolution 692 (1991) the
Security Council decided to establish the Fund and the Commission referred to
in paragraph 18 of resolution 687 (1991) in accordance with section I of the
Secretary-General's report, and directed the Governing Council to implement
the provisions of section E of resolution 687 (1991), taking into account the
recommendations in section II of the Secretary-General's report.

2.   The Governing Council will hold its meetings in private but will open
them to the public as and when it deems it necessary for the enhancement of
the effectiveness of the Governing Council.

3.   As provided for in paragraph 10 of the Secretary-General's report,
decisions of the Governing Council on the method of ensuring that payments are
made to the Fund should be taken by consensus. Other decisions will be taken
by a majority of at least nine of its members. No veto will apply in the
Governing Council.

4.   As provided for in paragraph 10 of the Secretary-General's report, if
consensus is not achieved on any matter for which it is required, the question
will be referred to the Security Council on the request of any member of the
Governing Council.

5.   The Governing Council may invite States that it considers to have
particular interest in its work to participate without a vote in its
discussions. It may also invite members of the United Nations Secretariat or
other persons to supply it with information or to give other assistance in
examining matters within its competence.

6.   Information on the work of the Governing Council will be made publicly
available by the President when so decided in consultation with the members of
the Governing Council.

7.   The Governing Council will be provided with summary records of all its
meetings in all official languages.

8.   The success of the work of the Governing Council depends upon the
cooperation of all States.

9.   Prior to the close of each session, the Governing Council will decide on
the dates and duration of its next session. In between sessions, if any
member of the Governing Council or the Executive Secretary raises a matter

0052

- 34 -

that requires prompt consideration by the Governing Council, the President will hold consultations with the members of the Governing Council and could decide to convene it. Members will be informed of the opening date of the session as well as the provisional agenda at least five days in advance.

10. The Governing Council will, on behalf of the Commission, report periodically to the Security Council.

Annex II

Criteria for expedited processing of urgent claims

1.   The following criteria will govern the submission of the most urgent claims pursuant to resolution 687 (1991) for the first categories to be considered by the Commission. It provides for simple and expedited procedures by which Governments may submit consolidated claims and receive payments on behalf of the many individuals who suffered personal losses as a result of the invasion and occupation of Kuwait. For a great many persons these procedures would provide prompt compensation in full; for others they will provide substantial interim relief while their larger or more complex claims are being processed, including those suffering business losses.

2.   These criteria are without prejudice to future Council decisions with respect to criteria for other categories of claims, which will be approved separately as promptly as possible, with expert advice from Commissioners as may be required.

3.   The following criteria are not intended to resolve every issue that may arise with respect to these claims. Rather, they are intended to provide sufficient guidance to enable Governments to prepare consolidated claims submissions. It will probably be necessary for the Council to make further decisions on the processing of claims after receiving expert advice where needed.

4.   Each Government may submit one or more consolidated claims for each category established by the Council. Thus, each Government may make separate consolidated submissions covering claims in each of the categories set forth below; and it may later submit separate consolidated claims for each additional category to be established by the Council.

5.   The Council will promptly establish criteria for additional categories of claims, to permit consolidated submissions by Governments for all losses covered by paragraph 16 of resolution 687 (1991). Business losses of individuals may be part of consolidated claims under the expedited procedures set forth below. The Council will provide further advice on an urgent basis as to the types of business losses eligible for consideration under the expedited procedures. Business losses of corporations and other legal entities will be covered in other criteria to be established. The Council will also consider separately claims on behalf of third parties, such as Governments, insurance companies, relief agencies and employers, which have made payments or provided relief to persons suffering compensable losses.

6.   The Council will consider promptly, after receiving expert advice, the circumstances in which claims for mental pain and anguish may be admitted, the amounts to be awarded, and the limits to be imposed thereon.

7.   The Council will separately examine the question of the eligibility or otherwise of claims by or in respect of members of the allied coalition armed

- 36 -

0054

forces of the Member States that cooperated with the Government of Kuwait; the Executive Secretary will have available, _inter alia_, the provisions of the relevant national legislation of the Governments concerned.

8. The Commission will process the claims in the initial categories in paragraphs 10 to 16 on an expedited basis. While decisions on the precise method of processing these claims will be made at a later stage, the following steps are contemplated. As the claims are received they would be submitted to a panel of Commissioners for review within a set time-limit. If, as expected, the volume of claims in these categories is large, the Commissioners would be instructed to adopt expedited procedures to process them, such as checking individual claims on a sample basis, with further verification only if circumstances warranted. The Commissioners would be asked to report to the Council on the claims received and the amount recommended for the claims submitted by each Government. The Council would then decide on the total amount to be allocated to each Government. To the extent necessary, the Council would seek expert advice (for example, on what constitutes serious personal injury) at any stage of the process.

9. As contributions are made to the Fund, the Council will allocate those funds among the various categories of claims. If resources of the Fund are insufficient with respect to all claims processed to date, _pro rata_ payments would be made to Governments periodically as funds become available. The Council will decide on the priority for payment of various categories of claims.

PAYMENT OF FIXED AMOUNTS

10. These payments are available with respect to any person who, as a result of Iraq's unlawful invasion and occupation of Kuwait: (a) departed from Iraq or Kuwait during the period of 2 August 1990 to 2 March 1991; (b) suffered serious personal injury; or (c) whose spouse, child or parent died.

11. In the case of departures, $2,500 will be provided where there is simple documentation of the fact and date of departure from Iraq or Kuwait. Documentation of the actual amount of loss will not be required. Claims submitted under this procedure for departure from Iraq or Kuwait cannot be resubmitted for a greater amount in any other category. If the loss in question was greater than $2,500 and can be documented, it may instead be submitted under paragraph 14 and in other appropriate categories.

12. In addition, in the case of serious personal injury not resulting in death, $2,500 will be provided where there is simple documentation of the fact and date of the injury; and in the case of death, $2,500 will be provided where there is simple documentation of the death and family relationship. Documentation of the actual amount of loss resulting from the death or injury will not be required. If the actual loss in question was greater than $2,500, these payments will be treated as interim relief, and claims for additional amounts may also be submitted under paragraph 14 and in other appropriate categories.

13. These amounts are payable cumulatively where more than one situation applies with respect to a particular person. However, no more than $10,000 will be paid for death, and no more than $5,000 for departure, with respect to any one family (consisting of any person and his or her spouse, children and parents).

CONSIDERATION OF CLAIMS FOR UP TO $100,000 OF ACTUAL LOSSES PER PERSON

14. These payments are available with respect to death or personal injury, or losses of income, support, housing or personal property, or medical expenses or costs of departure, as a result of Iraq's unlawful invasion and occupation of Kuwait. The Commission will give expedited priority consideration to claims for such losses up to $100,000 per person.

15. (a) Such claims must be documented by appropriate evidence of the circumstances and the amount of the claimed loss. The evidence required will be the reasonable minimum that is appropriate under the circumstances involved, and a lesser degree of documentary evidence would ordinarily be required for smaller claims, such as those below $20,000.

(b) If the loss in question was greater than $100,000, claims for additional amounts may also be submitted in other appropriate categories. Criteria for the submission of claims in excess of $100,000 will be approved separately. Claims larger than $100,000 may be submitted in their entirety at a later date under those separate procedures, or the first $100,000 may be submitted at this time and the remainder separately.

16. Compensation will not be provided for losses suffered as a result of the trade embargo and related measures, nor will costs of attorneys' fees or other expenses for claims preparation be compensated under this category. Any compensation, whether in funds or in kind, already received from any source will be deducted from the total amount of losses suffered.

REQUIREMENTS APPLICABLE UNDER BOTH CATEGORIES

17. Claims will not be considered on behalf of Iraqi nationals who do not have bona fide nationality of any other State.

18. Claims must be for death, personal injury or other direct loss to individuals as a result of Iraq's unlawful invasion and occupation of Kuwait. This will include any loss suffered as a result of:

(a) Military operations or threat of military action by either side during the period 2 August 1990 to 2 March 1991;

(b) Departure from or inability to leave Iraq or Kuwait (or a decision not to return) during that period;

(c) Actions by officials, employees or agents of the Government of Iraq or its controlled entities during that period in connection with the invasion or occupation;

(d) The breakdown of civil order in Kuwait or Iraq during that period; or

(e) Hostage-taking or other illegal detention.

19. Claims will be submitted by Governments. Each Government will normally submit claims on behalf of its nationals; each Government may, in its discretion, also submit the claims of other persons resident in its territory. In addition, the Council may request an appropriate person, authority or body to submit claims on behalf of persons who are not in a position to have their claims submitted by a Government. Each Government shall make one or more consolidated submissions of all such claims for each category. The Council encourages the submission of such claims within six months from the date on which the Executive Secretary circulates to Governments the claims forms described below; and the Commission will thereupon give consideration to such claims as provided herein. The Council will consider at a later time the period within which all such claims must be submitted.

20. Each consolidated claim must include:

(a) A signed statement by each individual covered containing:

(i) His or her name and address, and any passport number or other identifying national number;

(ii) For claims under paragraph 14, the amount, type, and reason for each element of the loss, and any compensation, whether in funds or in kind already received from any source for the claim asserted;

(iii) Any documents evidencing the matters set forth in the definition of each category, as well as the items set forth in the preceding subparagraph; and

(iv) His or her affirmation that the foregoing information is correct, and that no other claim for the same loss has been submitted to the Commission;

(b) The affirmation of the Government submitting the claim that, to the best of the information available to it, the individuals in question are its nationals or residents, and the affirmation of the Government or of the person, authority or body as referred to in paragraph 19 that it has no reason to believe that the information stated is incorrect.

21. The Executive Secretary (or a Commissioner) will prepare and the Executive Secretary will distribute a standard form for submission of claims within each category, incorporating the above elements in a clear and concise

- 39 -

0057

manner. Except as may otherwise be agreed between the Executive Secretary and the Government in question, claims will be submitted to the Executive Secretary by Governments or by persons, authorities or bodies as referred to in paragraph 19 on the standard form and must include the information in an official language of the United Nations. Each Government may adopt such procedures as it finds appropriate in preparing its consolidated claim. The Executive Secretary (or a Commissioner) will be available to answer questions or provide assistance to any Governments which may request it.

0058

<u>Annex III</u>

<u>Decision taken by the Governing Council of the United Nations
Compensation Commission, at its 10th meeting, held on
2 August 1991</u>

<u>Arrangements for ensuring payments to the Compensation Fund</u>

The elaboration of a system for ensuring payments to the Fund with respect to future Iraqi oil exports is too complex for adoption at the first session of the Governing Council. It is clear that the Governing Council will require adequate factual information to understand the pre-invasion and current oil situation and on options for holding revenues from Iraqi exports of petroleum and petroleum products. The Governing Council taking into account the decision of the Security Council, decides:

(a) To request the Executive Secretary, with the assistance of an expert in the oil trade, to report to the Governing Council by early September on the following: the legal, financial, market and other technical aspects of Iraq's pre-invasion oil trade; the quantity, quality and value of oil subject to paragraph 6 of Security Council resolution 692 (1991); the capacity of Iraq to resume oil exports, in what quantities, quality and time-frame, and the estimated value of resumed oil exports under various possible scenarios; the technical possibilities for monitoring Iraq's oil exports, including oil pipeline flows, metering, measurements at terminals (tank and/or flange), and the resources needed to implement various options;

(b) To request the Executive Secretary, with the assistance of an expert or experts in international financial transactions, and after contacting appropriate institutions, to report to the Governing Council by early September on options for holding and managing revenues from Iraqi exports of petroleum and petroleum products;

(c) To request a Working Group of Governing Council members, after consultation with an expert or experts in the oil trade and in related financial transactions, to meet in September to develop a proposal for a mechanism for ensuring payments to the Fund for presentation to the second session of the Governing Council in October. The Working Group would take into account the reports of the Executive Secretary and the experts' advice, as well as paragraph 19 of Security Council resolution 687 (1991) and the Secretary-General's report.

외 무 부

관리
번호 91
-1519

종 별 :

번 호 : AEW-0364   일 시 : 91 0825 0930

수 신 : 장관(중동일,중동이,정일),사본:외연원 홍순용대사

발 신 : 주 UAE대사대리

제 목 : 대이라크 피해보상청구(자응30호)

대:WAE-0384

1. 대호, 소직은 금 2.25. <u>주재국 ABDULLAH 정무국장</u>을 면담, 대호 탐문한바, 동인 반응 아래와 같음을 보고함.

가. 주재국은 쿠웨이트사태시 주재국 국민이 받은 피해액 규모를 현재조사중에 있으나 피해액 청구여부는 상금 검토하지 않고 있음

나. 동 적립금이 계획대로 실현된다면 <u>피해보상보다는 의약품및 생필품 지원등</u> <u>인도적인 차원에서 쿠웨이트 복구를 위하여 우선적으로 쓰여져야 할것임</u>

2. 동인은 이어 안보리결의 705 호는 수행과정에 있어서 어려움이 많음을 지적하고 현실적으로 피해액을 정확히 산정하는 것도 용이치 않다고 첨언하였음을 보고함. 끝.

(대사대리 오기철-국장)

예고:91.12.31 까지

91. 12. 31. 일반

중아국   차관   1차보   2차보   중아국   외연원   외정실

PAGE 1

원 본

외 무 부

종 별 :

번 호 : SKW-0554   일 시 : 91 0826 1135

수 신 : 장관(중동일,아서)

발 신 : 주 스리랑카 대사

제 목 : 대이라크 피해배상 청구

대:WSK-0318

대호 주재국 정부의 대이라크 피해배상 청구 방안을 아래 보고함.

1. 당초 주재국측은 90.9.5. 자 및 11.30 자 유엔안보리에 대한 메모란덤에서

가)주재국 주요산품인 홍차등 수출타격

나)약 10 만명 현지근무 자국근로자들의 취업 상실및 본국 송금타격

다)원유가격 인상

라)스리랑카 경제에 미친 인플레 영향등을 보상해주어야 함을 주장한바 있었음.

2. 주재국 정부는 최근 8 월중순 유엔측에 스리랑카의 피해근로자 1 인당 1 만불 이상을 보상해줄것과 걸프전으로 인해 현지에서 자산을 잃은 자국민에 대하여 문서상 증명이 있을경우에 10 만불 까지를 별도로 보상해줄것을 요청하였음.

3. 주재국 정부의 발표에 의하면 현지 근로자 약 10 만명중 최근까지 당국에 보상요청을 등록해온 근로자의 수는 약 5 만 2 천명이라고함.

(대사 장관-국장)

예고:91.12.31 일반

91. 12. 31. 일반

중아국   차관   2차보   아주국   정와대   안기부

원 본

외 무 부

종 별 : 지 급

번 호 : USW-4257

일 시 : 91 09826 2003

수 신 : 장 관(중동일,미일,기정)

발 신 : 주 미 대사

제 목 : 대이라크 피해 배상 청구

대 WUS-3806

1. 금 8.26 당관 노광일 서기관은 국무부 MISENHEIMER 이락 담당관및 RONALD BETTAMER 법무담당관실 국제 청구 담당관을 접촉, 대호 대이락 피해 배상 청구 문제 현황을 탐문한바, 동 내용 하기 보고함.

가. 전쟁 기간 피해 배상

O 안보리 결의안에 의거 이락 원유 판매 대금의 일부를 전쟁 배상금으로 활용하는 문제를 협의하기 위한 관리위(GOVERNING COUNCIL)가 지난 7 월말 제네바에서 개최되었음.

O 동회의시 십만불 이하의 개인 청구권에 대해서는 우선적으로 처리한다는 원칙이 채택되었으며, 여타 청구권(기업 및 국가)문제, 청구 방법 및 절차 문제는 10 월 개최 예정인 2 차 회의시 협의토록 결정되었음.

나. 이락 동결 자산 활용 문제

O 각국은 동결한 이락 자산을 활용, 피해 배상을 해주는것도 가능할것으로 봄.

-단, 전쟁 기간중 피해는 유엔 절차에 의해 이루어지는바, 전쟁기간을 제외한 기간의 피해에만 한정될것임.

O 상금 미국정부는 동결 이락 자산을 활용하여 피해를 배상해 줄것인가에 대해 결정을 내린바는 없으나, 하나의 가능한 방안으로 보고 있음. 이방안이 채택될 경우에는 미국 정부만이 독자적으로 결정하지는 않고 기타 이락 자산 동결국과 협의해서 공동 보조를 취할것으로 보고 있음.

-상기 공동 행동은 전쟁 기간 피해 배상을 위한 유엔 절차와는 별개이며, 따라서 유엔 관리위원회의에서 협의될 성질의 문제가 아님.

3. 상기 유엔 관리위 1 차회의 관련 자료 별전 FAX 송부예정임.끝.

중아국	장관	차관	1차보	2차보	미주국	분석관	청와대	안기부

PAGE 1

(대사 현홍주-국장)
예고:91.12.31 일반

91. 12. 31. 일반

외 무 부

종 별 :

번 호 : SBW-1260

일 시 : 91 0828 1510

수 신 : 장관(중일,기정,국방)

발 신 : 주 사우디 대사

제 목 : 대이라크 피해보상 청구

대:WSB-920

1. 주재국 외무부의 LAQUANI 국제기구국장은 주재국은 대이라크피해보상 청구와 관련한 부처간 협조를 위하여 외무부, 국방부, 석유광물부, 재무부등의 실무급으로 위원회를 구성하기를 했으나, 유엔에 배상기금이 정식으로 발족되고 구체적인 청구절차등을 알게된 연후에야 피해보상 청구액 산정방안등에 관한 구체적작업이 가능할것으로 본다고 말함.

2. 추후 동위원회 활동사항등 수시보고위계임.끝

(대사주병국-국장)

예고:91.12.31 일반

중아국	장관	차관	1차보	2차보	청와대	안기부	국방부

원 본

외 무 부

종 별 :

번 호 : JAW-4926   일 시 : 91 0828 1822

수 신 : 장관(중동일,아일,봉일)

발 신 : 주 일 대사(경제)

제 목 : 대이라크 피해배상 청구

대:JAW-3737

연:일(경)764-5485

대호, 표제 관련 주재국 외무성 영사이주부에 확인한바 아래 보고함.

1. 일본은 연호 양식에 의한 피해조사를 하고 있으며(현재 80-90 프로 정도조사됨), 손해배상 청구는 유엔 결의에 정한바대로 유엔을 통해 배상청구 예정이며 이라크에 대해 직접 배상청구는 않을 것임.(91.7.23-8.2. 간 제네바에서 개최된 유엔 배상 위원회 제 1 차 회의 결과 및 10 월 개최 예정인 동 제 2 차 회의 결과등에 의거 손해배상 청구 예정)

2. 일본은 일본내 이라크의 자산을 동결하고 있으나, 유엔에서 동결 자산을 배상에 활용 안하기로 한바, 동결 중인 일본내 이라크 자산을 손해배상에 활용하지 않을 것임.끝.

(대사 오재희-국장)

예고:91.12.31. 까지

91. 12. 31. 일어 [서명]

중아국 안기부	장관	차관	1차보	2차보	아주국	통상국	외정실	정와대

PAGE 1

외 무 부

종 별 :

번 호 : PAW-0912   일 시 : 91 0828 1500

수 신 : 장관(중동일,아서)

발 신 : 주 파 대사

제 목 : 대이락 피해배상청구

대 WPA-543, 연 PAW-282

1. 대호관련, 당관 박서기관은 금 8.28(수)TARIQ OSMAN HYDAR 외무성경제국장을 면담한바, 결과 아래보고함.

　가. 주재국 피해액 산정

　0 주재국정부는 걸프전으로인한 제반 경제적손실(근로자 송금중단, 유가 상승, 교역감소, 근로자 귀국및 재정착지원경비등)총액을 약 12 억불로 산정하고,중동전 기간중 안보리를 통해 배상청구하였으나, 성사되지못함(90.11. 주재국외무성은 주요 선진우방국에도 특별지원을 요청하는 AID-MEMOIRE 발송)

　0 주재국은 걸프전 발생시 쿠웨이트, 이락지역에 체류중인 약 10 만명의 근로자를 대부분 철수시킨바, 이로인한 근로자 송금 감소액을 약 1 억 3 천만불로산정함.

　나. 대이락 배상청구 절차참여

　0 걸프전 종전후 유엔안보리에 구성된 UN CLAIMS COMMISSION 은 지난 7월제네바에서 회의를 개최, 쿠웨이트, 이락지역에서 철수한 외국근로자들의 개인적 손실을 배상해주는데 우선 순위를 두고 미국제안으로 우선 철수 근로자 1 인당2,500 미불을 지원하여 주는방안을 검토하고있음.

　0 주재국은 7.26. 제네바에서 개최된 유엔 배상위 GOVERNING COUNCIL 회의시아래 기본입장을 천명함.

　1)동 배상위원회의 활동(절차)의 부명성을 높이고 주재국을 비롯한 비율빈,방글라데시등 피해가 많은 국가들의 참여를 제고시킬것.

　2)배상위가 우선적으로 철수근로자들에 대한 배상문제를 처리하기로 한데동의하나 기본배상액 2,500 미불은 너무 적으며, 피해국들이 자국근로자를 대신하여 적절한 배상액을 청구할수 있는 MOALITY 를 마련하여야 할것임.

중아국	장관	차관	1차보	2차보	아주국	분석관

다. 향후 대책

0 유엔 배상위 활동에 적극참여, 우선적으로 주재국철수 근로자들에 대한배상절차를 가속화하고 배상액을 극대화하도록 노력할것임.

0 기타 국가 및 기업의 COMMERCIAL CALIMS 에 대해서는 아직 관련국가간의의견수렴이 되지못한 상태인바, 주재국은 유엔 배상위및 관련국과의 협의를 계속할것임.

2. 상기 유엔 배상위 GOVERNING COUNCIL 회의시 주재국대표 STATEMENT 는파편 송부위계임.끝.

(대사 전순규)

예고 91.12.31 일반

PAGE 2

0067

외 무 부

종 별 :

번 호 : CNW-1228   일 시 : 91 0828 0745

수 신 : 장관(중동일,미일,정보)

발 신 : 주 카나다대사

제 목 : 대이라크 피해보상 청구

대:WCN-1084

연:CNW-0294

1. 안참사관이 8.27.(화) 주재국 외무부 경제통상법규과 S J 담당관 및 M V담당관과 각각 접촉, 파악한 주재국 현황을 아래 보고함.

가. 피해 신고 접수현황(91.8.26 현재)

- 총신고건수: 225 건(기업피해 12 건 포함)

- 신고액누게: 약 150 백만 카불(단, 동신고의 절반은 구체적 평가 단계에서 제외될 것으로 예측 된다고함.

나. 주요 피해신고내역(91.7 월말 현재, 단위 백만카불)

- 자동차, 가구등 동산(M P):14.8

-은행 예금:13.6

-보수 및 사회복지:11.3

-기업체 장비, 재고품 등:5.6

-신체적 피해(부상등):6.9

-기업체 투자지분:12.5

-기타 개인 및 기업체 재산손실:21.0

-여행경비:1.0

다. 피해신고자

-피해신고자의 과반수가 비 카나다인으로서 카나다에 거주중인 레바논, 팔레스타인, 이락인등이 포함되어 있는바, 현재 상기인들이 카나다에 거주하고 있다는점, UN 을 통한 피해보상인 점에 비추어 국적에 의한 신고접수 보다는 우선 공정한 피해내역을 파악하는 것이 필요하다는 점에서 이들을 신고대상에 포함시켰음.

중아국   장관   차관   2차보   미주국   외정실   분석관   청와대   안기부

PAGE 1   91.08.29   08:20

외신 2과 롱제관 BS

0068

378 걸프 사태 유엔안전보장이사회 동향 8

라. 금후 피해보상 청구방안

- 지난 7.23-8.2 간 제 1 차 UN 피해보상위원회(UN C C)회의가 개최된데 이어 오는 10 월 2 차 회의가 개최 예정이며, 동 회의종료후 피해보상을 위한 UN 신청서 양식을 배포 예정이므로 동양식을 UN 으로부터 접수하는대로 증거서류를 첨부하여 UN 당국에 제출 계획임.

마. 동결자산 활용문제

- 이라크의 쿠웨이트 침공 직후 동결된 주재국내 이라크 자산처리와 대이라크 피해보상을 아직 연관시키지 않고 있으며, 동결 자산 사용에 관한 안보리 결정을 대기중임.

2. J 담당관 면담시 입수한 8.27. 자 외무부의 피해보상 청구 안내서한 및 8.2 자 UN 피해 보상위원회(UNCC) 활동 관련 안보리 문서(S/22885) 사본을 8.30 당관발 파편 송부하니 참고 바람. 상기 담당관 추가접촉 에 필요하니 상기 면담시 카측이 문의한 아래사항 회신바람

가. 아국의 피해 청구 현황

나. 아국 대표의 제 1 차회의 UNCC 회의 파견여부 및 제 2 차 회의 파견계획

다. UNCC 에 아국 법률 자문 파견 여부(카측에 의하면 미국의 경우 60 여명의 법률 자문을 UNCC 에 파견중이라함.

라. 기타 아국의 대이라크 인도적 원조(식량, 의료품 등)제공 현황등 참고사항.

끝.

(대사 - 국장)

예고:91.12.31 까지

	분류번호	보존기간

발 신 전 보

번   호 : **WCN-1174**   910912 1814 FN   종별 :

수   신 : 주 카나다 대사. 총영사

발   신 : 장 관   (중동일)

제   목 : 대 이라크 ~~피해~~배상 청구

대 : CNW - 1228 (91.8.28)

대호 2항에 대하여 아래 회보함.

1. 아국의 피해배상 청구현황

   ㅇ 현재 UN에 구체적으로 ~~피해~~배상을 청구하지는 않고 있으며, 이라크 및 쿠웨
   이트내 아국교민등 피해 현황파악 및 동 배상청구를 위한 국내 절차 ~~수립~~중

2. 우리대표의 제1차 UNCC회의 참석여부

   ㅇ UN 배상위(UNCC)는 안보리 이사국 각국 대표 1명으로 구성되는 15인 집행
   ~~위원회~~(GOVERNING COUNCIL)이 실질기관으로 동회의는 비공개가 원칙이며
   필요시 각 이해당사국을 동회의 초청, 발언토록함.   따라서, 우리나라는
   동 회의에 참석한바 없으며, 필요시 10월 제2차 회의에 참석 검토예정

3. UNCC에의 한국인 법률자문 파견

   ㅇ UNCC는 ~~피해~~배상 청구를 실질적으로 심사할 전문가(COMMISSIONER)로서 재정,
   법률, 회계, 보험 및 환경훼손평가 분야 전문가들을 각국에 추천 요청 중인바,
   우리도 현재 3명을 추천했음. (상주파견이 아니라 UNCC 필요시 추천된 자중
   에서 선발하여 업무를 수행토록함.)

4. 우리의 대이라크 인도적 원조 현황

   ㅇ 쿠르드난민 지원 목적으로 정부차원에서 현금 60만미불, 쌀1천톤을 지원했고
   민간 차원에서는 대한 적십자사가 27만불 전달.   끝.

(중동아프리카국장   이 해 순)

예 고 : 1991. 12. 31. 까지

91. 12. 31. 일반

	보안통제	주

외 무 부

종 별 :

번 호 : NDW-1382   일 시 : 91 0829 1930

수 신 : 장 관(중동일, 아서, 정보, 기정)

발 신 : 주 인도 대사대리

제 목 : 대이라크 피해배상 청구

대:WND-0726

대호 관련, 당관 김원수서기관은 금 8.29 주재국 외무부 SACHDEV 걸프지역 과장을 면담하였는 바, 동인의 언급요지 아래 보고함.

1. 인도정부는 쿠웨이트 사태로 인해 인도가 입은 피해에 대한 배상청구를 UN 결의에 따라 행할 예정이며, 이를위해 현재 취하고 있는 조치는 다음과 같음.

가. 동 청구문제를 전담하는 특별대책반(SPECIAL KUWAIT CELL)을 지난 7 월경 외무부 걸프국내에 임시로 설치하였으며, 동 대책반은 청구문제가 완료될때까지 한시적으로 운영될 것임.

나. 쿠웨이트사태 이전에 이라크 및 쿠웨이트에 거주하던 인도인 17 만여명이 입은 개인적인 피해에 대해서는 신문광고등을 통해 외무부에 신고토록 안내하여 현재 접수중에 있음.

다. 당초에는 상기 개인피해 접수를 8 월말까지 마감하여 국가 및 기업피해까지 포함, UN 측에 인도측 청구를 가능한 한 조속히 제출할 계획이었으나 워낙많은 인원이 관련되어 있기 때문에 필요한 경우에는 마감시한을 다소 연장할것을 검토하고 있음.

2. 최종적인 액수가 집계되지는 않고 있으나, 현재로서는 인도의 청구액이 국가가 입은 피해(인도인 철수 소요비용 포함) 약 40 억불, 기업이 입은 피해(주로 이라크측의 연체대금)약 9 억불, 개인이 입은 피해 약 2 억불정도가 될 것으로 예상됨.

연이나, 쿠웨이트사태로 피해를 입은 국가가 많기 때문에 피해국들의 청구액수는 엄청날 것인 반면 이라크측의 배상의사와 능력은 제한되어 있음을 감안할때, 과연 어느정도의 배상을 받을수 있을지에 대해서는 솔직히 회의적인 생각이 앞섬.

(대사대리-국장)

91. 12. 기. 장은

중아국	차관	1차보	2차보	아주국	외정실	분석관	청와대	안기부

우리 철수비용 청구를

예고:91.12.31 일반.

0072

주 파 키 스 탄 대 사 관

주파(정)760 - 205   1991. 8. 28.
수신 외무부장관
참조 아중동국장
제목 대 이락 피해 배상

        연 ; PAW - 912

     연호, 유엔 배상위원회 Governing Council 회의 (7.26. 제네바)시
     주재국 대표의 statement를 별첨 송부합니다.

     첨 부: 동 statement 사본. 끝.

        주   파   키   스   탄

                                                    0073

P-4/6

PERMANENT MISSION OF PAKISTAN, GENEVA

Statement by Mr. Ahmad Kamal, Ambassador and Permanent
Representative of Pakistan, at the meeting of the Governing
Council of the United Nations Compensation Commission, in
Geneva, on 25 July 1991

Mr. Chairman,

I am happy to be able to express the preliminary views of
the Government of Pakistan at this meeting of the Governing
Council of the United Nations Compensation Commission. Pakistan
appreciates this opportunity because it is amongst those countries
which were most seriously affected by the Gulf crisis.

2.   The adverse financial and economic effects suffered by
Pakistan fall into a number of separate categories. A
preliminary, indicative, and non-exhaustive list would include the
following:

   i)   Some 100,000 Pakistani nationals were forced to flee
         Kuwait and Iraq leaving behind their contractual jobs,
         enterprises, property, and bank balances.

   ii)   The return of a major portion of these returnees was
         arranged and financed by the Government of Pakistan. On
         their arrival in Pakistan, each returnee was given a
         cash grant because most of them had lost everything.

   iii) A tremendous burden has been placed on the Government of
         Pakistan to attempt to try to facilitate the
         reabsorption and reintegration of these returnees since

1

0074

job creation at this level of quantity requires a major
reallocation of already scarce resources.

iv)   The returnees were providing a significant source of
foreign exchange remittances beneficial to their
extended families in Pakistan, and to the foreign
exchange reserves of the country.

v)   Pakistan has had to pay the substantial cost of a higher
import bill for oil and petroleum products as a result
of the Gulf crisis.

vi)   The higher oil import costs, and other contributing
factors arising from this crisis, had a multiplier
effect, raising prices, more inflation, and reducing
productivity and growth.

vii)   The region constituted an important area for existing
Pakistani exports. There was a substantial loss of
export earnings.

viii)   Private Pakistani firms and business individuals lost
heavily as a result of contractual agreements with
governmental and private concerns and organizations in
Iraq and Kuwait because deliveries of commodities or
services had been made, but were not paid for until now,
in some cases or because cargoes for delivery were on
the high seas when the crisis broke out.

3.   It is because of those reasons, and because of this concern,
that we have addressed a letter to you Sir, to express our deep
interest in the procedures that will be adopted, the priorities
that will be set, and the modalities and mechanisms which will be

2

0075

evolved, by the Commission.

4.   For Pakistan it would therefore be very important to keep abreast of the deliberations of the Governing Council of the Compensation Commission, and to be given access to the documentation being considered and generated by the Governing Council. We have appreciated having been given, by the originator, an important working paper concerning one of the areas to be examined by the Governing Council.

5.   It would therefore be important for Pakistan to participate in the work of the Governing Council of the United Nations Compensation Commission. Participation in the work of the Governing Council, by non-members, would be by observing its work, and by requesting to be invited to speak whenever it is found that there could be a contribution made. It is in no way any suggestion for the expansion of the Governing Council.

6.   I have outlined the general compensation problem as relevant to Pakistan, within which the place of the individual claims of the some 100,000 Pakistani returnees from Kuwait and Iraq, have a very high priority for Pakistan. We would welcome and support the Governing Council giving a high priority to the issue of small claims and the evolution of a modality permitting States to submit a consolidated claim on behalf of their nationals.

7.   I thank you Mr. Chairman for this opportunity to address the Governing Council, and I am completely at the disposal of its members to respond to any queries that they may wish to make.

3

0076

관리번호	91/1558

외　무　부

종　별 :

번　호 : POW-0551

수　신 : 장 관(중동일,구이)

발　신 : 주 폴투갈 대사

제　목 : 대 이라크 피해배상

일　시 : 91 0830 1900

대:WECM-0040

1. 당관 주참사관은 8.30 주재국 FRANCISCO 신임 중동국장을 면담, 대호건 문의함. 동국장은 폴투갈도 일부 제약회사의 쿠웨이트내 합작투자 공장이 피격당한것등 피해를본바 있으나, 현재 유엔 안보리의 제 결의에 따른 대 이라크 배상청구문제는 검토단계에만 있다고 말함

2. 또 주재국의 이라크재산 동결여부와 이에따른 대호 3 과같은 별도 배상움직임 여부에 대해서는 추가확인, 알려주겠다고 하였는바, 본건 추가확인될시 보고하겠음. 끝.

(대사조광제-국장)

예고:91.12.31 까지

---

91. 12. 31. 일반

중아국	1차보	2차보	구주국

관리 91
번호 /1566

외 무 부

종   별 :

번   호 : SDW-0722   일   시 : 91 0902 1800

수   신 : 장관(중동일)

발   신 : 주 스웨덴 대사

제   목 : 대이라크 피해배상 청구

대:WSD-0450

1. 당관 황공사가 9.2 외무성 영사, 법규 1 국의 A.VESTERSKOELD 담당관에게 대호건 문의하였던바, 스웨덴 정부는 유엔으로부터 대이락 배상청구에 관한 구체적인 절차를 통보받은 후에 구체적인 방안을 검토하게 될것이며, 현재로서는정부 및 기업, 개인의 피해를 조사중에 있으나, 피해액은 수백만 스웨덴 크로나 (환율: 미화 1 불당 약 6 크로나)가 될것으로 추정하고있다함.

2. 또한 동담당관은 주재국이 동결한 이락크 재산으로 기업이나 개인의 피해를 보상하는 방안은 전혀 검토된바 없다함. 끝

(대사 최동진-국장)

예고:91.12.31 까지

91. 12. 31. 있난

중아국   2차보

91.09.03   08:16
외신 2과 통제관 BN

0078

외 무 부

종   별 :

번   호 : UKW-1802　　　　　　　　　　　일   시 : 91 0904 1700

수   신 : 장관(중동일,구일)

발   신 : 주 영 대사

제   목 : 대이라크 피해배상 청구

대: WECM-0040

대호관련, 외무성 중동과 DAVID HOPE 이라크 담당관 및 손해배상과 B.PUGH 담당관에 문의한 바, 이들의 언급내용 아래 보고함.

　1. 피해배상 요청방법

　-이라크의 쿠웨이트 침공으로 피해를 입은 국민은 외무성 손해배상과에 비치된 양식에 손해사실 (물품 및 추정액) 을 작성, 제출토록 하고있음. (외무성은90.11. 경에 상기 절차를 신문광고를 통하여 국민에게 주지시킨바 있음)

　-그러나 이것은 단지 손해사실에 대한 보고이며, 손해배상의 청구가 아님. 손해배상 청구에 대하여는 제네바의 유엔 손해배상위원회(COMPENSATION COMMISSION)에서 청구기준 (청구가능 품목등)을 결정하여 홍보해 줄 것이라고함.

　2. 이라크 자산 활용문제

　-주재국은 대 이라크 경제제재 조치에 따라 주재국내의 이라크 자산을 동결하고 있으나, 주재국 기업 및 개인의 피해 배상을 위하여, 동결된 이라크 자산을활용하는 것은 주재국 국내법(은행법 및 회사법등)에 의하여 금지되어 있음.

　3. 경제제재

　-주재국은 현재 이라크에 억류중인 자국민(IAN RICHKER)이 석방될 경우, 유엔의 경제제재위원회의 동의를 얻어 인도적인 분야(식량, 의약품등)에 한하여 경제제재의 일부를 해제할 예정임.끝

　(대사 이홍구-국장)

　예고: 91.12.31 일반

91. 12. 31. 일반

중아국	차관	2차보	구주국	분석관	정와대	안기부

외 무 부

종   별 : 지급
번   호 : GEW-1790   일   시 : 91 0905 1140
수   신 : 장 관(중동이)
발   신 : 주 독 대사
제   목 : 대이락 손해배상 청구

대:WECM-0040

대호 관련 전참사관이 9.4. 외무부 DASSEL 중동과장을 면담, 파악한 바를 다음보고함.

1. 90.8.2-91.3.2. 이락의 쿠웨이트 점령에 따라 발생한 주재국의 피해(국가및 개인)에 관하여는 일반개인으로 부터의 배상청구도 접수하여 그내용및 피해액수등을 조사중에 있다함. 동 피해에는 인질로 억류된바 있던 독일인의 정신적 피해등도 포함됨으로 조사에 어려움이 많다고 함.

2. 또한 주재국 정부는 유엔 안보리및 사무처에 주재국의 배상청구의사를 이미 전달(SINGNALED)한바 있으며, 동 배상 기금을 관장하고 있는 유엔 구주사무소가 배상청구에 관한 구체적인 방법및 절차등에 관하여 10 월 중순경 발표할 것이라는 주제네바 독일대표부의 보고를 접하고, 이에 대비하고 있으나, 현실적으로 만족할만한 배상은 받을수 있을지에 관하여는 회의적이라함

3. 주재국은 주재국내 이락자산(약 10 억 마르크상당)을 동결한바 있으나, 상기 이락의 쿠웨이트 점령에 따른 직접 피해보상문제 해결이 우선되어야 함으로90.8.2. 이전의 대이락 채권배상문제는 상금 구체적으로 검토되지 않고 있다함.끝.

(대사-국장)

예고:91.12.31. 일반

91. 12. 31. 216/

중아국	장관	차관	1차보	2차보	구주국	분석관	청와대	안기부

분류번호	보존기간

발 신 전 보

WGE-1466   910912 1812 FN

번   호 :   종별 :

수   신 : 주   목   대사. 총영사

발   신 : 장   관   (중동일)

제   목 : 대 이라크 피해 배상 청구

대 : GEW - 1790 (91.9.5)

대호 2항, "귀 주재국 정부가 UN 안보리 및 사무처에 주재국의 배상 청구 의사를 이미 전달 했다는 것과 관련, 구체적으로 어떤 방법(문서등)으로 전달했는지 파악 보고 바람. 끝.

(중동아프리카국장   이 해 순)

예   고 : 1991. 12. 31. 까지

91.12.31. 인터.

보안통제	연 주

앙고재	91년 9월 12일	중동1과	기안자 성명	주		과장		국장	전결		차관	장관

외신과통제

외 무 부

관리 91
번호 -1602

종 별 :

번 호 : GEW-1865   일 시 : 91 0912 1630

수 신 : 장관(중동일)

발 신 : 주 독 대사

제 목 : 대이라크 배상청구

대:WGE-1466

연:GEW-1790

대호 DASSEL 중동과장은 휴가중이므로, 동 배상문제와 관련한 실무작업을 담당하고 있는 DINDSEIL 국제사법담당 과장에 재확인한바, 주재국측의 배상의사 전달은 주 유엔대표부 혹은 주 제네바 독일대표부 관계관이 구두로 독일정부의 청구의사를 표명(SIGNALED)한 것으로 알며, 공식문서 전달문제는 유엔 구주사무소의 구체적 발표에 관한 보고를 접한후 결정될 것이라 함. 끝

(대사-국장)

예고:91.12.31. 까지

91. 12. 31. 인맡.

중아국

PAGE 1

91.09.13   03:55
외신 2과 통제관 FM

0082

392 걸프 사태 유엔안전보장이사회 동향 8

외　무　부

종　별 :

번　호 : FRW-1959　　　　　　　　　일　시 : 91 0906 1030

수　신 : 장관(중동일,재무부)

발　신 : 주 불 대사

제　목 : 대이라크 피해 배상청구

대:WECM-0040

　　1. 대호관련 당관 재무관이 주재국 재무성 금융국 D.MAITRE 중동.구.아주과장을 면담조사한 내용을 보고함.

　　1) 이라크의 쿠웨이트 침공으로 인한 손실 및 피해 배상청구에 관하여는 이미 UN 의 결의내용을 신문공고하여 피해신고를 받고 있는바

　　- 기업이 입은 피해에 관하여는 재무성 대외경제협력국(D.R.E.E) 에서, 개인이 입은 피해에 관하여는 외무성 교민국에서 신고를 받고 있으며

　　- 전체적으로는 외무성에서 손실 및 피해내용을 총괄하여 UN 에 제출할 계획이라고 함.

　　2) 90.8 월의 주재국내 이라크 자산에 대한 동결조치는 현재 해제되지 않고 계속되고 있으나, 동결자산을 이라크의 채무변제에 활용하는 것을 고려되지 않고 있다함. 끝.

　　(대사 노영찬-국장)

　　예고:91.12.31. 까지

신문공고내용, 보고로록지시

91.12.31. 일반.

중아국	차관	1차보	2차보	분석관	재무부

발 신 전 보

WFR-1901   910912 1813 FN   종별 :

번 호 : _____

수 신 : 주 불 대사. ~~총영사~~

발 신 : 장 관 (중동일)

제 목 : 대 이라크 ~~피해~~ 배상 청구

대 ; FRW-1959 (91.9.6)

대호 주재국 정부가 피해배상청구 신고접수를 위해 신문에 공고한 내용을 입수 보고 바람. 끝.

(중동아프리카국장 이 해 순)

예 고 : 1991. 12. 31. 까지

91. 12. 31. 일반

보안통제	& 주

앙고재	91년 9월 12일	중동1과	기안자 성 명 주	과 장	심의관	국 장 전결	차 관	장 관	외신과통제

0084

외 무 부

종 별 :

번 호 : BHW-0407   일 시 : 91 0910 1600

수 신 : 장관(중동일)

발 신 : 주 바레인 대사

제 목 : 대 이라크 피해배상 청구

    대:WBH-325

    연:BHW-225(91.4.7)

    1. 대호, 우선 아래 보고함.

    가. 정부

    0 주재국 정부는 지난 4 월 초순 금번 사태로 인한 주재국의 경제적 손실 규모를 언론을 통해 발표한바 있었음(연호 보고 참조)

    0 상기 발표에도 불구, 현재로서는 주재국 정부 차원에서의 동 배상 청구와관련한 별다른 움직임은 없는 것으로 파악되고 있음.

    0 당지 외교단 등에서는 동 발표를 동 배상 청구를 위한 것이라기 보다는 금번 사태로 인한 피해 부각을 통하여 사태 해결을 위해 주재국이 감내한 희생및동 희생을 통한 참여도를 강조함으로서 주재국의 대외 이미지를 거양키 위한 것으로 보고 있음.

    나. 기업및 개인

    0 주재국 상의 관계관들에 따르면 바레인의 기업이 입은 직접적 손실은 별로 크지 않다고함.

    0 이에따라, 주재국 정부는 항만 또는 공항 폐쇄등으로 인한 간접적 손실등의 경우 형제국 해방을 위해 당연히 감내해야할 정도의 희생이라는 점을 강조하면서, 바레인 기업및 개인들의 배상 청구자제를 직.간접 경로등을 통해 종용하고있다고함.

    0 한편, 당지 불란서 대사관에는, 지난 8.15. 안보리 결의안 706 호 채택이후 바레인 기업인들로 부터 동 배상 청구절차에 대한 문의가 수차례 있었다고함.

    다. 상기에 비추어, 주재국이 입은 피해는 대부분이 간접적인 것으로서 입증자료 구비등에 사실상의 어려움이 있는점, 배상청구시 주재국이 금번사태를 이용 경제적 이득을 얻으려하고 있다는 인상을 아랍권 내에 줄 수도 있다는 점등을감안,

---

중아국   차관   2차보   분석관   정와대   안기부

현재로서는 동 배상 청구에 소극적 입장을 취하고 있는것으로 사료됨.

2. 본건 주재국 관계당국 등과 계속 접촉, 결과 있는대로 추보 위계임.끝.

(대사 곽희정-국장)

예고:9112.31 일반

91. 12. 31. 일반

외 무 부

종 별 :

번 호 : OMW-0189

수 신 : 장관(중동일)

발 신 : 주 오만 대사

제 목 : 대이락 피해보상 청구

일 시 : 91 0911 1350

대:WOM-0185

9.10 본직이 주재국 외무부 아주국장 AL TOOBI 대사와 면담시 대호건에 관하여 탐문하였는바, 동국장은 자국이 걸프전쟁시 입은 피해가 타국에 비해 상대적으로 적을뿐 아니라 같은 아랍국가인 입장에서 이락크에 대한 피해보상청구를 하지 않을 것이라고 말하였음. 끝

(대사 강종원-국장)

예고:91.12.31. 까지

91. 12. 31. 인수

중아국   장관   차관   2차보

분류번호	보존기간

발 신 전 보

WIT-1018   910912 1812 FN

번   호 :   종별 :

WAV -0986	WPH -0821
WCP -1537	WQT -0218
WCA -0623	

수   신 : 주   수신처 참조   //대사//총영사

발   신 : 장   관   (중동일)

제   목 : 대 이라크 ~~피해~~ 배상 청구

표제관련, 연호 파악 내용을 조속 보고 바람. 끝.

(중동아프리카국장   이 해 순)

예 고 : 1991. 12. 31. 까지

수신처 : ✓주 이태리(WECM 0040), ✓오지리(WAV 0884), ✓필리핀(WPH 0742),
　　　　북경(WCP-1319),　　　　　　　✓카타르(WQT 0197),
　　　　　　✓주 카이로총영사(WCA-0577)

91. 12. 31. 이해. (서명)

	보안통제	(서명)

앙고재	91년 9월 일	중동1과	기안자성명	과장 심의관	국장		차관 장관	
			주	(서명)	전결		(서명)	

외신과통제

0088

외 무 부

종 별 :

번 호 : CAW-0982

일 시 : 91 0912 1705

수 신 : 장관(중동이)

발 신 : 주 카이로 총영사

제 목 : 대이라크 피해배상 청구

대:WCA-0577

대호 당관 송응엽영사가 ABDUL KADER EL ASSAR 주재국 노동부 국제관계국장및 AHMED ABDUL WAHAB 외무부 영사국 공사와 접촉, 탐문한바, 요지 아래 보고함.

1. 주재국 노동부는 90.8.2 이라크의 쿠웨이트 침공이래 쿠웨이트 및 이라크에서 철수한 주재국 기업 및 개인을 상대로 근무기간, 근무장소, 월봉급, 두고온재산등을 포함한 설문지를 통해 주재국측 손실및 피해액을 조사, 이를 최종집계후 외무부에 봉보함.

2. 외무부는 상기 집계를 토대로 UN 피해배상 위원회를 통해 배상을 청구함.

3. 주재국측은 피해총액이 약 300 억불에 달한다고 주장하고 있으나, 동피해액의 상세는 비밀을 유지하고 있으며, 주재국 외무부측은 현재 UN 의 배상청구절차 협의를 예의주시하고 있는 상태임.끝.

(총영사 박동순-국장)

예고:91.12.31. 까지

91. 12. 31. 인수

분류번호	보존기간

발 신 전 보

WBA-0298   910913 1550 FN

번   호 : _____   종별 : _____

수   신 : 주   방글라데시   대사. 총영사

발   신 : 장   관   (중동일)

제   목 : 대 이라크 배상 청구

연 : WBA - 0268 (91.8.22)

표제관련, 연호 파악내용을 조속보고 바람.   끝.

(중동아프리카국장   이 해 순)

예 고 : 1991. 12. 31. 까지

ok

91.12.31. 인반

보 안 통 제	

앙고재	91 년 9 월 13 일	중동 1 과	기안자 성명		과 장		국 장		차 관	장 관
			주				전결			

외신과통제

0090

외 무 부

종 별 :

번 호 : PHW-1249

일 시 : 91 0913 1640

수 신 : 장관(중동일)

발 신 : 주 필리핀 대사

제 목 : 대이라크 피해 배상청구

대:WPH-742

대호관련, 당관 황참사관이 유엔 보상위원회 위원으로 위촉받은 당지 ENRIQUE SYQUIA 변호사 및 외무부 중동국 담당자로 부터 탐문한 내용을 아래 보고함.

1. 필리핀측은 현재 걸프전으로 피해를 입은 개인 및 기업에 대한 피해자료를 수집중이며 아직 이에관한 정확한 수치를 갖고 있지 못하다고함.

2. 그러나 필리핀측은 우선 개인 피해에 대한 보상을 청구할 계획이며, 현재 유엔에서 1 인당 2,500 불 보상을 제시하고 있는데 대하여 10 월중 제네바에서 개최될 유엔 보상위원회에서 동 액수를 5,000 불로 인상 하도록 요구할 계획이라고 함.

SYQUIA 위원은 보상 대상이 될 필리핀인은 자기 추산으로 약 50 만명이 될것이라고 본다고 함.

3. 필리핀 기업중 주요 보상 청구주체는 필리핀 항공사와 건설회사가 될것으로 보고 있음.

(대사 노정기-국장)

예고:91.12.31. 까지

91. 12. 31. 까지

중아국   장관   차관   1차보   외정실   청와대

PAGE 1

관리
번호 91/1609

외 무 부

종 별 :

번 호 : ITW-1327

일 시 : 91 0913 1720

수 신 : 장 관(중동일)

발 신 : 주 이태리 대사

제 목 : 대이라크 피해 배상 청구

대:WIT-1018, WECM-40

대호관련 주재국 관계관을 접촉코 파악한 내용 아래 보고함.

1. 대이라크 배상청구 문제에 대해 주재국 정부는 UN 결의를 따르는 입장임.

주재국 일부업체가 이미 피해보상청구를 정부에 제출한 바 있으나 현재로서는 이라크가 배상능력이 없는데다, 주재국 자체적으로 보상절차, 소관부서등도 정해지지 않는 상태로 특별히 강구중인 방안은 없는 실정임.

2. 주재국이 동결하고 있는 이라크 자산을 채무면제, 배상에 활용하는 안은 가정적으로 거론되는 사항으로 EC 차원에서 동문제가 논의될 가능성이 있으며 상기 문제에 대한 이태리의 기본적인 입장은 EC 합의를 따르는 것임.끝

(대사 김석규-국장)

예고:91.12.31. 까지

91. 12.31. 종결

중아국   장관   차관   1차보   2차보

91.09.14   06:20

외신 2과 통제관 FK

0092

외 무 부

종 별 :

번 호 : AVW-1132   일 시 : 91 0913 1930

수 신 : 장 관(중동일)

발 신 : 주 오스트리아 대사

제 목 : 대이라크 피해 배상청구

대:WAV-0986

1. 대호관련 주재국측은 우선 유엔 배상위원회 관계 회의에 적극 참여 중인바, 9.16 부터 제네바 개최 전문가 회의(10 월 제 2 차 회의 준비회의)결과등을 보아가며 세부적인 청구 방안을 강구하게 될것 이라함.

2. 또한 주재국은 주재국내에 동결되어 있는 이락의 자산을 피해 보상에 활용하는 방안도 고려하고 있으나 동 자산의 규모는 미미하다고 하며 구체적인 조치는 상기 1 항 경과를 보면서 검토 할것이라함. 끝.

예고:91.12.31 까지.

중아국

관리
번호 91/1612

외 무 부

종 별 :

번 호 : BAW-0465

일 시 : 91 0915 1200

수 신 : 장관(중동일,아서)

발 신 : 주 방 대사

제 목 : 배상청구

대: WBA-268, 298

1. 당관 배영진 참사관은 9.14 외무성 ALAM 극동과장과 면담 확인한 내용은 아래와 같음.

　가. 직접피해

　0 쿠웨이트 및 이락의 노무자 은행예치금: 2 천 7 백만불

　0 중동노무자 10 만명 철수경비: 5 천만불

　나. 간접피해

　0 노무자 외환송금: 2 억불

　0 원유가 추가부담: 2 억불

　0 중동지역 수출감소: 1 억 2 천만불

　0 쿠웨이트등의 원조: 4 억불

　다. 피해지원

　IMF 가 2 억 6 천만불 저리 장기 차관 제공

2. 동과장은 주재국은 걸프전쟁중 사우디에 성지수호군 명목의 군대를 파견하여 사우디로부터 원유등을 공급받았고 전후 쿠웨이트, 사우디등으로부터도 원조를 약속받은 상태이며 직접피해가 적은 점, 회교국가인점등을 고려하여 배상청구 방안을 확정치 않고 있다고 언급하고 있는바, 이는 피해보상 청구보다는 다액의 원조를 획득하여 실리를 추구코저 하는 것으로 관측됨.

　(대사 신성오-국장)

　예고: 91.12.31 까지

91.12.31. 일반

중아국　　아주국

PAGE 1

91.09.16　00:12

외신 2과　통제관 DO

0094

외 무 부

종   별 :

번   호 : QTW-0209

일   시 : 91 0917 1230

수   신 : 장관(중동일)

발   신 : 주 카타르 대사

제   목 : 대이라크 배상청구

대:WQT-197,218

주재국 외무성의 ALI-AL-BADR 정무국 심의관 및 ALI AHMED AL-MAUMOUD 경제영사국 경제과장에 의하면 대호관련 상부로 부터 아무런 지시도 없고, 주재국으로서는 정부 단위로 피해보상청구를 취합해서 이에 관한 조치를 취할 방침이 아닌것으로 생각한다고 함. 끝.

(대사 유내형-국장)

예고:91.12.31 일반.

예. 91. 12.31. 일반

중아국

PAGE 1

91.09.17   20:25

외신 2과 롱제관 CH

0095

유엔안전보장위원회 이라크 배상위원회, 1991-92. 전6권 (V.6 각국 동향) 405

관리번호 91/1635

외 무 부

종 별 :

번 호 : USW-4725   일 시 : 91 0920 1829

수 신 : 장 관 (중동일,미일,미이,정안)사본:주시애틀(총)경유 주미대사-직송

발 신 : 주 미 대사

제 목 : 미군 중동지역 재배치설(UN 사찰및 이락 원유수출 결의안)

대: WUS-4334

연: USW-4703

   금 9.20. 노광일 서기관은 국무부 ALAN MISENHEIMER 이락담당관및 정보조사실
STEPHEN GRUMMON 중동담당관을 접촉, 연호 BUSH 대통령의 UN 헬기 엄호결정및작일의
이락산 원유수출 허가 UN 안보리 결의안에 대해 탐문한바, 동 내용 하기 보고함.

   1. 미군용기의 UN 헬기 엄호 비행

   0 이락은 UN 안보리결의 687 및 707 에 따라 대량 살상무기 철폐를 목적으로 UN
사찰을 무조건으로 수용해야 할 의무가 있고, 따라서 UN 사찰단의 헬기비행에 대해
조건을 부과할 수는 없으나 이락측은 이를 거부하거나 조건을 붙였음.

   0 이는 UN 결의안에 대한 명백한 위반으로서 미국을 위시한 주요 연합국은 UN 을
통해 동 문제를 조용히 해결하려고 노력하였으나, 이락측의 거부자세로 금번 BUSH
대통령의 미군기 엄호비행 결정이 내려졌음.

   0 금일 UN 에서 안보리 의장국인 불란서와 이락측이 접촉, 이락측에게 UN 헬기의
자유로운 비행을 포함 안보리 결의의 무조건 수용을 다시한번 종용할 예정으로
있으며, 이락측이 계속 거부하면 미국을 포함한 연합국측은 일정기간 시한을 설정하고
무력사용을 암시하는 수단을 사용할 수밖에 없을 것임.

   0 이락측이 UN 사찰을 거부하고 있는 것은 최근의 소련 쿠데타및 중동 평화회담
추진을 계기로 이락에 대한 연합국의 관심이 저하되었다는 판단하에 연합국측의
결의를 시험하고 있는 것으로 보여지며, 결국 이락이 헬기의 자유스런 비행을 포함
광범위한 UN 사찰을 수락할 수 밖에 없을 것으로 보고 있음.

   2. 이락 원유의 제한적 수출

   0 작 9.19 UN 안보리는 이락내 인도주의적 물품의 공급과 이락에 대한 배상자금

중아국	장관	차관	1차보	2차보	미주국	미주국	외정실	분석관
정와대	안기부							

PAGE 1

91.09.21   08:47

외신 2과 통제관 BW

0096

확보를 위해 향후 6 개월이내 16 억불 상당의 이락 원유 판매를 허가하였음.(안보리 결의안 712 호)

- 상금 이락측은 동 조치는 이락의 주권 침해임을 들어 거부하고 있으나, 식량및 의약품 부족난을 해결할 다른 방안이 없으므로 결국 수락할수 밖에 없을 것으로 전망

0 동 원유 수출은 UN 측이 직접 관장을 하고 대금도 UN 이 관리하게 되며, 식량및 의약품의 구매및 국내배분은 기존 이락측의 시설및 유통망을 이용하게 될것임.

- 구매품목은 이락측의 소요판단을 보아가며, UN 이 결정하게 되나, 어느국가로부터 얼마만한 물량을 구매하느냐등의 상담은 이락측이 하게될 것임.(대금은UN 측이 직접 지급)

- 쿠르드족 및 시아파 밀집지역등 이락내 일부지역에 대해서는 UN 이 직접 구매물품을 배분하고, 기타지역에 대해서는 UN 의 감독하에 이락측이 물품을 배분하게 될 것임.끝.

(대사 현홍주-국장)

예고: 91.12.31. 일반

PAGE 2

외 무 부

종 별 :

번 호 : TUW-0711

일 시 : 91 0923 1400

수 신 : 장 관(구이,정보,중동일)

발 신 : 주 터키 대사

제 목 : 주재국 정세(자료응신 제89호)

1. 주재국 CHAL VRAKS 은 루마니아 방문에 이어 9.22-23 간 체코슬로바키아를 공식 방문, 체코 HAVEL대통령과 회담을 갖고 최근 유고 및 소련 사태등 주변정세에 대해 의견을 교환하고 양국간투자 보장협정에 서명하였음.

2. PKK 게릴라 부대의 한 지휘관이 영자일간지 TDN 과 가진 기자회견에서 PKK는 금번 총선거와 관련, 터키 동남부 지역 쿠르드족을 지지기반으로 한 HEP 후보가 선거법상의 제약으로 SHP티켓으로 출마하는데 대해 이를 지지할 것이며, 또한 쿠르드 문제에 동정을 갖고 있는 무소속후보도 지원할 것이라고 밝혔음. 또한 터키주둔 미군이 터키군의 PKK 소탕작전과 같은 적대행위에 직접 개입하지 않는 한 미군을 공격하지 않을 것이라고 밝힘.

한편, 아라랏드산 노아의 방주 탐사중 PKK게릴라에 납치되었던 고고학자를 비롯한 5명의 외국인들이 9.21 석방되었음.

3. 유엔 안보리가 이라크에 대해 식량 미 의약품구입을 위한 16억불 상당 원유수출을 허가키로한 결의와 관련, 이에 따른 부대조건을 이라크 정부가 동의하는 IMZ지 QPBELVW분명한 가운데 걸프기간중 연합군 공습에서 손상되지 않은 터키내 2개이라크 송유관 사용을 위한 터키와 UN사무국간의 협상은 터키정부가 그 사용료로 2억6천4배만달러의 고액을 요구하므로서 송유관재개문제도 현재 타결을 보지 못하고있음.

(대사 김내성-국장)

구주국   1차보   중아국   외정실   분석관   정와대   안기부

PAGE 1

91.09.24   09:40 FH

외신 1과 통제관

0098

408   걸프 사태 유엔안전보장이사회 동향 8

발 신 전 보

번 호 : **WUN-3249**   910925 1917 FO   종별 :

WGV -1286   WMEM-0069

수 신 : 주   수신처 참조   대사//총영사

발 신 : 장 관   (중동일)

제 목 : UN 대이라크 배상 청구관련 관계부처 대책회의 개최

1. 정부는 9.24. 외무부 제2차관보 주재로 표제 회의를 개최(9개 부처 참석), UN배상위 회의 진전에 따른 우리의 ~~참고~~ 대책을 논의하였음.

2. 동 회의에서 「UN 대이라크 배상 대책반」을 구성, 운영키로 하고 공식배상 신청에 앞서 피해액 규모 파악을 위해 예비조사를 실시키로하여 9.30.까지 신고서를 배포, 동 신고서를 10.7.까지 외무부에서 취합, 검토하여 필요시 배상에 관한 우리정부의 입장을 수립, UN배상위에서 개진키로 하였음.

3. 다음 회의는 2차회의(10.14-18) 개최결과를 지켜본후 필요시 개최키로 함.

4. 동 회의 자료 및 결과를 파편 송부 하겠음.   끝.

(중동아프리카국장   이 해 순)

예 고 : 1991. 12. 31.까지

수신 : 주UN, 제네바 및 ~~유엔 및 대사~~ 중동지역 전공관

91. 12. 31. 인□

점코 → 수신처 ⊕ 조사대상공관

		기안자 성 명		과장	심의관	국장		차 관	장 관		보 안 통 제	ㅃㅋ
앙 고 재	91 년 월 일	중동1 과	주			전결						

외신과통제

0099

발 신 전 보

번 호 :	WAG-0321 910926 1729 FH	종별 :	

		WLY -0384	WTN -0247
		WMO -0324	WMT -0170 ✓
		WJO -0578	WYM -0310 ✓
		WSS -0284	WTH -1452 ✓

수   신 : 주   수신처 참조   대사 // 총영사

발   신 : 장 관   (중동일)

제   목 : UN 대이라크 배상 청구

1. UN은 91.4.3. 안보리 결의안 제687호 채택이후 UN배상위를 구성하는등 일련의
   조치를 통하여 대이라크 배상청구 절차를 협의중에 있음.

2. UN 지침에 의하면 90.8.2 - 91.3.2.간 이라크의 불법적인 쿠웨이트 침공 및 점령으로
   인해 적접적으로 입은 손실 및 피해에 대하여 각국은 UN을 통하여 대 이라크
   배상청구를 할수 있게 되었는바 이와 관련 귀 주재국이 국가, 기업 및 개인이
   입은 피해에 대한 배상청구를 위해 강구중인 방안에 대하여 탐문 보고 바람.

3. 동건 관련 UN 문서집을 파편 송부 하겠음.   끝.

(중동아프리카국장   이 해 순)

예 고 : 1991.12.31.까지

수신처 : 주 알제리, 리비아, 튀니지, 모로코, 모리타니, 요르단, 예멘, 수단,
         ~~시라운과여~~, 태국 대사 ✓

		기안자 성 명		과 장	신의악	국 장		차 관	장 관		보 안 통 제	
앙 고 재	91 년 8 월 일	주				선호						외신과통제

0100

34917

분류번호 문서번호	중동일 720-	기안용지 (720-2327)		시행상 특별취급	
보존기간	영구.준영구 10. 5. 3. 1	장 관			
수신처 보존기간		仅 구			
시행일자	1991. 9. 27.				

보조기관	국 장		협조기관		문검인통 제 1991.9.27 주재관
	심의관				
	과 장	전 결			
기안책임자		주복룡			발송인
경유 수신 참조		수신처 참조	발신명의		발송 1991. 9. 27 외무부

제 목	UN 대이라크 배상청구 관련 문서집 송부

연호, UN의 대 이라크 배상청구 관련 UN의 문서집 별첨 송부하니

업무에 참고 하시기 바랍니다.

첨 부 : 동 문서집 1부. 끝.

수신처 : 주 알제리(WAG-0321), 리비아(WLY-0384), 튀니지(WTN-0247),

모로코(WMO-0324), 모리타니(WMT-0170), 요르단(WJO-0578)

예멘(WYM-0310), 수단(WSS-0284), 태국 대사(WTH-1452)

더 맑은 마음을, 더 밝은 사회를, 더 넓은 미래를

0101

관리번호 91/1656

외 무 부

종 별 :

번 호 : AVW-1214

일 시 : 91 0926 1230

수 신 : 장 관(중동일)

발 신 : 주 오스트리아 대사

제 목 : 대이라크 피해 배상청구 문제

대:WAV-0986

연:AVW-1132

9.25 조창범공사가 연호 유엔배상위원회 제2 차 GOVERNING COUNCIL 회의 준비 전문가회의(9.16-20 제네바 개최)에 참석했던 외무성 CEDE 국제법규 관계관과 면담한 결과를 아래 보고함.

1. 지난주 제네바 전문가 회의에선 우선 개인의 긴급한 배상청구 절차 기준에 관해 중점협의, 3 가지 카테고리의 피해 청구 절차기준(개인의 정신적 피해등SMALL CLAIM, 개인의 SERIOUS INJURY OR DEATH, 10 만불이하에 상당하는 개인의 경제적 손해)과 신청서 양식에 관해 합의하여 10 월 중순 제네바 개최 제 2 차 GOVERNING COUNCIL 회의에 회부 최종확정키로 하였으며, GOVERNING COUNCIL 사무국(제네바 소재)에선 동회의 직후 상기 양식을 각국정부에 배포, 이로부터 6 개월내 각국 정부로 부터 동신청서를 접수하게 될 것이라함.

2. 개인의 10 만불 이상의 피해 청구와 기업의 피해 청구및 정부의 피해 청구와 관련된 문제에 관해서는 아직 구체적인 협의를 갖지 못한 상태이며, 10 월 제2 차 GOVERNING COUNCIL 회의시부터 본격적인 협의가 개시될 것으로 본다함.

3. 오스트리아 정부로서는 상기 유엔배상위 관계회의 활동과 병행하여 현재외무성, 재무성, 상공회의소등 관계 부처, 기관으로 대책반을 구성, 주재국의 개인, 기업등이 입은 피해를 IDENTIFY 하는 작업을 진행하면서 우선 상기 유엔 배상위의 피해청구 신청서 배포를 기다리고 있는 중이라함.

4. 한편 동결된 이락의 자산을 피해 보상에 활용하는 문제에 관하여는 자신이 금번 제네바 전문가 회의에 참석한 각국대표에게 회의장 외에서 비공식 건론, 의견 교환해 본바, 대부분이 상기 UN 의 배상제도와 별도로 여사한 방안을 추가적으로

중아국   차관   1차보   2차보   분석관

강구하는데는 법적인 문제점이 있다는 의견이었으며 일단 UN 배상위의 배상기금을 활용한 모든 피해청구의 수렴이 바람직하다는 의견이었다고 함.

　동문제는 각국의 국내법제도와도 관련 계속적인 검토가 필요할것으로 보나 오스트리아 정부로서는 UN 을 통한 배상제도를 최대한 활용한다는 입장이라고함.

　5. 금번 제네바 전문가 회의에서 합의된 10 월 제 2 차 GOVERNING COUNCIL 회의의 의제(안)은 별첨(FAX)와 같은바, GOVERNING COUNCIL 의 비회원국도 "사전 사무국과 접촉 자국의 입장을 개진할수 있는 기회가 허용된다"함. (금번 전문가회의 세부 결과와 관련 문서, 향후대책등에 관한 구체적인 사항은 제네바 소재 GOVERNING COUNCIL 사무국의 ALZAMORA 사무국장(EXECUTIVE SECRETARY)과 직접 접촉희망.)

　첨부:상기 의제(안) FAX AVW(F)-030 (2 매)(표지포함). 끝.

　예고:91.12.31 까지

91. 12. 31. 일여

원 본

외 무 부

종   별 :

번   호 : YMW-0527   일   시 : 91 0930 1620

수   신 : 장 관(중동일)

발   신 : 주 예멘 대사

제   목 : UN 대이라크 배상청구 관련 대책회의 개최

대:WYM-0310

연:YMW-0190(91.3.17)

1. 주재국 정부는 예멘이 걸프전 피해국으로서 유엔 결의 661 호에 의거, 특별 경제원조를 국제적으로 호소하여 왔으나 이라크와의 유대 관계상, 대 이라크 배상 청구 제기 움직임은 현재로서는 보이지 않고 있음.

2. 당지 AL-THAWRA 9.23 일자 보도에 의하면,"이라크 수호 대중 위원회" 재정 분과 위원장 MUJAHED ABU SHAWRED 준장(현 내무담당 부총리)은 주 예멘 이라크 대사에게 동 위원회가 갹출한 헌금 내역(9,500 만리알, 미화 12 만불, 은 116KG, 및 금 12 KG)을 밝히고 이중 리알 헌금으로는 밀가루를 구입, 현물로 잔액과 함께 이라크에 곧 송부할 계획임을 알린것으로 알려졌으며, 한편 프랑스 및 영국을 방문중인 기획성 장관 FARAJ BEN GHANEM 이 기자회견을 통해 예멘의 피해총액을 17 억불로 추산한것으로 보도되었음을 참고 바람. 끝.

(대사 류 지호-국장)

예고:91.12.31. 까지

91. 12. 31. 일반

관리번호 91/1681

외 무 부

종 별 :

번 호 : THW-1967

수 신 : 장 관(중동일)

발 신 : 주 태 국 대사

제 목 : UN 대이라크 배상청구

일 시 : 91 1002 1800

대 : WTH-1452

문참사관이 9.30 SAIYUD NOKNOY 주재국 외무성 국제기구 정무과장에게 문의한바, 동인은 관계부처들과 접촉, 태국기업및 민간인 피해상황에 대한 자료를 수집하고 있으며 주 유엔 태국대표부에 배상청구절차에 대한 조회를 하고 있는바 동 결과가 나오는대로 태국정부의 입장을 정리, 유엔에 청구할 예정이라함. 본건추보함

(대사 정주년-국장)

예고 : 91.12.31. 까지

91. 12. 31. 인0? ~

중아국   차관   2차보   분석관

외 무 부

외신 2과 통제관 BN
91.10.08   17:47

종   별 :

번   호 : MTW-0213   일   시 : 91 1007 1710

수   신 : 장관(중동일)

발   신 : 주 모리타니 대사대리

제   목 : UN 대 이락 배상청구

대:WMT-0170

대호 관련, 당관 김원철 대사대리가 10.7 주재국 외무성 JIDDOU 차관을 면담,
확인한바, 모든 국가가 대 이락 배상청구를 한다 하더라도 주재국으로서는 어려웠을때
주재국을 도와준 같은 아랍 형제국 이락에 대하여 여하한 배상도 청구할수 없으며,
전혀 고려조차 하지도 않을것이라고 답변함.

(대사대리 김원철-국장)

PAGE 예고:91.12.31 일반

91. 12. 31. 일반

중아국

관리번호 91/1704

외　무　부

종　별 :

번　호 : MOW-0469

수　신 : 장관(중동일,중동이)

발　신 : 주 모로코 대사

제　목 : 대 이라크 배상청구

일　시 : 91 1008 1000

대:WMO-0324

1. 대호 이락 배상 청구건에 관련하여 10.7. 당관 박참사관은 외무성 중동과장 및 유엔과장을 접촉한바, 주재국의 입장을 다음과 같이 보고함.

　가. 걸프전때 본바와 같이 모로코 국민은 이락편이었고 정부는 사우디에 군대를 파견하는 등 양면적인 행동을 취하였음.

　나. 전쟁개시전 쿠웨이트 거주 모로코인 2 천여명은 정부예산으로 모두 귀국시켰으며 따라서 모로코국민 및 회사 또는 국가가 입은 손해는 극소하며 손실이 있다하더라도 형제국가인 이락에 배상을 청구할 생각은 없음. 이는 사우디 파병을 못마땅해하는 이락을 무마하는 방편도 됨.

2. 동인들은 한국이 유엔조치에 적극 참여하는 가를 물었으므로 아국은 다만 우호국가들과의 보조를 맞추기 위한 것이라 답변함. 끝

　(대사허리훈-국장)

　예고 91.12.31 일반

91. 12. 31. 일반

중아국	장관	차관	1차보	2차보	중아국	외정실	청와대	안기부

PAGE 1

외 무 부

종 별 :

번 호 : PAW-1070

수 신 : 장 관(중동일)

발 신 : 주 파키스탄 대사

제 목 : 대 이락 피해배상 청구

일 시 : 91 1010 2000

대:중동일 720-34952

연 : PAW -912

연호관련, 주재국 외무성은 지난 10.2. AZMATHASSAN 경제차관보 주최로 관계부처 대책회의를 개최한바, 결정사항 아래 보고함.

1. 개인에 대한 기본 배상액 인상 및 청구절차간소화

-유엔 배상위 집행이사회 1차 회의시(91.7.제네바)결정된 개인에 대한 기본 배상액 2,500불 인상 및 청구절차 간소화 노력

2. 개인 배상외 국가,기업의 배상청구를 위하여 관련부처(기관)간 업무분장

-재외교민 재단(OVERSEAS PAKISTANIS FOUNDATION):청구서 양식 배포 및 접수

-상무성 :기업의 COMMERCIAL CLAIMS 관련

-환경처 :환경피해 배상 청구 관련

-기획성(수전력성) :건설회사 배상청구

-재무성:국가 배상청구

-외무성 :정책총괄,조정.끝.

(대사 전순규 - 국장)

중아국 /차보

91.10.11   07:49 WH

외신 1과 통제관

0108

관리 번호	91 ~1733

외 무 부

종 별 :

번 호 : PAW-1105

일 시 : 91 1019 1800

수 신 : 장 관(중동일,아서)

발 신 : 주 파키스탄 대사

제 목 : 걸프전 피해보상 관련 파키스탄 정부 입장

연: PAW-1070,912

1. 당관 이상완 공사는 10.17. 주재국 외무부 HYDER 경제고정국장을 면담, 걸프전 피해 보상청구 관련 UN 보상위 가이드 라인에 대한 주재국 입장에 관한 PAPER 를 입수(부분적)한바, 이중 주재국 기본 입장을 아래 보고함. 동 PAPER 는 금명 제네바의 동 위원회에 제출 예정이라함.

A. INADEQUACY OF THE PROPOSED FIXED AMOUNT PAYMENTS

HENCE, IT CAN BE CLEARLY SEEN THAT THE TOTAL OVERALL AVERAGE LOSS SUFFERED BY THE PAKISTANI RETURNEES IS APPROXIMATEY US 35,487DOLLAR PER PERSON. FOR THE LARGEST CATEGORY OF OCCUPATIONAL GROUPS, RELATING TO PAKISTANI PRODUCTION AND RELATED WORKERS, TRANSPORT EQUIPMENT OPERATORS, AND LABOURERS, AMOUNTING TO AROUND 55,500DOLLAR PERSONS OR 74 PERCENT OF THE PAKISTANIS WORKING IN KUWAIT, THE AVERAGE LOSS AMOUNTED TO 30,551 DOLLAR PER PERSON.

B.SPECIFIC RECOMMENDATIONS OF THE GOVERNMENT OF PAKISTAN

THEREFORE, THE GOVERNMENT OF PAKISTAN, IN BRINGING THIS INFORMATION BEFORE THE GOVERNINGH COUNCIL, WOULD REITERATE THE FOLLOWING POINTS:

A) THE MINIMUM SIMPLIFIED PROPOSED CLAIM AMOUNT OF US 2,500 DOLLAR PER RETURNEE, HAS NO RELEVANCE TO THE ACTUAL FACTS ON THE GROUND.

B) THE PROPOSED AMOUNT OF US 2500 DOLLAR FOR SERIOUS PERSONAL INJURY, OR DEATH, SHOULD BE RAISED TO A MORE REALISTIC FIGURE IN ACCORDANCE WITH INTERNATIONAL STANDARDS.

C) ON THE GROUNDS OF EQUITY, FOR PAKISTANI RETURNEES THE MINIMUM SIMPLIFIED CALIM AMOUNT SHOULD BE US 30,500 DOLLAR.

중아국   차관   2차보   아주국

PAGE 1

91.10.20   15:31

외신 2과   통제관 FM

D) SHOULD THE GOVERNING COUNCIL DECIDE ON A LESSER MUNIMUM SIMPLIFIED CLAIM AMOUNT FOR RETURNEES, IT MUST BE IN THE MATURE OF AN INTERIM PAYMENT WITHOUT PREJUDICE TO THE RIGHT OF THE INDIVIDUAL, OR HIS FAMILY, TO PRESENT THE REMAINING PART OF THE CLAIM SUBSEQUENTLY.

E) IT WOULD BE USEFUL FOR THE GOVERNING COUNCIL OF THE UNITED NATIONS COMPENSATION COMMISSION TO MODIFY THE SOMEWHAT ISOLATED PROCEDURE OF WORK THAT IT, AND ITS WORKING GROUP, ARE CURRENTLY EMPLOYING. THIS WOULD ENABLEA MUNBER OF AFFECTED COUNTRIES, INCLUDING PAKISTAN, TO ENGAGE IN A CONSTRUCTIVE DIALOGUE WITH THE GOVERNING COUNCIL. THIS DEVELOPMENT WOULD PERMIT THE EVOLUTION OF MORE PRACTICAL AND EQUITABLE DECISIONS AND CRITERIA ON THE ISSUE NOW UNDER CONSIDERATION, OF URGENT CLAIMS OF INDIVIDUALS, AND ALSO FOR SUBSEQUENT SUBJECTS TO BE TAKEN UP BY THE GOVERNING COUNCIL.

2. 상기 발췌 자료 파편 송부함. 끝. (대사 - 국장)

예고 91.12.31. 일반

주 파 키 스 탄 대 사 관

주파(정)760 - **267**   1991. 10. 17.
수신   외부부장관
참조   중동아프리카국장
제목   걸프전 피해보상

       연 : PAW - **1105**

연호, 걸프전 피해보상 관련 주재국 정부 입장 관계자료를 별첨송부합니다.

첨 부 : 관련자료. 끝.

        주   파   키   스   탄

                                               0111

GOVERNMENT OF PAKISTAN RESPONSE
TO THE GUIDELINE CRITERIA
PROPOSED BY THE GOVERNING COUNCIL OF THE UNITED NATIONS
COMPENSATION COMMISSION
FOR THE EXPEDITED PROCESSING OF
URGENT CLAIMS AND PAYMENT OF
FIXED AMOUNTS

The Governing Council of the United Nations Compensation Commission meeting in Geneva has proposed to limit the urgent compensation due to the most numerous and needy small claimants who were forced to leave Kuwait and Iraq in the following way:

i)   compensation for simple departure from Iraq and Kuwait at the rate of US $ 2500 per individual, with a ceiling of US $ 5000 per family;

ii)   claims for serious personal injury or death at the rate of US $ 2500 per individual, with a ceiling of US $ 10,000 per family;

iii) claims for damages upto US $ 100,000 to be documented in relatively greater detail, with a lesser degree of documentary evidence for smaller claim below US $ 20,000.

2.   Claims submitted for departure under the first category of US $ 2500 per individual, can not be resubmitted for a greater amount in any other category. Hence, if this procedure was finalized, those in most urgent need, in return for some limited and immediate compensation, would have to forego any subsequent claim to what was morally, legally, and rightfully, due to them.

3.   The compensation of US $ 2500 per individual for serious injury, or death, also places an unworthy value on the lives of essentially the largest class of affected persons who belong to the developing countries.

4.   The proposed claims forms are far too complex for many of the affected returnees from Kuwait and Iraq, and should be simplified as far as possible.

Detailed Study carried out by the Overseas Pakistanis Foundation

5.   The Overseas Pakistanis Foundation which is a Government Organization functioning under the Ministry of Labour, Manpower, and Overseas Pakistanis, carried out a detailed statistical survey of Pakistani returnees from Kuwait and Iraq.

0112

Number of Pakistani Workers in Kuwait

6.   After the occupation of Kuwait migrant Pakistanis employed in both Kuwait and Iraq started to leave for Pakistan in large numbers. From Kuwait some 61,000 Pakistanis working there, and their families, arrived in Pakistan and were monitored by the OPF. Another approximately 14,000 Pakistanis working in Kuwait were already on leave in Pakistan, when the Gulf crisis started. Some 11,000 Pakistanis employed in Kuwait stayed on in neighbouring Gulf countries or in Kuwait itself. Therefore, it can be estimated that the approximate number of Pakistanis employed in Kuwait at the time of the Gulf crisis was around 75,000. Dependent family members resident in Kuwait can be estimated to be around another approximately 30,000.

7.   The registration of the returning Pakistanis was started by the OPF as soon as they started arriving in Pakistan. A form was designed for this purpose in which, amongst other questions, the returnees were asked to list their losses suffered in Kuwait as a direct result of the Gulf crisis. A total of 46,854 Pakistanis who had been employed in Kuwait, on their return, filled in the form designed by the OPF. Dependent family members were not asked to fill in a separate form but were listed, if appropriate, by the 46,854 returnees who can be considered as family heads. 30,022 Pakistanis who had been working in Kuwait, in filling in this form, primarily at the points of entry into Pakistan, were in an immediate position to provide an assessment of the losses they had suffered. Some, for reasons of fatigue, emotional stress, health reasons, family problems, etc., were not able to concentrate on the issue of compensation at this moment of entry.

8.   The replies furnished at that time from the 30,022 returnees, who constitute approximately 40% of the estimated 75,000 Pakistanis working in Kuwait, provides a very fair statistical sample of the claims of the Pakistanis in Kuwait, and should therefore be of great utility to the Governing Council of the United Nations Compensation Commission.

Estimate of Losses

9.   A breakdown summary, based on this statistical data, of the average losses suffered by the Pakistani returnees from Kuwait, is given below category wise for occupational groups:

2

0113

Occupational Group	No.	Average Amount (in K.D.)			
		of Bank Deposit	of Durables	of Dues from Employers	Total
Professional, Technical & Related Workers	5,025	2,283	8,311	4,299	14,893
Administrative & Managerial Workers	375	5,834	9,012	6,497	21,343
Clerical & Related Workers	1,800	1,508	5,913	4,191	11,611
Sales Workers	3,750	3,118	24,489	3,575	31,182
Service Workers	3,225	630	3,517	1,318	5,465
Agricultural Workers	675	340	1,863	1,265	3,468
Production & Related Workers, Transport Equipment Operators & Labourers	55,500	1,020	5,458	2,429	8,907
Workers Not Classified By Occupation	4,650	1,274	4,527	2,973	8,774
Total:	75,000	1,239	6,469	2,650	10,346

Source: OPF Kuwait Returnees Database

3

0114

10. At Annex-I, the actual statistical data for the summary table given above is appended.

Inadequacy of the Proposed Fixed Amount Payments

11. Hence, it can be clearly seen that the total overall average loss suffered by the Pakistani returnees is approximately US $ 35,487 per person. For the largest category of occupational groups, relating to Pakistani production and related workers, transport equipment operators, and labourers, amounting to around 55,500 persons or 74% of the Pakistanis working in Kuwait, the average loss amounted to US $ 30,551 per person.

Specific Recommendations of the Government of Pakistan

12. Therefore, the Government of Pakistan, in bringing this information before the Governing Council, would reiterate the following points:

a) The minimum simplified proposed claim amount of US $ 2500 per returnee, has no relevance to the actual facts on the ground.

b) The proposed amount of US $ 2500 for serious personal injury, or death, should be raised to a more realistic figure in accordance with international standards.

c) On the grounds of equity, for Pakistani returnees the minimum simplified claim amount should be US $ 30,500.

d) Should the Governing Council decide on a lesser minimum simplified claim amount for returnees, it <u>must</u> be in the nature of an interim payment without prejudice to the right of the individual, or his family, to present the remaining part of the claim subsequently.

e) It would be useful for the Governing Council of the United Nations Compensation Commission to modify the somewhat isolated procedure of work that it, and its working groups, are currently employing. This would enable a number of affected countries, including Pakistan, to engage in a constructive dialogue with the Governing Council. This development would permit the evolution of more practical and equitable decisions and criteria on the issue now under consideration, of urgent claims of individuals, and also for subsequent subjects to be taken up by the Governing Council.

4

0115

Annex - 1

OVERSEAS PAKISTANIS FOUNDATION
<u>ASSETS LEFT IN KUWAIT</u>

PRINTED ON : 05/10/91   (FIGURES IN KD)

PROFESSION IN KUWAIT	TOTAL PERSONS	BALANCE IN BANK	VALUE OF ASSETS	DUES FROM EMPLOYER	TOTAL
CHEMISTS	9	11,995	58,300	40,000	110,295
PHYSICAL SCIENTISTS AND RELATED TECHNICIANS					
TOTALS :	9	11,995	58,300	40,000	110,295
Averages :		1,332.78	6,477.78	4,444.44	12,255.00
ARCHITECTS AND TOWN PLANNERS	17	28,793	31,650	99,504	159,947
CIVIL ENGINEERS	37	195,993	443,700	176,692	816,385
ELECTRICAL AND ELECTRONICS ENGINEERS	23	123,636	694,600	621,133	1,439,369
MECHANICAL ENGINEERS	5	73,560	21,300	41,875	136,735
CHEMICAL ENGINEERS	9	25,092	86,483	93,000	204,575
ENGINEERS NOT ELSEWHERE CLASSIFIED	211	729,477	1,916,491	1,665,529	4,311,497
SURVEYORS	61	79,828	431,996	318,069	829,893
DRAUGHTSMEN	133	210,110	404,070	434,913	1,049,093
CIVIL ENGINEERING TECHNICIANS	0	0	0	0	0
ELECTRICAL AND ELECTRONICS ENGINEERING TECHNICIANS	157	243,845	1,023,219	533,860	1,800,924
MECHANICAL ENGINEERING TECHNICIANS	13	9,326	36,155	72,945	118,426
CHEMICAL ENGINEERING TECHNICIANS	1	10,756	1,220	0	11,976

5

0116

OVERSEAS PAKISTANIS FOUNDATION
<u>ASSETS LEFT IN KUWAIT</u>

PROFESSION IN KUWAIT	TOTAL PERSONS	BALANCE IN BANK	VALUE OF ASSETS	DUES FROM EMPLOYER	TOTAL
ENGINEERING TECHNICIANS NOT ELSEWHERE CLASSIFIED					
	263	339,334	2,827,547	643,755	3,810,636
ARCHITECTS, ENGINEERS AND RELATED TECHNICIANS					
TOTALS :	930	2,069,750	7,918,431	4,701,275	14,689,456
Averages :		2,225.54	8,514.44	5,055.13	15,795.11
AIRCRAFT PILOTS, NAVIGATORS AND FLIGHT ENGINEERS					
	2	5,801	4,800	8,400	19,001
SHIPS' DECK OFFICERS AND PILOTS					
	3	830	5,000	13,000	18,830
SHIPS' ENGINEERS					
	4	5,000	23,500	19,700	48,200
AIRCRAFT AND SHIPS' OFFICERS					
TOTALS :	9	11,631	33,300	41,100	86,031
Averages :		1,292.33	3,700.00	4,566.67	9,559.00
LIFE SCIENCES TECHNICIANS					
	23	15,255	99,758	114,483	229,496
LIFE SCIENTISTS AND RELATED TECHNICIANS					
TOTALS :	23	15,255	99,758	114,483	229,496
Averages :		663.26	4,337.30	4,977.52	9,978.09
MEDICAL DOCTORS					
	21	122,126	219,600	232,625	574,351
VETERINARY ASSISTANTS					
	2	700	10,200	682	11,582
PHARMACISTS					
	24	42,551	150,950	83,783	277,284

6

0117

OVERSEAS PAKISTANIS FOUNDATION
ASSETS LEFT IN KUWAIT

PRINTED ON : 05/10/91   (FIGURES IN KD)

PROFESSION IN KUWAIT	TOTAL PERSONS	BALANCE IN BANK	VALUE OF ASSETS	DUES FROM EMPLOYER	TOTAL
PROFESSIONAL NURSES	262	247,441	1,148,361	780,945	2,176,747
NURSING PERSONNEL NOT ELSEWHERE CLASSIFIED	1	500	3,000	400	3,900
MEDICAL X-RAY TECHNICIANS	2	0	1,700	1,949	3,649
MEDICAL, DENTAL, VETERINARY AND RELATED WORKERS NOT ELSEWHERE CLASSIFIED	32	60,639	332,410	98,173	491,222

MEDICAL, DENTAL, VETERINARY AND RELATED WORKERS

TOTALS :	344	473,957	1,866,221	1,198,557	3,538,735
Averages :		1,377.78	5,425.06	3,484.18	10,287.02

STATISTICIANS	3	1,700	28,500	28,000	58,200
SYSTEMS ANALYSTS	31	85,104	123,370	75,855	284,329

STATISTICIANS, MATHEMATICIANS, SYSTEMS ANALYSTS AND RELATED TECHNICIANS

TOTALS :	34	86,804	151,870	103,855	342,529
Averages :		2,553.06	4,466.76	3,054.56	10,074.38

ACCOUNTANTS	148	382,413	733,712	814,656	1,930,781

ACCOUNTANTS

TOTALS :	148	382,413	733,712	814,656	1,930,781
Averages :		2,583.87	4,957.51	5,504.43	13,045.82

JURISTS

TOTALS :	0	0	0	0	0
Averages :		***,***.**	***,***.**	***,***.**	***,***.**

7

0118

OVERSEAS PAKISTANIS FOUNDATION
<u>ASSETS LEFT IN KUWAIT</u>

(FIGURES IN KD)

PROFESSION IN KUWAIT	TOTAL PERSONS	BALANCE IN BANK	VALUE OF ASSETS	DUES FROM EMPLOYER	TOTAL
LAWYERS	0	0	0	0	0
UNIVERSITY AND HIGHER EDUCATION TEACHERS	3	8,475	2,518,500	24,500	2,551,475
TEACHERS NOT ELSEWHERE CLASSIFIED	150	306,562	969,610	416,397	1,692,569

TEACHERS

TOTALS :	153	315,037	3,488,110	440,897	4,244,044
Averages :		2,059.07	22,798.10	2,881.68	27,738.85

WORKERS IN RELIGION NOT ELSEWHERE CLASSIFIED	29	33,098	140,876	45,835	219,809

WORKERS IN RELIGION

TOTALS :	29	33,098	140,876	45,835	219,809
Averages :		1,141.31	4,857.79	1,580.52	7,579.62

AUTHORS JOURNALISTS AND RELATED WRITERS NOT ELSEWHERE CLASSIFIED	38	64,541	111,035	111,409	286,985

AUTHORS, JOURNALISTS AND RELATED WRITERS

TOTALS :	38	64,541	111,035	111,409	286,985
Averages :		1,698.45	2,921.97	2,931.82	7,552.24

COMMERCIAL ARTISTS AND DESIGNERS	1	1,850	3,500	0	5,350
PHOTOGHRAPHERS AND CAMERAMEN	114	110,605	814,268	131,480	1,056,353

SCULPTORS, PAINTERS, PHOTOGRAPHERS AND RELATED CREATIVE ARTISTS

TOTALS :	115	112,455	817,768	131,480	1,061,703
Averages :		977.87	7,111.03	1,143.30	9,232.20

8

0119

외 무 부

종 별 :

번 호 : ITW-0122　　　　　　　　　　　일 시 : 92 0129 1730

수 신 : 장관(중동일,경일)

발 신 : 주 이태리 대사

제 목 : 이라크 자산 동결 부분해제

　　　주재국정부는　주재국내　동결된　이라크　자산을　일부　해제하였는　바
주재국내대이라크 배상청구 동향 포함, 주요 내용 다음 보고함.

　　①. 이라크 재산 동결 부분해제

　　0 주재국 수상령 (92.1.10. 발효) 에 의거 주재국내 동결 이라크 자산의 약10
프로(약 1 억불정도) (동결자산 총액 약 10 억불 추산)를 해제.

　　이라크가 이태리로부터 의약품을 구입하는데 사용토록 허용함. 이는 UN 결의안
범위내에서 이루어진 결정이라고 함.

　　②. 대이라크 배상청구 동향(1.28. 이태리 국고성 RUBINO 국장 언급내용)

　　0 주재국 기업이 이라크에 수출하면서 이태리 수출보험 특별반(SACE) 의
수출보험에 가입치 않고 입은 피해는 이태리 국고성이 종합하고 있으며, 국고성이
지금까지 접수한 기업은 10 개정도로 배상청구 금액은 1.5 조리라(약 12.5 억불)에
달함. 따라서 SACE 의 보험에 가입한 피해액 1.5 조리라(약 12.5 억불)를 포함
이태리가 이라크에 배상청구 가능한 피해 총액은 3 조리라(25 억불)로 추산됨.

　　0 한편 SACE 보험가입 피해액은 SACE 자체적으로 피해보상을 해결하고 있으나,
국고성 접수분 피해는 전혀 보상되지 못하고 있다 함. 이는 UN 피해배상기금또는 동결
자산 해제를 통한 피해배상도 전혀 이루어지지 않고 있기 때문이라 함. 끝

　　(대사 김석규-국장)

　　예고:92.6.30. 까지 ~~빵빵빵~~

외 무 부

종 별 :

번 호 : JOW-0265   일 시 : 92 0402 1730

수 신 : 장 관(중동일,기정)

발 신 : 주 요르단 대사

제 목 : 걸프사태 관련 배상

　　1.AL-KABARITI 주재국 노동장관은 4.1. 기자회견을 갖고 주재국정부는 걸프사태와 관련 쿠웨이트로부터 퇴거된 자국민들의 배상청구 접수를 위해 사무국을 설치하였으며, 동 사무국을 통해 접수된 배상청구는 제네바 소재 'UN 걸프전 배상기금'(UN GULF WAR COMPENSATION FUND)에 제출될 것이라고 밝힘.

　　2.상기 조치는 UN 배상기금이 쿠웨이트 퇴거 주재국민(대부분 팔레스타인계로 30만명 추산)에 대한 배상청구를 6개월 이내 제출토록 요청함에 따른것이며, 피해당사자 1 인당 최고 2500미불을 배상해줄 계획이라 함.(동배상재원은 UN이 허용한 이라크의 원유판매대금 16억불중 전쟁배상금 명목에서 조달 예정).끝.

　　(대사 이한춘-국장)

중아국　　외정실　　안기부

정 리 보 존 문 서 목 록

기록물종류	일반공문서철	등록번호	2012090516	등록일자	2012-09-17
분류번호	731.33	국가코드	IQ	보존기간	영구
명 칭	유엔안전보장이사회의 대이라크 제재 조치, 1992				
생 산 과	국제연합1과	생산년도	1992~1992	담당그룹	
내용목차	* 3.27　　 대이라크 경제제재 지속 결정 9.24　　 대이라크 경제제재 지속 결정 10.2　　 이라크 해외자산 압류 결의안 채택(안보리 결의 778호) 11.23-24 안보리 본회의, 대이라크 제재조치 지속 결정				

0001

외 무 부

종 별 :

번 호 : UNW-0263   일 시 : 92 0128 1900

수 신 : 장관(연일,동구이,중동일,기정)

발 신 : 주 유엔 대사

제 목 : 안보리(비공식협의)

안보리는 금 1.28 비공식협의를 갖고 유고 평화유지군 배치, 대이락 제재조치
정기심사, 유엔레바논 평화유지군(UNIFIL) 임무기간연장 문제를 토의한바, 당관
원종찬 참사관이 탐문한 동협의 주요경과를 아래보고함.

    1. 유고 평화유지군 배치문제

    가. B.BOUTROS-GHALI 사무총장은 유엔 군사연락장교단(군요원 47 명, 민간지원
인원 15 명) 파견현황 및 M.GOULDING 사무차장의 유고방문 중간 결과에 관해
설명하였으며, 일부 위반사례에도 불구하고 휴전이 전반적으로 유지되고 있다는
평가를 보였음.

    나. 오지리, 불, 헝가리, 러시아는 유엔평화유지군의 조기 배치입장을
피력하였으며, 특히 불란서는 BOUTROS-GHALI 총장이 동 배치를위한 구체적 제의를
다음주초 까지는 해주기를 희망하였음.

    다. 미, 영국도 휴전요지를 적극적 평가하고 금주 GOULDING 차장 당지 귀임후
최종보고를 기대한다고 언급함.

    라. 끝으로 BOUTROS-GHALI 총장은 유엔의 유고 평화유지 활동과 관련하여
지방무장세력으로 인한 장애와 어려움에 대한 우려를 표명하였다고함.

    2. 대이락 제재조치 정기심사

    가. 미, 불은 이락의 계속적인 안보리휴전결의 위반행태에 비추어 제재조치를
현행대로 유지해야 한다는 입장을 표명하였으며, 1.27 이락방문중인 유엔화생무기
사찰반에 대한 시위방치 사건과 관련 이를 용인할수 없는 이락측 안보리결의
위반행위라고 지적하였음.

    나. 당초 의장은 금일 비공식협의후 발표할 다음요지의 문안을 준비하였으나,
금일협의시 비동맹이사국(CAUCUS 6 개국)을 대표하여 카포베르데가 본건에 관해 더

| 국기국 | 장관 | 차관 | 1차보 | 2차보 | 구주국 | 중아국 | 외정실 | 분석관 |
| 정와대 | 안기부 | | | | | | | |

92.6.30. 깐도쯔

숙고할 필요를 제기해옴에 따라 동 발표는 일단 연기되었음.

    1)제재조치 변경조건 충족 미합의(제재조치 유지)

    2)이락의 안보리결의 이행현황에 관한 사무총장 보고서 언급및 이락의 결의불이행 지적

    3)일정 품목반입절차 변경문제 계속협의

    4)이락원유 수출문제에 관한 이락-유엔간 협의 결실기대

    다.1.27 유엔사찰반에 대한 시위방치 사건에 대해서는 의장이 이락대사를 초치, 항의조치 토록 결정됨.

    3.UNIFIL 임무기간 연장문제

    사무총장 권고대로 동기간을 6 개월 연장조치키로 하였으며, 동 감축안(10 프로)도 추진키로 합의됨.(1.29 관련결의안 채택예정)

    첨부:1. 유엔사찰반 관련 발표내용(1.27)

    2. 대이락 제재조치 정기심사 결과관련 안보리 발표문(안):UNW(F)-97 끝

    (대사 노창희-국장)

    예고:92.12.31. 까지

UNW(㈜)-97 20128
(연일.동구이.중동인.기정)   총404

#변정

"Today at around 7:20 a.m. Eastern time, an incident occurred upon the arrival from Bahrain of a United Nations inspection team at the Sheraton Hotel Baghdad.

"The 18 members of a United Nations Special Commission Chemical and Biological Weapons inspection team were confronted by some 40 male demonstrators in and outside the hotel.

"The Deputy Chief Inspector, Karen Jansen, upon entering the hotel, together with two other team members, was jostled, shouted at and pinned against the wall of the lobby, while Iraqi police looked on, until the team members finally managed to force their way through the hostile crowd.

"Despite requests for the police to intervene, the remainder of the inspection team were trapped inside a bus in front of the hotel for a further 20 to 25 minutes before they decided to force their way through into the hotel. The police, in response to questions about why they did not do anything, said they were not allowed to. The team members remaining in the vehicle watched while demonstrators, shouting slogans, jumped up and down on United Nations vehicles.

"The entire incident was filmed by members of a CNN camera crew who were present at the hotel prior to the team's arrival.

"According to the Commission, the incident represents a clear breach by Iraq of various special arrangements, undertakings and Security Council resolutions concerning the immunities, privileges, safety and access of United Nations inspection teams, in particular the status agreement of 14 May 1991 and Security Council resolution 707 (1991).

"The Executive Chairman of the Special Commission has informed the President of the Security Council and the Office of the Secretary-General of the incident. Oral and written protests are being addressed to the Iraqi Government by the Special Commission." (Press Release IK/82)

97-4-(1)

"A five-person mission arrived in Baghdad today to discuss with the Iraqi authorities the need for fuller compliance with Security Council resolutions that require Iraq to disclose detailed information concerning its weapons of mass destruction and related research and industries. Iraq's failure to provide requested information is viewed as a serious obstacle to the implementation of the long-term monitoring and verification of Iraq's obligations under the relevant Council resolutions.

"Rolf Ekeus, Executive Chairman of the Special Commission created by the Security Council to carry out the removal or destruction of Iraq's weapons of mass destruction, designated two Commission members to head the mission. They are John Gee of Australia and Peter von Butler of Germany. They will be accompanied by Patrice Palanque of France, Johan Santesson of Sweden and Nikita Smidovich of Russia.

"The team will specifically ask Iraq to come forward with more detailed information, as required under Council resolution 715 (1991). By that resolution, the Council approved plans for the long-term monitoring of the disarmament of Iraq, including a demand for additional information on industries and research programmes with dual-use potential in the areas of chemical and biological weapons and ballistic missiles with a range of over 150 kilometres. While Iraq did respond with a submission of some data, it did not meet the requirements of the resolution, the Special Commission found.

"The special mission, which will be in Baghdad through Wednesday, 29 January, is also expected to raise with the Iraqis various requests for information made by the Special Commission's past inspection teams which have not been met. Twenty-six inspections have been carried out since the Commission was created under the Iraq-Kuwait cease-fire resolution of 3 April 1991." (Press Release IK/83)

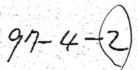

DRAFT PRESS STATEMENT

The Members of the Security Council held informal
consultations on 28 January 1992 pursuant to paragraph 21 of
Resolution 687 (1991). The Members of the Council expressed
their thanks to the Secretary-General for his factual report
on Iraq's compliance with all the obligations placed upon it
by Resolution 687 (1991) and subsequent relevant resolutions.

After taking note of the Secretary-General's report and
hearing all the opinions expressed in the course of the
consultations, the President of the Council concluded that
there was no agreement that the necessary conditions existed
for a modification of the regime established in paragraph 20
of Resolution 687 (1991), as referred to in paragraph 21 of
that Resolution.

In connection with the Secretary-General's factual report on
Iraq's compliance with all the obligations placed upon it by
Resolution 687 (1991) and subsequent relevant resolutions,
the Members of the Security Council note that while much
progress has been made, much remains to be done. There is
serious evidence of Iraqi non-compliance over its programmes
for weapons of mass destruction and the repatriation of
Kuwaitis and other third country nationals detained in Iraq.

97-4-3

There is still much Kuwaiti property to be returned. The
Members of the Council urge Iraq to comply fully with
Resolution 687 and subsequent relevant resolutions.

The Members of the Security Council note the report of the
Chairman of the Committee established by Resolution 661
(1990) concerning the situation between Iraq and Kuwait on
the study of those materials and supplies for essential
civilian and humanitarian needs that might be transferred
from the "no objection" procedure to a simple notification
procedure. They express their appreciation for the efforts
the Chairman has made to reach a conclusion and request him
to continue his consultations with the Members of the
Committee on the study and to report to the Council at an
early date.

The Members of the Council note that contacts are continuing
between the Secretariat and the Iraqi authorities about
implementation of Resolutions 706 (1991) and 712 (1991),
which gave to Iraq the possibility for oil sales to finance
the purchase of foodstuffs, medicines and materials and
supplies for essential civilian needs for the purpose of
providing humanitarian relief.   They trust that
these contacts will lead to the early implementation of the
scheme set out in those resolutions to enable humanitarian
supplies to reach the Iraqi people.

97-4-4

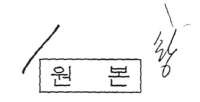

```
┌─────────┐
│관리 92  │
│번호 -95 │
└─────────┘
```

외 무 부

종   별 :

번   호 : UNW-0346   일   시 : 92 0205 1730

수   신 : 장관(연일,중동일,기정)

발   신 : 주 유엔 대사

제   목 : 안보리 비공식협의(대이락 제재조치 정기심사)

1. 안보리는 금 2.5 비공식협의를 가진바, 걸프휴전결의(687 호 본문 21 항)에 의거 대이락 제재조치 정기심사에 관한 토의결과 아래요지의 언론발표 문안에 합의하였음.

가. 현 제재조치 변경을위한 조건이 충족되었다는데 대해 합의없었음.(제재조치존속)

나. 최근 유엔사찰반 바그다드 방문중에 발생한 시위사건 우려표명

다. 이락의 안보리결의 전면이행 촉구(사무총장 보고서, 92.1.31 안보리정상회의 선언문 언급): 대량파괴 무기 폐기불이행, 외국인 억류, 쿠웨이트 재산 미반환

라. 안보리 제재위의 민수인도품 반입절차 완화문제 조기타결 요망

마. 이락의 자국 원유수출 문제관련 대유엔 접촉중단 결정 개탄및 동접촉 재개희망

2. 안보리는 의장으로 하여금 상기 합의문안을 언론에 발표하게 하는한편, 주유엔 이락대사를 초치하여 본건 안보리 토의결과를 통보토록 결정하였음. 끝

첨부:UNW(F)-134 끝

(대사 노창희-국장)

예고:92.12.31. 까지

국기국 안기부	장관	차관	1차보	2차보	중아국	외정실	분석관	정와대

PAGE 1   92.02.06   10:07

                                                외신 2과 통제관 BD

                                                        0008

4155E
ad

UNW(F)-134 20205 개정
(연일. 중도일. 기정)

Wednesday, 5 February 1992
12 noon

중 504

DRAFT PRESS STATEMENT

The members of the Security Council held informal consultations on 28 January
and 5 February 1992 purusant to paragraph 21 of resolution 687 (1991). The members
of the Council expressed their thanks to the Secretary-General for his factual
report on Iraq's compliance with all the obligations placed upon it by resolution
687 (1991) and subsequent relevant resolutions.

After taking note of the Secretary-General's report and hearing all the
opinions expressed in the course of the consultations, the President of the Council
concluded that there was no agreement that the necessary conditions existed for a
modification of the regime established in paragraph 20 of resolution 687 (1991), as
referred to in paragraph 21 of that resolution.

In the context of compliance, the Council members noted with concern the
recent incident in Baghdad, which demonstrates a lack of Iraqi cooperation in
complying with the resolutions of the Council.

In connection with the Secretary-General's factual report on Iraq's compliance
with all the obligations placed upon it by resolution 687 (1991) and subsequent
relevant resolutions, the members of the Security Council note that while much
progress has been made, much remains to be done. There is serious evidence of
Iraqi non-compliance over its programmes for weapons of mass destruction and the
repatriation of Kuwaitis and other third country nationals detained in Iraq. There
is still much Kuwaiti property to be returned. The members of the Council are
disturbed by the lack of Iraqi cooperation. Iraq must implement fully resolution
687 and subsequent relevant resolutions as was stated in the statement read out by
the President of the Council on behalf of its members in the meeting held on 31
January 1992 with the participation of the Heads of State and Government.

The members of the Security Council note that with a view to alleviating the
humanitarian conditions of the civilian population of Iraq and facilitating the
utilization of paragraph 20 of resolution 687, the 661 Committee had been requested
to prepare a study of those materials and supplies for essential civilian and
humanitarian needs, other than medicines which have not been subject to sanctions
and food shipments which have been permitted to move freely, that might be
transferred from the "no objection" procedure to a simple notification procedure.
The members of the Council also note the report of the Chairman of the Committee in
this regard. They express their appreciation for the efforts the Chairman has made
to reach a conclusion and encourage him to continue his consultations with the
members of the Committee on the study and to report to the Council at an early
date.

The members of the Council strongly deplored that the Iraqi authorities have
decided and communicated that decision to the Secretariat to discontinue contacts
with the Secretariat regarding implementation of resolutions 706 (1991) and
712 (1991), which give to Iraq the possibility for oil sales to finance the
purchase of foodstuffs, medicines and materials and supplies for essential civilian
needs for the purpose of providing humanitarian relief. They underscore that the
Government of Iraq, by acting in this way, is forgoing the possibility of meeting
the essential needs of its civilian population and therefore bears the full
responsibility for their humanitarian problems. They hope that a resumption of
these contacts may lead to the early implementation of the scheme set out in those
resolutions to enable humanitarian supplies to reach the Iraqi people.

134-5-1   0009

Enclosure

REPORT ON THE NINTH IAEA ON-SITE INSPECTION IN IRAQ

UNDER SECURITY COUNCIL RESOLUTION 687 (1991)

11 - 14 January 1992

SALIENT POINTS

- The main objective of the ninth IAEA on-site inspection was to verify recent information obtained from Governments of Member States, and in particular from the Government of Germany, about the procurement of large quantities of stock materials and components needed in the manufacturing of gas centrifuge machines for the production of enriched uranium.

  The materials and components in question included purpose-designed aluminium alloy extrusions used in the production of centrifuge vacuum housings and molecular pumps, and ferrite magnets used in the stators of the centrifuge motors. The quantities involved, which would have been sufficient for the manufacture of the basic static parts of several thousand centrifuges, had not been included in any previous Iraqi declaration.

- This information was discussed with the Iraqi Minister of State for Foreign Affairs in the presence of technical experts from both sides. Subsequent to the discussion, the Iraqi authorities acknowledged the procurement of these materials and components, but stated that all had been destroyed or "rendered harmless" by melting and crushing before the beginning of nuclear inspections in Iraq under resolution 687.

- Further, they acknowledged the procurement of 100 tons of the special high-tensile-strength steel (maraging steel) needed for producing several thousand centrifuge rotors and rotor internal fittings and the procurement of a few thousand aluminium forgings for the vacuum housing top and bottom flanges.

  The Iraqi authorities explained that in this case also the stockpile of maraging steel and aluminium forgings had been "rendered harmless" by melting before the start of the nuclear inspections and offered to present to the team all the materials which they had procured at the location where they were currently stored after being rendered harmless.

134-5-2   0010

S/23505
English
Page 4

The inspection team verified and sampled the melted maraging steel stockpile and the powder resulting from the crushing of the ferrite magnets, leaving for the next inspection the remaining verifications. A rough estimate of the quantities made on-site appears consistent with the quantities procured. Full verification must await the results of sample analyses and a more accurate assessment of mass.

The results of this inspection have resolved a number of inconsistencies regarding the Iraqi centrifuge programme remaining from previous inspections. In the opinion of the experts who took part in the nuclear inspection, Iraq had not reached the point where it could start centrifuge production on a sizeable scale, but given time, it would have been successful.

However, the centrifuge enrichment programme had reached the point where the materials necessary for certain key centrifuge components had been identified, and these materials were being procured as opportunities presented themselves even though the final design had not been completely fixed nor the manufacturing process fully implemented. The operation of any production-oriented centrifuge cascade would have required the procurement of large numbers of finished components, but the nuclear inspection teams have found no evidence of this.

Initiatives taken by the German Government have greatly assisted the ongoing inspection effort as it relates to the Iraqi centrifuge enrichment programme.

134-5-3

0011

IRAQIS DEFYING U.N. ON ARMS INDUSTRY AND OIL SALE TERMS

A TEST FOR U.S. AND ALLIES

Baghdad Thought to Be Probing Cohesiveness of Coalition in the Security Council

By PAUL LEWIS
Special to The New York Times

UNITED NATIONS, Feb. 4 — Iraq has rejected a United Nations plan for monitoring of its armaments industry and has broken off talks about selling oil to pay for imports of vitally needed food and medicine and for compensation of victims of the invasion of Kuwait.

These two moves, coming on top of the tight economic blockade that President Saddam Hussein has imposed on the Kurdish region of Iraq since last October, has propelled him into a potential confrontation with the Security Council, diplomats and officials here said today.

These diplomats and officials said in interviews that they believe President Hussein is bent on testing the cohesiveness of the coalition ranged against him during the war by refusing to comply with the Security Council's terms for ending the Persian Gulf war. He has backed down in the past.

New Help for Kurds

But uncertain whether Iraq will again yield, the diplomats and officials said the Council may soon be forced to consider further steps against Mr. Hussein and to provide fresh help for the Kurds if he continues to be recalcitrant.

President Bush appeared to allude to the possibility of such further action in his speech to last week's meeting of leaders of the Security Council, when he said, "We must deal resolutely with these renegade regimes, if necessary by sanctions or stronger measures, to compel them to accept international standards of behavior."

The United States is said to have stepped up its U-2 spy plane patrols over Iraq to hunt for secret weapon sites, sending an average of two flights a week over Iraq from a base in Saudi Arabia.

On Wednesday, the United Nations special commission set up to destroy Iraq's most dangerous weapons is scheduled to report to the Security Council that Baghdad has rejected its long-term plan for monitoring its military industries to insure that it never tries to make nuclear, chemical or biological weapons again.

Diplomats said the United States, which is this month's Council president, will issue a statement announcing that Iraq is still in breach of the Council's cease-fire terms and that sanctions, including the restrictions on the sale of Iraqi oil, cannot be lifted.

In its latest report on Iraqi compliance with the Security Council's demands, Rolf Ekeus, the Swede who heads the commission, says Iraq has refused to provide a detailed report on its defense industries, as demanded by the Security Council in Resolutions 707 and 717.

The report says that Iraq "does not recognize" that it has "any obligations" under these resolutions and that at a meeting with commission members in Baghdad on Jan. 12, senior Iraqi officials said that Iraq "would not make any further declarations" on weapons production plans, effectively challenging United Nations inspectors to go and find whatever they are looking for.

Iraq today punctured hopes it might soon agree to start selling oil under terms set by the Security Council, by canceling a second planned round of talks in Vienna on the oil sale plan with United Nations officials.

Plan for Oil Sales

After last month's initial meeting, the head of the United Nations team, Koffi Annan of Ghana, appeared optimistic that Iraq would soon accept the plan, selling some $1.6 billion worth of oil, with two-thirds of the proceeds being spent on food and humanitarian aid that the United Nations would distribute around the country.

The remaining third of the proceeds would be used to start compensating the victims of Iraq's invasion of Kuwait.

Iraq's United Nations representative, Abdul Amir al-Anbari, indicated that Baghdad has now lost all interest in the proposal. "We decided that the talks were no longer useful or productive, given the conditions imposed by the Security Council," he said today.

Western Governments had been hoping that Baghdad would ease the worsening plight of the Kurds by selling oil and thus allowing the United Nations to give them their share of the food and other supplies the proceeds would have bought.

But this hope has now disappeared, prompting some diplomats to speculate that governments may be forced to launch a new humanitarian relief operation in Kurdish areas before the warm weather comes, as they did last spring when they sent in armed forces to establish safe havens for refugees fleeing the Iraqi Army.

Economic Blockade of Kurds

United Nations officials say that since last October the Iraqi Army has established a fortified military line across northeastern Iraq, imposing a tight economic blockade on some three million Kurds living beyond the line.

The line starts north of Qasr-i-Shirin on the Iranian frontier and runs just east of Kifri and Kirkuk and south of Erbil to Zakho on the Turkish border.

United Nations relief workers in Iraq estimate that the blockaded portion of Iraq is only receiving about 10 percent of the food, fuel and other essential supplies it usually gets from other parts of the country.

Travelers crossing the line are searched and made to surrender food and other goods in short supply, the relief workers say. Motorists are only allowed to take half a tank of gasoline into the blockaded area.

The assumption among United Nations officials is that President Hussein

134-5-4

0012

Baghdad facing a showdown with the Security Council.

...is using the blockade to encourage the Kurds to accept the modest autonomy offer he made them last year, which most have now rejected. However the economic deprivation they are suffering could also strengthen nationalist feelings among them.

Concealment of Nuclear Effort

The new report on Iraq's compliance with the Security Council's efforts to destroy its most dangerous weapons chronicles Iraq's continuing efforts to conceal the extent of its clandestine nuclear program, most recently by hiding centrifuge plants designed to make enriched uranium nuclear explosive.

It says that Iraq has also tried to conceal equipment used for making chemical weapons, saying that while Baghdad had 10 different types of chemical ordnance in its arsenal, United Nations inspectors have only found the plants used for making two of them so far.

Baghdad maintains an economic blockade against northern Kurds.

The report says Iraq has admitted conducting research into biological weapons development but still refuses to produce plans for their production.

The new United Nations Secretary General, Boutros Ghali, has so far refused to publish the report as a public Council document, apparently for fear of offending Arab states. But the United States is expected to demand publication when the Council reviews it tomorrow.

A new nuclear inspection team arranged by the Vienna-based International Atomic Energy Agency is scheduled to arrive in Baghdad on Wednesday, and is expected to visit several undisclosed sites where the special commission has received intelligence that Iraq may be hiding prohibited material.

Some of this intelligence, officials say, comes from Iraqi documents, removed from Baghdad by inspectors last year, which indicated that Iraq has imported nuclear material that has not so far been accounted for. The commission is also working with private companies, mainly European, which sold Iraq suspicious material or helped it build plants that appear to have been intended for military uses.

The latest nuclear inspection team, United Nations officials say, is causing tension between the special commission and the I.A.E.A.

Officials say the I.A.E.A. is an organization used to working with its member governments to safeguard their nuclear installations and feels uncomfortable in its present adversarial role. I.A.E.A. officials are also said to be embarrassed by the enormous scale on which Iraq evaded the program of safeguards they operated in the country in a futile effort to prevent Iraq from developing nuclear weapons.

134-5-5

0013

외 무 부

종 별 :

번 호 : UNW-0353   일 시 : 92 0206 1630

수 신 : 장관(연일,미이,동구이,중동일,기정)

발 신 : 주 유엔 대사

제 목 : 안보리(비공식협의)

    1. 안보리는 금 2.6 비공식협의를 갖고 유고사태를 토의하고 의장의 이락대사 접촉결과를 청취한바, 당관 원참사관이 탐문한 바에 의하면, 금일 협의 말미에 의장인 T.PICKERING 미대사는 북한대사와 면담예정이며, 용건은 IAEA 안전조치문제로 보인다고만 간단히 언급하였으며, 이에대한이사국들의 반응은 없었다고함

    2. 상기 비공식협의시 유고사태 토의경과 및 의장의 이락대사 접촉결과 보고 요지는 다음과같음.

    가. 유고사태

    1)B.BOUTROS-GHALI 사무총장은 기배치중인 유엔 연락장교단 증원안 (UNW-0345) 을 설명하였으며, 금일 CROATIA 공화국 F.TUDJMAN 대통령이 유엔안 전면수락을 통보해옴에 따라 KRAJINA 지방지도자 M.BABIC 의 유보입장이 현재 유엔 평화유지군 배치와 관련하여 남은 중요장애 요인이라고 지적

    2)불란서는 유엔 평화유지군 배치 지연으로 사태악화 가능성이 있음에 비추어 KRAJINA 지방을 제외한 다른 지역부터 점진적, 부분적인 배치에 착수하는 방안을 제의하였으며, 동 제의에 대해 항가리, 러시아, 오지리가 호의적인 반응을 보임.(특히, 오지리는 안보리 결의안에 이를 반영시키는 문제제기)

    3)비동맹이사국(CAUCUS 6 개국)을 대표하여 에쿠아돌은 사무총장의 관련 제의가 없는 상황에서 유엔평화 유지군 배치를 개시하는 것에 이의를 제기하였으며, 기존 대유고 부기금수조치이행 문제를 강조함.

    4)인도는 현단계에서 유엔 평화유지군 배치를 추진하는 경우 TUDJMAN 대통령의 유엔안 전면 수락재고를 유발할 가능성도 있다고 하면서, 불란서제안은 신중한 검토가 필요하다고 언급

    5)영국은 사무총장의 유엔 연락장교단 증원을 승인하는 안보리 결의안 추진문제에

국기국 분석관	장관 정와대	차관 안기부	1차보	2차보	미주국	구주국	중아국	외정실

92. 6. 30.

92.02.07   07:34

외신 2과 통제관 BD

0014

대해서는 이의가 없으며, 불란서의 유엔평화유지군 부분 배치안은 사무총장, C.VANCE 북사의 당사자들과의 추가협의 결과를 보아가며, 검토하자는 입장을취한바, 벨지움도 이에 동조함.

6)상기 결의안 문제관련 명 2.7 비공식협의개최 예정(동일 안보리 결의안 공식채택 가능성)

나. 이락문제

의장은 대이락 제재조치 정기심사 종결(UNW-0346) 에 따른 2.5 이락대사와의 접촉결과를 보고한바, 동 접촉시 이락대사 반응은 다음과 같았다고 함.

1)이락 원유수출문제에 관한 대유엔 협의중단 조치는 이락주권을 해치는 여러 조건들을 제기해 온 때문

2)유엔 사찰반에 대한 시위는 평화적 범주를 벗어난일 없음.

3)안보리의 제반 결의 위반사실 부인.끝

(대사 노창희-국장)

예고:92.12.31. 까지

예고문에 의거 일반문서로 재분류(1992.12.31.)

PAGE 2

0015

외 무 부

종   별 :

번   호 : UNW-0786

일   시 : 92 0319 2030

수   신 : 장 관 (연일,중동일,기정)

발   신 : 주 유엔 대사

제   목 : 안보리-이라크 경제제재

연: UNW-0697

안보리는 3.18. 공식회의를 개최, 연호 이라크측이 식량 및 의약품 구입을 위해 석유수출을 제안한데 대해 이를 환영하고 안보리결의 706 및 712 에 따라 이라크 및 유엔사무총장이 세부 추진방안을 협의토록 하는 별첨 안보리 의장성명을 발표함. 끝

(대사대리 전기목-국장)

첨부: UNW(F)-285

국기국   1차보   중아국   안기부

92.03.20   13:49 WG

외신 1과 통제관

0016

DRAFT PRESIDENTIAL STATEMENT ON 706/712

The Security Council welcomes the announcement of
the Iraqi authorities that they will resume discussions with
the United Nations Secretariat concerning implementation of
the scheme of sales of Iraqi petroleum and petroleum
products, as provided for in Security Council resolutions
706 and 712, and for the use of the proceeds of such sales
in accordance with the Secretary-General's report of 4
September 1991 (S/23006) and the above mentioned
resolutions.

The Council also welcomes the Secretary-General's
intention that these discussions be organised without delay.

The Council is prepared to authorise the regime
for the sale of Iraqi petroleum and petroleum products on
the above basis for a like period of time as that specified
in these resolutions as soon as the Secretary-General
indicates that the Iraqi authorities are prepared to proceed
on a date certain with the export of petroleum and petroleum
products in accordance with the scheme.

The members of the Council are prepared at an
appropriate time to consider possible further extensions of
time based upon Iraq's cooperation with the above and the
Council's ongoing assessment of the needs and requirements
in accordance with paragraph 1(d) of Security Council
Resolution 706.

UN 安保理, 對이락 經濟制裁 持續 決定

1. UN 安保理는 3.27 非公開 定例會議를 開催하고 對이락 經濟制裁를 持續하기로 決定했음.

2. UN의 對이락 經濟制裁와 관련한 動向을 보면

   가. 이락의 쿠웨이트 侵攻(90.8)直後 醫藥品·食糧을 제외한 對이락 物資 搬入 全面禁止 및 海外資産 凍結 등을 骨子로 한 包括的인 對이락 經濟制裁措置(安保理決議 661號)를 통해 安保理 理事國으로 構成된 制裁委員會가 對이락 物資搬入의 監視 및 許容與否를 管掌토록 한 가운데

   나. 걸프戰 終戰(91.2)을 계기로 該當國 政府의 事前通報와 함께 制裁委員會의 異議가 없을 경우에 한해 人道的 民需物品의 이락 搬入을 許容(91.3)하는 등 人道的 次元에서 制裁措置를 多少 緩和한데 이어

   다. 걸프戰 停戰決議案 687號를 採擇(91.4), 制裁委員會로 하여금 每 60日마다 이락의 安保理 決議 履行實態를 점검하고 이락의 大量破壞武器 廢棄履行에 따른 對이락 禁輸措置 解除與否를 決定하도록 規定한 바 있으나

   라. 安保理 制裁委는 이락측이 大量破壞武器 폐기이행에 非協調的인 態度를 보임에 따라 5차(91.6, 91.8, 91.10, 91.12, 92.1.28)에 걸친 會議를 통해 對이락 經濟制裁의 持續을 決定한 바 있음.

21-14

0018

3. 이번 安保理의 對이락 經濟制裁 持續 決定은

　가. 停戰決議案 687號에 의거 對이락 經濟制裁의 解除與否 決定을 위한 定
　　　期審査의 一環에서 이루어진 것이나

　나. 時期的으로 UN·이락間 制限的인 이락産 原油輸出 허용문제가 協議되
　　　고 있고, 이락측이 UN의 大量破壞武器 폐기에 協調하겠다는 立場을 밝
　　　힌 가운데 UN 核査察團의 이락訪問(4.5 -)을 앞두고 있다는 점에서

　다. 이락에 대해 大量破壞武器 廢棄履行 壓力은 물론 UN이 定한 條件下에
　　　이락産 原油를 販賣하도록 壓力을 加하는 要因으로 作用할 것으로 豫
　　　想됨.

21-15

0019

주 국 련 대 표 부

주국련20313- **422**   1992. 4. 16.

수신 장관

참조 국제기구국장, 중동아프리카국장

제목 걸프사태

걸프사태와 관련한 유엔 배포자료를 별첨 송부합니다.

첨 부 : 1. 이락-쿠웨이트간 상황에 대한 안보리의장 성명(S/23803)

        2. 이락외상의 유엔사무총장앞 서한(S/23809)

        3. 이락대사의 유엔사무총장앞 서한(S/23810)

        4. 안보리결의 687 이행과 관련한 유엔 사무총장 보고서(S/23801).

주 국 련 대 사

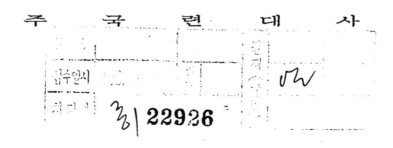

22926

0020

UNITED
NATIONS

S

Security Council

Distr.
GENERAL

S/23801
10 April 1992

ORIGINAL: ENGLISH

THE STATUS OF THE IMPLEMENTATION OF THE PLAN FOR
THE ONGOING MONITORING AND VERIFICATION OF IRAQ'S
COMPLIANCE WITH RELEVANT PARTS OF SECTION C OF
SECURITY COUNCIL RESOLUTION 687 (1991)

Report of the Secretary-General

Introduction

1.   The present report is submitted in pursuance of paragraph 8 of Security
Council resolution 715 (1991) adopted on 11 October 1991. This requests the
Secretary-General and the Director General of the IAEA to submit to the
Security Council reports, when requested and at least every six months after
the adoption of the resolution, on the implementation of the plans approved
under resolution 715 (1991), for the ongoing monitoring and verification of
Iraq's compliance with relevant parts of Section C of Security Council
resolution 687 (1991). The paragraphs below provide information, for the
first six-month period, on the implementation of the plan to be carried out by
the Special Commission established by the Secretary-General pursuant to
paragraph 9 (b) (i) of Security Council resolution 687 (1991). This plan
itself contains, in paragraph 25, the same reporting requirements on the
implementation of the plan as the Council's resolution 715 (1991).

2.   The Special Commission's monitoring and verification plan is contained in
document S/22781/Rev.1. It covers the long-term monitoring and verification
of Iraq's compliance with its unconditional obligations under Section C of
resolution 687 (1991) not to use, retain, possess, develop, construct or
otherwise acquire any weapons or related facilities and items prohibited under
paragraphs 8 and 9 of that resolution relating to proscribed ballistic
missiles, chemical and biological weapons and facilities. Monitoring and
verification under the plan will need to cover not only military but also
those civilian sites, facilities, material and other items or activities that
could be used in contravention of these obligations of Iraq under resolution
687 (1991). For that purpose the plan provides for inspections in Iraq,
aerial overflights and submission of information by Iraq so that the Special
Commission would be able to monitor and verify that no chemical or biological
weapons, ballistic missiles with a range greater than 150 kilometres, or any

92-16520 3791a (E)   100492   120492   /...

other facilities and items prohibited under resolution 687 (1991) were reacquired.

3.   Under paragraph 5 of resolution 715 (1991), Iraq is required to meet unconditionally all its obligations under the plan and to cooperate fully with the Special Commission in carrying out the plan.

4.   The first practical steps to be taken by Iraq under the plan were the submission, by 10 November 1991, of (a) initial information on the specific dual-purpose activities, facilities and items outlined in the plan and its annexes; and (b) a report on the legislative and administrative measures taken to implement resolutions 687 (1991), 707 (1991), other relevant Security Council resolutions and the plan. Iraq is further obliged to update the information in (a) above each 15 January and 15 July, and to report further on (b) when requested by the Special Commission. Ongoing monitoring and verification can only be carried out effectively if the Special Commission has the clearest picture of what Iraq's capabilities have been in the development, production and acquisition of weapons of mass destruction and prohibited ballistic missiles and what items, facilities and materials were at its disposal or would be from time to time acquired which, while devoted to civilian activities, could be converted with relative ease to proscribed military uses.

Developments during the period 11 October 1991-8 April 1992

5.   Iraq's position on resolution 715 (1991) and the monitoring and verification plan approved thereunder was formally stated in a letter of 19 November 1991 which the Minister for Foreign Affairs of Iraq addressed to the President of the Security Council. In the letter Iraq did not recognize any obligations under resolution 715 (1991) and strongly attacked the plan, claiming that it was "aimed at objectives incompatible with the letter and spirit of the United Nations Charter, the norms of international law and international and humanitarian pacts and covenants". In the view of the Special Commission, this position is tantamount to a rejection of the resolution and the plan.

6.   Only in late November did the Special Commission receive from Iraq a document that was stated in the letter of 19 November of the Minister for Foreign Affairs of Iraq to be "the information required under resolution 687 (1991) that comes under the mandate of the Special Commission". As described in paragraph 5 above, the letter does not recognize that Iraq has any obligations under resolution 715 (1991) and the plans approved thereunder. Instead Iraq arrogated to itself the right to decide what information it would provide to the Special Commission and, in this respect, the document transmitted to the Special Commission did little more than repeat information already supplied. It thus fell well short of the information required under the monitoring and verification plan. No information was provided by Iraq, as required by the plan, on the legislative and administrative measures taken to implement resolutions 687 (1991), 707 (1991), other relevant Security Council resolutions and the plan.

/...

0022

7.   The Executive Chairman of the Special Commission in a letter, dated
20 December 1991, to the Permanent Representative of Iraq to the United
Nations stated that the Special Commission could not accept that the document
provided by Iraq with the letter of 19 November constituted the submission of
information required under Security Council resolution 715 (1991). He further
stressed that Iraq's attitude was a serious obstacle to the implementation of
the monitoring and verification of Iraq's compliance with its obligations
under resolution 687 (1991). In the letter Iraq was requested to rectify the
situation immediately and fulfil its obligations under resolution 715 (1991)
and the monitoring and verification plan. The Special Commission asked Iraq
to provide by 15 January 1992 all the information and data specified in the
plan.

8.   Iraq has failed to respond to these requests, and has not provided its
first semi-annual declaration which under the plan was due from it on
15 January 1992. No notifications on specific activities, as stipulated by
the plan, were communicated by Iraq to the Special Commission.

9.   The failure by Iraq to acknowledge its obligations under resolution
715 (1991) and to comply with the monitoring and verification plan was
reported to the Security Council in the Secretary-General's notes and reports
(S/23268, S/23514, S/23606, S/23643 and S/23687) which also referred to steps
taken by the Special Commission to seek Iraq's compliance with Security
Council resolution 715 (1991) and the plan.

10.   As part of these efforts the Special Commission, at the end of
January 1992, sent a special mission headed by two members of the Commission
to Baghdad to underline the Commission's most serious concern with Iraq's
failure to comply with the resolution 715 (1991) and the plan. Iraq, at the
level of the Minister of State for Foreign Affairs, reiterated that the
Government maintained its position expressed in the letter of 19 November.

11.   In view of the attitude maintained by Iraq the Special Commission
reported on 18 February to the Security Council (S/23606) its conclusion that
"Iraq has no intention of meeting its obligations under the plans approved
under, and the provisions included in, Security Council resolution
715 (1991)".

12.   On 19 February 1992, the President of the Security Council issued a
statement on behalf of the members of the Council which noted that "ongoing
monitoring and verification of Iraq's obligations is an integral part of
Security Council resolution 687 (1991), which established a cease-fire and
provided the conditions essential to the restoration of peace and security in
the region". The statement of 19 February also determined that Iraq's failure
to acknowledge its obligations under resolution 715 (1991) and its rejection
of the two plans for ongoing monitoring and verification constituted a
continuing material breach of the relevant provisions of resolution
687 (1991). The members of the Council supported the decision of the
Secretary-General to dispatch a special mission headed by the Executive
Chairman of the Special Commission to visit Iraq immediately to meet and

/...

0023

discuss with the highest levels of the Government of Iraq for the purpose of securing the unconditional agreement by Iraq to implement all its relevant obligations under resolutions 687 (1991), 707 (1991) and 715 (1991).

13. The special mission headed by the Executive Chairman of the Special Commission was immediately dispatched and held talks with the Government of Iraq on 21, 22 and 23 February. The report on the proceedings and outcome of the mission's visit was communicated to the Security Council by a note of the Secretary-General of 26 February (S/23643). This report contained amongst its conclusions the statement by the Executive Chairman that he was not able to report to the Council that he had secured from the highest levels of the Government of Iraq unconditional agreement by Iraq to implement all its relevant obligations under Security Council resolutions 687 (1991), 707 (1991) and 715 (1991).

14. In order to achieve its objectives, the special mission specifically urged Iraq to acknowledge its obligations under resolution 715 (1991) and the plans approved under it as well as to take specific steps to implement its obligations such as submission of declarations required under the plans and an undertaking that Iraq would cooperate to ensure implementation of the plans. In response, Iraq stated that it did not reject the plans for ongoing monitoring and verification approved under Security Council resolution 715 (1991). In elaborating on this statement, Iraq indicated that it had accepted only the principle of ongoing monitoring and verification, and that this was subject to considerations of sovereignty, territorial integrity, national security and non-infringement on Iraq's industrial capabilities. The Executive Chairman could not conclude that such a statement constituted unconditional agreement by Iraq to implement its obligations under the plans for ongoing monitoring and verification.

15. On 28 February the President of the Security Council issued a statement in which the members of the Council approved in full the conclusions of the special mission, and deplored and condemned, *inter alia*, the failure of Iraq to comply with the plans for ongoing monitoring and verification approved by resolution 715 (1991). The statement reiterated the Council's determination that Iraq's behaviour constituted a material breach of resolution 687 (1991) and demanded that Iraq immediately implement all its obligations under Council resolution 687 (1991) and subsequent related resolutions.

16. Through the report of the Secretary-General on the status of compliance by Iraq with the obligations placed upon it under certain of the Security Council resolutions (S/23687), the Special Commission informed the Council on 7 March that the most important outstanding matters include: failure by Iraq to acknowledge its obligations under Council resolution 715 (1991) and under the plans approved by this resolution; failure by Iraq to agree to implement unconditionally all its obligations under resolution 715 (1991); and failure by Iraq to provide the declarations required under the plans for ongoing monitoring and verification. This information was brought to the attention of the Security Council in the statement made by the President of the Council at the opening of the 3059th meeting on 11 March.

/...

0024

17. The Security Council met on 11 and 12 March to consider all aspects of Iraq's compliance with resolution 687 (1991) and other relevant resolutions. The Executive Chairman of the Special Commission in his statement before the Council reiterated that Iraq's position towards the plans for ongoing monitoring and verification could not be understood otherwise than as rejection.

18. On 11 March, the Deputy Prime Minister of Iraq expressed before the Council Iraq's readiness to reach a practical solution to the question of the Security Council's verification of Iraq's capabilities to produce the weapons prohibited by resolution 687 (1991), while underlining the need for respect for Iraq's sovereignty and national security. He stated that "the understanding by the Security Council of the logical and legitimate principles, basis and requests which we have presented will naturally lead to an objective, equitable and just implementation of the substantive obligations placed upon Iraq in resolutions 707 (1991) and 715 (1991), in a manner which will satisfy the Council".

19. At the conclusion of the meeting of the Security Council on 12 March, the President of the Council made a statement indicating that, in the view of the Security Council, the Government of Iraq had not yet complied fully and unconditionally with its obligations, must do so and must immediately take the appropriate actions in this regard. The Council expressed its hope that the goodwill expressed by the Deputy Prime Minister of Iraq would be matched by deeds.

20. Following the consideration in the Security Council of Iraq's compliance with the relevant resolutions, officials from the Office of the Executive Chairman of the Special Commission met on 12 and 13 March with an Iraqi technical team. The Commission explained in detail to the team what it expected of Iraq by way of implementation of the plan for ongoing monitoring and verification (S/22871/Rev.1). In response to Iraq's requests the Special Commission provided during the meetings detailed explanations as to the format and modalities required by the plan for its implementation under its different sections and annexes. The delegation of Iraq promised to provide, by early April, the information under the plan except on the sources of imported items and on operational employment or disposition of relevant weapons. The Special Commission stressed that the information should be provided in full as required by the plan. The team handed over, by way of example, certain preliminary material on the content of Iraq's future official declarations. After review of the material, the Special Commission found that information contained therein did not meet the requirements of the plan and it therefore informed Iraq that the material needed further work to ensure that the declarations to be submitted by Iraq corresponded - both in substance and in format - to the requirements of the plan for ongoing monitoring and verification. As of 8 April no declarations or information as required by the plan has been received from Iraq by the Special Commission.

21. The Special Commission communciated on 20 December to Iraq that it would not be in a position to decide upon the requests of Iraq for the reuse of

/...

0025

certain dual-purpose items until it received all information and data under the plan for ongoing monitoring and verification, and obtained clear and unequivocal acceptance by Iraq of resolution 715 (1991) and the plan. Any such items that might be released by the Special Commission for reuse, after being rendered harmless, need to be covered by appropriate monitoring and verification procedures envisaged in the plan.

Conclusions

22.   At the moment the Special Commission has to report that, despite the Commission's best endeavour, it was not possible to begin the practical implementation of the plan for ongoing monitoring and verification (S/22871/Rev.1) approved by resolution 715 (1991) because of the positions maintained by Iraq since the adoption of this resolution.   It is apparent that during the period covered in this report Iraq was not in compliance with Security Council resolution 715 (1991) nor with the plan.

23.   Without clear acknowledgement by Iraq of its obligations under Security Council resolution 715 (1991) and the plans approved thereunder, as well as without its agreement to implement unconditionally these obligations the Special Commission will be neither legally nor practically able to initiate and operate effectively the monitoring and verification plan contained in document S/22871/Rev.1.   There would be no assurances on the full implementation of resolution 715 (1991) as envisaged by the Security Council and Iraq's position would still be a matter of great concern.   In the absence of these steps on the part of Iraq the credibility of Iraq's declarations on its capabilities related to resolution 715 (1991) would be greatly undermined.   As the statement, dated 19 February, of the President of the Security Council on behalf of the Council members indicated, unconditional agreement by Iraq to implement its obligations under resolution 715 (1991) is one of the essential preconditions to any reconsideration by the Council under paragraphs 21 and 22 of resolution 687 (1991) of the prohibitions referred to in those paragraphs.

24.   The Security Council in its resolution 715 (1991) demanded that Iraq meet unconditionally all its obligations under the plan for ongoing monitoring and verification (S/22871/Rev.1) and cooperate fully with the Special Commission in carrying out the plan.   If Iraq adopts such an approach and abides by its obligations, then the practical implementation of the plan could proceed in a smooth and unobtrusive manner, on a routine basis and without unnecessarily hampering or delaying the normal activities at locations which would be inspected.   The full cooperation, complete initial and periodic declarations and goodwill of the Government of Iraq will be the determining factor.

25.   Along with a clear acknowledgement by Iraq of its obligations under resolution 715 (1991) and the plans approved thereunder, the immediate step required to start the proper operation of the plan for ongoing monitoring and verification (S/22871/Rev.1) is for Iraq to file with the Special Commission the initial declarations required under the plan.   If and when Iraq's declarations are received, the Special Commission will evaluate them in order

/...

to determine the extent to which they meet the requirements - both in format and in substance - of the plan. Such declarations are essential so that the Special Commission will be in a position to begin and carry out effectively its inspections and other monitoring and verification activities under the plan of the nature and scope approved by the Security Council.

0027

UNITED NATIONS

Security Council

S

Distr.
GENERAL

S/23803
10 April 1992

ORIGINAL: ENGLISH

NOTE BY THE PRESIDENT OF THE SECURITY COUNCIL

After the consultations held on 10 April 1992, the President of the Security Council issued the following statement on behalf of the members of the Council in connection with the item entitled "The situation between Iraq and Kuwait":

"The members of the Security Council have learnt with grave concern from the Executive Chairman of the Special Commission of recent developments which appear to call for a halt in and constitute a threat to the safety and security of the Special Commission's aerial surveillance flights over Iraq. The members of the Council wish to point out that the surveillance flights are carried out under the authority of Security Council resolutions 687, 707 and 715 (1991). Reaffirming the right of the Special Commission to conduct such aerial surveillance flights, the members of the Council call upon the Government of Iraq to take all the necessary steps to ensure that the Iraqi military forces will not interfere with or threaten the security of the flights concerned and to comply with its responsibilities to secure the safety of the Special Commission's aircraft and personnel while flying over Iraq. The members of the Council warn the Government of Iraq of the serious consequences which would ensue from any failure to comply with these obligations."

100492

92-16496 3104g (E)   100492

0028

Security Council

Distr.
GENERAL

S/23809
14 April 1992
ENGLISH
ORIGINAL: ARABIC

LETTER DATED 13 APRIL 1992 FROM THE PERMANENT REPRESENTATIVE OF
IRAQ TO THE UNITED NATIONS ADDRESSED TO THE SECRETARY-GENERAL

On instructions from my Government, I have the honour to transmit
herewith a letter dated 12 April 1992 addressed to you by Mr. Ahmad Hussain,
Minister for Foreign Affairs of the Republic of Iraq, concerning the increase
in violations by the Kuwaiti regime in the demilitarized zone.

I should be grateful if you would have this letter and its annex
circulated as an official document of the Security Council.

(Signed) Abd al-Amir AL-ANBARI
Ambassador
Permanent Representative

ANNEX

<u>Letter dated 12 April 1992 from the Minister for Foreign Affairs
of Iraq addressed to the Secretary-General</u>

I should like to inform you that there has been a substantial increase in the number of violations by the Kuwaiti regime in the demilitarized zone. About 100 have been committed, as indicated in your report on UNIKOM covering the period 3 October 1991 to 31 March 1992 (document S/23766 of 31 March 1992). These violations are not even mentioned as possible sources of concern or as actions demanding an appropriate response. Nor is the Kuwaiti regime asked to put an end to such violations; the United Nations might have been expected to make such a request in such circumstances.

The silence concerning the increase in violations by the Kuwaiti regime could be interpreted as wilful negligence dictated by certain countries that are well known for exerting pressure on the United Nations for obvious political ends. Those very countries cried out in indignation over the Bubiyan incident when the Kuwaiti regime uttered what were known to be false charges, alleging that Iraqi troops had invaded the island on 28 August 1991. You examined those charges in your report of 3 September 1991 (S/23000), in which you refuted outright the outrageous inventions of the Kuwaiti leaders. The Governments of the Western countries have been quick to repeat, disseminate and magnify the lies uttered by the Kuwaiti leaders. They have tried to turn them into real events and to threaten Iraq, but they have remained unruffled and silent in the face of the actual brutalities described in your above-mentioned report. And now again they say not a word, finding nothing bad to say about these disturbing Kuwaiti violations.

In bringing the above to your notice, we hope and pray that the reports of the Secretariat will follow a single rule of neutrality and objectivity, without favouring either party at the expense of the other.

I should be grateful if you would have this letter circulated as a document of the Security Council.

(<u>Signed</u>) Ahmad HUSSAIN
Minister for Foreign Affairs
of the Republic of Iraq

0030

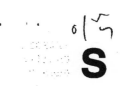

UNITED
NATIONS

Security Council

Distr.
GENERAL

S/23810
14 April 1992
ENGLISH
ORIGINAL: ARABIC

LETTER DATED 13 APRIL 1992 FROM THE PERMANENT
REPRESENTATIVE OF IRAQ TO THE UNITED NATIONS
ADDRESSED TO THE SECRETARY-GENERAL

On instructions from my Government, I should like to inform you that over the period 3-9 April 1992 United States aircraft have persisted in their violations of Iraqi airspace for purposes of observation and provocation.

3-4 April 1992

Six sorties, flown by one two-aircraft formation and four single aircraft at speeds of 600 to 900 kilometres per hour and at altitudes of 5,000 to 6,500 metres, centred over Mosul, Amadiyah, Zakho, northern Irbil and Tall Afar.

At 1232 hours on the same day, two F-16s overflew Tall Afar airfield at a speed of 700 kilometres per hour and at an altitude of 150 metres.

5-6 April 1992

Twenty-six sorties, flown by 12 two-aircraft formations and two single aircraft at a speed of 600-900 kilometres per hour and at altitudes of 4,000 to 7,000 metres, centred over Mosul, Irbil, Dohuk, Amadiyah and Zakho.

6-7 April 1992

Twenty sorties, flown by seven two-aircraft formations and six single aircraft at a speed of 900 kilometres per hour and at altitudes of 4,000 to 7,000 metres, centred over Mosul, Tall Afar, Dohuk, Irbil, Amadiyah and Zakho.

7-8 April 1992

Twenty-two sorties, flown by seven two-aircraft formations and eight single aircraft at speeds of 600 to 900 kilometres per hour and at altitudes of 3,500 to 6,000 metres, centred over Mosul, Irbil, Dohuk, Tall Afar, Amadiyah, Zakho and Ayn Zalah.

92-16872 2991c (E)   /...

0031

<u>8-9 April 1992</u>

Twenty-two sorties, flown by eight two-aircraft formations and six single aircraft at speeds of 600 to 900 kilometres per hour and at altitudes of 3,000 to 7,000 metres, centred over Mosul, Irbil, Amadiyah, Dohuk and Tall Afar.

I should be grateful if you would have this letter circulated as a document of the Security Council.

(<u>Signed</u>) Abdul Amir A. AL-ANBARI
Ambassador
Permanent Representative

0032

주 국 련 대 표 부

주국련20313- 524   1992. 5 . 14.

수신 장관

참조 중동아프리카국장

제목 걸프사태

　　　　걸프사태와 관련, 유엔 안보리문건을 별첨 송부합니다.

　　첨 부 : 안보리문건(S/23893, 895, 901, 903). 끝.

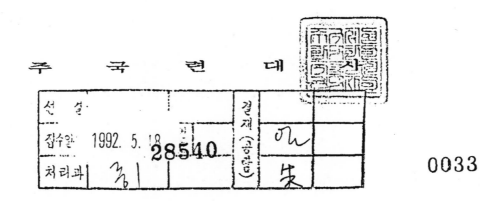

0033

UNITED NATIONS

Security Council

Distr.
GENERAL

S/23893
8 May 1992
ENGLISH
ORIGINAL: ARABIC

S

LETTER DATED 8 MAY 1992 FROM THE CHARGE D'AFFAIRES OF
THE PERMANENT MISSION OF KUWAIT TO THE UNITED NATIONS
ADDRESSED TO THE SECRETARY-GENERAL

On instructions from my Government and in response to the letter sent by the representative of Iraq (S/23751) concerning the demilitarized zone, I have the honour to inform you as follows:

1.   Iraq's allegations that an Iraqi was wounded in the frontier zone, at Safwan, on 12 March 1992 have no foundation. The aforementioned zone is traversed constantly by members of the United Nations Iraq-Kuwait Observer Mission (UNIKOM), which keeps a record of all the violations occurring there. There is also a set observer patrol by the aforementioned members of UNIKOM in the vicinity of the farms where Iraq maintains that the incident occurred. This patrol goes between the Kuwaiti police station at Al-Abdali and the Iraqi police post at Safwan. If there had been any violation on the part of the Kuwaiti police, UNIKOM would have alerted the Kuwaiti authorities.

2.   Iraq's allegations that a Kuwaiti patrol opened fire on the guard post of Umm Qasr on 18 and 19 March 1992 are also fallacious. The guard post of Umm Qasr is located close to the observer's command post in the northern sector. It is on the Mike Road, which our patrols are not authorized to use, by order of the observers. Furthermore, the observer patrols are constantly traversing the area of Umm Qasr. Accordingly, if there had been a violation on the part of the Kuwaiti police, UNIKOM would have alerted the Kuwaiti authorities.

3.   The existence of the Iraqi post of Umm Qasr is considered in itself a violation of the cease-fire and the integrity of Kuwaiti territory. This post, as UNIKOM reports attest (see para. 22 (d) of document S/23766), is one of five Iraqi posts located in Kuwaiti territory, according to the frontiers shown on the UNIKOM map. Although Kuwait and UNIKOM have repeatedly stated that these posts should be evacuated, Iraq continues to delay their evacuation.

92-19851 3407b (E)   080592 080592

090592

/...

0034

I should be grateful if you would have the text of this letter circulated as a document of the Security Council.

(Signed)   Mohammad S. AL SALLAL
Chargé d'affaires a.i.

0035

UNITED NATIONS

S

 Security Council

Distr.
GENERAL

S/23895
11 May 1992
ENGLISH
ORIGINAL: ARABIC

LETTER DATED 8 MAY 1992 FROM THE PERMANENT REPRESENTATIVE OF
IRAQ TO THE UNITED NATIONS ADDRESSED TO THE SECRETARY-GENERAL

On instructions from my Government and in reply to the letter from the Kuwaiti representative contained in document S/23819, I wish to inform you of the following:

When the Kuwaiti representative takes up secondary details addressed in your report (S/23766) and makes baseless and tendentious claims, he is simply trying to distort and falsify the essential subject of that report which Iraq felt had not benefited from the attention it deserved. The essential point is that the number of Kuwaiti violations, as stated in the report, amounted to 100 during the period from 3 October 1991 to 31 March 1992, as compared with 4 Iraqi violations established by the Observer Mission. The report noted simply that the aforementioned violations had been raised in writing with the party concerned. Thus, according to the report, the United Nations took no action vis-à-vis the Kuwaiti side's persistent infringements and violations. In the light of available evidence and precedents, Iraq considers that the report of the United Nations Secretariat did not treat the issue in a neutral and objective manner. It is, indeed, this approach which encourages the representative of Kuwait to persist in his pedantic presumptions and to make random accusations against Iraq at a time when the Kuwaiti regime continues to commit flagrant violations inside the zone of operations of the United Nations Observer Mission.

I should be grateful if you would have this letter circulated as a document of the Security Council.

(Signed) Abdul Amir A. AL-ANBARI
Ambassador
Permanent Representative

92-20019 3178j (E)   120592 120592   *120592*

0036

UNITED NATIONS

Security Council

Distr.
GENERAL

S/23901
11 May 1992
ENGLISH
ORIGINAL: ARABIC

LETTER DATED 11 MAY 1992 FROM THE PERMANENT REPRESENTATIVE OF
IRAQ TO THE UNITED NATIONS ADDRESSED TO THE SECRETARY-GENERAL

On instructions from my Government, I should like to inform you that over
the period 30 April-7 May 1992 United States aircraft have persisted in their
violations of Iraqi airspace for purposes of observation and provocation.

<u>30 April-1 May 1992</u>

Thirteen sorties, flown by three 2-aircraft formations and seven single
aircraft at speeds of 600-900 kilometres per hour and at altitudes of
2,000-5,500 metres, centred over Mosul, Irbil, Dohuk, Zakho, Tall Afar,
Amadiyah and Rawanduz.

<u>1-2 May 1992</u>

Thirteen sorties, flown by five 2-aircraft formations and three single
aircraft at speeds of 600-900 kilometres per hour and at altitudes of
4,500-7,000 metres, centred over Zakho, Dohuk, Mosul, Irbil, Tall Afar,
Amadiyah and Ayn Zalah.

<u>3-4 May 1992</u>

Twenty-two sorties, flown by eleven 2-aircraft formations at speeds of
600-900 kilometres per hour and at altitudes of 3,500-8,000 metres, centred
over Mosul, Irbil, Dohuk, Zakho and Amadiyah.

<u>4-5 May 1992</u>

Twenty-two sorties, flown by six 2-aircraft formations and 10 single
aircraft at speeds of 600-720 kilometres per hour and at altitudes of
2,000-18,000 metres, centred over Dohuk, Mosul, Amadiyah, Tall Afar, Irbil and
Dukan.

92-20212 3053c (E)   120592 120592 *120592*   /...

0037

<u>5-6 May 1992</u>

Twenty-six sorties, flown by twelve 2-aircraft formations and two single aircraft at speeds of 600-900 kilometres per hour and at altitudes of 2,000-8,000 metres, centred over Zakho, Dohuk, Mosul, Irbil, Amadiyah, Tall Afar and Dukan. At 1125 hours on 5 May 1992, a formation consisting of two United States aircraft flew 15 kilometres inside the 36th parallel in the area of Irbil at a speed of 800 kilometres per hour and at an altitude of 2,000 metres.

<u>6-7 May 1992</u>

Seven sorties, flown by one 2-aircraft formation and five single aircraft at speeds of 600-900 kilometres per hour and at altitudes of 5,500-6,500 metres, centred over Amadiyah, Irbil, Mosul, Dohuk and Tall Afar.

I should be grateful if you would have this letter circulated as a document of the Security Council.

(<u>Signed</u>)   Abdul Amir A. AL-ANBARI
Ambassador
Permanent Representative

0038

UNITED NATIONS

Security Council

Distr.
GENERAL

S/23903
12 May 1992
ENGLISH
ORIGINAL: ARABIC

LETTER DATED 12 MAY 1992 FROM THE PERMANENT REPRESENTATIVE OF
IRAQ TO THE UNITED NATIONS ADDRESSED TO THE SECRETARY-GENERAL

On instructions from my Government, I wish to inform you of further
Iranian violations of the cease-fire between the two countries for the period
from 2 to 7 May 1992.

1.   At 0855 hours on 2 May 1992, three Iranians were observed strengthening
the communications trench at geographical coordinates 035937 inside the area
of separation.

2.   At 1130 hours on 2 May 1992, an Iranian excavator was observed building a
road between the Ziyadi guardpost at geographical coordinates 162489 and the
Tariq bin Ziyadah guardpost at coordinates 204489 inside the area of
separation.

3.   At 1920 hours on 2 May 1992, 16 soldiers from the Iranian side occupied
the Tariq bin Ziyad guardpost at geographical coordinates 204489 inside the
area of separation.

4.   At 1000 hours on 3 May 1992, a group of between 12 and 14 Iranians was
observed laying barbed wire south of the Qal'at Lam guardpost at geographical
coordinates 689248 inside the area of separation.

5.   At 1130 hours on 7 May 1992, the Iranian side dug four slit trenches at
intervals of 25 metres near the Iranian zone at geographical coordinates
899302 inside the area of separation.

I should be grateful if you would have this letter circulated as a
document of the Security Council.

(Signed) Abd al-Amir AL-ANBARI
Ambassador
Permanent Representative

92-20425 3138f (E)   130592 130592   130592

0039

UN, 이락 海外資産 押留 檢討

1. UN 制裁委員會는 이락內 UN活動費用의 충당을 위해 이락의 海外資産을
   押留할 것을 검토하고 있다고 中東經濟調査誌(MEES)가 보도(5.25)하였음.

2. 그간 UN은

   가. 이락의 쿠웨이트 侵攻(90.8)직후 醫藥品·食糧을 제외한 對이락 物資
      搬入 全面禁止 및 海外資産(40-50億弗) 凍結 등을 골자로 한 포괄적인
      對이락 經濟 制裁措置(安保理 決議 661호)를 통해 安保理 理事國으로
      구성된 制裁委員會로 하여금 對이락 物資搬入의 감시 및 허용여부를
      관장토록 한 가운데

   나. 걸프戰 停戰決議案 687호를 채택(91.4), 制裁委員會로 하여금 매 60일
      마다 이락의 安保理 決議 履行實態를 점검하고 이락의 大量破壞武器
      廢棄履行에 따른 對이락 禁輸措置 解除與否를 결정토록 하는 한편
      ※ 同 制裁委는 이락側이 大量破壞武器 廢棄履行에 비협조적인 태도를
         보임에 따라 6차(91.6, 91.8, 91.10, 91.12, 91.1.28, 3.27)에 걸쳐 對이
         락 經濟制裁의 지속을 결정

   다. 決議案 706호를 채택(91.8)하여
      ○ 食糧·醫藥品등 緊急 民生物資 購入에 한해 제한된 기간(6개월)동안
         제한된 量(16億弗 상당)의 이락産 原油輸出을 허용하되

○ 原油販賣 대금을 UN 관리하에 두고 이락側이 필요로 하는 民生物資 購入(50%), 戰爭賠償(30%), 大量破壞武器 廢棄活動등 UN停戰決議 履行과 관련한 活動費用(20%)에 충당토록 하고

라. 이락側과 2차(1.8, 3.26 오스트리아)에 걸쳐 이락産 原油販賣 問題를 협의하였으나 이락側의 原油輸出 限度增額(16億弗→32億弗)·長期契約 締結 등을 주장함에 따라 進展을 이루지 못한 바 있음.

3. UN의 이락 海外資産 押留 檢討는

가. 旣 凍結된 이락의 海外資産을 임의 처분할 수 있는 押留措置를 통해 「후세인」退陣壓力을 加重시켜 나가면서

나. 현재 이락의 非協調로 전혀 조성되지 못하고 있는 걸프戰 배상기금 조달은 물론 難民救護등 이락內 活動經費 保全을 위해 이락에 대해 UN 決議案 706호 履行을 강요하기 위한 壓力手段의 일환에서 비롯된 것으로 評價되는 바

다. 최근 美 高位官吏들이 「후세인」政權에 壓力을 가하기 위해 이락의 海外資産을 이락內 UN活動費 등으로 쓰는"방안에 대해 協議해 왔다는 (3.16 WSJ紙)점 등에서 5월말 開催豫定인 UN制裁委員會를 통해 本格 제기될 可能性이 있어 注目됨.

주 국 련 대 표 부

주국련 2031- 619   1992. 6. 4.

수신 : 장관

참조 : 중동아프리카국장

제목 : 걸프전

　　　　이락-쿠웨이트 휴전에 관해 양국이 유엔에 제출한 서한을 별첨
송부합니다.

　　첨 부 : 유엔문건(S/24006, 24022, 24023, 24047). 끝.

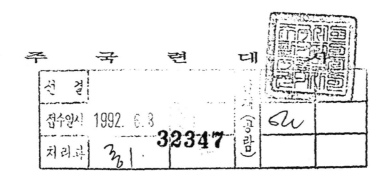

0042

Security Council

Distr.
GENERAL

S/24023*
1 June 1992
ENGLISH
ORIGINAL: ARABIC

LETTER DATED 27 MAY 1992 FROM THE PERMANENT REPRESENTATIVE
OF KUWAIT TO THE UNITED NATIONS ADDRESSED TO THE
SECRETARY-GENERAL

On instructions from my Government and in response to the contents of the
letter from the Iraqi representative (S/23857) concerning the demilitarized
zone, I wish to state the following:

1.   Iraq's claim that Kuwaiti boats gave chase to a number of Iraqi vessels
in the Khor Abdullah area on 5 April 1992 is false.   What in fact happened was
that on Friday, 3 April 1992, at 7.30 p.m. (local time), a Kuwaiti coastal
patrol arrested four Iraqi infiltrators after they had penetrated seven
nautical miles into territorial waters north-east of Faylakah.   Following
questioning, they were returned to Iraq under the auspices of the
International Committee of the Red Cross.

2.   Iraq's claim that a number of civilians and Kuwaiti policemen set up
signposts near Al-Shaheed guard post on 5 April 1992 is spurious.   As is well
known, Kuwait has made arrangements with civilian contractors to clear the
demilitarized zone south of the boundary line adopted by the United Nations
Iraq-Kuwait Observation Mission (UNIKOM).   A contractor was present at that
location purely for the purpose of carrying out legitimate work inside Kuwaiti
territory.   It should be noted that Al-Shaheed guard post is located inside
Kuwaiti territory at coordinates 659299.

3.   Iraq's claim that a Kuwaiti patrol fired on the Umm Qasr police post on
18 April 1992 is false.   As we have mentioned before, the post is situated
near the UNIKOM headquarters in the northern sector, which is constantly
patrolled by the Mission.   If there had been a violation by the Kuwaiti
police, UNIKOM would so have informed the Kuwaiti authorities.   As we have
also previously mentioned, the Umm Qasr police post is one of the five Iraqi
posts situated on the Kuwaiti side of the boundary line shown on the UNIKOM
map, as confirmed in the reports of the Mission (S/23766, para. 22 (d)).

---

*   Reissued for technical reasons.

92-23425   3195f (E)   010692 010692   010692   /...

4.   Iraq's claim that four vans approached the Iraqi Talha guard post on 19 April 1992, set up markers at that location and then headed for the Kuwaiti Ratqa guard post is also false. As noted in paragraph 2, Kuwait is determined to clear the area of mines and has made arrangements with contractors to carry out this task, which is being conducted in consultation with UNIKOM. Here also, we should like to point out that the existence of the Iraqi Talha guard post is in itself a flagrant violation of the provisions of the cease-fire because it is located inside Kuwaiti territory and is one of the five posts referred to by the Secretary-General in his reports.

5.   Iraq's claim that Kuwait carried out engineering work by building a dirt road on 20 April 1992 at geographical coordinates inside Iraqi territory is false. In fact, an engineering unit under contract to Kuwait carried out activity inside Kuwaiti territory.

6.   Iraq's claim that individuals fired in the direction of the Iraqi Abu Musa post on 25 April 1992 is also spurious. Suffice it to say that the Abu Musa post too is one of the five Iraqi posts which Iraq persists in attempting to remove from Kuwaiti jurisdiction.

    In short, Iraq's assertions prove in themselves - even without any response on our part - that the Iraqi regime is violating the provisions of the cease-fire by insisting on maintaining five police posts inside Kuwaiti territory, four of which were mentioned in its letter. Nor is it possible to ignore the regime's responsibility for the repeated acts of infiltration from Iraq into Kuwaiti territory.

    I should be grateful if you would have this letter circulated as a document of the Security Council.

                                  (Signed) Mohammad A. ABULHASAN
                                            Permanent Representative

-----

0044

UNITED NATIONS

S

Security Council

Distr.
GENERAL

S/24047
1 June 1992
ENGLISH
ORIGINAL: ARABIC

LETTER DATED 1 JUNE 1992 FROM THE PERMANENT REPRESENTATIVE OF
IRAQ TO THE UNITED NATIONS ADDRESSED TO THE SECRETARY-GENERAL

On instructions from my Government and further to our previous letters concerning violations of Iraqi airspace by United States aircraft, I should like to inform you of a number of fresh violations.

20-21 May 1992

Twenty-six sorties, flown by 12 two-aircraft formations and two single aircraft at speeds of 600-900 km/h and at altitudes of 4,000-6,000 metres, centred over Mosul, Zakho, Dohuk, Irbil, Tall Afar and Amadiyah.

21-22 May 1992

Twenty-three sorties, flown by 10 two-aircraft formations and three single aircraft at speeds of 600-900 km/h and at altitudes of 3,000-6,000 metres, centred over Zakho, Dohuk and Ayn Zalah.

22-23 May 1992

Twenty-one sorties, flown by 10 two-aircraft formations and one single aircraft at speeds of 750-900 km/h and at medium altitude, centred over Zakho, Dohuk, Tall Afar, Mosul, Irbil, west of Rawanduz and Amadiyah.

24-25 May 1992

Ten sorties, flown by five two-aircraft formations at speeds of 600-900 km/h and at altitudes of 5,000-6,000 metres, centred over Mosul, Dohuk, Amadiyah, Zakho and Tall Afar.

26-27 May 1992

Twelve sorties, flown by four two-aircraft formations and four single aircraft at speeds of 600-900 km/h and at altitudes of 3,000-6,500 metres, centred over Mosul, Irbil, Dohuk, Zakho, Tall Afar and Amadiyah.

92-23440 3912a (E)   010692 010692   010692

/...

27-28 May 1992

    Ten sorties, flown by two two-aircraft formations and six single aircraft at speeds of 600-900 km/h and at altitudes of 2,500-6,500 metres, centred over Zakho, Amadiyah, Mosul, Tall Afar, Dohuk and Irbil.

    I should be grateful if you would have this letter circulated as a document of the Security Council.

(Signed) Abd al-Amir AL-ANBARI
Ambassador
Permanent Representative

UNITED NATIONS

Security Council

Distr.
GENERAL

S/24023
27 May 1992
ENGLISH
ORIGINAL: ARABIC

LETTER DATED 27 MAY 1992 FROM THE PERMANENT REPRESENTATIVE
OF KUWAIT TO THE UNITED NATIONS ADDRESSED TO THE
SECRETARY-GENERAL

On instructions from my Government and in response to the contents of the letter from the Iraqi representative (S/23857) concerning the demilitarized zone, I wish to state the following:

1.   Iraq's claim that Kuwaiti boats gave chase to a number of Iraqi vessels in the Khor Abdullah area on 5 April 1992 is false. What in fact happened was that on Friday, 3 April 1992, at 7.30 p.m. (local time), a Kuwaiti coastal patrol arrested four Iraqi infiltrators after they had penetrated seven nautical miles into territorial waters north of Faylakah. Following questioning, they were returned to Iraq under the auspices of the International Committee of the Red Cross.

2.   Iraq's claim that a number of civilians and Kuwaiti policemen set up signposts near the Martyr guard post on 5 April 1992 is spurious. As is well known, Kuwait has made arrangements with civilian contractors to clear the demilitarized zone south of the boundary line adopted by the United Nations Iraq-Kuwait Observation Mission (UNIKOM). A contractor was present at that location purely for the purpose of carrying out legitimate work inside Kuwaiti territory. It should be noted that the Martyr guard post is located inside Kuwaiti territory at coordinates 659299.

3.   Iraq's claim that a Kuwaiti patrol fired on the Umm Qasr police post on 18 April 1992 is false. As we have mentioned before, the post is situated near the UNIKOM headquarters in the northern sector, which is constantly patrolled by the Mission. If there had been a violation by the Kuwaiti police, UNIKOM would so have informed the Kuwaiti authorities. As we have also previously mentioned, the Umm Qasr police post is one of the five Iraqi posts situated on the Kuwaiti side of the boundary line shown on the UNIKOM map, as confirmed in the reports of the Mission (S/23766, para. 22 (d)).

4.   Iraq's claim that four vans approached the Iraqi Talha guard post on 19 April 1992, set up markers at that location and then headed for the Kuwaiti Ratqa guard post is also false. As noted in paragraph 2, Kuwait is determined

92-22879 3231j (E)   290592 290592   290592   /...

to clear the area of mines and has made arrangements with contractors to carry out this task, which is being conducted in consultation with UNIKOM. Here also, we should like to point out that the existence of the Iraqi Talha guard post is in itself a flagrant violation of the provisions of the cease-fire because it is located inside Kuwaiti territory and is one of the five posts referred to by the Secretary-General in his reports.

5.   Iraq's claim that Kuwait carried out engineering work by building a dirt road on 20 April 1992 at geographical coordinates inside Iraqi territory is false. In fact, an engineering unit under contract to Kuwait carried out activity inside Kuwaiti territory.

6.   Iraq's claim that individuals fired in the direction of the Iraqi Abu Musa post on 25 April 1992 is also spurious. Suffice it to say that the Abu Musa post too is one of the five Iraqi posts which Iraq persists in attempting to remove from Kuwaiti jurisdiction.

In short, Iraq's assertions prove in themselves - even without any response on our part - that the Iraqi regime is violating the provisions of the cease-fire by insisting on maintaining five police posts inside Kuwaiti territory, four of which were mentioned in its letter. Nor is it possible to ignore the regime's responsibility for the repeated acts of infiltration from Iraq into Kuwaiti territory.

I should be grateful if you would have this letter circulated as a document of the Security Council.

(Signed)   Mohammad A. ABULHASAN
Permanent Representative

0048

Security Council

Distr.
GENERAL

S/24022
27 May 1992
ENGLISH
ORIGINAL: ARABIC

LETTER DATED 27 MAY 1992 FROM THE PERMANENT REPRESENTATIVE OF
IRAQ TO THE UNITED NATIONS ADDRESSED TO THE SECRETARY-GENERAL

On instructions from my Government and further to our letter concerning violations of the cease-fire by the Kuwaiti side, I wish to inform you of fresh occurrences of Kuwaiti violations, as follows:

1.   At 1815 hours on 6 April 1992, the farmer Salim Shaddad Azzafah was shot at by Kuwaiti patrols while he was on his farm trying to remove the markers set up by the Kuwaiti side inside his farm, which is estimated to lie 600 metres inside Iraqi territory.

2.   At 1800 hours on 29 April 1992, four fighter planes of unknown identity were seen flying at very high altitude and at medium speed from the direction of Kuwaiti airspace. They entered Iraqi airspace at geographical coordinates 555515.

3.   At 1915 hours on 29 April 1992, a large transport plane preceded by a number of fighter planes entered Iraqi airspace at geographical coordinates 555515. It was not identified and proceeded towards Kuwaiti airspace.

4.   On 20 May 1992, the Kuwaiti side pitched a 400-pound tent in front of the Himam control post at geographical coordinates 618332 on the road that runs across the common line to Kuwait. Three military personnel with a white GMC vehicle were in front of the tent.

These repeated acts of aggression perpetrated by the Kuwaiti side are clearly intended as a provocation and constitute a flagrant violation of the cease-fire provisions set forth in Security Council resolution 687 (1991). They also violate the directives relating to the demilitarized zone.

In drawing your attention to the significance of these acts, the Government of the Republic of Iraq lodges a vigorous protest against these blatant acts of aggression against the security of Iraq, its citizens and its frontier posts and emphasizes that the Kuwaiti side must bear responsibility for the consequences which these violations may have.

I should be grateful if you would have this letter circulated as a
document of the Security Council.

(Signed)   Abd al-Amir AL-ANBARI
Ambassador
Permanent Representative

0050

Security Council

Distr.
GENERAL

S/24006
26 May 1992
ENGLISH
ORIGINAL: ARABIC

LETTER DATED 25 MAY 1992 FROM THE PERMANENT REPRESENTATIVE OF
IRAQ TO THE UNITED NATIONS ADDRESSED TO THE SECRETARY-GENERAL

On instructions from my Government, I wish to inform you of further
violations by Iran of the cease-fire between the two countries for the period
from 11 to 18 May 1992.

1.   At 1920 hours on 11 May 1992, a Land Cruiser vehicle carrying three
persons, one of whom was wearing a turban and the other two military uniform,
was observed halting at geographical coordinates 902060 inside the area of
separation. The individuals fired three shots in the direction of Iraqi units
before withdrawing to the Iranian rear.

2.   At 1030 hours on 12 May 1992, a helicopter was observed proceeding from
the Iranian rear in the direction of the international border opposite the
Zayn al-Qaws slope. The aircraft returned to the Iranian rear at 1035 hours.

3.   At 1230 hours on 12 May 1992, an Iranian helicopter was observed
proceeding from the Iranian rear. It flew at medium altitude over the oil
wells in the area of Naft-e-Shah and returned to the Iranian rear at
1235 hours.

4.   At 1300 hours on 13 May 1992, the Iranian side completed the construction
of the Iranian guardpost opposite the Darraji border post at geographical
coordinates 131726 inside the area of separation.

5.   At 1430 hours on 15 May 1992, an Iranian helicopter was observed on the
ground at geographical coordinates 605501. It returned to the Iranian rear at
1900 hours.

6.   At 1450 hours on 15 May 1992, an Iranian helicopter proceeding from the
Iranian rear was observed landing at geographical coordinates 683320. It
returned to the Iranian rear after 10 minutes.

7.   At 1830 hours on 15 May 1992, eight persons from the Iranian side
occupied the building near the Bahramabad guardpost, opposite the Hasan
military guardpost, at geographical coordinates 010647 inside the area of
separation.

92-22580 3903a (E)   270592 270592   270592   /...

8.   Between 0930 and 1320 hours on 16 May 1992, an Iranian helicopter was observed flying at an altitude of 2,000 metres over Iraqi units. It landed at geographical coordinates 578493 inside the area of separation before returning to the Iranian rear.

9.   At 1000 hours on 16 May 1992, the Iranian side set up a PKC machine-gun by the Iranian position at geographical coordinates 035937 inside the area of separation.

10. At 1115 hours on 16 May 1992, an Iranian helicopter was observed landing at geographical coordinates 622325 inside the area of separation. After five minutes, the helicopter flew along the border embankment before returning to the Iranian rear.

11. At 1200 hours on 16 May 1992, an Iranian helicopter was observed landing at geographical coordinates 622325. It took off in the direction of the Iranian rear after five minutes.

12. At 1450 hours on 16 May 1992, an Iranian helicopter proceeding from the Iranian rear was observed landing at geographical coordinates 683321. It returned to the Iranian rear after five minutes.

13. At 1500 hours on 16 May 1992, an Iranian helicopter proceeding from the Iranian rear was observed landing at geographical coordinates 578493 inside the area of separation. It returned to the Iranian rear after unloading bags and crates.

14. At 0650 hours on 17 May 1992, a 106-millimetre gun mounted on a vehicle was observed in the Iranian zone opposite the Iraqi position at geographical coordinates 713216 inside the area of separation.

15. At 1020 hours on 17 May 1992, an Iranian helicopter proceeding from the Iranian rear was observed landing at geographical coordinates 578493 inside the area of separation. It returned to the Iranian rear at 1120 hours.

16. At 1150 hours on 17 May 1992, an Iranian helicopter proceeding from the Iranian rear was observed landing at geographical coordinates 578493 inside the area of separation. It returned to the Iranian rear at 1200 hours.

17. At 1600 hours on 17 May 1992, an Iranian helicopter proceeding at low altitude from the Iranian rear was observed landing behind the Iranian position at geographical coordinates 622325. It returned to the Iranian rear after 15 minutes.

18. At 1000 hours on 18 May 1992, an Iranian helicopter was observed proceeding from the Iranian rear. It flew for five minutes over the Iranian units at coordinates 578493 before landing there and taking off in the direction of the Iranian rear at 1100 hours.

/...

19. At 1200 hours on 18 May 1992, an Iranian helicopter proceeding from the Iranian rear was observed landing at geographical coordinates 578493 (Majnun al-Shimali) before returning to the Iranian rear.

I should be grateful if you would have this letter circulated as a document of the Security Council.

(Signed) Abd al-Amir AL-ANBARI
Ambassador
Permanent Representative

0053

USW(F) : 4708　년월일 : 92.7.16　시간 : 10:50

수 신 : 장 관 (머인, 연원, 중동인)

발 신 : 주미대사

제 목 : 이락의 유엔 결의 준수문리

(출처 :　　　)

보 안
품 체

STATE DEPARTMENT REGULAR BRIEFING
BRIEFER: RICHARD BOUCHER

Q　Richard, yesterday you had a rather strong statement about Iraq and I was a little confused because when I asked you specifically about a letter that the Iraqis had sent to the UN, demanding certain things from the UN, among them the rescission of UN resolutions, you were not reacting to that yesterday, right? You did not seem to be aware of that yesterday.

MR. BOUCHER: What we were reacting to yesterday was the standoff in Baghdad that does continue. The letter, I think I told you that we were aware of it from wire reports or something like that --

Q　I wonder -- what I wonder is you were actually --

MR. BOUCHER: I'll be glad to explain.

Q　(Off mike) -- before the letter came. Now you are reacting today to the letter. It was reported by some people yesterday that what you said yesterday was in reaction to the letter. That was not the case, right?

MR. BOUCHER: I'm not going to get into what people might have reported. I didn't see people reporting one way or the other. I mean yesterday we were talking about the letter and I gave some general comments on the situation with Iraqi compliance, which I'll be glad to explain further what's in these various letters that the Iraqis sent and what our views are, if that's your question today.

(4708 - 4 -1)

외신 1과
등 제

배부처	장관실	차관실	一차보	二차보	외경실	문석관	아주국	미주국	구주국	중아국	국기국	강재국	동상국	문협국	의연원	청와대	안기부	공보처	경기원	상공부	재무부	동자부	한경처	기치
	0	/	/	/	/			0	/	/				/									

First, with the standoff in Baghdad, the members of the UN Special Commission inspection team continue to monitor the entrances to the Ministry of Agriculture building in Baghdad. UN Special Commission Chairman Rolf Ekeus left New York last night for Baghdad to meet with Iraqi authorities. His goal is to underline the Security Council's commitment to see Iraq comply with its obligations under the Security Council resolution.

As you know from what I did say yesterday, the Secretary told Boutros-Ghali the other night that Ekeus' effort had our full support.

The Iraqi refusal to grant access to UNSCOM is just one part of a continuing pattern of Iraqi rejection of its obligations under the UN Security Council resolutions. And I'd like to talk about some other of those today.

0708 - 4 - 2

UN Security Council resolution 688 demanded at Iraq end repression of the Iraqi civilian population and insisted that Iraq allow immediate access by international humanitarian organizations to all those in need of assistance. The Iraqi government is clearly not fulfilling its obligations under this resolution. Continued repression in the north and south and interference with the work of humanitarian workers by harassment, restriction of travel, and delaying visa issuance all make this failure clear.

Iraq has turned a blind eye to harassment of officials of international organizations. Such harassment has included things like a grenade attack on UN guards, firing at official vehicles, and violent demonstrations against UN personnel.

Iraq sent a July 11th letter to the Security Council in which the government of Iraq appears to refuse to implement Security Council resolutions 706 and 712. These resolutions were intended to provide humanitarian assistance to those in need, to fund UN activities in Iraq, and to provide compensation to the victims of Iraqi aggression in Kuwait. In that letter, the Iraqi government reiterated a false claim that it has fulfilled the requirements of UN Security Council resolution 687 to disclose and destroy all weapons of mass destruction and related equipment. However, Iraq's failure to allow UN Special Commission members access to the building in Baghdad only underscores Iraq's continuing violation of UN Security Council resolutions 687 and 707. We do not believe that Iraq has made a full disclosure at this point of its weapons of mass destruction program.

Q   What do you think is in the building?

MR. BOUCHER: Excuse me?

Q   What do you think is in the building?

MR. BOUCHER: I believe that Ekeus gave a press conference in New York last week that it was documents relating to a ballistic missile program. I'll have to double-check if he said anything more

Q   And in the meantime --

MR. BOUCHER: Jim, let me finish and go through another letter, okay?

There was another letter that was sent July 12th to the Security Council. In that letter, the government of Iraq reneged on its commitment to participate in the work of the Iraq-Kuwait boundary demarcation commission that was established pursuant to UN Security Council resolution 687, thus again raising doubt about Iraq's willingness to honor its obligation under Resolution 687 to respect the Kuwait-Iraq border. This commission, which is currently meeting in New York, is carrying out the technical task necessary to demarcate the precise coordinates of the boundary between Iraq and Kuwait. The work of the commission addresses one of the principal underlying causes of instability in the region.

708 - 4 -3

As we said yesterday, the United States is determined to see
that Iraq meets all its international obligations under Security
Council resolutions. We hold Iraq responsible for the safety of all
UN personnel in Iraq, and we're consulting with key coalition
partners on steps to ensure Iraqi compliance.

        Q   Well, let me simplify the question. In the US view,
would another UN Security Council resolution be required in view of
Iraq's non-compliance with the past resolutions?

        MR. BOUCHER: At this point, Jim, I think that would be
speculation by me on a particular course of action, and I don't want
to get into that.

0057

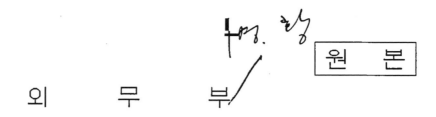

외 무 부

종   별 :

번   호 : UNW-1939　　　　　　　　　일   시 : 92 0717 2000

수   신 : 장 관 (연일,중동일,기정)

발   신 : 주 유엔 대사

제   목 : 이락주둔 유엔 경비병 피살

　　1.7.17. 안보리는 본회의를 개최하여 7.16. 이락에서 발생한 유엔 경비병 피살사건을 규탄하고 이락에 배치된 유엔 경비병과 유엔 직원에 대한 공격을 즉시 중지할것을 요청하는 성명을 채택함.

　　2.유엔 대변인의 발표에 의하면 7.16. 바그다드북쪽 210마일에 위치한 DOHUK (쿠르드족지역)에서 휘지 출신 유엔 경비병 (R. DAKIA) 이 침실에서 총격으로 피살되었다함.

　　3.현재 이락에는 구호물자 지원을 위해 500명의 유엔 소속 직원과 이들의 보호를 위해 500명의 유엔 경비병이 배치되어 있는바 이들의 주둔에관한 유엔-이락 간의 합의서가 92.7.1.종료되었으나 이락측은 유엔 경비병의 철수를 요청하면서 동 합의서의 연장을 거부하고 있어 현재 유엔-이락 간의 현안이 되고 있음. 끝

　　(대사 유종하-국장)

　　첨부: FAX (UNW(F)-603)

국기국　　중아국　　안기부

PAGE 1　　　　　　　　　　　　　　　　　　　92.07.18　　11:12 WG

　　　　　　　　　　　　　　　　　　　　　　　외신 1과　통제관

0058

STATEMENT BY THE PRESIDENT OF
THE SECURITY COUNCIL

The Security Council deeply deplores the murder of a member of the United Nations Guards Contingent in Iraq on 16 July 1992 in the Governorate of Dohuk. It supports the Secretary-General's decision to order an immediate and thorough investigation of this appalling crime. Members of the Council wish to express their sincere condolences to the family of the victim, Mr. Ravuama Dakia, and to the Government of Fiji.

The Security Council wishes to register its profound concern at the deteriorating security conditions affecting the safety and well-being of United Nations personnel in Iraq. The Council demands that attacks perpetrated against the United Nations Guards Contingent and other humanitarian personnel deployed in Iraq cease immediately and that maximum co-operation be extended by the authorities in the investigation of this crime, as well as in the protection of United Nations personnel.

외 무 부

종 별 :

번 호 : UNW-2040

일 시 : 92 0727 2030

수 신 : 장 관(연일,중동일,기정)

발 신 : 주 유엔 대사

제 목 : 대 이라크 제재

1. 금 7.27 안보리는 비공개 협의회를 개최, 안보리 결의 687 및 700 에 의하여 매 60 일마다 대 이라크 제재조치에 대한 검토를 위하여 "이라크-쿠웨이트간사태"의제로 논의하였는바, 동 회의에서 이라크에 대한 제재 조치를 수정하여야할 만한 조건이 이루어지지 않았다는 결론을 내렸음

2. 일본대표부에 의하면 과거 제재조치 검토 회의시에는 일부 국가들이 이라크에 대한 제재조치의 완화를 거론한 경우가 흔히 있었으나 금일 회의에서는 여사한 발언을 한 국가가 없었다는바 이는 농무성 사찰 거부를 위요한 이라크측에 대한 모든 이사국들의 강한 반대입장을 반영한 것으로 보이며 이라크는 농무성 사찰 문제로 국제적으로 더욱 많은 불신을 산것으로 평가됨

(대사 유종하-국장)

예고:92.12.31 일반
첨부:UNW(F)-0631

국기국   장관   차관   1차보   중아국   분석관   청와대   안기부

27 July 1992

D R A F T

NOTE BY THE PRESIDENT OF THE SECURITY COUNCIL

After the consultations held on 27 July 1992, the President of the Security Council issued the following statement on behalf of the members of the Council in connection with the item entitled "The situation between Iraq and Kuwait":

"The members of the Security Council held informal consultations on 27 July 1992 pursuant to paragraphs 21 and 28 of resolution 687 (1991) and paragraph 6 of resolution 700 (1991).

"After hearing all the opinions expressed in the course of the consultations, the President of the Council concluded that there was no agreement that the necessary conditions existed for a modification of the regimes established in paragraph 20 of resolution 687 (1991), as referred to in paragraph 21 of that resolution; in paragraphs 22, 23, 24 and 25 of resolution 687 (1991), as referred to in paragraph 28 of that resolution; and in paragraph 6 of resolution 700 (1991)."

631-1-1

0061

주 미 대 사 관

USW(F) : 4981   년월일 : 92.7.29   시간 : 11:30

수 신 : 장 관 (미일, 중동일, 연일)   보안   통제 : 훕

발 신 : 주미대사

제 목 : 이락 제재동향   (출처 : WP. WSJ)

White House Says Iraq Crisis Has Eased

Military Response Played Down; U.N. Team Enters Baghdad Ministry

By R. Jeffrey Smith and Trevor Rowe
Washington Post Staff Writers

The Bush administration sought yesterday to quash speculation about imminent military action against Iraq, as Baghdad, acting after a three-week delay, finally allowed a United Nations team to inspect its Agriculture Ministry headquarters.

"The situation has been defused for the moment," White House press secretary Marlin Fitzwater said. His statement followed a week in which senior U.S. officials raised the possibility of military force to press Iraq to allow inspection of the ministry and comply with other U.N. orders.

"I guess I would say very directly that I am not here to threaten military action," Fitzwater told reporters. Secretary of Defense Richard B. Cheney, testifying on Capitol Hill, also played down the prospect of military action in connection with the latest crisis.

At the same time, other officials made clear the administration and its allies continue to plan for a more rapid diplomatic and military response if Iraq obstructs U.N. inspectors again.

"We all want to pop him," one official said, referring to Iraqi President Saddam Hussein. But the official added that the administration has decided any action would have to await a new Iraqi provocation.

Several U.S. and diplomatic officials said leading members of the international coalition that went to war against Iraq last year have not ruled out taking steps in coming days to halt flights of Iraqi fixed-wing aircraft and helicopters, which are being used in a battle against Shiite rebels in southern Iraq. But other officials said such measures may be too difficult to implement.

"It is genuinely difficult to understand what people can do" that they have not already done to force Iraqi compliance with U.N. cease-fire resolutions, another official said.

At a White House meeting yesterday morning, President Bush conferred with congressional leaders about the potential use of military force against Iraq.

"I didn't get the impression that immediate use of force was contemplated," House Speaker Thomas S. Foley (D-Wash.) said after attending the session. "There's a possibility in the future, if there are circumstances that lead to international and other U.N. resolutions."

Sen. Richard G. Lugar (Ind.), the acting ranking Republican on the Foreign Relations Committee, said legislators at the meeting were divided over whether "you wait for another crisis" with Iraq or act now to force its compliance with U.N. orders on issues ranging from repression of ethnic and religious minorities to the supervised sale of Iraq's crude oil.

Lugar said the president did not indicate his position but rather "just soaked it all in."

Although Foley and Senate Majority Leader George J. Mitchell (D-Maine) emphasized their willingness to work with Bush on Iraq policy, several other prominent Democrats sharpened their criticism yesterday of Bush's handling of the

92.7.29
WP

(4981 - 4 - 1)

외신 1과
폄   제

0062

crisis, which they said was allowed to go on too long and was settled on terms that were too favorable to Iraq.

"It looks like Saddam Hussein has more to cheer about than George Bush does," said House Armed Services Committee Chairman Les Aspin (D-Wis.). Democratic vice-presidential nominee Albert Gore Jr. criticized the administration for enabling Saddam to "thumb his nose at the entire world and . . . [proclaim] victory."

Under the terms of an agreement reached last weekend between U.N. and Iraqi officials, none of the inspectors who entered the ministry building yesterday were citizens of countries that fought Iraq in the Persian Gulf War. Two U.S. members of the inspection team were left to stand outside the building while other inspectors went inside.

Critics of this arrangement in Congress, at the United Nations and in the administration said it created the appearance that Iraq was able to dictate the composition of a U.N. team, which Baghdad had not previously been allowed to do. As a result, the critics argued, U.N. Security Council authority to supervise implementation of cease-fire resolutions has been weakened.

While some U.S. officials last weekend blamed the U.N. Special Commission on Iraq for striking the compromise, U.S. officials yesterday publicly emphasized their support for the commission and the work of its chairman, Swedish Ambassador Rolf Ekeus, who participated in yesterday's inspection of the agriculture ministry.

U.N. and diplomatic officials involved in the intensive negotiations that led to Iraq's acceptance of the inspection said, moreover, that they had consulted continuously with Washington, Paris and London, and even presented in advance a list of proposed inspectors who would be allowed to enter the building.

"Throughout, we enjoyed the full support of the three members for our plans to proceed with the inspection," a U.N. official said. U.S. and diplomatic officials familiar with the negotiations did not deny this account yesterday.

Initially, U.S. officials including Bush hailed the agreement worked out by the United Nations as proof that Saddam had "caved in" by allowing inspection of the agriculture ministry. But on the issue of the U.N. inspection team's composition, Fitzwater acknowledged yesterday that "he [Saddam] won on that point."

Fitzwater added, however, that the composition was "not relevant to the quality of the inspection," which is due to be completed today, because the U.N. personnel allowed to go inside are "outstanding people." He noted further that U.S. personnel are slated to participate fully in other inspections in Iraq.

"These arrangements apply only to this inspection," State Department spokesman Richard Boucher told reporters during lengthy questioning about the arrangement yesterday. Diplomatic officials said Ekeus also conveyed that message to Iraq during the negotiations.

Smith reported from Washington, Rowe from the United Nations. Staff writer Helen Dewar contributed to this report.

4981- 4-2

92.7.29
WP

0063

주 미 대 사 관

USW(F) :　　　　　년월일 :　　　　　시간 :

수 신 : 장　관

발 신 : 주 미 대 사

제 목 :

보　안
통　제
(출처 :　　　　)

Charles Krauthammer

Saddam Won

President Bush's claim that Saddam "caved in" on the great confrontation at the Agriculture Ministry is the kind of empty loser's boast that one expects from defeated Arab tyrants, not from an American president. Not only did Saddam have 21 days to clean the place out of any incriminating documents. He also gained a veto over the composition of the U.N. inspection team. The U.N. inspection regime thus gave up its two principal weapons: surprise and independence.

Despite his public statements, Bush knows he suffered a defeat. That is why he is laying down new markers and ordering a stepping up of U.N. weapons monitoring. The point is either to make Saddam really back down next time or to provoke punitive allied military action.

No doubt the president's calculations about Iraq are influenced by the election. Nonetheless, there are real issues in the world, election year or not, and Iraq is one of them. Saddam is stirring and unless beaten back promises deadly problems for the United States and its gulf allies in the future.

The issue is not the Agriculture Ministry. Nor is it Saddam's thwarting U.N. authority over his weapons of mass destruction. The issue is Saddam's general resurgence and his new bid for power in the region.

Saddam's first aim is to run international organizations out of his country. U.N. soldiers and inspectors have been harassed and roughed up. A Fijian U.N. soldier has already been killed. Even Save

the Children is on the run. The group pulled all but two of its people out of Iraq after finding a bomb under its truck.

Second, Saddam is moving to crush all internal opposition. He has stepped up the war against Shiite rebels in Iraq's south, bombing them now with fixed-wing aircraft in violation of the gulf war cease-fire.

Third, and most ominous, Saddam is reviving his regional ambitions. The official press is raising once again the issue of the annexation of, yes, Kuwait. Four weeks ago, Iraq's envoy to the U.N. in Geneva (Saddam's step-brother) published a call for redrawing the boundaries of the gulf region. It was an ill-disguised attempt to buy off U.S. allies: Saudi Arabia would absorb Bahrain and Qatar. Oman would absorb the United Arab Emirates. Iraq would absorb Kuwait.

Here we go again. Saddam is getting up off the floor. It is no use decrying Bush's appalling mishandling of the gulf war aftermath. What's done is done. The question is what to do now.

Picking targets for some air raid is not a policy. An air raid might demonstrate to Saddam the costs of his new game. But unless it kills him—and we had no such luck during the 40-day air war—it will have achieved very little.

We need a new strategy for Iraq and it must be this: Turn Iraq into Afghanistan. After the Soviet invasion of Afghanistan, the United States waged its most successful proxy war ever. Use the model of the Afghan resistance. Bring down the regime, over many years if necessary, through massive assistance to those already in place and quite willing to do the job themselves: the Shiite guerrillas in the south and the Kurds in the north.

In Afghanistan our policy took a decade to succeed, but succeed it did with a generous dose of arms, money and intelligence. Saddam will be a harder target. Proxies, while necessary, may not be

sufficient. The anti-Saddam insurgents will need, in addition, both diplomatic and military help:

(1) Start war crimes trials against Saddam for crimes against humanity. Urged on us a year ago by the Europeans, they would once again focus public attention on Saddam's criminality and provide legitimacy for an allied campaign to remove and/or kill him. We have all the evidence we need in captured documents of his campaign of genocide against the Kurds.

(2) Withdraw diplomatic recognition of Saddam's regime. Begin the delegitimization of the Baath dictatorship by recognizing in its place a provisional government based in Iraqi Kurdistan and composed of opposition leaders.

(3) Supplement Kurdish and Shiite guerrilla forces with allied air and naval power to provide air cover and deliver air strikes at selected strategic and tactical targets. This is a far better use of U.S. and allied military power than the delivery of "messages" through purely punitive strikes.

The quick fix, once available after Desert Storm but rejected by a conflicted president, is now beyond our reach. In the absence of a lucky air strike, the only way to counter Saddam is with a longer, more drawn-out strategy borrowed from the Afghan model.

Long-run plans are not designed for winning political points, certainly not in an election year. But it is hard to see how Bush can win any political points on Iraq, a victory he bungled away. What he might win now, however, is the kind of historical credit due a recent one-term president, Jimmy Carter, for having initiated a far-reaching policy that brought victory in Afghanistan long after he himself had been forcibly retired.

외신 1과
통　제

4981-4-3

92.7.29　WP

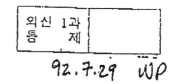

0064

주 미 대 사 관

USW(F) :   년월일 :   시간 :

수 신 : 장 관

발 신 : 주미대사

제 목 :

보 통
안 제

(출처 :   )

U.S., Seeking to Boost Pressure on Iraq, Prepares to Meet With Opposition Group

By ROBERT S. GREENBERGER
And GERALD F. SEIB
Staff Reporters of THE WALL STREET JOURNAL

WASHINGTON—The Bush administration set a strategy to escalate pressure on Iraq, as a coalition of Iraqi opposition leaders prepared to ask the U.S. for political, financial and military support to help topple Saddam Hussein.

The opposition leaders are scheduled to meet today with Secretary of State James Baker, the highest-level U.S. official to see them yet. They will lay out a plan to establish a broad-based provisional government of Kurdish, Shiite and Sunni Muslim groups. The opposition leaders believe that with international recognition and U.S. support, the provisional government could persuade some Iraqi military units to join them, gradually isolating Saddam Hussein in Baghdad.

Jalal Talabani, a major Kurdish leader, said in an interview that the opposition is seeking "some kind of moral support, political support, even financial support." He added: "We also must be supplied with sufficient arms to at least resist when Saddam Hussein attacks. This is what we will explain to American officials."

Military Force Weighed

Meanwhile, Bush administration aides said they have decided on a two-pronged strategy to continue confronting Saddam Hussein and build international support for reining him in, perhaps through use of military force.

First, the U.S. will push for a series of new United Nations weapons inspections, in essence daring the Iraqi leader to try again to get in the way of efforts to ferret out and destroy his weapons of mass destruction. Second, the Bush administration will try in coming weeks to focus international attention on what officials call a pattern of Iraqi violations of the U.N. resolutions Iraq accepted to end last year's Persian Gulf War.

In particular, the administration will point out Iraqi violations of a resolution that bars Saddam Hussein's government from repression of Iraqi citizens. That suggests the U.S. will be watching closely for more Iraqi attacks against Shiite Muslims in southern Iraq and against Kurds in northern Iraq. In recent weeks, the Iraqi government, which is dominated by Sunni Muslims, has stepped up pressure and harassment of both of those groups.

Mr. Talabani said yesterday that during the past few days Saddam Hussein has moved his 20th armored brigade, along with surface-to-surface missiles, heavy artillery and tanks, further north into Iraqi Kurdistan. The Kurdish leader also said there have been increasing attacks with similar equipment as well as fixed-wing aircraft in the marshlands of the south, where many of Iraq's Shiite Muslims live.

Waiting for Opening

While administration aides don't specifically say they are looking for a pretext for military action, they clearly wouldn't be unhappy if intransigence by Saddam Hussein gives the U.S. and its allies an opening to move in coming weeks. But at the moment, one official said, "there is no consensus" among the U.S. and its allies about what circumstances would justify military action.

U.S. officials said their response to the request for help from Iraqi opposition leaders will depend on its details, but they noted that are interested in discussing a joint game plan. In the past, the U.S. has shied away from high-level cooperation with Iraqi opposition factions. But administration aides say they are more willing to work with the opposition group now visiting Washington because it represents the kind of unified Sunni, Shiite and Kurdish front the U.S. has been urging Saddam Hussein's foes to form.

Mr. Talabani said opposition leaders hoped that today's meeting with Mr. Baker would send a signal to Saddam's opponents that the U.S. is serious about removing the Iraqi dictator. He expressed little regard for last weekend's U.N. compromise in its standoff with Baghdad. To Iraqis, he said, Saddam Hussein prevailed by effectively setting ground rules for the U.N. inspection of an Agriculture Ministry building that was a suspected site of documents on weapons programs.

"It is not good policy to permit Saddam Hussein to dictate the agenda," he said.

(4981 - 4 - 4)

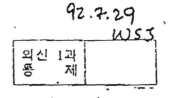

92.7.29
WSJ

외신 1과
통 제

0065

USW(F) : 4599   년월일 : 92.7.29 시간 : 18:50

수 신 : 장 관 (미일, 중동일, 연일)

발 신 : 주미대사

제 목 : 이락 제재동향 (백악관 브리핑)   (출처 : FNS)

보안통제 제 46

THE WHITE HOUSE WASHINGTON, DC REGULAR BRIEFING   BRIEFER: MARLIN
FITZWATER   TUESDAY, JULY 28, 1992

Okay. Let me briefly summarize the congressional meeting this
morning, and then we'll go to any questions you want to ask. Just
that the President met with the bipartisan congressional leadership
to discuss the situation in Iraq. As you know, he met with his
national security advisers last night in the residence for about an
hour to discuss the situation as well.

I would summarize the situation by saying that we are
continuing to monitor the inspection regime and the general
compliance with the UN resolutions in Iraq. All of the tensions
have not been defused. We still seek some compliance with all of
the resolutions, and obviously, we watch this very closely. One of
the points the President made to the leadership this morning was
that he is seeking their advice -- was seeking their advice in this
meeting, that these were real-time consultations in advance of any
anticipated action we might have to take in the days or weeks ahead.

The congressional members, obviously, each of them have their
own views and I'll let them speak for themselves. Many of them did
in the driveway. But I think there was a very high degree of
general support for the UN resolutions and for any US action in
support of those resolutions. So we felt it was a very good and
productive meeting.

The only quote I can give you from the President was he said,
quote, "We will continue to show our resolve in enforcing the UN
resolutions and strengthening the UN peacekeeping abilities." End
quote.

Q   Three things. One: As you suggest, there's some
evident dissatisfaction with the terms that were worked out with
Saddam for the inspection of the agricultural ministry, and a number
of outstanding alleged violations of various agreements and UN
resolutions that still trouble the administration. Number one, is
there any indication that the coalition partners are equally as

(4999 - 5 - 1)

외신 1과	
통 제	

백부처	장관실	차관실	일차보	이차보	외정실	문석관	미주국	구주국	중아국	국기국	경대국	통상국	문립국	외연원	청와대	안기부	공보처	경기원	상공부	재무부	농수부	동자부	환경처	과기처
	/	/		/			O		/	/				/										

0066

upset as the White House is about those alleged outstanding
violations, to the point where it is as willing as the White House
seems to be to take some action to deal with them? And second, is
there any sense that Congress would go along with any such (action
?)?

MR. FITZWATER: I would say that the coalition is supportive,
and certainly they want the UN resolutions complied with. They
share the UN concern for the violations that have been demonstrated
in recent weeks. They certainly share the concern of the UN for the
inspectors not being able to go about their business at the
agriculture building a few days ago. And I would say that the
members of Congress were even more supportive; that -- again, I
would hesitate to speak for everybody, but I think they would all
say that they were -- with the possible exception of Senator Pell --
they were very supportive of whatever action might be taken in a
general sense and assuming consultation and so forth in support of
the UN resolutions.

Q   Let me come at it a slightly different way. Would you
disagree with the notion, then, that the cave-in, as the President
called it, on the agriculture ministry has had the effect -- the
practical effect of defusing the matter for the moment as far as any
immediate military action by the coalition is concerned?

MR. FITZWATER: I would not like to speculate on military
action but would agree to the idea that the situation has been
defused for the moment.

Steve?

Q   Did the President present to the leaders a scenario in
which the US might have to go it alone here because the coalition is
not full force behind military action; and how would Congress
respond to that?

MR. FITZWATER: Well, we anticipate coalition support in one
form or another for whatever we would do. We certainly have had
their support in the past. They have been supportive on this issue
and in this specific situation. So that is the assumption that we
make in looking down the road, as well.
There were some members of Congress who said they would be
supportive of unilateral action regardless, but our purpose and
intent is to seek and we believe we would sustain coalition support.

Q   The President didn't say to these leaders, "Look,
there's this possibility that we might have to go it alone, how do
you feel about it?"

MR. FITZWATER: Well, the President asked for their general
views on all of these issues. Some were specific to that question
but the President's request was pretty general. Michael?

499-5-2

Q   Marlin, have we asked, first of all, the UN to speed up inspections and are we looking for some way to test whether Saddam will meet the requirements?

MR. FITZWATER: Not in a specific sense as was kind of implied by those stories this morning, but we have told the UN that we are interested in carrying out the inspection regimes as rapidly as possible, that we do believe that they should be tested, that although the resolutions are expected to be complied with, and we would like to force that issue at every opportunity.

Q   What I'm getting at kind of is what the United States is doing now, what we're looking for in the future. We've got the Patriots going to Kuwait, an aircraft carrier headed in that direction and you have Dole out in the driveway saying a confrontation appears inevitable at some point, but Cheney up on the Hill after the meeting said people are making too much out of this.

MR. FITZWATER: Yeah, I think -- of course you know you get into all the nuances of this, but I would try to square some of those comments by saying -- by pointing to the history first of all of Saddam's cheat and retreat methods up until the last month or two, and that is that he has pushed the matter to the brink on inspections and on a number of other issues, and then when he is faced with overwhelming opposition, either diplomatically or militarily from the coalition and from the UN, he retreats and that's somewhat similar to what happened in the case of the Ag Ministry building.

However, we are concerned that over the last month or two we have seen a broader pattern of non-compliance which the President outlined to the nation in his comments returning from Camp David yesterday, which I would only summarize to include first of all the inspection and destruction of weapons, their failure to participate in the Iraq-Kuwait Boundary Demarcation Commission, their refusal to account for Kuwaiti citizens seized during the occupation, their refusal to return stolen Kuwaiti property, Iraq's refusal to renew the memorandum of understanding with the UN -- that's the MOU after

the war regarding humanitarian assistance. They have stepped up harassment of UN officials and they have flagrantly increased persecution of the Iraqi population including recent use of jet fighters against the Shi'ite and maintaining an economic blockade in the north.

So there are -- all of these refusals or defiance episodes tend to portray a pattern that to us is very disturbing, and one that should be monitored very closely.

←999—5—3

0068

Q   Was the President aware on Sunday that the agreement the
United Nations had reached with Iraq meant that no coalition member,
no inspector from a coalition member country would be on that team?

MR. FITZWATER: Yeah, that was one of the -- one of the issues --

Q   One of their demands, wasn't it?

MR. FITZWATER: Yeah, it's not that crucial a point with us
because first of all we have Americans on the team, they just aren't
going in the building. Secondly, it's just this team -- more teams
which will go in very soon will have Americans on them, so there's
no precedent setting.

Q   Two questions. One, would you deny the report, the --
Mike Gordon's story that there is division within the White House
and the administration, unhappiness over the compromise that was
reached on the team to go into the ag building, some apparently
within the White House and the administration feeling that (a
precedent was set ?)? And two, did Bush actually say today at this
meeting, as he was quoted by somebody in the driveway, talking about
not taking Saddam out? Did he say that whose son -- something like
whose son is going to be a volunteer? Who's going to volunteer to
get somebody killed to take Saddam out? Was that talked about
today?

MR. FITZWATER: There was --

Q   Marlin, can we all get in on the little secret up there,
what his question was?

MR. FITZWATER: Yes. Mr. Cochran's question was whether or
not the issue was raised of going after Saddam Hussein and what was
the President's response. And one of the members did raise that
issue. And the President's response was that that was not a part of
the UN resolutions, and he also said, as John asked about, whose son
do you want to go to Baghdad to try to find Saddam Hussein, and is
that what American really wants?

There is no disagreement. The President's national security
advisers met here last night. They were agreed on the regime on the
way the inspections had been completed and on the process that we're
going forward with. I don't doubt that Michael had a source, but
that does not represent the top national security advisers,
including the secretaries of State, Defense, et cetera that are
advising the President.

Now, your question was --

Q   Do you have any analysis you're willing to share about
why you think -- why the White House thinks that Saddam is behaving
in this way? There's been some suggestion from the overseas press
that he's actually seeking a military confrontation so that he can
create a martyr -- he can be a martyr, or something of that sort.

MR. FITZWATER: There is no understanding Saddam in that sense

4997-5-9

that -- as -- there never has been for the simple reason that he reacts irrationally and does not respond the way one would anticipate a leader who is concerned about his people's welfare would respond. We have found that, to his dissatisfaction, I'm sure, that he's not predictable in that sense. I would say that the only general conclusion that we're able to make is that there does appear to be an attitude on his part that he can get away with more than he can get away with, and that he is pushing the limits on every front, and that he is trying to use that as a propaganda weapon within his country to engender support. But whether that's why he's doing it or to what degree, there's really no way for us to say.

Q   Marlin? But you have been spending most of this briefing making the case for US military action, even though you've said that the immediate situation has been defused. My question is, if Bush decides to go ahead with this military action after having said publicly that Saddam Hussein in this case capitulated, how can he explain it to the American people so that it does not look like a campaign ploy?

MR. FITZWATER: Well, I think, first of all --

Q   Or are you saying that he would wait for another provocation?

MR. FITZWATER: First of all, I've tried to point out that the immediate situation is defused, without speculating on specific actions. Secondly, I would say that we are carrying out the inspection in the ag ministry today. I saw the wire service's report that that was underway. Secondly, we are demanding compliance. And, thirdly, I guess I would say very directly that I am not here to threaten military action. I am here to simply point out the status of the situation and where we are at this point and that we expect full compliance. But this is not a political matter, as far as we're concerned. The President intends to stay strong and steady and principled in his response and in his judgments about when and if we need to act.

Q   Could I just follow up, Marlin? Are you saying that there will be no military action unless there is another provocation from Saddam --

MR. FITZWATER: No, I never want to rule anything out, specifically rule in or out.

K999-5-5

0070

외 무 부

종 별 :

번 호 : UNW-2116

수 신 : 장 관(연일,중동일,기정)

발 신 : 주 유엔 대사

제 목 : 이라크 사태

일 시 : 92 0805 2030

1.금 8.5 안보리 비공개 협의회에서 미국대표부 WATSON 대사는 이라크의 남부 시아파에 대한 인권침해에 관한 7.30 자 인권위원회 보고서를 언급하고 동보고서 보고자인 VAN DER STOEL 을 안보리에 초청하여 브리핑을 청취할 것을 제의함(상기 인권위 보고서는 상금 유엔 문서로 배포되지 않았는바, 이사국요청으로근일중 배포될 것이라함)

2. 이에 대하여 일부 이사국들은 안보리는 유엔의 다른 기관의 고유권한 사항도 존중하여야 한다는 의견(에쿠아돌)과 안보리와 인권위간의 조심스러운 협조가 필요(일본)하다는 의견등이 개진되었고 이에 대하여 미국과 선진국들은 이미 안보리는 결의 688 을 통하여 이라크의 인권위반에 대한 계속적인 관심을 결의한바 있으므로 동건은 안보리의 권한에 속한다고 주장함

3. 영국대사는 동 브리핑을 안보리 본회의에서 청취함을 선호하나 만일 일부국가들이 이에대해 이견이 있다면 비공개 협의회에서 청취하는 안도 가능할 것이라 하여 타협안을 제시함

4. 결국 금일회의에서는 각 이사국들이 본국정부에 훈령을 받아 차기 협의회에서 재논의키로 함

(대사 유종하-국장)
예고:92.12.31 까지

국기국   장관   차관   1차보   중아국   분석관   정와대   안기부

PAGE 1

* 원본수령부서 승인없이 복사 금지

92.08.06   10:08
외신 2과 통제관 BX
0071

유엔안전보장이사회의 대이라크 제재 조치, 1992 503

외 무 부

관리 92
번호 ー 780

종 별 :

번 호 : UNW-2152

일 시 : 92 0810 2200

수 신 : 장 관 (연일, 중동일, 기정)

발 신 : 주 유엔 대사

제 목 : 안보리 (이라크사태)

연 : UNW - 2116

1. 금 8.10 안보리 비공식 협의회는 미, 영, 불, 벨기에등 4 개국의 요청에 의하여 명 8.11 안보리 본회의를 개최, 이라크 남부 시아파에 대한 탄압문제를 심의키로 함.

2. 명일 본회의에서는 의사규칙 제 39 조에 따라 연호 유엔 인권위원회 특별보고자 VAN DER STOEL 의 안보리 초청여부를 결정키로 하였으며, 이어 동인의 브리핑과 토의가 있을 예정임.

3. 연호 보고와 같이 중국, 인도, 짐바붸등 일부 비상임 이사국들은 인권문제를 전담하는 인권위원회가 동건을 심의중에 있음에도 불구하고 동 위원회가 임명한 RAPPORTEUR 를 안보리에 초청하여 브리핑을 청취함은 안보리의 월권이라고 주장하고 있는 바, 금일 회의에서 영국대사는 안보리 결의 688 에 의거, 이라크 인권문제에 대한 정보를 제공받기 위하여 안보리가 동인을 개인자격으로 초청하여 이라크 인권상황에 관한 의견을 청취함에는 아무런 문제가 없다고 주장하였음. 이에 대해 중국 대사 (안보리 의장)는 STOEL 의 초청문제를 안보리 본회의에서 정식 논의하여 필요하면 표결처리 (절차 문제로 9 개국 찬성으로 가결)할 것을 제의함에 따라 명일 본회의가 개최케 된 것임.

4. 금일 배포된 STOEL 의 보고서에 관한 안보리 문건은 금파편 송부함. 끝

(대사 유종하 - 국장)

예고 : 92.12.31 까지

국기국   장관   차관   1차보   중아국   분석관   청와대   안기부

92.08.11   13:11
외신 2과 통제관 FS
0072

외 무 부

종 별 :

번 호 : UNW-2162

수 신 : 장관 (연일, 중동일, 기정)

발 신 : 주 유엔 대사

제 목 : 안보리(이라크사태)

일 시 : 92 0811 2100

연 : UNW-2152

1. 금 8.11. 안보리는 본회의를 개최하여, 인권위원회의 이라크 인권문제 특별 보고자 VAN DER STOEL(전 화란외상)로 부터 이라크의 인권상황에 대한 브리핑을 청취하고 이에대한 이라크 대사의 반박발언과 이라크정부를 규탄하는 안보리 이사국들의 발언이 있었음.

2. 금일회의에서 STOEL 은 북부 쿠르드족 거주지역과 남부 시아파 거주지역에 식량 및 유류의 공급중단 또는 공급방해와 시아파에 대한 공습 및 포격등 이라크정부의 안보리결의 688 위반 행위를 열거하고 이지역의 인권상황이 매우 위험한 상태에 있음을 경고하였음.

3. 이에대하여 AI-ANBARI 이라크대사는 STOEL 이 인권위의 RAPPORTEUR 직을사임한후 안보리에 출석했어야 한다고 언급하면서 동인의 보고는 사실을 왜곡한 것이며 특히 시아파가 거주하는 지역에서 추진되고 있는 MAIN DRAIN(THIRD RIVER) PROJECT 를 시아파에 대한 위협이라고 지적한 것은 동사업을 전혀 이해하지 못한데서 기인한다고 주장하고 이라크정부의 인권위반 행위를 부인함.

4. 미, 영, 불, 러시아, 일본등 대부분의 이사국들은 STOEL 의 보고에 의해이라크의 안보리결의 688 위반은 명백하다고 주장하고 식량공급 방해중지, 무력등에 의한 탄압중지, 구호물자지원 요원 체류연장을 위한 유엔과의 양해각서 조속연장등을 요구하였음.

5. 금일 회의 벽두, STOEL 초청문제와 관련하여 인도, 에쿠아돌, 짐바뷔, 중국등 4 개국은 인권문제는 총회와 인권위원회의 권한에 속함을 주장하고 다만 안보리가 정보를 얻고자 하는 목적으로 동인을 개인자격으로 초청한다는 조건하에 동인의 초청에 반대하지 않을 것임을 밝힘. 특히 에쿠아돌 대사는 91.4 월 채택된 안보리

국기국   장관   차관   1차보   중아국   분석관   청와대   안기부

결의 688(이라크 인권문제)은 당시 쿠르드족에 대한 탄압으로 수많은 난민이 발생, 인접국으로 유입되는 상태에 있어 국제평화와 안전에 위협이 된다는 판단하에서 이를 지지하였다고 언급하였으며 인도 대사는 미, 영, 불등이 안보리결의 688 을 원용하나 안보리는 인권문제를 심의할 권한이 없다는 판단으로 인도는 동 결의안 채택시 기권한바 있음을 상기시켰음. 중국 대사 역시 안보리는 국제평화와 안전에 위협이 되는 문제를 심의하는 것이며 인권은 인권위원회소관사항이라는 입장에서 STOEL 의 초청은 적절치 않다는 의견을 개진하였음.

6. 한편 구호물자 공급을 위한 유엔요원의 체류문제와 관련, 8.10 유엔사무국은 이라크정부가 유엔과의 양해각서 연장 협상을 위하여 유엔대표를 이라크에 초청 함에 따라 ELIASSON 사무차장(긴급구호 및 인권담당)을 파견, 8.17 부터 협상을 재개한다고 발표함. 끝

(대사 유종하 - 국장)

PAGE 2

0074

주 미 대 사 관

USW(F) : 5206   년월일 :92.8.12   시간 : 14:50

수 신 : 장 관 (미인, 연인, 중동인)

발 신 : 주미대사

제 목 : 대 이락 제재   (출처 :   )

보 안
통 제

U.S. Warns Iraq on Shiites

U.N. Might Intervene If Abuses Continue

By Trevor Rowe
Special to The Washington Post

UNITED NATIONS, Aug. 11—In a veiled warning, the United States today hinted that if Baghdad continues its bloody repression of the Shiite population in southern Iraq the U.N. Security Council may have to intervene and create a protected zone there as it did in the Kurdish north of the country.

The warning came during an urgent meeting of the council to discuss mounting human rights violations in Iraq. During the session, Max van der Stoel, the U.N. special investigator of human rights abuses in Iraq, presented a report in which he expressed concern that "thousands of innocent people are in danger of losing their lives" throughout the country as a result of forced starvation and military attacks.

The U.S. warning, which was echoed by Britain, appears intended both to prod Baghdad to end its suppression of Iraq's Shiite and Kurdish populations and to force it to cooperate with the world body. Iraq so far has refused to renew a memorandum of understanding covering U.N. and humanitarian personnel in Iraq and has rebuffed a plan for it to sell $1.6 billion in oil to pay for food and medicine for its people.

The warning was contained in a statement by U.S. Ambassador to the United Nations Edward Perkins. Referring to the council's decision last year to protect the Kurdish population from Iraqi forces by creating U.N. protected camps, Perkins suggested the situation among the Shiites in the south appeared to require a similar response.

It was unclear if he was threatening to repeat the 1991 military intervention by thousands of U.S. and allied troops to help Kurdish refugees, or proposing to emulate the subsequent dispatch of U.N. guards to set up protected zones.

"We have reason to believe that additional villages will be attacked, bombed, destroyed, and civilian casualties will rise," Perkins said. "In 1991 the council condemned the repression of civilian populations.... Additional measures had to be taken to prevent further Iraqi repression."

At the moment, it is not known whether the council will support creating a protected zone for the Shiites. And, if the plan were approved,

it is uncertain whether it could be properly implemented should it involve U.N. guards since Iraq continues to deny visa renewals to U.N. guards and humanitarian personnel. Baghdad also is refusing to sell fuel to the United Nations, thereby impeding its distribution of relief and monitoring of humanitarian needs.

Perkins said Iraq's refusal to renew visas meant that the normal contingent of 500 U.N. guards assigned to Iraq would be reduced to 127 within one week.

During his speech, van der Stoel also appealed for "massive" humanitarian aid for Iraq. He said that in

92.8.12 WP

외신 1과
통 제

5206-2-1

recent weeks Baghdad had intensified its economic embargo of the Kurdish area and that no food supplies are entering. He said Iraq also had imposed a food embargo on the Shiite inhabitants of the south, many of whom live in marshlands.

The increase in military attacks against the Shiites included artillery bombardments, he said, and "causeways" are being built to drain large sections of the marshes, depriving the inhabitants of food.

Iraq has charged that van der Stoel is part of a "campaign of hostility" waged by the United States and its allies. It denies that it has attacked Shiite population centers and says it has merely been protecting the inhabitants from crimes committed by groups linked to Iran.

During the debate in the council, Iraqi Ambassador Abdul Amir Anbari accused van der Stoel of failing to properly research his charges.

92. 8. 12
WP

506-2-2

0076

報 告 事 項

報 告 畢

1992. 8. 13.
國 際 機 構 局
國際聯合1課(23)

題 目 : 이라크의 유엔決議 違反現況

8.12(水) 駐韓 美大使館側은 이라크의 諸般 유엔決議 不履行 및 違反에 관한 아래 要旨의 現況資料를 修交해 왔음을 報告드립니다.

---

1. 資料要旨

가. 이라크側 態度 評價

○ 후세인 政權은 大量破壞武器 廢棄에 관한 유엔 決議를 完全 遵守할 의향이 전혀 없음이 분명함.

○ 또한 武器 廢棄分野이외의 諸般 유엔決議 遵守에도 非協助的이며 유엔 努力에 대해 包括的 妨害策動을 하고 있음.

나. 이라크가 履行하지 않고 있는 諸般 유엔決議 內容

○ 安保理決議 687호 (91.4.3)

- 쿠웨이트·이라크 國境線 尊重 (2-3항)

- 生化學武器, 미사일등 大量殺傷武器 廢棄 및 使用, 開發, 生産 禁止 (8-10항)

- NPT 協定 遵守義務 (11항)

- 核武器, 核關聯 物質等 保有, 利用, 開發, 生産禁止(12-13항)

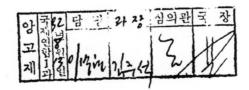

0077

ㅇ 安保理決議 688호(91.4.5)

  - 이라크 國民 抑壓中止 및 國際 救護機關 出入國 保障

ㅇ 安保理決議 707호(91.8.15)

  - 大量殺傷武器 廢棄 및 NPT 協定遵守 義務 再確認

  - 유엔 및 IAEA 査察團 活動保障

ㅇ 安保理決議 661호(90.8.6)

  - 食糧 및 유엔 허가하 人道的 品目을 除外한 모든 物資의 對이라크

    禁輸 및 金融支援 禁止

ㅇ 安保理決議 706호(91.8.15) 및 712호(91.9.19)

  - 食糧購入, 걸프戰 被害報償 및 유엔 査察團 活動 財源調達을 위한

    石油輸出 一部 許容方案 受諾促求

ㅇ 安保理決議 715호(91.10.11)

  - 大量 殺傷武器 統制檢證을 위한 유엔特委(UNSCOM) 및 IAEA와의

    協調 무조건 受諾

다. 上記 決議에 대한 이라크側 主張 및 違反事例 詳細 說明

2. 言論對策 : 해당없음.

- 끝 -

0078

報 告 事 項

題 目 : 이라크의 유엔決議 違反現況

8.12(水) 駐韓 美大使館側은 이라크의 諸般 유엔決議 不履行 및
違反에 관한 아래 要旨의 現況資料를 修交해 왔음을 報告드립니다.

1. 資料要旨

가. 이라크側 態度 評價

ㅇ 후세인 政權은 大量破壞武器 廢棄에 관한 유엔 決議를 完全 遵守할
의향이 전혀 없음이 분명함.

ㅇ 또한 武器 廢棄分野이외의 諸般 유엔決議 遵守에도 非協調的이며
유엔 努力에 대해 包括的 妨害策動을 하고 있음.

나. 이라크가 履行하지 않고 있는 諸般 유엔決議 內容

ㅇ 安保理決議 687호 (91.4.3)

- 쿠웨이트·이라크 國境線 尊重 (2-3항)

- 生化學武器, 미사일등 大量殺傷武器 廢棄 및 使用, 開發, 生産
禁止 (8-10항)

- NPT 協定 遵守義務 (11항)

- 核武器, 核關聯 物質等 保有, 利用, 開發, 生産禁止(12-13항)

0079

o 安保理決議 688호(91.4.5)

- 이라크 國民 抑壓中止 및 國際 救護機關 出入國 保障

o 安保理決議 707호(91.8.15)

- 大量殺傷武器 廢棄 및 NPT 協定遵守 義務 再確認

- 유엔 및 IAEA 査察團 活動保障

o 安保理決議 661호(90.8.6)

- 食糧 및 유엔 허가하 人道的 品目을 除外한 모든 物資의 對이라크

禁輸 및 金融支援 禁止

o 安保理決議 706호(91.8.15) 및 712호(91.9.19)

- 食糧購入, 걸프戰 被害報償 및 유엔 査察團 活動 財源調達을 위한

石油輸出 一部 許容方案 受諾促求

o 安保理決議 715호(91.10.11)

- 大量 殺傷武器 統制檢證을 위한 유엔特委(UNSCOM) 및 IAEA와의

協調 무조건 受諾

다. 上記 決議에 대한 이라크側 主張 및 違反事例 詳細 說明

2. 言論對策 : 해당없음.

- 끝 -

0080

외 무 부

관리 92
번호 -1094

원 본

종 별 :

번 호 : UNW-2256

일 시 : 92 0819 2030

수 신 : 장 관 (연일,중동일,미일,구일,기정)

발 신 : 주 유엔 대사

제 목 : 이라크 사태

    1. 이라크의 시아파에 대한 탄압방지를 위하여 미, 영, 불간에 합의한 것으로
보도된 북위 32도 이남에 대한 비행금지 조치의 법적근거와 관련, 당관 이수혁
참사관이 영국 WOOD 참사관 및 미국 ROSENSTOK 참사관을 접촉, 파악한 바를 아래
보고함

    가. 영국측 입장

    - 이라크 정부의 민간인 탄압중지를 요청한 안보리결의 688 은 정치적 의미가 있는
결의이나 결의 미이행에 대한 제재조치를 규정하고 있지 아니하므로 그자체가
비행금지 조치의 법적근거는 될수 없음

    - 일반 국제법상 집단학살등 중대한 인권위기에 대하여는 이를 중지하기 위한 제 3
국의 개입이 허용된다고 봄. 이미 선례로서 작년 미, 영, 불은 쿠르드족에 대한
탄압방지를 위하여 36 도 이북에 대한 비행금지조치를 취한 바 있음

    나. 미국측 입장

    - 법적근거와 관련, 영국측과 약간의 견행차이가 있음. 미국으로서는 안보리결의
678, 687 및 688 등 3 개의 결의가 시아파 탄압 방지를 위한 개입의 근거가 된다는
입장임. 즉 안보리결의 678 제 2 항은 국제평화와 안전회복을 위하여 필요한 모든
조치를 취할권리를 유엔 회원국에 부여하였고 비록 동기는 다르더라도 결의 687 제 4
항에서도 필요한 모든 조치를 취하도록 되어 있으며 결의 688 은 민간인 탄압중지를
요청하고 있음

    - 상기 3 개의 결의의 정신을 감안할때 이라크의 인권탄압은 이지역의 국제평화와
안전을 위협하는 것이며, 국제평화와 안전을 위하여 이라크에 대하여는 필요한
모든조치를 허용하고 있다고 해석하여야 함

    - 영국측과 다소 해석상의 차이가 있으나 만일 공동조치가 취해질경우 미, 영 간의

국기국   장관   차관   1차보   미주국   구주국   중아국   분석관   정와대
안기부

견해차이가 없도록 GENERAL TERM 으로 입장이 발표되어야 할것임

　2. 당관 관찰로서는 미. 영. 불이 32 도 이남에 대한 비행금지 조치를 취할 경우 새로운 안보리 결의없이 비행금지 조치를 선언하고 이를 시행할 것으로 전망됨

　(대사 유종하-국장)

　예고 : 92.12.31 일반

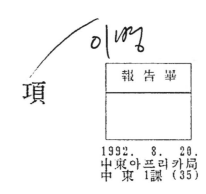

1992. 8. 20.
中東아프리카局
中 東 1課 (35)

報 告 事 項

題 目 : 美國等의 對이라크 攻擊 可能性

> 이라크가 UN 決意를 違反, 南部地域의 시아파에 대한 彈壓을 繼續하고
> 있음에 따라 美國의 對이라크 軍事攻擊 可能性이 높아지고 있는바, 關聯事項
> 을 主要 公館報告를 綜合, 아래 報告합니다.

1. 現 況
   - 美國은 이라크가 UN 安保理 決意 688을 무시하고 航空機까지 動員하여
     시아파에 대한 軍事攻擊을 계속하자, 英國, 프랑스等 友邦國들과 協議,
     北緯 32° 線 以南을 飛行禁止區域으로 設定할 것을 檢討中
   - 同 措置時 이라크는 91.4 쿠르드人 保護를 위해 취해진 北緯 36° 線 以北
     에서의 飛行禁止 措置와 함께 領土의 2/3地域에서 航空機를 運航할 수
     없게됨.

2. 分析 및 展望
   - 美國은 걸프戰後 이라크의 諸般 UN決意 遵守態度를 Creep and Cheat 戰略
     으로 看做, 보다 철저한 이라크의 UN決意 遵守를 위해 對이라크 軍事攻擊
     을 計劃하고 있으나, 對이라크 攻擊이 大統領 選擧를 유리하게 이끌기
     위한 부시 行政府의 戰略이라는 一部 言論의 批判을 意識, 그 時期 選擇
     에 있어 愼重을 기하고 있는 것으로 보임.
   - 그러나 英國, 프랑스等 主要 友邦國 및 UN과의 "協議"를 마칠 境遇, 美國
     은 언제라도 空襲等을 통해 이라크를 攻擊할 準備를 갖추고 있는 것으로
     判斷되는바, 사담 후세인 大統領이 UN의 大量破壞 武器査察 活動이나 시아파
     彈壓과 關聯, 繼續 美國을 刺戟할 境遇 電擊的 軍事措置 可能性이 높아지고
     있음.

3. 關聯措置
   - 現在 이라크 居住 우리國民은 21名으로 有事時 緊急待避 計劃을 樹立해
     놓고 있으며 모두 바그다드의 比較的 安全地域에 居住中
   - 關聯部處 및 業體에 繼續 事態進展에 留意토록 喚起 (8.17)

4. 言論對策 : 滯留者 安全對策에 대해 수시로 出入記者들에 說明.   끝.

0083

이락의 飛行禁止區域 設定關聯 對應 動向

1. 이락은 美·英·佛의 對이락 飛行禁止區域 設定(8.27)과 관련

   가. 8.29 「알 주베이디」總理가 모든 수단을 동원해 저항할 것임을 재천명
   한 데 이어

   나. 8.30 「후세인」大統領은 성명을 통해

   ○ 아랍地域의 石油에서 나오는 富를 장악하기 위한 西方의 아랍分割 의
     도에서 나온 것이라고 비난, 아랍政府들에 대해 지원하지 말것을 촉
     구하고

   ○ 西方의 이락分割 기도에 끝까지 저항할 것이라고 宣言하였음.

2. 이락은 飛行禁止區域 設定이후

   가. 南部地域에서 軍隊 撤收를 시작하고 執權 바트黨의 黨員들과 文書들을
   이동시키고 있는 것으로 알려지고 있는 가운데(8.29 在野消息通)

   나. 바그다드市民 수천명을 동원한 反美示威 展開(8.27)와 함께 西方側이
   이락領土를 분할하고 아랍을 宗派·種族別로 분열시키려 하고 있다고
   주장하면서 이락國民은 이에 굴복해서는 안된다고 강조(8.27이래 바그
   다드TV 및 라디오放送) 하고 있으며

18 - 5

0084

다. 美·英·佛 空軍機의 偵察飛行(1일 100회 이상 출격)에 대한 이락 空軍機들의 飛行禁止區域 近接飛行을 증가(8.29「크램블」사우디配置 美비행대대장) 시키고

라. 聯合國측이 이락을 자극시켜 挑發行爲를 유도하려 하고 있으나 이락은 忍耐心을 지킬 것이라고 言及(8.29「무바라크」保健長官)하면서

마. 시아派 탈영병들이 투항하고 있으며 수만명의 시아派 回教徒들이 飛行禁止區域 設定에 對應키 위해「후세인」大統領의 攻擊命令만을 기다리고 있다고 주장(8.30 알타우라紙)하고

바. 아랍측 지지를 모색키 위한 外交的 措置一環에서 오만·바레인·카타르·UAE 指導者들에 메시지를 발송(8.29 AFP 통신)한 바 있음.

3. 評 價

가. 이락측의 强硬對應 姿勢 誇示는

○ 對內的으로 反美·反西方 敵對感情 고취를 통한 국민결속 기회로 활용,「후세인」體制 공고화를 도모하면서

○ 對外的으로는

− 主要 아랍국들이 西方側의 飛行禁止區域 設定에 반대하고 있는 점을 감안, 西方側과 아랍諸國을 이간시키고 아랍國家와의 연대를 강화시켜

18 - 6

0085

- 國際社會의 對이락 制裁解除 雰圍氣 조성과 함께 아랍권內 影響力을 회복해 나가고

- 특히 美國의 威信 실추를 통한 「부시」美大統領의 落選을 도모하려는 政治的 意圖에서 비롯된 것으로 評價됨

나. 앞으로 「후세인」政權은

○ 이락이 通信體制, 레이다망 등을 복구하지 못한 상태이기 때문에 對西方 軍事對應이 어려운 실정인 데다

○ 美國이 飛行禁止區域 設定措置가 미흡하다고 판단할 경우 시아派 回敎徒들을 위한 안전지대 설정과 함께 空襲을 단행할 것으로 보여 (8.29 WP 紙)

○ 西方을 刺戟할 軍事行動은 자제하면서 對內外的으로 對美 적개심 鼓吹에 주력하는 한편 리비아등 反西方 아랍諸國과의 紐帶強化를 圖謀해 나갈 것으로 豫想됨.

18 - 7

0086

외　무　부　　　　　　원　본

종　별 :

번　호 : UNW-2410

일　시 : 92 0902 2140

수　신 : 장 관(연일,중동일,기정)

발　신 : 주 유엔 대사

제　목 : 이라크 사태

1. 금 9.2 안보리는 본회의를 개최하여 이라크가 국제구호물자 수송을 위한유엔 요원의 체류연장을 거부하고 있는 사태 및 최근 유엔 요원에 대한 위해사건과 관련하여 이를 시정할 것을 요청하는 별첨 성명을 발표함

2. 금일 본회의에 앞서 개최된 비공식 협의회에서 ELIASSON 사무차장은 8.29 이라크내 유엔 요원차량에 폭탄 부착사건과 관련, 주유엔 이라크대사에게 엄중하였으나 이라크측은 책임을 부인하고 이라크 사태에 개입된 연합국측의 도발행위라는 반응을 보였다고 보고함

3. 동 사무차장은 현재 이라크내에는 117 명 (이중 15 명은 바그다드에, 나머지는 북부지역에 배치)의 경비요원과 75 명의 구호요원이 있다고 밝히고 이라크측은 당초 MOU 에서 합의된 경비요원 500 명 대신 150 명만을 허용하고, 동경비 요원의 배치도 바그다드와 쿠르드족이 거주하는 북부지역에만 배치하고 시아파가 있는 남부에 배치는 불허한다는 입장을 고수하고 있어 MOU 연장교섭에 진전이 없다고 보고함

(대사 유종하-국장)

예고:92.12.31.까지고문에
첨부:UNW(F)-0706

국기국	장관	차관	1차보	중아국	외정실	분석관	청와대	안기부

UNWOHOПоб 20902 2160 #청부도

DRAFT PRESIDENTIAL STATEMENT

The Security Council is deeply concerned at the current situation of the Inter-Agency Humanitarian Programme in Iraq, as outlined in the Secretary-General's letter of 24 August 1992 to the President of the Council (S/24509), including its reference to Iraq's failure to renew its Memorandum of Understanding with the United Nations.

The Security Council recalls the statement of 17 July 1992 (S/24309), in which the Council expressed its profound concern at the deteriorating conditions affecting the safety and well-being of UN personnel in Iraq. The Council is particularly disturbed by Iraq's continuing failure to ensure the safety of UN personnel and the personnel of non-governmental organizations (NGOs).

The Security Council expresses its concern regarding the conduct and statements of Iraq on the Inter-Agency Humanitarian Programme which are inconsistent with the previous Security Council resolutions that demand that Iraq cooperate with the international humanitarian organizations.

The Security Council affirms that the critical humanitarian needs of vulnerable groups in Iraq require the speedy conclusion of arrangements that would ensure the continuation of the Inter-Agency Humanitarian Programme. In this respect, the Council considers unrestricted access throughout the country and the assurance of adequate security measures as essential prerequisites for the effective implementation of the programme. To this end, the Council fully endorses the Secretary-General's insistence upon appropriate field offices for participating UN agencies and programmes and the continuing deployment of the UN Guards. The Council strongly supports the Secretary-General's continuing efforts to sustain a United Nations and NGO humanitarian presence throughout Iraq, and urges him to continue to use all resources at his disposal to help all those in need in Iraq. The Council urges Iraq in the strongest possible terms to cooperate with the United Nations.

0088

외 무 부

종 별 :

번 호 : UNW-2725

일 시 : 92 0924 2130

수 신 : 장 관(연일,중동일,기정)

발 신 : 주 유엔 대사

제 목 : 대 이라크 제재조치

    금 9.24 안보리 비공개 협의회는 안보리 결의 687 제21항에 의거, 동결의 제 20항에의한 대 이라크 제재조치(민수용품 이외의 품목 수출금지) 변경여부를 검토 (60일마다 검토)한 결과 변경할 만한사유가 없으므로 현제재조치를 계속키로 결정함.

    (대사 유종하-국장)

국기국   중아국   안기부

PAGE 1

원 본

외 무 부

종 별 :

번 호 : UNW-2780

일 시 : 92 0929 1940

수 신 : 장 관(연일,중동일,기정)

발 신 : 주 유엔 대사

제 목 : 대 이라크 제재

1. 유엔 안보리의 대이라크 제재와 관련, 미국및 EC 국가들은 쿠르드족등에대한 인도적 물자지원, 쿠웨이트 침공에 의한 희생자들에 대한 보상, 대량파괴무기 폐기 사찰단 활동경비등을 지급하기 위하여 유엔모든 회원국들에게 안보리 결의에 의해 동결된 이라크의 해외자금등을 안보리 결의 706 및 712 에 의하여 설치된 유엔 계정에 이체할 것을 요구하는 별첨 결의안 초안을 협의중임

2. 이라크의 해외자산은 약 10 억불로 추정되고 있다고함. 미.영, 불등은 겨울이 다가오고 있어 북부 쿠르드족에 대한 구호품 공급이 시급한 실정이나, 이라크측이 안보리 결의 706(식량 구입등 상기 1 항목적을 위한 16 억불 상당의 석유수출 허가)의 이행을 거부하고 있음에 따라 이라크의 해외자산을 압류하는 상기 결의안을 제안한 것임

3. 이에대하여 이라크측은 안보리 706 이행을 위한 협상재개 의사를 밝히고현재 이라크에 잔류중인 구호물자 수송 유엔요원의 비자기간을 10 월말까지 연장을 허가하고 유엔요원의 추가 파견문제에 대한 융통성 있는 입장을 표명한 것으로 알려지고 있음. 그러나 이에 대하여 미.영.불등은 해외자산을 압류하기 위한 안보리 결의를 지연시키기 위한 책략으로 간주하고 가능한한 조속 동결의안을채택토록 추진하고 있는 것으로 탐문됨

4. 상기결의안 초안에 대하여는 현재 안보리 이사국간에 비공식 협의중인바, 진전사항 추보예정임

(대사 유종하-국장)

첨부;UNW(F)-0779

국기국 장관 차관 1차보 미주국 중아국 외정실 분석관 청와대
안기부

0090

PAGE 1

92.09.30 10:32

OIIWUTROIIP 20824 1940   #435.82

THE SECURITY COUNCIL,

RECALLING ITS PREVIOUS RELEVANT RESOLUTIONS AND IN PARTICULAR 706 (1991), AND 712 (1991),

TAKING NOTE OF THE REPORT OF THE SECRETARY-GENERAL (S/--) ON IRAQ'S COMPLIANCE WITH THE OBLIGATIONS PLACED ON IT BY RESOLUTION 687 AND SUSEQUENT RESOLUTIONS,

CONDEMNING IRAQ'S CONTINUED FAILURE TO COMPLY WITH THOSE OBLIGATIONS,

REAFFIRMING ITS CONCERN ABOUT THE NUTRITIONAL AND HEALTH SITUATION OF THE IRAQI CIVILIAN POPULATION, AND THE RISK OF A FURTHER DETERIORATION OF THIS SITUATION,

RECALLING AND REAFFIRMING IN THIS REGARD ITS RESOLUTION 688 (1991), WHICH PROVIDES A BASIS FOR HUMANITARIAN RELIEF TO THE IRAQI POPULATION,

RECALLING THAT THE ESCROW ACCOUNT PROVIDED FOR IN RESOLUTIONS 706 (1991) AND 712 (1991) WILL CONSIST OF IRAQI FUNDS ADMINISTERED BY THE SECRETARY GENERAL WHICH WILL BE USED TO PAY CONTRIBUTIONS TO THE COMPENSATION FUND, THE FULL COSTS OF CARRYING OUT THE TASKS AUTHORIZED BY SECTION C OF RESOLUTION 687 (1991), THE FULL COSTS INCURRED BY THE UNITED NATIONS IN FACILITATING THE RETURN OF ALL KUWAITI PROPERTY SEIZED BY IRAQ, HALF THE COSTS OF THE BOUNDARY COMMISSION, AND THE COST TO THE UNITED NATIONS OF ITS ROLES UNDER RESOLUTION 706 (1991) AND OF OTHER NECESSARY HUMANITARIAN ACTIVITIES IN IRAQ,

DEPLORING IRAQ'S REFUSAL TO COOPERATE IN THE IMPLEMENTATION OF RESOLUTIONS 706 (1991) AND 712 (1991), WHICH PUTS ITS CIVILIAN POPULATION AT RISK, AND WHICH RESULTS IN THE FAILURE BY IRAQ TO MEET ITS ABOVE OBLIGATIONS,

RECALLING ITS DECISION IN RESOLUTION 692 THAT THE REQUIREMENT FOR IRAQI CONTRIBUTIONS TO THE COMPENSATION FUND APPLIES TO CERTAIN IRAQI PETROLEUM AND PETROLEUM PRODUCTS EXPORTED FROM IRAQ BEFORE APRIL 2, 1991, AS WELL AS TO ALL IRAQI PETROLEUM AND PETROLEUM PRODUCTS EXPORTED FROM IRAQ AFTER APRIL 2, 1991,

HAVING REGARD TO THE FACT THAT THE PERIOD OF SIX MONTHS REFERRED TO IN RESOLUTIONS 706 (1991) AND 712 (1991) EXPIRED ON MARCH 18, 1992,

ACTING UNDER CHAPTER VII OF THE CHARTER OF THE UNITED NATIONS

0091

1.   DECIDES THAT IN ALL STATES IN WHICH THERE ARE FUNDS OF THE
GOVERNMENT OF IRAQ, OR ITS STATE BODIES OR CORPORATIONS, THAT
REPRESENT THE PROCEEDS OF SALE OF IRAQI PETROLEUM OR PETROLEUM
PRODUCTS, PAID FOR BY OR ON BEHALF OF THE PURCHASER ON OR AFTER
AUGUST 6, 1990, SHALL CAUSE THE TRANSFER OF THOSE FUNDS (OR
EQUIVALENT AMOUNTS) AS SOON AS POSSIBLE TO THE ESCROW ACCOUNT
PROVIDED FOR IN RESOLUTIONS 706 (1991) AND 712 (1991); PROVIDED
THAT THIS PARAGRAPH SHALL NOT REQUIRE ANAY STATE TO CAUSE THE
TRANSFER OF SUCH FUNDS IN EXCESS OF 200 MILLION DOLLARS OR TO
CAUSE THE TRANSFER OF MORE THAN FIFTY PERCENT OF THE TOTAL FUNDS
TANSFERRED OR CONTRIBUTED PURSUANT TO PARAGRAPHS 1,2, AND 3 OF
THIS RESOLUTION; AND FURTHER PROVIDED THAT STATES MAY EXCLUDE
FROM THE OPERATION OF THIS PARAGRAPH ANY FUNDS WHICH HAVE ALREADY
BEEN RELEASED TO A CLAIMANT OR SUPPLIER PRIOR TO THE ADOPTION OF
THIS RESOLUTION, OR ANY OTHER FUNDS INSOFAR AS THEY ARE SUBJECT
TO OR ARE REQUIRED TO SATISFY THE RIGHTS OF THIRD PARTIES

2.   DECIDES THAT IN ALL STATES IN WHICH THERE ARE PETROLEUM OR
PETROLEUM PRODUCTS OWNED BY THE GOVERNMENT OF IRAQ, OR ITS STATE
BODIES, CORPORATIONS, OR AGENCIES, SHALL TAKE ALL FEASIBLE STEPS
TO POURCHASE OR ARRANGE FOR THE SALE OF SUCH PETROLEUM OR
PETROLEUM PRODUCTS AT FAIR MARKET VALUE, AND THEREUPON TO
TRANSFER THE PROCEEDS AS SOON AS POSSIBLE TO THE ESCROW ACCOUNT
PROVIDED FOR IN RESOLUTIONS 706 (1991) AND 712 (1991);

3.   URGES ALL STATES, IN PARTICULAR THOSE STATES THAT DO NOT
CAUSE TRANSFERS TO BE MADE TO THE ESCROW ACCOUNT PURSUANT TO
PARAGRAPHS 1 OR 2 OF THIS RESOLUTION, TO CONTRIBUTE SUBSTANTIAL
FUNDS FROM OTHER SOURCES TO THE ESCROW ACCOUNT AS SOON AS
POSSIBLE;

4.   DECIDES THAT ALL STATES SHALL PROVIDE EACH OTHER AND THE
SECRETARY GENERAL WITH ANY INFORMATION NEEDED FOR THE EFFECTIVE
IMPLEMENTATION OF THIS RESOLUTION AND THAT THEY SHALL TAKE THE
NECESSARY MEASURES TO ENSURE THAT BANKS AND TO OTHER BODIES AND
PERSONS PROVIDE ALL RELEVANT INFORMATION NECESSARY TO IDENTIFY
THE FUNDS AND DETAILS OF ANY TRANSACTIONS RELATING THERETO, OR
THE SAID

0092

PETROLEUM OR PETROLEUM PRODUCTS, WITH A VIEW TO SUCH INFORMATION
BEING UTILIZED BY ALL STATES AND BY THE SECRETARY GENERAL IN THE
EFFECTIVE IMPLEMENTATION OF THIS RESOLUTION;

5.   DIRECTS THE SECRETARY GENERAL: (A) TO ASCERTAIN THE
WHEREABOUTS AND AMOUNTS OF THE SAID PETROLEUM AND PETROLEUM
PRODUCTS AND THE PROCEEDS OF SALE REFERRED TO IN PARAGRAPHS 1 AND
2 OF THIS RESOLUTION, DRAWING ON THE WORK ALREADY DONE UNDER THE
AUSPICES OF THE COMPENSATION COMMISSION, AND REPORT THE RESULTS
TO THE SECURITY COUNCIL AS SOON AS POSSIBLE; AND (B) TO TAKE THE
FOLLOWING ACTIONS:

(I)   TRANSFER TO THE COMPENSATION FUND, FROM THE FUNDS REFERRED
TO IN PARAGRAPHS 1 AND 2 OF THIS RESOLUTION, THE PERCENTAGE
REFERRED TO IN PARAGRAPH 10; AND

(II)   USE THE REMAINDER OF FUNDS REFERRED TO IN PARAGRAPHS 1, 2,
AND 3 OF THIS RESOLUTION FOR THE COSTS OF UNITED NATIONS
ACTIVITIES CONCERNING THE ELIMINATION OF WEAPONS OF MASS
DESTRUCTION, THE PROVISION OF HUMANTARIAN RELIEF IN IRAQ, AND THE
OTHER UNITED NATIONS OPERATIONS SPECIFIED IN PARAGRAPHS 2 AND 3
OF RESOLUTION 706 (1991);

6.   DECIDES THAT FOR SO LONG AS OIL EXPORTS TAKE PLACE, PURSUANT
TO THE SYSTEM PROVIDED IN RESOLUTIONS 706 (1991) AND 712 (1991)
OR TO THE EVENTUAL LIFTING OF SANCTIONS PURSUANT TO PARAGRAPH 22
OF RESOLUTION 687 (1991), IMPLEMENTATION OF PARAGRAPHS 1 TO 5 OF
THIS RESOLUTION SHALL BE SUSPENDED AND ALL PROCEEDS OF THOSE OIL
EXPORTS SHALL IMMEDIATELY BE TRANSFERRED BY THE SECRETARY
GENERAL, IN THE CURRENCY IN WHICH THE TRANSFER TO THE ESCROW
ACCOUNT HAD BEEN MADE, TO THE ACCOUNTS OR STATES FROM WHICH FUNDS
HAD BEEN PROVIDED UNDER PARAGRAPHS 1, 2, AND 3 OF THIS
RESOLUTION, TO THE EXTENT REQUIRED TO REPLACE IN FULL THE AMOUNTS
SO PROVIDED (TOGETHER WITH APPLICABLE INTEREST); AND THAT, IF
NECESSARY FOR THIS PURPOSE, ANY OTHER FUNDS REMAINING IN THE
ESCROW ACCOUNT SHALL SIMILALRY BE TRANSFERRED TO THOSE ACCOUNTS
OR STATES; PROVIDED, HOWEVER, THAT THE SECRETARY GENERAL MAY
RETAIN AND USE ANY FUNDS URGENTLY NEEDED FOR THE PURPOSES
SPECIFIED IN PARAGRAPH 5 OF THIS RESOLUTION;

7.   DECIDES THAT THE OPERATION OF THIS RESOLUTION SHALL HAVE NO
EFFECT ON RIGHTS DEBTS AND CLAIMS EXISTING WITH RESPECT TO FUNDS
PRIOR TO THEIR TRANSFER TO THE

mp-4-3

0093

ESCROW ACCOUNT; AND THAT THE ACCOUNTS FORM WHICH SUCH FUNDS WERE
TRANSFERRED SHALL BE KEPT OPEN FOR RETRANSFER OF THE FUNDS IN
QUESTION;

8.   REAFFIRMS THAT THE ESCROW ACCOUNT REFERRED TO IN THIS
RESOLUTION WILL ENJOY THE PRIVILIGES AND IMMUNITIES OF THE UNITED
NATIONS, INCLUDING IMMUNITY FROM LEGAL PROCEEDINGS, OR ANY FORM
OF ATTACHMENT, GARNISHMENT OR EXECUTION; AND THAT NO CLAIM SHALL
LIE AT THE INSTANCE OF ANY PERSON OR BODY IN CONNECTION WITH ANY
ACTION TAKEN IN COMPLIANCE WITH OR IMPLMENTATION OF THIS
RESOLUTION;

9.   DIRECTS THE SECRETARY GENERAL TO REPAY, FORM ANY AVAILABLE
FUNDS IN THE ESCROW ACCOUNT, ANY SUM TRANSFERRED UNDER THIS
RESOLUTION TO THE ACCOUNT OR STATE FROM WHICH IT WAS TRANSFERRED,
IF THE TRANSFER IS FOUND AT ANY TIME TO NOT TO HAVE BEEN OF FUNDS
SUBJECT TO THIS RESOLUTION;

10. CONFIRMS THAT THE PERCENTAGE OF THE VALUE OF EXPORTS OF
PETROLEUM AND PETROLEUM PRODUCTS FROM IRAQ FOR PAYMENT TO THE
COMPENSATION FUND SHALL, FOR THE PURPOSE OF THIS RESOLUTION AND
EXPORTS OF PETROLEUM AND PETROLEUM PRODUCTS SUBJECT TO PARAGRAPH
6 OF RESOLUTION 692 (1991), BE THE SAME AS THE PERCENTAGE DECIDED
BY THE SECURITY COUNCIL IN PARAGRAPH 2 OF RESOLUTION 705 (1991),
UNITL SUCH TIME AS THE GOVERNING COUNCIL OF THE COMPENSATION FUND
MAY DECIDE OTHERWISE;

11. DECIDES THAT NO FURTHER IRAQI ASSETS SHALL BE RELEASED FOR
THE PURPOSES SET FORTH IN PARAGRAPH 20 OF RESOLUTION 687 EXCEPT
TO THE SUB-ACCOUNT OF THE ESCROW ACCOUNT, ESTABLISHED PURSUANT TO
PARAGRAPH 8 OF RESOLUTION 712, OR DIRECTLY TO THE UNITED NATIONS
FOR HUMANITARIAN ACTIVITIES IN IRAQ;

12. DECIDES THAT, FOR THE PURPOSES OF THIS RESOLUTION AND OTHER
RELEVANT RESOLUTIONS, THE TERM "PETROLEUM PRODUCTS" DOES NOT
INCLUDE PETROCHEMICAL DERIVATIVES;

13. CALLS UPON ALL STATES TO COOPERATE FULLY IN THE
IMPLEMENTATION OF THIS RESOLUTION; _____

14. DECIDES TO REMAIN SEIZED OF THIS MATTER.

119-4-4

0094

외 무 부

종 별 :

번 호 : UNW-2835

일 시 : 92 1002 2200

수 신 : 장 관(연일,중동일,기정)

발 신 : 주 유엔 대사

제 목 : 이라크 자산동결

연: UNW-2780

1. 금 10.2 안보리는 비공개협의회에서 이라크자산 동결에 관한 연호 초안을 수정하여 본회의에서 찬성 14, 기권 1(중국)으로 채택함(결의 778 별첨)

2. 이로서 유엔은 동결된 이라크의 해외자산을 배상금 기여, UNSCOM 활동경비(결의 687), 쿠웨이트 자산반환 경비, 국경핵정위원회 경비, 안보리 결의 706 집행경비및 기타 이라크내 구호활동 경비등으로 사용할수 있게됨

3. 동안보리 결의에 의해 모든 회원국은 자국에 있는 이라크 정부 또는 기관등의 자금과 석유등의 판매대금을 유엔계정에 이체하여야함

4. 동결의 채택과정에서 이라크측은 유엔측과 안보리 결의 706 을 위한 협상재개와 유엔 요원 체류문제에 대하여 융통성 있는 입장을 밝히고 이라크 국민의 식량등 구호품에 사용하기 위해 40 억불 상당의 석유판매 허용(이중 5%는 소말리아 난민에 제공)등을 요청하였으나 서방국가들은 동결의안 채택 지연을 위한술책으로 간주하고 특히 구호품 구입을 위한 40 억불 석유수출에 대하여는 먼저 안보리 결의를 준수한후 검토할 문제라는 입장을 취하여 이를 거부함

(대사 유종하-국장)

예고:92.12.31 까지 고문에
첨부:UNW(F)-0798

국기국　　장관　　차관　　1차보　　중아국　　외정실　　분석관　　청와대　　안기부

* 원본수령부서 승인없이 복사 금지

UNW.(5 798   *X002 X-00*   *#청부문*

UNITED NATIONS

Security Council

PROVISIONAL

S/24605
30 September 1992

ORIGINAL: ENGLISH

Belgium, France, Russian Federation, United Kingdom of Great Britain and Northern Ireland and United States of America; Hungary, Japan draft resolution

The Security Council,

Recalling its previous relevant resolutions and in particular resolutions 706 (1991) and 712 (1991),

Taking note of the 15 July 1992 letter from the Secretary-General to the President of the Security Council on Iraq's compliance with the obligations placed on it by resolution 687 and subsequent resolutions,

Condemning Iraq's continued failure to comply with its obligations under relevant resolutions,

Reaffirming its concern about the nutritional and health situation of the Iraqi civilian population, and the risk of a further deterioration of this situation, and recalling in this regard its resolution 706 (1991) and 712 (1991), which provide a mechanism for providing humanitarian relief to the Iraqi population, and resolution 688 (1991), which provides a basis for humanitarian relief efforts in Iraq,

Having regard to the fact that the period of six months referred to in resolutions 706 (1991) and 712 (1991) expired on 18 March 1992,

Deploring Iraq's refusal to cooperate in the implementation of resolutions 706 (1991) and 712 (1991), which puts its civilian population at risk, and which results in the failure by Iraq to meet its obligations under relevant Security Council resolutions,

Recalling that the escrow account provided for in resolutions 706 (1991) and 712 (1991) will consist of Iraqi funds administered by the Secretary-General which will be used to pay contributions to the Compensation Fund, the (full) costs of carrying out the tasks authorized by section C of resolution 687 (1991), the full costs incurred by the United Nations in facilitating the return of all Kuwaiti property seized by Iraq, half the costs

4214a

/...

798-4-1

S/24605
English
Page 2

of the Boundary Commission, and the cost to the United Nations of implementing
resolution 706 (1991) and of other necessary humanitarian activities in Iraq,

Recalling that Iraq, as stated in paragraph 16 of resolution 687 (1991),
is liable for all direct damages resulting from its invasion and occupation of
Kuwait, without prejudice to its debts and obligations arising prior to
2 August 1990, which will be addressed through the normal mechanisms,

Recalling its decision in resolution 692 that the requirement for Iraqi
contributions to the Compensation Fund applies to certain Iraqi petroleum and
petroleum products exported from Iraq before 2 April 1991, as well as to all
Iraqi petroleum and petroleum products exported from Iraq after 2 April 1991,

Acting under Chapter VII of the Charter of the United Nations,

1.   Decides that all States in which there are funds of the Government
of Iraq, or its State bodies, corporations, or agencies that represent the
proceeds of sale of Iraqi petroleum or petroleum products, paid for by or on
behalf of the purchaser on or after 6 August 1990, shall cause the transfer of
those funds (or equivalent amounts), as soon as possible to the escrow account
provided for in resolutions 706 (1991) and 712 (1991); provided that this
paragraph shall not require any State to cause the transfer of such funds in
excess of 200 million dollars or to cause the transfer of more than
fifty per cent of the total funds transferred or contributed pursuant to
paragraphs 1, 2 and 3 of this resolution; and further provided that States may
exclude from the operation of this paragraph any funds which have already been
released to a claimant or supplier prior to the adoption of this resolution,
or any other funds subject to or required to satisfy the rights of third
parties, at the time of the adoption of this resolution;

2.   Decides that all States in which there are petroleum or petroleum
products owned by the Government of Iraq, or its State bodies, corporations,
or agencies, shall take all feasible steps to purchase or arrange for the sale
of such petroleum or petroleum products at fair market value, and thereupon to
transfer the proceeds as soon as possible to the escrow account provided for
in resolution 706 (1991) and 712 (1991);

3.   Urges all States to contribute funds from other sources to the
escrow account as soon as possible;

4.   Decides that all States shall provide the Secretary-General with any
information needed for the effective implementation of this resolution and
that they shall take the necessary measures to ensure that banks and other
bodies and persons provide all relevant information necessary to identify the
funds referred to in paragraphs 1 and 2 above and details of any transactions
relating thereto, or the said petroleum or petroleum products, with a view to
such information being utilized by all States and by the Secretary-General in
the effective implementation of this resolution;

/...

0097

5.   Requests the Secretary-General:

(a) To ascertain the whereabouts and amounts of the said petroleum and petroleum products and the proceeds of sale referred to in paragraphs 1 and 2 of this resolution, drawing on the work already done under the auspices of the Compensation Commission, and report the results to the Security Council as soon as possible;

(b) To ascertain the costs of United Nations activities concerning the elimination of weapons of mass destruction, the provision of humanitarian relief in Iraq, and the other United Nations operations specified in paragraphs 2 and 3 of resolution 706 (1991); and

(c) To take the following actions:

(i)   Transfer to the Compensation Fund, from the funds referred to in paragraphs 1 and 2 of this resolution, the percentage referred to in paragraph 10 of this resolution; and

(ii) Use of the remainder of funds referred to in paragraphs 1, 2 and 3 of this resolution for the costs of United Nations activities concerning the elimination of weapons of mass destruction, the provision of humanitarian relief in Iraq, and the other United Nations operations specified in paragraphs 2 and 3 of resolution 706 (1991), taking into account any preference expressed by States transferring or contributing funds as to the allocation of such funds among these purposes;

6.   Decides that for so long as oil exports take place pursuant to the system provided in resolutions 706 (1991) and 712 (1991) or to the eventual lifting of sanctions pursuant to paragraph 22 of resolution 687 (1991), implementation of paragraphs 1 to 5 of this resolution shall be suspended and all proceeds of those oil exports shall immediately be transferred by the Secretary-General in the currency in which the transfer to the escrow account had been made, to the accounts or States from which funds had been provided under paragraphs 1, 2 and 3 of this resolution, to the extent required to replace in full the amounts so provided (together with applicable interest); and that, if necessary for this purpose, any other funds remaining in the escrow account shall similarly be transferred to those accounts or States; provided, however, that the Secretary-General may retain and use any funds urgently needed for the purposes specified in paragraph 5 (c) (ii) of this resolution;

7.   Decides that the operation of this resolution shall have no effect on rights, debts and claims existing with respect to funds prior to their transfer to the escrow account; and that the accounts from which such funds were transferred shall be kept open for retransfer of the funds in question;

/...

598-4-3

0098

S/24605
English
Page 4

8.   Reaffirms that the escrow account referred to in this resolution,
like the Compensation Fund, enjoys the privileges and immunities of the United
Nations, including immunity from legal proceedings, or any forms of
attachment, garnishment or execution; and that no claim shall lie at the
insistence of any person or body in connection with any action taken in
compliance with or implementation of this resolution;

9.   Requests the Secretary-General to repay, from any available funds in
the escrow account, any sum transferred under this resolution to the account
or State from which it was transferred, if the transfer is found at any time
by him not to have been of funds subject to this resolution; a request for
such a finding could be made by the State from which the funds were
transferred;

10.   Confirms that the percentage of the value of exports of petroleum
and petroleum products from Iraq for payment to the Compensation Fund shall,
for the purpose of this resolution and exports of petroleum or petroleum
products subject to paragraph 6 of resolution 692 (1991), be the same as the
percentage decided by the Security Council in paragraph 2 of resolution
705 (1991), until such time as the Governing Council of the Compensation Fund
may decide otherwise;

11.   Decides that no further Iraqi assets shall be released for purposes
set forth in paragraph 20 of resolution 687 except to the sub-account of the
escrow account, established pursuant to paragraph 3 of resolution 712, or
directly to the United Nations for humanitarian activities in Iraq;

12.   Decides that, for the purposes of this resolution and other relevant
resolutions, the term "petroleum products" does not include petrochemical
derivatives;

13.   Calls upon all States to cooperate fully in the implementation of
this resolution;

14.   Decides to remain seized of this matter.

유엔안전보장이사회의 대이라크 제재 조치, 1992 531

美國, UN安保理에 이락 海外資産 沒收決議案 提出

1. 美國은 9.30 UN制裁로 凍結된 이락의 海外資産중 原油關聯 資産을 沒收 하여 UN의 對이락 武器査察活動, 걸프戰 被害補償 및 이락內 UN의 人道 的 救護活動에 使用할 수 있도록 許容하는 것을 內容으로 하는 決議案을 UN安保理에 提出했음.

2. 그간 美國은

가. 이락의 쿠웨이트侵攻(90.8) 直後 醫藥品 및 食糧을 除外한 모든 분야 에서의 對이락 交易中止등 포괄적인 對이락 經濟制裁(安保理 決議案 661호)에 의거, 이락의 海外資産(40-50億弗 추산)에 대한 凍結措置를 취하는 한편

나. 決議案 706호(90.8)를 통해
   ○ 6個月間 16億弗의 이락産 原油輸出을 許容하되
   ○ 原油販賣代金을 UN管理하에 두고 이락의 民生物資 購入(50%), 戰爭 賠償金 지불(30%) 및 걸프戰 終戰協定履行 관련 UN活動費用(20%)으 로 使用하려 하였으나 이락측의 拒否로 挫折됨에 따라

다. 英·佛 등과 함께 이락의 海外凍結 資産중 一部를 沒收하여 使用하는 方案을 推進해 왔음.

3. 評　價

가. 美國이 이락의 海外資産 沒收 決議案을 推進하고 있는 것은

○ UN이락武器査察團의 지속적인 活動保障을 위한 資金을 確保하는 한편

○ 이락 反政府勢力들에 대한 支援資金으로 活用함으로써「후세인」이락 大統領의 早期逐出을 도모하려는 데 主目的이 있는 것으로 評價

나. 同 決議案은

○ 이락 石油代金(10億弗 추산)을 多量 保有하고 있는 英・佛・日 등의 支持를 얻고 있어 安保理내 表決에 부쳐질 경우 통과될 可能性이 큰 것으로 보이는 바

○ 이는 이락南部 飛行禁止區域 設定(8.26)에 이어「후세인」의 政治的 立地를 더욱 弱化시키는 要因으로 作用할 것으로 展望.

27 - 8

0101

외 무 부

종   별 :

번   호 : JOW-0682   일   시 : 92 1005 1240

수   신 : 장관(중동일,경이,유엔일)

발   신 : 주 요르단대사

제   목 : 유엔의 해외 이락자산 압류조치에 대한 현지반응

유엔안보리의 해외 이락자산압류 조치 이후 현지 반응 및 관련사항 아래 보고함.

1. 이락 HAMED 공보장관은 성명을 통해 금번 유엔안보리 결의는 미국의 선동에 의하여 이락에 대하여 유엔이 취한 불평부당한 결의이며 이러한 조치는 미국 텍사스 스타일의 은행강도와 같은 불법약탈 행위라고 맹렬히 규탄하였음.

2. 한편 이락 AHMED 재무장관은 유엔의 해외 이락자산 압류 결의는 불법인바, 이락 자산을 보유하고 있는 모든 은행들이 불법적인 유엔의 결의에 응하지 말아줄것과 국제은행의 법률에 따라 이락자산을 보호해 줄것을 촉구하였음.

3. 당지 언론에서는 금번 조치로 이락 정부와 해외 무역업자들간의 모든 결제와 가능한 계약들도 완전히 정지케 될것으로 보고 이결과로 이락의 생필품 수입이 현격히 감소될것이며 2-3 개월내에 이락 시장은 더욱 악화될 것으로 보고 있음. 그간 유엔의 대이락 경제 제재조치에도 불구하고 이락의 해외자산이 이락의 수입에 담보가 되어 생필품을 구입할수가 있었으나 동조치 이후 이락의 생필품 수입에 타격이 클것으로 보고 있음.

4. 금번 유엔안보리 결의는 이락의 수입 및 모든 거래가 원천적으로 차단되는 결과를 초래하여 장래 이락의 생필품 부족, 물가폭등, 이락디나 가치폭락은 더욱 심화되어 이락 사담 후세인 정권에 대한 압박은 가중될것으로 봄.

5. 최근 이락내 아국업체(현대건설)의 식품 및 사무용품도 아카바항에서 통관이 지연되어 당관에서 주재국 관계당국에 협조를 요청한바, 주재국 관계당국(외무부 및 관세청)의 말에 의하면 대이락 경제 제재조치의 강화로 인해 최근 이락으로 반입되는 모든 물자는 예외가 없으므로 행선지를 요르단으로 하여 당지에서 봉관후 소량씩 바그다드로 송부하는것이 좋을 것이라는 의견이 있었음을 참고로 보고함. 끝.

(대사 이한춘-국장)

중아국   차관   2차보   국기국   경제국   분석관   정와대   안기부

예고:92.12.31. 까지

1992.12.31. 에 예고문에
의거 일반문서로 재분류

PAGE 2

주 국 련 대 표 부

866 UN Plaza #300, New York, N.Y. 10017, U.S.A.　　　　Tel(212)371-1280
　　　　　　　　　　　　　　　　　　　　　　　　　　　　FAX(212)371-8873

문서번호 주국련 2031- **1157**
시행일자 1992.10.20.
수　신　장　관
참　　조　국제기구국장

선결			지시	
접	일자 시간		결재·공람	
수	번호	60738		
처리과				
담당자				

제　　목　안보리결의 관련 공한 송부

　　이락-쿠웨이트 사태 관련 안보리 결의 778 (이락 해외자산 압류)에 관한
유엔 사무국 공한을 별첨 송부합니다.

　　첨부 : 동 공한 1부.　끝.

주　국　련　대

0104

UNITED NATIONS NATIONS UNIES

POSTAL ADDRESS—ADRESSE POSTALE: UNITED NATIONS, N.Y. 10017
CABLE ADDRESS—ADRESSE TELEGRAPHIQUE: UNATIONS NEWYORK

REFERENCE: SCPC/11/92(11)

The Secretary-General of the United Nations presents his compliments to the Permanent Representative of the Republic of Korea to the United Nations and has the honour to refer to resolution 778 (1992), adopted by the Security Council at its 3117th meeting, on 2 October 1992, in connection with the item entitled "The situation between Iraq and Kuwait".

The text of resolution 778 (1992) was transmitted to the Foreign Minister immediately upon its adoption.

The Secretary-General has the honour to draw attention, in particular, to paragraphs 1 to 4 and 6, 7, 9, 11 and 13 of resolution 778 (1992), which read as follows:

"The Security Council,

...

"Acting under Chapter VII of the Charter of the United Nations,

"1. Decides that all States in which there are funds of the Government of Iraq, or its State bodies, corporations, or agencies, that represent the proceeds of sale of Iraqi petroleum or petroleum products, paid for by or on behalf of the purchaser on or after 6 August 1990, shall cause the transfer of those funds (or equivalent amounts), as soon as possible to the escrow account provided for in resolutions 706 (1991) and 712 (1991); provided that this paragraph shall not require any State to cause the transfer of such funds in excess of 200 million dollars or to cause the transfer of more than fifty per cent of the total funds transferred or contributed pursuant to paragraphs 1, 2 and 3 of this resolution; and further provided that States may exclude from the operation of this paragraph any funds which have already been released to a claimant or supplier prior to the adoption of this resolution, or any other funds subject to or required to satisfy the rights of third parties, at the time of the adoption of this resolution;

"2. Decides that all States in which there are petroleum or petroleum products owned by the Government of Iraq, or its State bodies, corporations, or agencies, shall take all feasible steps to purchase or arrange for the sale of such petroleum or petroleum products at fair market value, and thereupon to transfer the proceeds as soon as possible to the escrow account provided for in resolutions 706 (1991) and 712 (1991);

"3. Urges all States to contribute funds from other sources to the escrow account as soon as possible;

"4. Decides that all States shall provide the Secretary-General with any information needed for the effective implementation of this resolution and that they shall take the necessary measures to ensure that banks and other bodies and persons provide all relevant information necessary to identify

Annex enclosed

the funds referred to in paragraphs 1 and 2 above and details of any transactions relating thereto, or the said petroleum or petroleum products, with a view to such information being utilized by all States and by the Secretary-General in the effective implementation of this resolution;

...

"6.   Decides that for so long as oil exports take place pursuant to the system provided in resolutions 706 (1991) and 712 (1991) or to the eventual lifting of sanctions pursuant to paragraph 22 of resolution 687 (1991), implementation of paragraphs 1 to 5 of this resolution shall be suspended and all proceeds of those oil exports shall immediately be transferred by the Secretary-General in the currency in which the transfer to the escrow account had been made, to the accounts or States from which funds had been provided under paragraphs 1, 2 and 3 of this resolution, to the extent required to replace in full the amounts so provided (together with applicable interest); and that, if necessary for this purpose, any other funds remaining in the escrow account shall similarly be transferred to those accounts or States; provided, however, that the Secretary-General may retain and use any funds urgently needed for the purposes specified in paragraph 5 (c) (ii) of this resolution;

"7.   Decides that the operation of this resolution shall have no effect on rights, debts and claims existing with respect to funds prior to their transfer to the escrow account; and that the accounts from which such funds were transferred shall be kept open for retransfer of the funds in question;

...

"9.   Requests the Secretary-General to repay, from any available funds in the escrow account, any sum transferred under this resolution to the account or State from which it was transferred, if the transfer is found at any time by him not to have been of funds subject to this resolution; a request for such a finding could be made by the State from which the funds were transferred;

...

"11.   Decides that no further Iraqi assets shall be released for purposes set forth in paragraph 20 of resolution 687 (1991) except to the sub-account of the escrow account, established pursuant to paragraph 3 of resolution 712 (1991), or directly to the United Nations for humanitarian activities in Iraq;

...

"13.   Calls upon all States to cooperate fully in the implementation of this resolution".

14 October 1992

S. B.

0106

Security Council

Distr.
GENERAL

S/RES/778 (1992)
2 October 1992

RESOLUTION 778 (1992)

Adopted by the Security Council at its 3117th meeting,
on 2 October 1992

The Security Council,

Recalling its previous relevant resolutions and in particular resolutions 706 (1991) and 712 (1991),

Taking note of the letter of 15 July 1992 from the Secretary-General to the President of the Security Council on Iraq's compliance with the obligations placed on it by resolution 687 (1991) and subsequent resolutions,

Condemning Iraq's continued failure to comply with its obligations under relevant resolutions,

Reaffirming its concern about the nutritional and health situation of the Iraqi civilian population, and the risk of a further deterioration of this situation, and recalling in this regard its resolution 706 (1991) and 712 (1991), which provide a mechanism for providing humanitarian relief to the Iraqi population, and resolution 688 (1991), which provides a basis for humanitarian relief efforts in Iraq,

Having regard to the fact that the period of six months referred to in resolutions 706 (1991) and 712 (1991) expired on 18 March 1992,

Deploring Iraq's refusal to cooperate in the implementation of resolutions 706 (1991) and 712 (1991), which puts its civilian population at risk, and which results in the failure by Iraq to meet its obligations under relevant Security Council resolutions,

Recalling that the escrow account provided for in resolutions 706 (1991) and 712 (1991) will consist of Iraqi funds administered by the Secretary-General which will be used to pay contributions to the Compensation Fund, the full costs of carrying out the tasks authorized by section C of resolution 687 (1991), the full costs incurred by the United Nations in facilitating the return of all Kuwaiti property seized by Iraq, half the costs

92-47554 4379Z (E) 021092

021092

/...

0107

of the Boundary Commission, and the cost to the United Nations of implementing resolution 706 (1991) and of other necessary humanitarian activities in Iraq,

Recalling that Iraq, as stated in paragraph 16 of resolution 687 (1991), is liable for all direct damages resulting from its invasion and occupation of Kuwait, without prejudice to its debts and obligations arising prior to 2 August 1990, which will be addressed through the normal mechanisms,

Recalling its decision in resolution 692 (1991) that the requirement for Iraqi contributions to the Compensation Fund applies to certain Iraqi petroleum and petroleum products exported from Iraq before 2 April 1991, as well as to all Iraqi petroleum and petroleum products exported from Iraq after 2 April 1991,

Acting under Chapter VII of the Charter of the United Nations,

1.   Decides that all States in which there are funds of the Government of Iraq, or its State bodies, corporations, or agencies, that represent the proceeds of sale of Iraqi petroleum or petroleum products, paid for by or on behalf of the purchaser on or after 6 August 1990, shall cause the transfer of those funds (or equivalent amounts) as soon as possible to the escrow account provided for in resolutions 706 (1991) and 712 (1991); provided that this paragraph shall not require any State to cause the transfer of such funds in excess of 200 million dollars or to cause the transfer of more than fifty per cent of the total funds transferred or contributed pursuant to paragraphs 1, 2 and 3 of this resolution; and further provided that States may exclude from the operation of this paragraph any funds which have already been released to a claimant or supplier prior to the adoption of this resolution, or any other funds subject to or required to satisfy the rights of third parties, at the time of the adoption of this resolution;

2.   Decides that all States in which there are petroleum or petroleum products owned by the Government of Iraq, or its State bodies, corporations, or agencies, shall take all feasible steps to purchase or arrange for the sale of such petroleum or petroleum products at fair market value, and thereupon to transfer the proceeds as soon as possible to the escrow account provided for in resolution 706 (1991) and 712 (1991);

3.   Urges all States to contribute funds from other sources to the escrow account as soon as possible;

4.   Decides that all States shall provide the Secretary-General with any information needed for the effective implementation of this resolution and that they shall take the necessary measures to ensure that banks and other bodies and persons provide all relevant information necessary to identify the funds referred to in paragraphs 1 and 2 above and details of any transactions relating thereto, or the said petroleum or petroleum products, with a view to such information being utilized by all States and by the Secretary-General in the effective implementation of this resolution;

/...

0108

5.   Requests the Secretary-General:

(a) To ascertain the whereabouts and amounts of the said petroleum and petroleum products and the proceeds of sale referred to in paragraphs 1 and 2 of this resolution, drawing on the work already done under the auspices of the Compensation Commission, and report the results to the Security Council as soon as possible;

(b) To ascertain the costs of United Nations activities concerning the elimination of weapons of mass destruction, the provision of humanitarian relief in Iraq, and the other United Nations operations specified in paragraphs 2 and 3 of resolution 706 (1991); and

(c) to take the following actions:

(i)   transfer to the Compensation Fund, from the funds referred to in paragraphs 1 and 2 of this resolution, the percentage referred to in paragraph 10 of this resolution; and

(ii) use of the remainder of funds referred to in paragraphs 1, 2 and 3 of this resolution for the costs of United Nations activities concerning the elimination of weapons of mass destruction, the provision of humanitarian relief in Iraq, and the other United Nations operations specified in paragraphs 2 and 3 of resolution 706 (1991), taking into account any preference expressed by States transferring or contributing funds as to the allocation of such funds among these purposes;

6.   Decides that for so long as oil exports take place pursuant to the system provided in resolutions 706 (1991) and 712 (1991) or to the eventual lifting of sanctions pursuant to paragraph 22 of resolution 687 (1991), implementation of paragraphs 1 to 5 of this resolution shall be suspended and all proceeds of those oil exports shall immediately be transferred by the Secretary-General in the currency in which the transfer to the escrow account had been made, to the accounts or States from which funds had been provided under paragraphs 1, 2 and 3 of this resolution, to the extent required to replace in full the amounts so provided (together with applicable interest); and that, if necessary for this purpose, any other funds remaining in the escrow account shall similarly be transferred to those accounts or States; provided, however, that the Secretary-General may retain and use any funds urgently needed for the purposes specified in paragraph 5 (c) (ii) of this resolution;

7.   Decides that the operation of this resolution shall have no effect on rights, debts and claims existing with respect to funds prior to their transfer to the escrow account; and that the accounts from which such funds were transferred shall be kept open for retransfer of the funds in question;

/...

8. _Reaffirms_ that the escrow account referred to in this resolution, like the Compensation Fund, enjoys the privileges and immunities of the United Nations, including immunity from legal proceedings, or any forms of attachment, garnishment or execution; and that no claim shall lie at the instance of any person or body in connection with any action taken in compliance with or implementation of this resolution;

9. _Requests_ the Secretary-General to repay, from any available funds in the escrow account, any sum transferred under this resolution to the account or State from which it was transferred, if the transfer is found at any time by him not to have been of funds subject to this resolution; a request for such a finding could be made by the State from which the funds were transferred;

10. _Confirms_ that the percentage of the value of exports of petroleum and petroleum products from Iraq for payment to the Compensation Fund shall, for the purpose of this resolution and exports of petroleum or petroleum products subject to paragraph 6 of resolution 692 (1991), be the same as the percentage decided by the Security Council in paragraph 2 of resolution 705 (1991), until such time as the Governing Council of the Compensation Fund may decide otherwise;

11. _Decides_ that no further Iraqi assets shall be released for purposes set forth in paragraph 20 of resolution 687 (1991) except to the sub-account of the escrow account, established pursuant to paragraph 3 of resolution 712 (1991), or directly to the United Nations for humanitarian activities in Iraq;

12. _Decides_ that, for the purposes of this resolution and other relevant resolutions, the term "petroleum products" does not include petrochemical derivatives;

13. _Calls upon_ all States to cooperate fully in the implementation of this resolution;

14. _Decides_ to remain seized of this matter.

0110

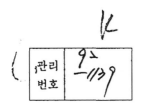

외   무   부

종   별 :

번   호 : UNW-3166   일   시 : 92 1026 1930

수   신 : 장 관(중동이,연일,기정)

발   신 : 주 유엔 대사

제   목 : 이라크 자산 압류

연: UNW-2904

1. 연호 안보리 결의 778 제 3 항의 "OTHER RESOURCES"는 결의 문맥만을 볼때 이라크 자산중 석유관련 이외의 자산은 해당되지 않음을 명시하고 있지 않으므로 이라크의 은행 예치금등 석유관련 이외 자산도 포함되는 것으로 해석할수도있으나, 동결의 작성과정어서 미, 영, 일간에는 동결의안을 통하여 이라크 자산중 석유관련 자산만을 압류한다는 대전제가 있었고 연호 보고와 같이 1 항과 2 항의 이행에 있어 문제점이 제기되어 회원국들에게 자발적으로 기여금을 제공토록 촉구한다는 양해가 있어 동 결의가 채택된 것임

2. 이러한 과정을 종합하여 판단할때 비록 안보리의 어떤 결의도 이라크의 비 석유관련 자산을 압류하여 유엔 계정에 이체함을 금지하고 있지 않으므로 제 3국이 그렇게 하고자 할경우 제 3 국의 독자적 판단으로 가능할 것이나, 결의 778 의 기본 취지는 석유관련 자산만을 압류하는 것이며, 따라서 제 3 항의 "여타재원"은 각국의 자발적 기여금을 의미하는 것으로 해석함이 타당함

3. 주요 자발적 기여금 제공 국가로 예상되는 영, 불, 일등은 미국측의 기여금 제공촉구에 대하여 우선 동결의 제 5 항(B)에 의거, 사무총장으로 부터 유엔 활동경비에 관한 보고서를 접수한후 구체적 기여금을 결정할 것이라는 입장을 밝히고 있다함. 현재까지 기여금 제공 의사를 밝힌 국가는 쿠웨이트(2 천만불) 임.

(대사 유종하-국장)

예고:92.12.31 까지 고문에
의기 인만표서   결

중아국   장관   차관   2차보   국기국   분석관   청와대   안기부

관리
번호 92-1169

외 무 부

종 별 :

번 호 : UNW-3282

일 시 : 92 1102 1900

수 신 : 장 관(연일,중동일,기정)

발 신 : 주 유엔 대사

제 목 : 이락 해외자산 압류

연:UNW-2904, 주국련 2031-1157(92.10.20)

대:WUN-2798

유엔 사무총장은 별첨 본직앞 공한을 통해 이락 해외자산 압류조치에 관한 유엔결의 778 관련, 동결의 이행에 관한 회원국들의 보고의무에 관한 4 항 규정에 따라 관련사항 있을 경우에는 제반 관련 상세 정보를, 없을 경우에는 없다는 사실을 92.11.30 까지 유엔사무총장에게 알려줄것을 요청해온바, 회시바람

(대사 유종하-국장)

예고:92.12.31 까지

첨부:UNWF-0987

국기국   장관   차관   1차보   중아국   분석관   청와대   안기부

PAGE 1

* 원본수령부서 승인없이 복사 금지

92.11.03   09:18

외신 2과 통제관 BX

0112

544 걸프 사태 유엔안전보장이사회 동향 8

UNITED NATIONS ⚛ NATIONS UNIES

POSTAL ADDRESS—ADRESSE POSTALE. UNITED NATIONS. N.Y. 10017
CABLE ADDRESS—ADRESSE TELEGRAPHIQUE· UNATIONS NEWYORK

REFERENCE: SCPC/1/92(12)

The Secretary-General of the United Nations presents his compliments to the Permanent Representative of the Republic of Korea to the United Nations and has the honour to refer to resolution 778 (1992), adopted by the Security Council at its 3117th meeting, on 2 October 1992. Immediately upon its adoption, resolution 778 (1992) was transmitted by telegram to the Ministers for Foreign Affairs of all States. By a note dated 14 October 1992 (SCPC/11/92(11)) the Secretary-General brought resolution 778 (1992) to the attention of all Permanent Representatives and Permanent Observers to the United Nations.

Paragraph 4 of resolution 778 (1992) reads as follows:

"The Security Council,

...

"Acting under Chapter VII of the Charter of the United Nations,

...

"4. Decides that all States shall provide the Secretary-General with any information needed for the effective implementation of this resolution and that they shall take the necessary measures to ensure that banks and other bodies and persons provide all relevant information necessary to identify the funds referred to in paragraphs 1 and 2 above and details of any transactions relating thereto, or the said petroleum or petroleum products, with a view to such information being utilized by all States and by the Secretary-General in the effective implementation of this resolution".

It is requested, therefore, that His/Her Excellency's Government provide all relevant information to the Secretary-General necessary to identify any place under its jurisdiction, including all territories for whose international relations it has responsibility, in which there are funds of the Government of Iraq, or of its State bodies, corporations, or agencies, that represent the proceeds of sale of Iraqi petroleum or petroleum products, paid for by or on behalf of the purchaser on or after 6 August 1990.

His/Her Excellency's Government is requested to provide for each such deposit of funds the following specific information as at the date of resolution 778 (1992):

(a) name of the bank or other institution, and the branch or location, in which the deposit is held;

0113

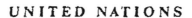

-2-

(b)   name of the account holder and account number;

(c)   amount and currency of the funds in the account subject to the provisions of resolution 778 (1992);

(d)   details of the transaction(s) which generated said amount of currency, including:

     (i)   name and address of the purchasing party;

     (ii)   quantity, price, and description of the petroleum or petroleum products purchased;

     (iii) shipping dates and shipping agent(s).

If any such listed funds have already been released to a claimant or supplier prior to the adoption of resolution 778 (1992), or if the funds are subject to or required to satisfy the rights of third parties at the time of the adoption of resolution 778 (1992), they may be excluded from the requirement of being transferred to the United Nations escrow account. For each deposit of funds listed it should be indicated whether any amount of the currency received cannot or will not be transferred to the United Nations escrow account and the specific reason for its exclusion from the transfer provisions of paragraph 1 of resolution 778 (1992).

It is further requested that His/Her Excellency's Government provide all relevant information to the Secretary-General necessary to ascertain the whereabouts and amounts of any petroleum or petroleum products owned by the Government of Iraq, or by its State bodies, corporations, or agencies, which are currently under the jurisdiction of His/Her Excellency's Government. This information should include the specific quantities of petroleum or petroleum products stored at each location by grade or type along with estimated market values for each and estimates of related sales costs.

If His/Her Excellency's Government determines that under its jurisdiction there are no petroleum or petroleum products or funds of the Government of Iraq, or of its State bodies, corporations, or agencies, that represent the proceeds of sale of Iraqi petroleum or petroleum products subject to the provisions of resolution 778 (1992), it would be appreciated if this could be specifically confirmed to the Secretary-General in a note.

The Secretary-General would be grateful if the requested information could be communicated to him by 30 November 1992.

26 October 1992

M. R.

0114

발 신 전 보

번 호.: WUN-3265   921105 1058 WJ   종별 : _____

수 신 : 주 UN   대사.//총영사

발 신 : 장 관 (중동일, 연일)

제 목 : 이라크 해외자산 압류

대 : UNW - 3282 (92.11.2)

1. 대호관련, 우리국내에는 이라크의 자산이 없다는 사실을 UN측에 똥보바람.

2. 똥건 관련 우리는 90.8.9 외무차관 명의 성명을 똥해 우리 국내에는 이라크의 자산이 없음을 대외적으로 발표한바 있음.   끝.

(중동아국장 최상덕)

예고 :19 1993. 6.30 까자
         의거 인빈문서 고문에

0115

수 미 대 사 는

USR(F) : 7026   년월일 : 92.11.5   시간 : 16:20
수 신 : 장 관 (미일, 연일, 중동인)
발 신 : 주미대사
제 목 : 이락의 유엔결의안 준수

보 안
통 제

(출처 :   )

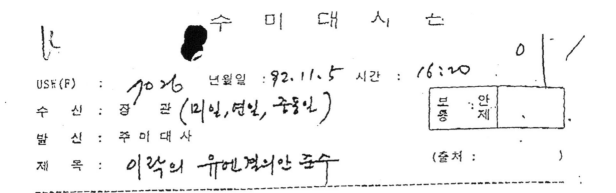

U.N. Team Says Iraq May Be Hiding Scud Missiles

UNITED NATIONS, Nov. 4 (Reuter) — The head of the United Nations commission in charge of eliminating Iraq's weapons of mass destruction said today that he could not yet say with authority whether Iraq was hiding Scud missiles.

Under terms of the cease-fire in the Persian Gulf war, the easing of the United Nations ban on Iraq's oil exports depends on Baghdad's destruction of its war machine, and the commission chairman, Rolf Ekeus, said he was not ready to certify that this had been accomplished.

Mr. Ekeus said he was pursuing the views of the United States, Britain and France, the Western permanent members of the United Nations Security Council, on what would happen if he decided that Iraq had complied with the weapons provisions of the Security Council's cease-fire demands, which require Iraq to destroy its nuclear, ballistic, chemical and biological stockpiles.

Both President Bush and Prime Minister John Major of Britain have vowed not to ease United Nations trade sanctions against Iraq while President Saddam Hussein is still in office, and President-elect Bill Clinton has given no indication that he disagrees with this position.

The commission is seeking an interpretation of the resolutions, which make no mention of Mr. Hussein's removal from power in Iraq, in order to encourage Baghdad to comply with weapons inspectors.

"It is a question of how to encourage Iraq to be more forthcoming," Tim Trevan, the commission's spokesman, said of the approach to Council members. "They have argued with us they are damned if they do, damned if they don't."

The Baghdad Government issued a new protest of the sanctions today. In a letter to the United Nations Secretary General, Boutros Boutros-Ghali, Iraq's Foreign Minister, Mohammed al-Salaf, said that continued sanctions against Baghdad "in effect means the commission of genocide against the people of Iraq."

Mr. Ekeus said Iraq could not be expected to remove its Government to get sanctions lifted. But he said the weapons destruction could be solved "quite quickly if Iraq really decided to go for it."

"The decision is in Baghdad," he added.

Iraq Has Not Complied

Mr. Ekeus said that Iraq has not yet complied with demands for long-term monitoring of its weapons potential and "there are still serious problems in getting the full data, such as the names of foreign suppliers."

"There is a way to go," he said.

Mr. Ekeus's remarks came after a news conference by Nikita Smidovich, head of a United Nations inspection team that recently returned from Iraq. Mr. Smidovich said that debris and data from destroyed Scud missile launchers was still being analyzed to determine how many missiles were used and how many possibly remained.

United Nations experts had estimated that about 100 ballistic missiles may have survived the war. United States intelligence has put the number at 200.

Mr. Ekeus praised Iraq's military for its cooperation, but said Baghdad's intentions to comply with the terms of the cease-fire agreement were still suspect after harassment of Mr. Smodivich's team, including death threats in their hotel, and statements from President Hussein referring to United Nations inspectors as "stray dogs."

배부처	장관실	차관실	일차보	이차보	외정실	분석관	아주국	미주국	구주국	중아국	국기국	경제국	통상국	문협국	외연원	청와대	안기부	공보처	경기원	상공부	재무부	농수부	등자부	찬경처	과기처
		/	/	/	0		/	/	/			/	/											

(7026 - 1 - 1)

92.11.05 NYT

외신 1과 동 제

0116

548   걸프 사태 유엔안전보장이사회 동향 8

관리
번호 92-1247

외 무 부

종 별 :

번 호 : JOW-0775   일 시 : 92 1121 1100

수 신 : 장관 (중동일, 유엔일, 북미일, 기정)

발 신 : 주 요르 단대사

제 목 : 이락 부총리 유엔향발

1. TAREQ AZIZ 이락 부총리는 11.21. MOHAMMED AL-SAHAF 외무장관등 6 명으로 구성된 사절단을 인솔, 당지경유 (11.20-21) 뉴욕 향발함.

2. TAREQ AZIZ 의 금번 방문 목적은 11.23(월) 유엔안보리에서 연설 계획에있으며 유엔안보리와 경제제재 해제문제를 협의할 예정인바, 그간 미부쉬 행정부의 압력에 의해 유엔안보리가 이락에 대하여 장기간에 걸쳐 취하여진 제재 조치에 대한 해제를 호소하고, 향후 현안 해결방안에 대하여 논의할 것으로 알려짐.

3. 이락 관영봉신 (INA) 보도에 의하면 TAREQ AZIZ 부총리의 말을 인용, UN이 미국 대통령 당선자인 BILL CLINTON 시대는 이락에 대하여 보다 동정적이길 희망하면서, 부쉬 미행정부도 비록 가까운 시일내에 대이락 경제 제재를 해제하여 주리라고 기대하지는 않지만 이락의 입장을 더욱 이해하여 줄것을 희망한다고 밝혔음.

4. 이락정부가 걸프전 당시 외무장관이었던 TAREQ AZIZ 부총리를 단장으로한 사절단을 유엔 및 미국에 파견하는것은 미대통령 선거이후 부쉬 행정부와의 감정을 해소하고 신행정부와 관계를 개선하려는 대미 접근 노력의 일환인 것으로보이며 유엔안보리와도 이락 경제제재 해제방안을 구체적으로 협의코자 하는 이락의 태도로 보임. 끝.

(대사 이한춘 - 국장)

예고: 93.6.30. 일반

중아국 장관 차관 1차보 미주국 국기국 외연원 외정실 분석관
정와대 안기부

PAGE 1   92.11.21   19:11

* 원본수령부서 승인없이 복사 금지   외신 2과 통제관 DI

0117

외 무 부

종 별 :

번 호 : KUW-0720   일 시 : 92 1122 1300

수 신 : 장관(중동일)

발 신 : 주 쿠웨이트 대사

제 목 : 대이라크 안보리 경제제재조치

연:KUW-717

1. 안보리의 대이장관 경제제재조치위원회 대변인(TIMOTY TREVIN)은 11.20 쿠웨이트 국영통신(KUNA)과의 회견에서 이라크의 대량살상무기를 제거시키는데에 진전이 있는것은 사실이지만(이라크의 협조를 의미-당관주), 장기에 걸친감시의무 수락을 기피하고 있고, 대량살상무기와 그생산장비를 공급한 외국회사를 밝히기를 거부하고 있기때문에 경제제재 조치해제가 어려울것이라고 언급하였음.

2. 동인은 또 미국, 영국, 프랑스가 훗세인정권이 존속하는한 이라크는 안보리 결의안을 이행치않을것이라는 의견을 견지하고 있는데 비해, ROLY EKEUS 위원장(경제제재조치위원회)은 다른 견해를 보였다고 말함으로서 경제제재조치해제시기를 둘러싸고 ~~ELOUS~~ EKEUS 위원장과 안보리사이에 의견다툼이 일고 있다는 그간의 풍문을 확인하였음.

3. 위 TREVIN 대변인의 언급으로 보아 이라크는 대량살상무기 제거협조 의무 이외에 무기또는 그생산장비를 공급한 외국회사도 밝힐것을 요구받고 있는것으로 보임.끝

(대사이종무-국장)

중아국	장관	차관	2차보	분석관	청와대	안기부	

* 원본수령부서 승인없이 복사 금지

92.11.22   22:04

외신 2과   통제관 FK

0118

외 무 부

종 별 :

번 호 : UNW-3545   일 시 : 92 1123 2230

수 신 : 장 관(연일,중동일,기정)

발 신 : 주 유엔 대사

제 목 : 안보리 회의

　　1. 금 11.23 안보리 회의는 안보리 결의 687(1991) 및 관련 결정사항에 관한 이락의이행상태를 점검한바, 안보리 의장성명을 발표한후,미,영,불을 포함한 13개 안보리이사국의 평가발언및 BLIKS IAEA 사무총장, EKEUS유엔특위의장,ELIASSON 긴급구호조정담당사무차장 및 VAN DER STOEL 이락 인권조사위 특별보고자의 보고를 청취하고,이락및 쿠웨이트측 요청에 의해 특별초청된 TARIQ AZIZ 이락 부수상과 SAUD 쿠웨이트 공보장관 발언을 청취하였음

　　2. ERDOS(헝가리) 안보리 의장은 성명(별첨)을 통해 이락이 현재까지 안보리 결의에 따른 의무사항을 선별적, 부분적으로 이행하고 있다고 선언하고 이락-쿠웨이트 사태와 관련한 안보리 결의를 충족시키지 못하고 있다고 말하였음.동의장은 특히 이락이 BOUNDARY DEMARCATION COMMISSION에 불참하고 있음과 UNIKOM 원칙에 따른 국경초소의 철수를 거부하고 있음을 지적하고 687결의에 따른 대량 무기 관련진상 공개(생산 및 공급과 생산능력에 관한 증거 문서 공개등)미흡 및 이와 관련한 경비제공 책임을 게을리하고 있음을 비난하면서 이락내의 실종 또는 억류되고 있는 사람들에 대한관련자료 미제공 등 인권측면에서도 안보리 결의 준수에 크게 미흡하고 있다고 강조하였음

　　3. 영,미,불,러 및 모로코등 안보리이사국(13개국)은 일제히 이락이 아직까지도 결의 687등 안보리결의안이 요구하고 있는 제반사항(이-쿠 국경선 획정준수, 쿠웨이트가 이락영토의 일부라는 주장,대량 파괴 무기 사찰,억류자 문제,이락국민대우문제등)을 이행하지 않고 있음을 강력히 비난하고 이락에 대한 경제 제재조치 해제를 고려할 단계가 아님을 역설하였음. 특히 PERKINS 미국 대사는 이락의 비타협적 태도를 보아안보리의 재재노력이 가일층 계속되어야 함을 강조하고 지난 3.11-12 시행된 제 1차안보리-이락간 의견교환 회의 이후 이락으로 부터 아무런 긍정적 회신을 받은바

국기국　　중아국　　외정실　　분석관　　안기부

PAGE 1

92.11.24　　13:39 EJ
외신 1과 통제관

0119

없다고 하면서 이락의 안보리 제반결의의 전면적이고 완벽한 이행을 추궁하고 이락측의긍정적 답변을 촉구하였음

　　4.한편 이락의 안보리 결의 이행사태를 보고하기 위해 이락의 요청에 따라 안보리에 초청된 AZIZ 이락 부수상은 경제 제재조치로 인해 무고한 이락국민이 고통속에 빠져 있음을 지적하면서,이락은 안보리 제반 결의, 특히 결의 687 의SECTION C 를 충실하게 이행해 왔다고 강변하고 안보리가 결의 687 의 22항에 따른 경제제재조치 해제를 게을리하고 있다고 말하였음. 동부수상은 대이락 안보리의 제반 제재 결의가 BUSH행정부의 특별정책적 고려에 의해 특별한 상황하에서 채택되었다고 하고 여사한 특별상황이 사라지고 이락과 유엔특위, IAEA 간관계도 안정화된점을 고려, 동결의 내용의재고가 필요함을 역설하였음

　　5. SAUD 쿠웨이트 공보장관은 이락측의 이-쿠 국경문제 관련 위반사실 및 쿠웨이트의 주권을 불인적하는 정책을 계속하고 있는점등을 들어가면서 이락측이 안보리 결의를 준수치 않고 있다고 맹비난하고 어떠한 제재조치의 해제도 반대함을 분명히 함

　　6.BLIKS IAEA 사무총장, EKEUS 유엔특위의장,ELIASSON 사무차장및 VAN DER STOEL보고자등도 일제히 이락측이 아직 안보리 제결의 준수에 미흡함을 지적하였음

　　7.안보리는 이락측과의 질의응답을 명일 계속할것인바, 관련내용 추보함

　　(대사 유종하-국장)

　　첨부:UNWF-1108

PAGE 2

0120

2̶3̶ November 1992

~~DRAFT~~ STATEMENT BY THE PRESIDENT OF THE SECURITY COUNCIL

I.   General obligation

"1. The resolutions concerning the situation between Iraq and Kuwait impose a number of general and specific obligations upon Iraq.

"2. As regards the general obligations, Iraq is required, under paragraph 33 of Security Council resolution 687 (1991), to give official notification to the Secretary-General and to the Security Council of its acceptance of the provisions of that entire resolution.

"3. Iraq signified its unconditional acceptance in letters dated 6 and 10 April 1991 (S/22456 and S/22480, respectively) and 23 January 1992 (S/23472).

II.   Specific obligations

"4. In addition to the general obligation to accept the provisions of resolution 687 (1991) in their entirety, several Security Council resolutions impose specific obligations upon Iraq.

(a)   Respect for the inviolability of the international boundary

"5. By paragraph 2 of resolution 687 (1991) the Security Council demands that Iraq respect the inviolability of the international boundary and the allocations of islands previously agreed upon between Iraq and Kuwait. Pursuant to paragraph 3 of that resolution, the Secretary-General established a Boundary Demarcation Commission to demarcate the boundary between Iraq and Kuwait. Paragraph 5 of the same resolution requires Iraq and Kuwait to respect a demilitarized zone (DMZ) established by the Security Council.

"6. Iraq did not participate in the work of the Boundary Demarcation Commission at its July 1992 and October 1992 sessions. Iraq has refused up to now to withdraw a number of police posts that are not in line with UNIKOM's principle that both sides should stay 1,000 metres from the boundary line shown on UNIKOM's map. The Council in paragraph 2 of resolution 773 (1992)

92-73956   3610g (E)

/...

welcomed the Commission's land demarcation decisions and, by paragraph 5, the intention of the Secretary-General to carry out at the earliest practicable time the realignment of the DMZ to correspond to the international boundary demarcated, by the Commission, with the consequent removal of the Iraqi police posts.

"7. In response to the Iraqi Foreign Minister's 21 May 1992 letter to the Secretary-General (S/24044), the Security Council in a 17 June 1992 statement (S/24113) stressed to Iraq the inviolability of the international boundary between Iraq and Kuwait being demarcated by the Commission and guaranteed by the Council pursuant to resolution 687 (1991). The Presidential statement also noted with dismay that the Iraqi Foreign Minister's letter recalled past Iraqi claims to Kuwait without also recalling Iraq's subsequent repudiation of these claims. The members of the Council firmly rejected any suggestion that tended to dispute the existence of Kuwait. Resolution 773 (1992) underlined the Council's guarantee of the above-mentioned international boundary and its decision to take as appropriate all necessary measures to that end in accordance with the Charter, as provided for in paragraph 4 of resolution 687 (1991).

(b) Weapons-related obligations

"8. Section C of resolution 687 (1991) imposes certain specific obligations upon Iraq with respect to its chemical and biological weapons programmes, its ballistic missile programmes with a range greater than 150 kilometres and its nuclear programmes. These obligations are elaborated upon in resolutions 707 (1991) and 715 (1991). The obligations are defined in paragraphs 8, 9, 10, 11, 12 and 13 of resolution 687 (1991) and they are elaborated upon in paragraphs 3 and 5 of resolution 707 (1991) and paragraph 5 of resolution 715 (1991).

"9. By resolution 699 (1991), the Security Council decided that the Government of Iraq shall be liable for the full costs of carrying out the tasks authorized by section C of resolution 687 (1991). No funds have so far been received from Iraq to meet this liability.

"10. The Council has noted that since the adoption of resolution 687 (1991) progress has been made in the implementation of section C of that resolution but that much remains to be done. In particular, Iraq needs to provide the full, final and complete disclosure of all aspects of its programmes for weapons of mass destruction and ballistic missiles with a range greater than 150 kilometres. There is a particular and vital requirement for complete information, including credible documentary evidence on Iraq's post production, suppliers and consumption of all prohibited items, and its past capacity to produce such items.

"11. Iraq must also acknowledge clearly its obligations under Security Council resolution 715 (1991) and the two plans for ongoing monitoring and verification approved thereunder. It must agree to implement these obligations unconditionally. In this connection the Council notes the letter

/...

of 28 October 1992 from Iraq's Minister of Foreign Affairs to the Secretary-General seeking a review of the terms and provisions not only of resolution 715 (1991) but also Security Council resolution 707 (1991). It is accordingly clear that Iraq seems unprepared to comply with the obligations already prescribed.

"12. The Special Commission has informed the Council about the outstanding matters that would at the present time appear to be the most important. The Council has noted document S/24661 of 19 October 1992 entitled 'The Status of the Implementation of the Plan for the Ongoing Monitoring and Verification of Iraq's Compliance with Relevant Parts of Section C of Security Council resolution 687 (1991).'

"13. The Council has also noted the document S/24722 of 28 October 1992 containing the second report of the Director General of the International Atomic Energy Agency (IAEA) on the implementation of the Agency's plan for the future ongoing monitoring and verification of Iraq's compliance with paragraph 12 of resolution 687 (1991).

"14. In a statement issued on behalf of the members of the Council (S/23803) on the Special Commission's right to conduct aerial surveillance flights in Iraq, the President stated on 10 April 1992 that:

'The members of the Council wish to point out that the surveillance flights are carried out under the authority of Security Council resolutions 687 (1991), 707 (1991) and 715 (1991). Reaffirming the right of the Special Commission to conduct such aerial surveillance flights, the members of the Council call upon the Government of Iraq to take all the necessary steps to ensure that the Iraqi military forces will not interfere with or threaten the security of the flights concerned and to comply with its responsibilities to secure the safety of the Special Commission's aircraft and personnel flying over Iraq.'

The President also said:

'that the members of the Council warn the Government of Iraq of the serious consequences which would ensue from any failure to comply with these obligations'.

14. bis. The Special Commission, on 15 October 1992, informed the Council of actions endangering the safety and security of the Commission's inspection teams in Iraq, including a systematic campaign of harassment, acts of violence, vandalism to property and verbal denunciations and threats at all levels. The President of the Council issued on the same day a statement to the press stressing the Council's particular concern for the safety of the Commission's inspectors.

"15. In a further statement made on 6 July 1992 on behalf of the Council (S/24240) concerning the Government of Iraq's refusal to permit access to certain premises by a team of inspectors, the President said:

/...

7-3

'Iraq's present refusal to permit access to the Inspection Team currently in Iraq to the premises designated by the Special Commission constitutes a material and unacceptable breach by Iraq of a provision of resolution 687 (1991) which established the cease-fire and provided the conditions essential to the restoration of peace and security in the region. The members of the Council demand that the Government of Iraq immediately agree to the admission to the premises concerned of the inspectors of the Special Commission as required by the Chairman of the Special Commission, so that the Special Commission may establish whether or not any documents, records, materials, or equipment relevant to the responsibilities of the Commission are located therein.'

Security Council resolution 707 (1991) demands that Iraq allow the Special Commission, the IAEA and their inspection teams immediate, unconditional and unrestricted access to any and all areas, facilities, equipment, records and means of transportation which they wish to inspect. Therefore, the Council cannot accept Iraq's insistence that there must be a limit on access by the inspection teams.

    (c) Repatriation of and access to Kuwaiti and third-country nationals in Iraq

"16. As regards Kuwaiti and third-country nationals in Iraq, Security Council resolutions 664 (1990), 666 (1990), 667 (1990), 674 (1990), 686 (1991) and 687 (1991) impose an obligation on Iraq to release, facilitate repatriation of, and arrange for immediate access to them, as well as the return of the remains of any deceased personnel of the forces of Kuwait and of the member States cooperating with Kuwait pursuant to resolution 678 (1990). Furthermore, paragraph 30 of resolution 687 (1991) requires Iraq to extend all necessary cooperation to the International Committee of the Red Cross (ICRC) in facilitating the search for Kuwaiti and third-country nationals still unaccounted for.

"17. In spite of ICRC's best ongoing efforts, ICRC has not received information as to the whereabouts of the persons reported missing in Iraq. Nor has it received detailed and documented information on the search conducted by the Iraqi authorities. Following the 11-12 March 1992 Council meeting with the Iraqi Deputy Prime Minister, Iraq published in its press lists of those believed missing/detained inside Iraq. ICRC has still not received permission to visit Iraqi prisons and detention centres in accordance with standard ICRC criteria. Very few missing persons/detainees have been released since March 1992, while hundreds are believed still to be inside Iraq.

    (d) Iraq's liability under international law

"18. Another obligation concerns Iraq's liability under international law. In resolution 674 (1990), the Security Council reminds Iraq that under international law it is liable for any loss, damage or injury arising in regard to Kuwait and third States and their nationals and corporations, as a

/...

result of the invasion and illegal occupation of Kuwait by Iraq'. Its
liability under international law is reaffirmed in paragraph 2 (b) of
resolution 686 (1991) and paragraph 16 of resolution 687 (1991). Resolution
687 (1991) further specifies that it 'is liable under international law for
any direct loss, damage, including environmental damage and the depletion of
natural resources, or injury to foreign governments, nationals and
corporations, as a result of Iraq's unlawful invasion and occupation of
Kuwait'.

"19. By paragraph 18 of the same resolution, the Security Council created a
fund to pay compensation for claims that fall within paragraph 16, to be
financed by a percentage of the value of the exports of petroleum and
petroleum products from Iraq. In view of the existing economic sanctions
against Iraq under resolution 661 (1991), Iraq was permitted by the Security
Council under resolutions 706 (1991) and 712 (1991) to sell a limited quantity
of oil, as an exception, a portion of the proceeds from which would be used to
provide financial resources for the fund. To date, it has not availed itself
of this possibility. The Council noted that this authorization lapsed on
18 March 1992 but indicated its readiness to authorize the regime for the sale
of Iraq; petroleum and petroleum products for a like period of time as that
specified in the resolutions and also its readiness to consider possible
further extensions (S/23732, 19 March 1992). Since then Iraq has not shown
any willingness to resume discussions about implementing these resolutions.
The members of the Council are aware of a previous request by Iraq for a
five-year moratorium on meeting its financial obligations, including payments
into the Compensation Fund.

"20. In view of Iraq's refusal to cooperate in the implementation of
resolutions 706 (1991) and 712 (1991) after several rounds of technical
discussions with the Secretariat, the Security Council adopted resolution
778 (1992) which mandates that certain frozen Iraqi assets be transferred to a
United Nations escrow account. A portion of these funds will be transferred
to the Compensation Fund.

    (e) Repayment and servicing of Iraq's foreign debt

"21. With regard to another obligation, the Security Council, in paragraph 17
of resolution 687 (1991), demands that Iraq scrupulously adhere to all of its
obligations concerning servicing and repayment of its foreign debt.

    (f) Nonentitlement to claims deriving from the effects of the measures
        taken by the Security Council in resolution 661 (1990) and related
        resolutions (para. 29 of resolution 687 (1991)) of the Security
        Council

"22. According to information received with regard to this item, Iraq has
attempted to enforce some claims under which it would have benefitted from a
contract frustrated by the coming into effect of the terms of resolution
661 (1990), in particular, through the confiscation of the property of foreign
companies and organizations left in Iraq.

/...

—6—

(g) Return of property

"23. I now turn to the question of return of property. The Security Council, in paragraph 2 (d) of resolution 686 (1991), demands that Iraq immediately begin to return all Kuwaiti property seized by it, to be completed in the shortest possible period. The members of the Council have previously noted with satisfaction that Iraqi officials involved with the return of property have extended cooperation to the United Nations to facilitate the return. However, much property, including military equipment and private property, remains to be returned.

(h) Monthly statements of gold and foreign currency reserves

"24. Another obligation is set out by paragraph 7 of resolution 706 (1991), under which the Government of Iraq is required to provide to the Secretary-General and appropriate international organizations monthly statements of its gold and foreign currency reserves. To date, no such statements have been provided to the Secretary-General or to the IMF.

(i) Undertaking not to commit or support acts of international terrorism

"25. By paragraph 32 of resolution 687 (1991), Iraq is required not to commit or support acts of international terrorism or allow any organization directed towards commission of such acts to operate within its territory and to condemn unequivocally and renounce all acts, methods and practices of terrorism.

"26. The Council notes Iraq's statements contained in letters dated 11 June 1991 (S/22687 and S/22689) and 23 January 1992 (S/23472) that it is a party to international conventions against terrorism and that it has never pursued a policy favourable to international terrorism as defined by international law.

(j) Security Council action with respect to the Iraqi civilian population

"27. Resolutions 706 (1991) and 712 (1991) provide a means for Iraq to meet its obligations to supply its civilian population with needed humanitarian assistance, particularly food and medicine. Resolution 778 (1992) mandates that certain frozen Iraqi assets be transferred to a United Nations escrow account and urges States to contribute funds from other sources to the escrow account. A portion of these funds will be used for humanitarian assistance.

III. Security Council resolution 688 (1991)

"28. I should now like to refer to the demands by the Security Council with respect to the Iraqi civilian population. In paragraph 2 of resolution 688 (1991), the Security Council demands that Iraq, as a contribution to removing the threat to international peace and security in the region, end the repression of its civilian population. In paragraphs 3 and 7, the Security Council insists that it allow immediate access by international humanitarian

/...

7-6

organizations to all those in need of assistance in all parts of Iraq, and demands its cooperation with the Secretary-General to these ends.

"29. The Security Council remains deeply concerned at the grave human rights abuses that, despite the provisions of resolution 688 (1991), the Government of Iraq continues to perpetrate against its population, in particular in the northern region of Iraq, in southern Shi'a Centres and in the southern marshes (Commission on Human Rights resolution 1992/71 of 5 March 1992). The Security Council notes that this situation is confirmed by the reports of the Special Rapporteur of the Commission on Human Rights (E/CN.4/1992/31, also circulated as document S/23685 and Add.1, and part I of the interim report circulated as document S/24386). The members of the Council recall their public meeting with Mr. Max van der Stoel on 11 August 1992.

"30. The members of the Council are particularly concerned at the reported restrictions on the supplies of essential commodities, in particular food and fuel, which have been imposed by the Government of Iraq on the three northern governorates of Dohuk, Erbil and Suleimaniya. In this regard, as the Special Rapporteur has noted in his reports, inasmuch as the repression of the population continues, the threat to international peace and security in the region mentioned in resolution 688 (1991) remains.

IV. Concluding observation

"In view of the observations on the record of Iraq's performance, and without prejudice to further action by the Security Council on the question of the implementation of its relevant resolutions by Iraq, the Security Council has considered itself justified in concluding that Iraq has up to now only selectively and then partially complied with the obligations placed upon it by the Council. It is the Council's hope that this meeting will prove a valuable opportunity to impress once again upon Iraq the imperative need for full compliance and to obtain from Iraq undertakings which would constitute an advance in the consideration of this issue as required in the interest of world peace and security, as well as that of the Iraqi people."

```
관리
번호  92-1265
```

외 무 부

종   별 :

번   호 : UNW-3559   일   시 : 92 1124 2030

수   신 : 장 관(연일,중동일,기정)

발   신 : 주 유엔 대사

제   목 : 안보리 회의(이락사태)

연:UNW-3545

1. 11.24 속개된 이락사태 관련 안보리 회의는 어제 발표된 안보리 의장성명, 안보리 이사국 평가발언에 대한 AZIZ 이락부수상 답변과 SAUD 쿠웨이트 공보장관의 반박 발언을 청취한후 아래요지의 안보리 의장 폐회성명 (별첨)을 발표하고 종료함

-이락측의 안보리 재결의 준수의향 결여및 안보리, IAEA 등에 위협에 대한 유감 표명

-11.23 발표된 안보리 의장성명 전폭지지

-일부 긍정적 조치가 있었음을 인정하나 이락정부가 상금 완벽하고 조건없는 의무 이행을 수행치 않고있는바, 즉각 적절한 조치를 취할것을 촉구

2. AZIZ 이락부수상은 11.23 발표된 안보리 의장성명 내용에 대해 약 1 시간 30 분간 항목별로 이락측 입장을 아래요지로 개진함

-이락은 EMBARGO 와 관련된 모든 약속사항을 이행하였음

-이.쿠간 국경획정위에 불참한것은 동위원회가 이락의 의견을 개진할 상황에 처해 있지 않기때문이며, 이락은 동위원회 활동을 방해할 어떠한 조치도 취한바 없음

-이락내에는 단 1 명의 억류자도 없으며 ICRC 와 긴밀히 협조하고 있음

-경제제재 조치로 인해 대외부채 상환능력이 없어졌으며, OIL EMBARGO 해제등 조치가 뒤따르지 않으면 대외 부채 변제는 불가능함

-수차에 걸쳐 제 3 국 및 쿠웨이트의 군용및 공공자산을 반환하는 조치를 취했으며, 개인재산에 대해서는 아직까지 반환 요청을 받은일이 없음

-KURD 족관련, 이락은 이들이 거주하는 여러나라중 문화, 교육등 제반 측면에서 헌법상 지위를 보장해 주고 있는 유일한 나라임

-이락은 안보리와의 계속적 대화를 갖기를 희망함

| 국기국 | 장관 | 차관 | 1차보 | 중아국 | 외정실 | 분석관 | 청와대 | 안기부 |
| 안기부 | | | | | | | | |

PAGE 1

3. SAUD 쿠웨트 공보장관은 반박발언을 통해 이란 억류자산, 억류자 문제를 비롯한 모든 문제에 대한 AZIZ 부수상의 답변이 허위와 속임수라고 맹렬하게 질타하면서 이락측의 제반 안보리 결의의 완벽하고 즉각적인 이행을 촉구함

4. 관찰및 평가

-지난 3월에 이어 안보리가 부여한 경제제재 조치를 완화하기 위해 이락측이 취한 금번 시도도 미국을 비롯한 안보리 이사국들의 강력한 반대에 부딪쳐 또다시 좌절되었으며, 안보리 -금번 이락측 STATEMENT 는 당초 보다 완화되고 타협적인 내용일 것으로 기대

되었으나 전반적으로 오히려 지난 3월 성명보다 더 위협적이며 도전적인 내용이 포함되므로서 다수 회원국들에서 의외로 받아들여지고 있으며, 일부에서는 이를 BUSH 행정부 퇴진을 겨냥, 국제사회의 관심을 재환기시켜 현상을 타파하려는 이락측 전략으로 분석하고 있음

-안보리 의장 폐회성명의 강도가 높으나 "SOME POSITIVE STEPS"을 인정하므로서 이락 측을 위한 긍정적 발전으로 보는 시각도 있음 (미국대표부 HANSON 이락 문제 담당관에 의하면 동귀절삽입은 중국과 짐바브웨등 제 3 세계 국가들의 요청을 수용한 결과라함)

(대사 유종하-국장)

예고:92.12.31 까지

첨부:UNWF-1109

PAGE 2

0129

UNCO두 9 세/24 2030 11 채명요

"In concluding the present stage of the consideration of the item on the agenda, I have been authorized, following consultations among members of the Security Council, to make the following statement on behalf of the Council:

'The views of the Security Council having been expressed through its President and by the statements of its members on the extent of compliance by the Government of Iraq with its obligations under the relevant Security Council resolutions, the Council has listened with close attention to the statements by the Deputy Prime Minister of Iraq. The Council regrets the lack of any indication in the statements by the Deputy Prime Minister of Iraq of how the Government of Iraq intends to comply with the resolutions of the Council. It also regrets the baseless threats, allegations and attacks launched by the Deputy Prime Minister of Iraq against the Council, the Special Commission, the International Atomic Energy Agency (IAEA), the Boundary Demarcation Commission and the Committee established by resolution 661 (1990). The Council rejects in toto these threats, allegations and attacks.

'Having heard all the interventions in the debate, the Council reiterates its full support for the statement made by the President of the Council on its behalf at the opening of the 3139th meeting (S/24836).

'In the view of the Security Council, while there have been some positive steps, the Government of Iraq has not yet complied fully and unconditionally with its obligations, must do so and must immediately take the appropriate actions in this regard.'"

H

P.1   NOV 24 '92 20:21 KOREAN MISSION

0130

562 걸프 사태 유엔안전보장이사회 동향 8

UN安保理, 이락制裁 解除問題關聯 會議 開催

1. UN安保理는

   ○ UN의 對이락 制裁措置 解除問題와 관련 11.23 - 24간 公式會議를 소집하고

   ○ 安保理 議長(「에르도스」駐UN 헝가리大使)이 11.23 開幕演說을 통해 이락이 UN 終戰決議 의무를 제대로 이행치 않고 있음을 비난, 당분간 •對이락 制裁措置의 緩和는 없을 것이라고 밝혔음.

2. UN安保理는 이락의 쿠웨이트 侵攻(90.8)이후

   가. 決議 661호(90.8)를 통해 醫藥品·食糧을 제외한 對이락 輸出入 全面 禁止 및 海外資産(40 - 50億弗) 凍結措置를 취하고

   나. 終戰決議案인 687호(91.4)를 통해

   ○ 大量破壞武器 廢棄 및 開發潛在力 除去를 위해 生化學武器와 彈道미사일(사정거리 150km이상) 관련 物質·研究施設의 確保·開發을 포기하고 關聯地域과 施設의 현장사찰을 받을 것으로 규정하고

   ○ 安保理 理事國으로 구성된 制裁委員會를 통해 60일마다 이락의 UN決議 履行實態를 점검, 解除與否를 결정토록 하였으며

   다. 쿠르드人을 비롯한 이락內 모든 시민에 대한 彈壓의 중지를 촉구하고 이락 難民에 대한 모든 가능한 措置를 취할 것임을 決議(688호, 91.4)하는 한편

라. 705, 706호(91.8)를 통해 인도적 필요에 의한 條件附 石油輸出(6개월 간 16億弗 수출, 代金은 UN관리)을 허용한 바 있음.

3. 이에 대해 이락側은

가. 大量破壞武器 廢棄와 관련

  ○ 核査察團의 秘密書類 搬出을 막기 위해 査察團 강제억류, 알 아티르 공단內 核施設 廢棄拒否(이상 91.9), 스커드 미사일 부품 및 생산설 비 파괴를 위한 査察拒否(92.2)를 비롯 化學武器 査察團의 農務部 査察을 거부(92.7)하는 등 방해활동을 지속하면서

  ○ 최근의 15차 核査察(11.8 - 18)에서도 核開發을 지원한 外國과 企業 의 名單提出을 거부하고 스커드 미사일 등 大量破壞武器 生産情報의 완전공개를 거부하는 한편

나. UN의 條件附 석유수출 허용에 대해 販賣量 및 代金의 UN管理에 대한 不滿을 이유로 이를 拒否(92.3) 하고

다. UN國境劃定委가 설정한 이락·쿠웨이트 國境을 불인정하면서 쿠웨이 트에 대한 領有權 主張을 견지(8.2 「알 주베이디」總理, 9.3 「라마단」 副統領) 하고

라. 北部 쿠르드族 및 南部 시아派 주민 구호활동을 위한 UN요원 滯留期 限(92.6.30) 延長 거부(10.17 延長 同意), 쿠르드 地域內 UN차량에 대 한 爆發物 設置사건(8.27) 등으로 UN의 活動을 방해하여 왔음.

25-19

0132

4. 이번 UN 安保理 會議는

　가. 이락側이

　　○ 부시 大統領의 選擧敗北에 따라 예상되는 美 國內情勢의 變化와 制裁
　　　의 長期化로 인해 國際的 關心이 낮아진 시기를 이용하여

　　○ 經濟制裁의 지속으로 인한 이락國民의 고통을 호소하고 UN 감독하에
　　　시행되고 있는 主要 核關聯 施設의 파괴와 化學武器廢棄 등 자국의
　　　UN決議 履行을 부각시켜 UN의 制裁解除를 촉구하기 위해 요청, 開
　　　催(「아지즈」이락 副首相 參席)되었으나

　나. UN側은

　　○ 이락이 終戰決議에 의한 諸義務를 선택적으로만 지키고 있을 뿐 아니
　　　라 UN이 정한 쿠웨이트와의 國境線 인정, 걸프戰 당시 실종자에 대
　　　한 생사확인 등 基本的 義務를 이행하지 않고 있고

　　○ 특히 이락이 核開發과 관련된 外國과 企業에 대한 자료, 스커드미사
　　　일 生産情報 등의 완전한 공개를 계속 거부하고 있는 한 이락에 대한
　　　制裁措置의 완화가 고려될 수 없다는 從前立場을 고수하고 있어

　다. 이락의 國際的 孤立과 制裁脫皮를 위한 획기적인 태도변화가 없는 한
　　　經濟封鎖 및 武器査察 活動 등 制裁措置를 지속해 나갈 것으로 豫想됨.

외교문서 비밀해제: 걸프 사태 25
걸프 사태 유엔안전보장이사회 동향 8

초판인쇄 2024년 03월 15일
초판발행 2024년 03월 15일

지은이 한국학술정보(주)
펴낸이 채종준
펴낸곳 한국학술정보(주)
주 소 경기도 파주시 회동길 230(문발동)
전 화 031-908-3181(대표)
팩 스 031-908-3189
홈페이지 http://ebook.kstudy.com
E-mail 출판사업부 publish@kstudy.com
등 록 제일산-115호(2000. 6. 19)

ISBN 979-11-6983-985-3 94340
      979-11-6983-960-0 94340 (set)